american RABBIS

american RABBIS

FACTS AND FICTION

David J. Zucker

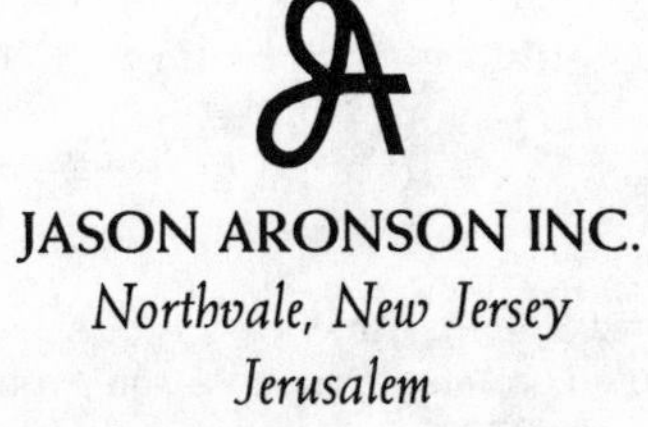

JASON ARONSON INC.
Northvale, New Jersey
Jerusalem

This book was set in 10 pt. Carmina Light by Alpha Graphics of Pittsfield, New Hampshire.

10 9 8 7 6 5 4 3 2 1

Library of Congress Cataloging-in-Publication Data
Zucker, David J., 1942–
American rabbis : facts and fiction / by David J. Zucker
p. cm.
Includes bibliographical references and index.
ISBN 0-7657-9989-8 (alk. paper)
1. Rabbis—United States—Office. 2. Rabbis in literature.
3. Judaism—United States—History—20th century. I. Title.
BM652.Z83 1998
296.6'1'0973—DC21 97-35822
CIP

Manufactured in the United States of America. Jason Aronson Inc. offers books and cassettes. For information and catalog write to Jason Aronson Inc., 230 Livingston Street, Northvale, New Jersey 07647.

I dedicate this to my parents-in-law,
and my parents,
who instilled in their children
a love of lifelong learning.

Fred R. and Lorraine R. Hofeld
and (the late Rabbi John J.) and Lilian R. Zucker

Contents

Acknowledgments

I should like to acknowledge the help of . . .

Rabbi Daniel Goldberger, a wonderful colleague, friend, and mentor here in Denver. He read through an earlier draft of the book; he shared his extensive collection of articles on the rabbinate for the last fifty years. This book is improved through his critical insights, any mistakes are mine.

Professor Dan Cohn-Sherbok, who urged me to follow through with this project.

Professor Stanley F. Chyet, who wrote the foreword for this book.

Colleagues and laity, men and women, literally locally, as well as coast-to-coast, north to south, and in Great Britain—right across the religious spectrum: Orthodox, Conservative, Reconstructionist, Reform—who lent me books and articles from their personal, institutional, and synagogue libraries, shared advice, read parts of chapters in earlier drafts, and answered questions.

The many people who gave permission to quote from their previously published works.

The staff of the Aurora Public Library and especially Interlibrary loans.

Joanna Willett, Head of Drama, SelecTV, London, England, for graciously sending me the twenty episodes of "Love hurts" and then answering questions about the production.

Rabbis Alan M. Ullman and Jennifer Weiner for sending me copies of their respective rabbinic theses.

The Library at Congregation Emanuel, Denver.

P.J. for reading, proofing, and offering insights.

The Denver/Boulder rabbinate, a cordial, friendly, respectful, sharing group of wonderful men and women.

The residents, men and women, Jews and non-Jews, at Shalom Park who listened to parts of these chapters and offered comments and advice.

Finally, my family who put up with my many hours on the computer—and especially my wife, Donna who supported this endeavor throughout and who, as a research librarian, tracked down many arcane articles and books for me.

Foreword

Prof. Stanley F. Chyet
Hebrew Union College- Jewish Institute of Religion

André Malraux, in his *Anti-Memoirs*, thought of culture as "first and foremost a vast resurrection." In a fundamental way, it seems to me, that notion of culture applies to what my dear friend, Rabbi David J. Zucker, has undertaken in this book on the American rabbinate. I do not mean that the rabbinate in America has ever been dead or moribund, or that Rabbi Zucker suggests anything of the sort—but his twelve chapters function, indeed, to "resurrect" an estimate of the American rabbinate as a cultural, as well as a spiritual phenomenon, and to revive our awareness of the rabbinic role or roles in Jewish life. The fact is that even those of us who lay claim to a rabbinical title have often forgotten or lacked a clear sense of the rabbinical territory we inhabit. Our awareness needs resurrection, and Rabbi Zucker has understood that.

It is a bold design he sets out to frame in these pages; charting the factors—religious, historical, social, cultural, psychological—making for at least a provisional definition of the rabbinate in contemporary America. There is not much of genuine significance he fails to mention in his survey of the territory, nor is it topographic features alone he seeks to assess. He displays a large consciousness of rich resources lying beneath the surface.

An especially noteworthy aspect of Rabbi Zucker's exploration is the attention he pays to depictions of rabbinical life and characters in the American Jewish fiction published during the second half of the twentieth century. Moreover, he has been wise enough to avoid confining himself to the fiction created by novelists of genius like Saul Bellow and Cynthia Ozick. Lesser works—which contribute their own valuable social and psychic details—have not been disdained by him.

Rabbi Zucker's is thus an intriguing approach, and one I judge happily in accord with Malraux's idea of culture. The rabbinate, as a *meaningful* phenomenon in Jewish life today, cannot, perhaps, be finally rendered so well in history or sociology as in imaginative literature.

I applaud Rabbi Zucker's effort and allow myself to hope that it will open many eyes and hearts to the treasure house of values and of experience that is the American rabbinate.

Prologue: What Is a Rabbi?

Rabbis, first and foremost, are teachers. They are primary Jewish role models. The objective of the rabbinate is to ensure the continuity of Jewish communal life by conveying the past messages of Judaism to the present generation so that this religious tradition will be followed in the future. The purpose of this book is to portray the "reality" of today's rabbinate and at the same time to compare and contrast how rabbis are depicted in contemporary American fiction.[1] I will quote extensively from contemporary descriptions of the rabbinate as a profession—material by both rabbis and laity—to allow the "factual" rabbinate to speak for itself. Fictional material is then used variously to enhance, illustrate, and occasionally to contrast with the factual statements. I have limited my fictional examples to rabbis who have appeared in novels and short stories published since 1950.

Rabbis have appeared as characters in television dramas and comedies. They also are portrayed as characters in cinematic productions. Nonetheless, with but one extraordinary exception, I made a conscious decision to offer examples only taken from rabbis in the print media.[2] Most rabbis in North America who serve professionally as rabbis function directly within the setting of a synagogue, though as I shall explain, this is not the exclusive venue of the rabbinate. I shall focus primarily on the practicing rabbi, the rabbi who works within the Jewish community, oftentimes as the leader of a congregation, as opposed to those rabbis who achieve ordination and then choose another occupation as their vocation.[3]

The rabbinate as an institution has changed significantly over the past 2,000 years. Today, congregational rabbis are Jewish religious role models: leaders at religious services, preachers, teachers, and pastoral counselors. This is in marked contrast to the earliest rabbis who were interpreters and expounders of both biblical law and the Oral Teaching which appears to owe a great deal to the Pharisees. Furthermore, today the rabbinate is a profession in its own right while two millennia ago rabbis almost invariably had an occupation from which they derived their livelihood.[4]

> As Rabbi David Small, the creation of author Harry Kemelman (found in the series which began with the 1964 novel *Friday the Rabbi Slept Late*, and, arguably the best-known "fictional" rabbi) explains, in the past, basically the rabbi's "job was to guide and teach the community. Well, that's still his job, only now his community is less plastic, less docile, less interested, and even less inclined to be guided. It's a much harder job than it used to be. . . .
>
> "We say it's hard to be a Jew, and it's even harder to be a rabbi, I suppose, who is a kind of professional Jew."[5]

While it is a difficult profession, as Murray Polner indicated in his book *Rabbi: The American Experience* (1977), "the rabbi nonetheless continues to play a central, if reduced, role in American Jewish life. But I believe he is the most significant person in that life today and for the years ahead."[6]

When, where, and how the early rabbinate came into being, as well as the names of the first rabbis, is not known. In his work *A Concise History of the Rabbinate* (1993), Simon Schwartzfuchs explains that the rabbinate appeared well after the establishment of the synagogue,[7] an institution which probably is a product of the Babylonian Exile, which took place over 2,500 years ago. The synagogue itself was developed to fill the void left following the destruction of the First Temple in Jerusalem by the Babylonian army in 586 BCE (Before the Common Era). It was further developed following the destruction of the Second Temple in Jerusalem by the Roman army in 70 CE (Common Era), but by then the rabbinate as an institution was in place. In time, the synagogue took on three functions: a place of assembly; a center for worship; and a location for education. The modern synagogue continues to fulfill these three important roles, and the congregational rabbi serves as the religious leader of the synagogue.

The term rabbi is derived from the Hebrew noun *rav*. It does not occur in the Bible as a word that refers to a teacher or communal leader, for the rabbinate is a post-Biblical institution. The term "rabbi" means literally "my master" and it initially referred to Sages who were ordained in the land of Israel. The Babylonian Sages of the Talmud bore the title *rav* as opposed to *rabbi*. The Sages of the Talmud, whether located in the land of Israel or Babylon were great scholars, teachers in the sense that they interpreted and expounded Jewish law, but they were not communal leaders as we would understand them today. "It was only in the Middle Ages that the rabbi became—in addition to, or instead of, the interpreter and decisor of the law—the teacher, preacher, and spiritual head of the Jewish congregation or community."[8]

Rabbis today take on that title through the process of *semikhah*, the "laying" on of hands by which a rabbi, usually as the head of the seminary, though in rarer cases, privately, "ordains" the student.[9] This tradition of passing on the mantle of leadership derives from the Biblical example of Moses who laid his hands on his successor, Joshua, to commission (ordain) him as God had commanded (Numbers 27:23). In time, the practice became a verbal acknowledgment of the student's having acquired sufficient knowledge to serve as a judge of the law. In the Talmudic period, the formula for ordination stated: *Yoreh yoreh; yadin yadin; yatir yatir—May he decide? He may decide. May he judge? He may judge. May he permit? He may permit*.

For the better part of two millennia, rabbis were ordained when they had achieved sufficient knowledge of Talmudic law and the subsequent codes. In the modern period, especially in the nineteenth century,

> a drastic change took place with regard to the position, requirements, and training of rabbis. The change originated in Germany, which became the center for the development of Reform Judaism and for the scientific study of Jewish history and the Jewish religion. Knowledge solely of the Talmud and codes was no longer deemed sufficient, and many communities now demanded that their rabbis be versed in the vernacular, secular studies, and auxiliary Judaic studies . . . curricula were evolved which . . . [in addition to Talmud and codes, taught such subjects as] Bible, homiletics, Jewish his-

> tory and philosophy, the grammar of Hebrew and of cognate languages, pastoral psychology, and synagogue administration.[10]

In the United States, the four major rabbinic seminaries differ in their approach to ordination. At Yeshiva University, the Rabbi Isaac Elchanan Theological Seminary ("Centrist" Orthodox)[11] ordains its graduates in a traditional fashion after they have completed a course of study which stresses Talmud and codes. The Jewish Theological Seminary (Conservative) does not grant a traditional ordination to its students. The Reconstructionist Rabbinical College has a ceremony of graduation and does not use the traditional formula. The Hebrew Union College-Jewish Institute of Religion (Reform) retains the traditional formula of *yoreh yoreh, yadin yadin* but this is only a formal acknowledgment of the ancient tradition.[12]

To appreciate the role of the contemporary rabbi, I shall sketch in some of the changes that have taken place in the rabbinate over the past 2,000 years. As mentioned above, the earliest rabbis were primary scholars who were well versed in both Biblical law and the Oral Teaching which was developed by the Pharisees. These rabbis taught students in a setting where they themselves studied, interpreted, and expounded on the law. The early rabbis developed a whole new body of literature, first the Mishna and then the major addition to the Mishna, the Gemara, which together form the Talmud. In fact there are two Talmuds, one which was developed in the land of Israel, known variously as the *Talmud Yerushalmi*, the Jerusalem Talmud or the Palestinian Talmud, and then the more authoritative and influential Talmud which was developed in Babylon, known as the *Talmud Bavli* or the Babylonian Talmud.

The ancient rabbis, like the rabbis of the Middle Ages, were religious authorities, scholarship and judgeship being central to their avocation. Unlike the contemporary rabbinate, which is a full-time profession, in earlier ages rabbis worked at different occupations and then devoted part of their day, or if it was seasonal work part of the year, to their rabbinic duties. In the past, rabbis did not officiate at services or lead people in prayer. Further, in contrast to contemporary congregational rabbis, they did not preside at life-cycle ceremonies. Those functions became part of the rabbinate only during the nineteenth century.

As Jewish communities spread throughout the world and as central institutions broke down, the rabbis over a period of time took on social-spiritual leadership. They were leaders in their communities but their regular duties were very different. Until modern times, the rabbi only gave a public sermon on very limited occasions. He may also have had responsibilities to oversee some of the religious institutions in the community such as the ritual bath or the proper slaughtering of meat for food. Yet the rabbi's major function was to decide matters of law, be it ritual or judicial law. To place this within a proper context, it needs be said that until the modern period, the Jewish community was legally deemed a separate population with a distinct jurisdiction in its own right. The Jews were regarded and treated as a nation within a nation. They had their own laws and statutes to guide them, *certainly in matters that involved only Jews themselves*. This meant that rabbis were concerned with a wide range of matters from business and commercial law to ethical, moral, ritual, marital, and inheritance issues, as long as they pertained to Jews within the Jewish community itself. It was only with the Emancipation in the late eighteenth and early nineteenth centuries that Jews became integrated into the wider non-Jewish communities.

Chapter 1 (The American Rabbi) explores the unique American rabbinical experience. As a post-Emancipation community, the rabbinate in America virtually from its start has had to deal with a very wide variety of issues. Addressing the "Scope of the Modern American Rabbi's Vocation," Simon Greenberg has written that

> [p]erhaps the most troublesome of the problems which has bedeviled the American Rabbinate from its inception is the bewildering number and variety of needs which its clients experience and expect the Rabbi to meet. . . . They are the needs to relate in a meaningful manner to:
>
> a) the transcendental—the mysteries that envelop us—to God;
> b) suffering and death;
> c) fellow human beings and the non-human environment;
> d) the awareness of one's Jewishness;
> e) one's self, one's instincts and aspirations.
>
> There are some professionals who are trained to help individuals meet one or another of these needs. [Yet . . .] the Rabbi is the only professional serving the community who is presumably expected to have been trained to deal with them all as elements in an indivisible complex.
>
> To prepare them for their vocation, the American Rabbinate generally requires its practitioners to undergo a lengthy period of post-graduate education in order to master a vast area of special knowledge and a considerable variety of practical skills.[13]

How the American Rabbinate has met these bewildering number and variety of needs—both in reality and as portrayed in fiction—is the very subject of this book.

While this book has been carefully researched, it is also written from an "insider's" viewpoint. I was ordained as a rabbi in 1970 and served as a traditional congregational rabbi for twenty-one years. I have served pulpits both in Great Britain and the United States. I now serve as the Chaplain in a long-term care community, where my congregants are largely in their eighties and nineties, with a few having achieved a century of years.

For both professional and personal reasons, I have had a strong interest in fictional portrayals of rabbis for many years.

Simon Greenberg's description of the "Scope of the Modern American Rabbi's Vocation" correctly notes that rabbis undergo a "lengthy period of post-graduate education" so that they will master a vast area of knowledge. Rabbis value this study and often feel that they should actively continue their learning when they enter the field. Some congregational boards, however, have other ideas about this. This matter highlights a difference in congregational and rabbinic expectations, a subject which is dealt with at length in chapter 6 (Congregants View Their Rabbis.) A fictional treatment of this issue is found in the short story by Stanley F. Chyet, "The Wise Men of Wentworth." When Rabbi Isaiah Gotthelf first comes to the town of Wentworth, he meets with his Board of Directors. He explains that he intends to take the weekday morning hours for study. His board is uniformly appalled. They ask him why he has to study if he is a rabbi. "You don't know, rabbi, we're running here a shul*—a synagogue—not a yeshiva! So who hired a rabbi he should study?" When Rabbi Gotthelf explains that a rabbi's studies are never completed, he is met with incredulity. The president groans, "When a rabbi graduates from the yeshiva, he's a scholar. So why do you need yet to study?" The board then fires Rabbi Gotthelf on the spot. They refer to him as an "*unfinished, a half-*baked rabbi." The next rabbinical candidate fares completely differently. He too, wishes to be left undisturbed in the mornings. "Mondays through Fridays." When the board asks why, Rabbi George Handler relates the fact that he is a married man, and he explains that he sleeps best in the morning. "A sigh of relief, of understanding, of satisfaction had welled up then from the assembled board members and from President Abrams, who turned triumphantly to the board.*

"'You see, Gentlemen, a rabbi what is a rabbi, a full, finished *rabbi, we got.'"*

"A full-*baked rabbi," another congregant caustically remarks.*[14]

NOTES

1. The overwhelming number of examples are drawn from fiction set in North America. Early in my career, I served as a congregational rabbi in Great Britain for nine years. During that time, I came across numerous examples of British fiction that featured rabbis as characters. In many cases, the rabbinic experiences were equally applicable in North America. Consequently I have taken the liberty of including about a dozen quotes from British fiction. In each and every case, I make it clear that the fictional situation is set in Britain. Though these are both earlier factual, and fictional, portrayals of rabbis in American life, notably Sidney Nyburg's 1917 novel, *The Chosen People*, I have limited my discussion to works published after 1950.

2. The one example where I feature a rabbi who is a character in non-print media is the role of the "fictional' Rabbi Diane Warburg, who appears in a television series by Laurence Marks and Maurice Gran, "Love hurts." Since fictional portrayals of women rabbis are so limited, I felt that I could make an exception in this case. Rabbi Warburg serves a congregation in London.

3. For example, some rabbis achieve ordination and then stay within the world of the yeshiva, the classical Talmudic school. Others achieve ordination and then go into some form of secular business.

4. Rabinowitz, L. I. (1972). "Rabbi, Rabbinate," in *Encyclopedia Judaica*, vol. 13 (Jerusalem: Keter), p. 1445.

5. Kemelman, H. (1973). *Tuesday the Rabbi Saw Red* (New York: Arthur Fields Books), pp. 258-259.

6. Polner, M. (1977). *Rabbi: The American Experience* (New York: Holt, Rinehart and Winston), p. xiii.

7. Schwartzfuchs, S. (1993). *A Concise History of the Rabbinate* (Oxford, UK and Cambridge, USA: Blackwell), p. ix.

8. Rabinowitz, p. 1445.

9. Jacob, W. (1997). "Private ordination—Need We Be Concerned?" *CCAR Journal* 44:1 (Winter): 3.

10. Rothkoff, A. (1972). "Semikhah," in *Encyclopedia Judaica* vol. 14, (Jerusalem: Keter) pp. 1146-1147.

11. A definition of the various divisions within Orthodoxy will be found in Chapter 2, Mainstream Rabbis and Sectarian Orthodox Rabbis.

12. For further information on the history and development of the rabbinate, as well as the institution of ordination, see the articles on "Rabbi, Rabbinate" and "Semikhah," in *Encyclopedia Judaica* (Jerusalem: Keter, 1972); Schwartzfuchs; "The Making of American Rabbis," in *Encyclopedia Judaica Yearbook 1983/5* (Jerusalem: Keter, 1985) pp. 84–105; Jacob, "Private Ordination—Need We Be Concerned?" pp. 3-8.

13. Greenberg, S. (1991). "The Rabbi as Darshan." *Judaism* 40:4 (Fall): 471.

14. Chyet, S. F. (1962). "The Wise Men of Wentworth." *Chicago Jewish Forum* 21:1 (Fall): 34–36.

1

The American Rabbi

THE FIRST ONE HUNDRED YEARS, 1840–1940

The history of the rabbinate in North America is considerably shorter than that of the history of the Jewish community on this continent. Jews first came here in the middle of the seventeenth century (1654), yet it would be nearly 200 years before a trained rabbi settled on these shores. Until the mid-nineteenth century, in terms of Jewish population, America was largely a backwater. There were millions of Jews living in the area of Eastern and Central Europe. Poland and Lithuania were major centers of rabbinic learning, and following the Emancipation, Jewish studies developed in Western Europe, primarily in Germany. In terms of both Jewish population and of Jewish culture, initially there was little to draw immigrants to the New World.

Though exact census figures are open to question, it is estimated that in 1700 there were about 200 to 300 Jews in America. By 1776, that number had grown tenfold, but it still was a very limited community. In the four decades leading up to 1860, relatively speaking, the Jewish population of the United States mushroomed, from an estimated 6,000 people in 1826 to well over to 150,000 in 1860. The vast majority of these settlers came from German lands.[1]

The typical congregation in colonial times had various lay leaders and a board of trustees, but the ritual aspects were delegated to a *hazzan* (cantor); a person to serve as a *shochet* (ritual slaughter of meat products); and a *shammash* (beadle), who dealt with daily ritual needs. There were no trained rabbis serving congregations until 1840, when Rabbi Abraham Rice came to Baltimore. Between 1840 and 1860, however, there would be a major expansion in the rabbinate. Prominent among them would be the leaders of the growing Reform movement, such stalwarts as Isaac Mayer Wise (first Albany, and then for much of his career, Cincinnati), David Einhorn (Baltimore), Bernard Felsenthal (Chicago), and Samuel Adler (New York). There also were voices in opposition to the ideas of Reform, most notable among them being Isaac Leeser of Philadelphia, though Leeser never claimed rabbinical status or authority.[2]

The next 25 years, approximately 1860–1885, saw significant changes. This period would see the flowering of German Jewry in America. Congregations were being formed throughout the Midwest and the South, both in the large cities and in small towns. Further, as Gilbert S. Rosenthal (1986) has noted, discerning "leaders realized that the American rabbinate could not develop properly without a rabbinic seminary."[3] A number of schools were started, but with the exception of the Hebrew Union College in Cincinnati they were not successful. German language newspapers—weeklies or monthlies—were published, the most important a supplement to the *Israelite* (renamed the *American Israelite* in 1874), which was edited by Rabbi Isaac Mayer Wise, arguably the "founder" of Reform Judaism in America. The Reform movement and its synagogues dominated Jewish life. The theological position of the movement was embodied in the "Pittsburgh Platform" of 1885, and it would characterize Reform Jewish thinking for fifty years, though it was never adopted as any sort of official creed. It described its understanding of Judaism as a "progressive religion, ever striving to be in accord with the postulates of reason," and further that it was capable of adapting to the advances of modern knowledge. The platform spoke of Judaism no longer being a "nation" but clearly "a religious community." As the American historian Sidney Ahlstrom (1972) has written, by "the time this declaration was published Reform Judaism had almost come to *be* American Judaism."[4] In this general period, the continuing institutions of Reform Judaism were all established, first the congregational organization, the Union of American Hebrew Congregations (1873); then the Hebrew Union College, the Reform rabbinical seminary (1875); and lastly the rabbinic organization, the Central Conference of American Rabbis (1889), though only the CCAR was established from its start as a Reform agency.

Just as America was rapidly growing in population at this time, so Jewish immigration was also burgeoning. From less than 300,000 Jews in 1880 (considerably less than one percent of the total population of the United States) to approximately 4.5 million out of a total population of 115,000,000 in 1925 (nearly four percent) was a phenomenal increase. The years 1880–1924 saw nearly 2.5 million Jews come to America, largely from Eastern Europe, from the Austro-Hungarian empire, Rumania, and the lands under Russian domination.

In Europe, the Jews had lived largely as a separate community, either in agricultural villages, the *shtetlach*, or some form of urban quarter, the ghetto. When they came to America, they sought to re-create Jewish life here. In many northern cities in the United States, but primarily among them New York, *voluntary* Jewish ghettoes were established. These were urban areas where an observant Jewish life could be lived. The Jewish population was largely an industrial- and labor-oriented community. Most of the immigrants were in their mid-teens to mid-forties.

The Reform institutions of America, and especially the synagogues (often called Temples), were doubly uninviting to the new immigrants. These institutions were German-dominated, as opposed to Eastern European; there were such radical religious changes that observant Jews felt alienated; and finally there was considerable social distance between those who had (relatively) "made it" and the new immigrants.

The influx of "East European Jewish immigrants brought about the firm establishment of Orthodoxy in the United States, although only a minority of the immigrants and few of their children actually remained Orthodox Jews. Several hundred East European rabbis settled throughout the country, but their influence was far more limited than it had been in their native lands."[5] This increase of Jews committed to an Orthodox religious expression also meant that there would be formal institutions in this land reflecting those values. In 1898, the Union of Orthodox Jewish Congregations of America was formed, and in 1902, the Union of Orthodox Rabbis of the United States and Canada was begun. The Rabbi Isaac Elchanan Theological Seminary (RIETS) in New

York had been formed in 1897. Originally, it was a transplanted East European Yeshiva which provided immigrant students and scholars alike a place to continue their studies. In time, this first would become part, of Yeshiva College, and then of Yeshiva University. "In this institution and in similar ones elsewhere a new English-speaking Orthodox rabbinate was trained, who in 1930 organized the Rabbinical Council of America. The Young Israel movement (founded in 1912) gave further scope to such activity."[6]

Jeffrey S. Gurock (1996) points out that RIETS' founding purpose as an East European Yeshiva was consciously changed.

> [Under] pressure from, among others, Americanized Orthodox East European lay leaders . . . RIETS [was] reorganized as the Rabbinical College of America. Under the leadership of Rabbi Bernard Revel, the school slowly began to produce rabbis knowledgeable in American ways and able to preach in English homiletic messages attractive to fellow second generation Jews—worthy opponents of JTS [the Conservative movement's rabbinical school—the Jewish Theological Seminary] graduates.[7]

Other communities also set up yeshivot (plural of yeshiva). In Chicago, the Orthodox community in 1922 started the Beth Hamidrash La-Torah, the Hebrew Theological College. Founded by a group of Midwest-based rabbis, it was committed "from its inception to produce 'modern leaders of Orthodox Jewry,'" explains Jeffrey S. Gurock. Its curriculum emphasized not only "intense study of the Talmud and the Codes . . . and mastery of the *Tanach* [Bible] but also a thorough knowledge of Jewish history and literature and a comprehensive grasp of the problem of contemporary Jewish life."[8]

In the minds of the more religious right-wing Orthodox communities, both the Rabbi Isaac Elchanan Theological Seminary and the Hebrew Theological College were suspect. Consequently, these Orthodox groups created their own higher yeshivot. Hundreds of rabbis have "come forth from Brooklyn's Torah Vadaat, Chaim Berlin, and Lubavitcher Yeshivah; Manhattan's Jacob Joseph and Tifereth Yerushalayim; Baltimore's Ner Israel; Cleveland's Telse [Telshe] Yeshivah; Lakewood's [Lakewood, New Jersey's] Beth Midrash Gavoha; and Spring Valley's [Spring Valley, New York's] Beth Midrash Elyon"[9] as well as many other smaller institutions. Most of these rabbis, however, do not serve congregations but become teachers or go into business.

William B. Helmreich in his ground-breaking work *The World of the Yeshiva* (1982) explains that the yeshiva is much more than an institution where Orthodox rabbis are ordained. Indeed many students who enroll in the yeshiva do not become practicing rabbis or teachers. They are "more likely to enter accounting, law, business, or other secular fields" or they enroll there for no other goal than to continue learning. This is in accord with the primary goals of the yeshiva, namely, to train pious, God-fearing Jews who are well informed in the laws and customs of Judaism.[10]

> Helmreich's thought is reflected in a novel where a rabbinical student attending Yeshiva University explains that in the Orthodox world one doesn't necessarily study for *semikhah* [ordination] to serve in the professional rabbinate; how in fact, the majority of his classmates did not intend to serve as rabbis at all; indeed many, after earning their *semikhah*, would go on to careers in law, business, and medicine.[11]

Today the Union of Orthodox Rabbis of the United States and Canada would be considered further to the religious right than the Rabbinical Council of America. Broadly speaking, the rabbis associated with the Union of Orthodox Rabbis reflect the Sectarian Orthodox "Litvishe" (Russian-Lithuanian) Yeshiva tradition of study as opposed to what is called "Centrist Orthodox" on its left and Hasidic Orthodox, which is another division within Sectarian Orthodoxy. As I explain in the following chapter, Mainstream Rabbis and Sectarian Orthodox Rabbis, there is no consensus on terminology to describe the Orthodox movement.

The opening decades of the twentieth century also saw the rise of Conservative Judaism in the United States.[12] Central to this endeavor was the reorganization of the Jewish Theological Seminary under the leadership of Rabbi Solomon Schechter, who was brought to America in 1902 to accomplish that task. The Seminary had been founded in 1886 and opened its doors a year later. It was under Schechter's leadership that a prominent faculty of biblical, Talmudic, and historical scholars as well as an excellent library would be established. The Seminary worked alongside the Rabbinical Assembly of America, which had been established in 1900. By 1913, again under Rabbi Schechter's leadership, the United Synagogue of America, the Conservative movement's federation of congregations, was formed. Conservative Judaism then, as today, sought to find a middle ground between what it perceived as the unacceptable radical stance of Reform Judaism and the unbending position of Orthodox Judaism.

The founder of the fourth branch of American Judaism, the Reconstructionist movement, taught at the Jewish Theological Seminary for many years. Rabbi Mordecai M. Kaplan (1881–1983) had served for a time as an Orthodox rabbi and in 1912 he was one of the founders of the Orthodox Young Israel movement. Then, in 1913, he helped Solomon Schechter with the founding of the United Synagogue of America. Kaplan characterized Judaism as an evolving religious civilization more than as a religion per se. He suggested that the Jewish religion exists for the Jewish people not the Jewish people for the religion. Key points in the development of Reconstructionist Judaism were Kaplan's founding of the Society for the Advancement of Judaism, a synagogue in New York City in 1922; his magnum opus, *Judaism as a Civilization*, published in 1934; and the establishment of the Reconstructionist Rabbinical College in 1968. As the Reconstructionist movement has grown, Kaplan's philosophy remained at the core of its ideology, but now "Kaplan's teachings are viewed not as the end of the story, but as the beginning."[13]

The development of American rabbinical seminaries has meant an American rabbinate that is "home grown" and reflective of American values and communal expectations.[14] Their experience, roles, and duties are a far cry from what existed in Europe. American rabbis have a secular education. If these rabbis serve a congregation, they preach in English. They are involved in community affairs, both Jewish and secular. Oftentimes they work with Christian clergy and do not necessarily avoid matters of controversy. They have greater prestige than their nineteenth century counterparts in America. As Rosenthal has described the modern rabbinate, these are professionals, community leaders who are "a mixture of pastor, preacher, priest, public relations expert, ambassador to the gentiles, teacher, psychologist, fund raiser, master of ceremonies, and organizer of numerous projects."[15]

THE AMERICAN RABBINATE: 1940–1970

Two Defining Events: the Holocaust and the Reestablishment of the State of Israel

The three decades from 1940 to 1970 saw tumultuous changes in the life of world Jewry as well as significant transformations in North

America generally. Many of these phenomena had a direct impact on the American rabbinate. There were two events which changed forever the fate and faith of Judaism. The first was the rise to power of the Nazi party in Germany and the subsequent Holocaust (1939–1945, with systematic slaughter dating from 1942) wherein six million innocent Jews—women, men, and children—were callously and brutally murdered. The second life-changing event was the reestablishment of the State of Israel in 1948.

In terms of the Holocaust, not only did the Jewish community have to deal with this horrible sense of loss but theologically questions were asked as well as to the nature and presence (or absence) of God. These issues were and are faced by both the factual and fictional rabbinate. In this general period, significant works by rabbis include Richard L. Rubenstein's *After Auschwitz: Radical Theology and Contemporary Judaism* (1966); Irving Greenberg's "Cloud of Smoke, Pillar of Fire: Judaism, Christianity, and Modernity After the Holocaust," in *Auschwitz: Beginning of a New Era*, Eva Fleishner, ed. (1977); Arthur A. Cohen's *The Tremendum: A Theological Interpretation of the Holocaust* (1981); and Emil Fackenheim's *To Mend the World: Foundations of Future Jewish Thought* (1982).

> Rabbi Chaplain David Cohen (*The Conversion of Chaplain Cohen*) says: "I've thought about it, I've questioned, I've sought the answer. But there is no ready one . . . not for me . . . and I can't pretend there is an ultimate answer that anyone can fathom . . . Yesterday, alas, another note fell due—notice not of God's failure, but of the world's."[16]
>
> Another rabbi, Rabbi Aaron Baltner (*A Marked House*) apportions blame to both God and human beings:
>
> "Millions of Jews humiliated, tortured and killed . . . Where was God when it took place, our omniscient, omnipotent and loving God?
>
> ". . . to Thee, Lord, I say . . . Be the God we were taught to believe in. Take pity on all. Let the Creator and all Creation atone. Let there be a new day from now on."[17]
>
> Rabbi Cohen suggests that humankind was to blame, that the "failure" was one which highlights a deep flaw in the moral life of men and women, but that God cannot be held responsible. Rabbi Baltner wrestles with God's apparent absence during the Holocaust, and while he, like Cohen, holds humanity

responsible, Baltner also suggests that God too has to atone for not acting out the role of an all-powerful, all-knowing, beneficent deity.

The reestablishment of the State of Israel in 1948 had a profound effect on world Jewry. Following the atrocity of the Holocaust, it has given Jews a way to work through their grief, it has provided a sense of hope for the future. When referring to the Holocaust and the subsequent establishment of Israel, Jews often use such linked terms as "tragedy" and "triumph."

Today, there are incredibly strong bonds between Jews worldwide and the State of Israel. Sociologist Jonathan S. Woocher (1986) writes that "American Judaism recognizes only one heresy which subjects the perpetrator to immediate excommunication: denial of support to the State of Israel."[18] With those ties so evident, it is easy to forget that there was a great controversy among American Jews and American rabbis over the wisdom of establishing an independent Jewish state. While the majority of the Conservative rabbinate had been strongly pro-Zionist from its early days, Orthodox Jewry was divided over this issue as was the Reform rabbinate. By the 1930s, however, that had changed, and many, if not actually most rabbis in all three branches of Judaism were committed to ideological Zionism.[19]

In the 50 years of Israel's existence, there certainly have been moments of high drama. While Israel does not escape criticism from Jews, and specifically from rabbis, it is absolutely clear that Israel is central to the life of many Jews in America, and its role is very complex. As Woocher has written:

> In practical terms, an enormous proportion of the energies of the institutions of the Jewish polity is devoted to work of one sort or another on behalf of the state and people of Israel. For many activists, Israel is the prime motivator and focus of their involvement. It remains the central theme and cause in communitywide fundraising campaigns. Jewish unity, mutual responsibility, and Jewish survival all come together in Israel; it is the symbolic center of the civil Jewish universe, the place where the lines of Jewish existence—of Jewish history and tradition, of the modern Jewish condition, and the response to that condition—intersect.
>
> Like all important religious symbols, Israel has multiple meanings.[20]

Israel at one and the same time claims to serve as a spiritual homeland for all Jews, as a place to nourish Judaism, a centerpiece of Jewish pride, and also a refuge for Jews in crisis anywhere in the world. When Israel was literally under attack in 1967 (and again in 1973), and her very existence seemed in question, the outpouring of support was phenomenal.[21]

> After explaining that Judaism is more than just a system of beliefs or ritual practices, Rabbi David Small (*Monday the Rabbi Took Off*) comments that it is "a way of life, but more than that, [Judaism is] . . . intertwined somehow with the people themselves, with the Jews as a nation. And the two, the religion and the people, are somehow tied in with the place, Israel . . . it is not significant merely because we happened to come from there, but rather because it is the particular place assigned to us by God."[22]

The Changing Demography of American Jewry

Jews generally live within the great suburban stretches of America. Many congregations, factual and fictional, are set within these environs. Charles E. Silberman (1985) notes that it was to the "suburbs, to which Jews flocked after the end of World War II" and likewise it was "there the consciousness of being a Jew suddenly came to the fore as Jews found themselves living in predominantly Gentile communities and neighborhoods. More was involved than just a shift from being part of the majority to being a tiny minority."[23] In the old neighborhoods, there had been non-Jews, but they were largely fellow-ethnics, Irish, Italian, and Polish Catholics. They were "outsiders" just as the Jews were. As one person remarked, the "Italians were really sort of Jewish." These Gentiles in the suburbs were different, "the Gentile neighbors were 'Americans'—white Protestants rather than fellow ethnics; they were insiders in an age in which Jews still felt themselves to be outsiders. . . . In this environment Jews felt awkward and ill at ease, and they were eager—in fact, anxious—to gain their neighbor's approval."[24] One way to gain that approval was to build a synagogue, to be like "them."

These new synagogues provided friendship and fellowship for the new Jewish communities. This was necessary, for the new suburbanites did not have the support of extended family as they had when growing up. The synagogue also provided a place for religious education for their children. According to a study of that period, very few Jews affiliated with a synagogue simply because they deemed themselves "religious." Some joined synagogues because the rabbi was "available for counseling in the many personal and family problems that dislocation" had brought with their move. In addition, the rabbi was a leader in the Jewish community and an "esteemed representative to the general community."[25]

> Building a synagogue or Jewish institution where there had not been one before is a significant issue in several works, among them Philip Ruth's "Eli the Fanatic" in the collection *Goodbye Columbus and Five Short Stories*; Arkady Leokum's *The Temple*; Jerome Weidman's *The Temple*; and Howard Fast's *The Outsider*. In these works, what their non-Jewish neighbors think is certainly an important matter for the congregants, though they differ in each of the books.[26]

The period encompassed by the three decades 1940–1970 was a time of stunning growth both in the establishment and construction of new religious institutions. Reform Judaism almost doubled its constituent congregations in the period between 1948 and 1966, reaching a figure of 664 congregational units. Reconstructionist Judaism also grew in this period. Conservative Judaism increased its numbers from 350 congregational units at the conclusion of World War II to 800 by 1965. Orthodox synagogues likewise saw a huge increase in growth as Young Israel and other modern Orthodox [now, more often called "Centrist" Orthodox] congregations emerged in urban and suburban areas.[27]

The increase, according to historian Jack Wertheimer (1989) was due to several factors. These included:

1. When G.I.s returned after World War II, they were eager to participate in "Americanized" religious services lead by American-trained rabbis, similar to the services they had encountered lead by their American-trained Jewish chaplains.
2. Having moved to suburbia, they "looked to the synagogue to provide them with a network of Jewish friends and peers" to re-create for them the Jewish neighborhoods in which they had grown up.
3. Since there were no natural Jewish neighborhoods where their children would learn Jewish customs, values and traditions al-

most "through a process of osmosis" these families had to join congregations to provide a Jewish education for their children.
4. Finally, by participating in the building of synagogues and sending their children to Sunday school, these Jews were acting as "quintessential midcentury Americans."[28] A catch phrase of that period is "to go to the church or synagogue of your choice."

The rabbis of these suburban congregations (in the 1940s, 1950s, and 1960s) on the whole, are not physically isolated from their colleagues or other Jews. Exceptions to this rule certainly can be found, often young rabbis early on in their careers. Some congregations in this period are decades old, while some have been established recently. These congregations, factual and fictional, reflect the broad spectrum of Jewish life in America. Many are from the middle class.

The fiction reflects similar locales both then and in succeeding decades. We learn of Rabbi Sam Weintraub's congregation (*The Rabbi Is a Lady*), Temple Shalom, which is located in the "prosperous, suburban Long Island community of Wilmette."[29] Rabbi Abraham Cohen (*Days of Judgment*) serves 400 families in Adamstown, New York,[30] and Rabbi Daniel Winter (*An Eye for an Eye*) serves a 700 member congregation in Los Angeles.[31] By way of contrast, Rabbi Deborah Luria's Congregation Beth Shalom (*Acts of Faith*) is located in Old Saybrook, "a relatively young and growing community" a part of "sylvan Connecticut and yet an easy journey to New York City."[32]

There are exceptions both small and large. Rabbi Davis' congregation (*Coat Upon a Stick*) is primarily poor, "a score of old men, from the nursing home and a few surrounding streets where a room was cheap enough to die in. . . ." There also are a few "little Jewish businessmen, doing what they have to, trying to stay alive."[33] Likewise, Rabbi Arthur Bloom's synagogue (*The Rabbi of Casino Boulevard*), located in unfashionable Gardena, California, is "composed of salesmen, bookkeepers, some small businessmen, owners of a newspaper route and of a coin-operated laundry or two, some civil-service workers, pensioners and some old soldiers." They are a "poorer, far more colorful group" than the "troublesome doctors, lawyers, and successful businessmen Bloom had struggled with at his previous jobs."[34] Rabbi David Hartman (*The Outsider*) takes on a congregation which, though it will grow over the years, initially has a very limited membership. "In the fourteen families, there are two Orthodox families and two Conservative families. They go along with the Reform movement because it's the only way they can have a synagogue."[35] On the other end of the scale we find in the Golden Ghetto in Los Angeles, a synagogue while

> not the oldest in Southern California, it was certainly the largest, the best known and the richest, full of patricians. It had as members the oldest Jewish families, the most solid because of social standing and a long preoccupation with local history. They were the cream of the film and television set, real estate speculators, furriers, collectors of modern art, the half-gentile, floaters of sailing boats, drivers of British or Italian cars, and a backlog of solid upper middle class, one time refugees.[36]

The struggle for Civil Rights, especially in the 1960s, brought many Jews into the realm of political activism. Jewish students were very active, especially in the "civil rights summers," and in many cases rabbis were there marching alongside with them. A very famous picture of that period shows Rabbi Abraham Joshua Heschel arm in arm with Ralph Bunche, Reverend Martin Luther King, Jr., and Reverend Ralph D. Abernathy on the march from Selma to Montgomery, March 22–26, 1965.

In the fiction, Rabbi Alvin Blumenfeld (*The Rabbi and the Nun*) "was one of the first rabbis who went down South in the early sixties to help Dr. Martin Luther King fight for what Blumenfeld called a 'just and humane society.'"[37] Rabbi David Hartman (*The Outsider*), is not only found marching in the Deep South, he also is attacked and bloodied for his efforts.[38]

THE JEWISH COMMUNITY AND THE AMERICAN RABBINATE: 1970–2000

The late 1960s saw great changes in American and American-Jewish life. These "currents reshaped the agenda of both religious institutions and individual Jews." Among many factors these years saw the leveling off of the Jewish population at about 5.8 million people; a "soaring rate of intermarriage" and with it various strategies as how best to face this phenomenon; a redefining of the meaning of the State of Israel for American Jewry, especially following the near-catastrophic 1967 Arab-Israeli War; the passing of the mantle of leadership from an immigrant generation to a cohort of "home-grown" Jews; the social and political activism which began in the 1960s themselves; the "resurgence of religious traditionalism and decline of secularism; and, finally, the women's movement."[39]

Though I shall deal with the matter further in Chapter 7 (Women Rabbis), already in the early 1970s there were strong stirrings for greater equality for women in all aspects of synagogue life. The year 1971 saw the formation of Ezrat Nashim, a "consciousness-raising" group for women. All sectors of Judaism were affected by the women's movement. American Orthodoxy would not be immune from the winds of change. Writing about the Orthodoxy community in the mid-1980s, Jeffrey S. Gurock noted that the majority of the membership of the Rabbinical Council of America resisted making accommodation to the women's requests. Yet a small group began searching for ways within an Orthodox reading of Jewish law to allow for change. "Accordingly, many Orthodox congregations now permit their women to serve on lay boards of trustees, and some even permit female membership on synagogue ritual committees. Most strikingly, a few rabbis have placed their imprimatur upon separate women's tefilot (prayer services) within their communities."[40]

As time moved from the 1970s to the 1990s, both the urban and suburban congregations were buffeted by many of the same winds assaulting mainstream Christian congregations. We live in a much more secular world than heretofore. Whether there has or has not been a real decline in religious values, there are those who have spoken of a decline in church and synagogue membership and participation.

Clearly, Jews belong to congregations for a variety of reasons. They do so because that is how they define their Jewishness; they want a place for their children to be Jewishly educated; and they want a place to pray on the High Holy Days. Jews may join a certain congregation because that is where their parents belong. Jews may join a particular congregation because of denominational issues. If they have a choice of several synagogues within the movement, or if denominational matters are not of great importance, they may join because of the personality of a particular rabbi.

Those involved with congregational life know that only a small percentage of the members are there because of a genuine interest in the synagogue or because they want a regular place to pray. "We have paying members, and praying members," a congregant once remarked to me. Several years ago, Conservative Rabbi Samuel H. Dresner (1963) labeled the phenomenon "Judaism by proxy." He wrote of the people who "join a synagogue—not because they feel the need to pray or study, but because David goes to Hebrew school and it is the proper thing to do." He laments the fact that synagogues have become so child-centered that adults are virtually left out of the picture. In many cases, after "the child is grown, membership in the synagogue is dropped." He also addresses those Jews who belong for the sake of their parents. "Although they see little meaning in the Jewish religion, they make Jewish life a 'family affair,' participating in it for one reason and one reason only: their parents. . . . They may attend the synagogue not out of desire to hear the teachings of the Torah but because their parents urge them to go."[41]

About a decade later Rabbi Martin Siegel met with a small group of his synagogue who were interested in broadening the activities of their congregation.

> In discussing the present temple membership, the group agreed that only a core of about thirty percent of the members have a genuine interest in the temple, in each other and in Judaism. Fifty percent, they said, have a general peripheral interest, fifteen percent a special interest (the Men's Club, the bowling league or the Sisterhood) and five percent have an ephemeral interest. Members of this last group join until the services they require (bar mitzvahs, confirmations, weddings) are completed, then quit.[42]

Beginning about the 1980s, there was another change in American Jewish life. Jews were more open about their Jewishness. Michael G. Berenbaum (1995) explains that, in the past, Jews who were active in political life were cautious about their religious background. That changed dramatically.

> In the 1980s, Jewish members of the House of Representatives came from Bozrah, Connecticut; Wichita, Kansas; and Dallas, Texas. They represented districts where the Jewish population was less than one-

> half of one percent. Politicians . . . take pride in their ethnicity and their support for Israel is nonapologetic and direct. They respond directly to critics. Barney Frank, [a] . . . Congressman from Massachusetts, responded to one of his colleagues who called America a "Christian country" by asking: "If this is a Christian country, what is an overweight Jewish boy from Boston doing up at 5:15 in the morning presiding over the House of Representatives?"[43]

Yet along with an acceptance in American life, Judaism and the place of the synagogue in Jewish life, also changed. Michael A. Meyer (1988) has written of the "new privatism in synagogue life." Congregants regard the synagogue as a "supplier of private needs . . . the religious ceremonies associated with birth, puberty, marriage, and death. They valued rabbis according to their ability to enhance individual lives rather than the collective life of the congregation."[44]

Sara Bershtel and Allen Graubard (1992) note that in recent years "Synagogue membership has dropped below half of the number of Jewish households, and even for the diminishing number of members, synagogue attendance continues to decline."[45] This decline may well be linked to a variety of reasons including assimilation, intermarriage, and a lessening of overt anti-Semitism. Others mention apathy and indifference. In addition, the general movement of people, Jews included, from the more urban centers to suburbia, from the "rust-belt" to the "sun-belt"—and the general drift of American population west, southwest and south—has meant that a number of congregations are losing members. While some new congregations are being formed, in many cases having moved to a new community, Jews are postponing the decision whether or not to join a congregation, if at all.

Yet attendance does not tell the whole picture. Marshall Sklare (1971) observed that were we to judge the synagogue merely by the criterion of attendance, that the conclusion would be that this is a struggling institution, "banished to the periphery of Jewish life. . . . Nothing could be further from the truth. The American synagogue is a vital institution." He goes on to point out that irrespective of "community size, membership is common in all segments of the population" though he notes that the more prosperous and families with children between five and 15 (the religion school years) belong in larger numbers. Furthermore, absence from "the membership rolls does not generally represent a clear commitment to any rival institution. It does mean of course that the individual has been strongly influenced by the secularization process. But any critical observer would be quick to point out that most synagogue members have been vitally affected by the same process."

Indeed, Sklare also mentions that the American synagogue is focused on Jewish survival, and rather than erect barriers to keep the secularists out, the synagogue "has accepted the secular Jew on his own terms" and simply seeks to transform him. "In most congregations membership is open to all; no test of the applicant's religious attitudes or observance of *mitzvot* is required."[46]

Identification with a certain movement is not the same thing as formal affiliation. Nonetheless, even verbal association does suggest something about the relative strengths of the three major movements. Connections with Orthodoxy in any large numbers is largely limited to the New York City area, and in particular the boroughs of Brooklyn and the Bronx.[47] Having said this, by the 1990s there are also large pockets of Orthodoxy in such cities as Baltimore, Boston (Brookline), Chicago, Cleveland, Los Angeles, and Miami. Wertheimer explains that the numerical strength of Orthodoxy in the largest Jewish community in the United States, New York City, gives that movement a visibility that is greater than its actual numbers. Identification with Conservative Judaism does continue, though in many cities it is being challenged by Reform Judaism. "The main beneficiary of Orthodox and Conservative losses seems to be the Reform movement (as well as the group of Jews with no preference.)"[48] Recent figures divide American Jews into these categories: "2 percent Reconstructionist, 9 percent Orthodox, 29 percent Reform, 34 percent Conservative, and 26 percent 'other' or 'just Jewish.'"[49] These figures suggest both a decline in the number who have associated with Orthodoxy and a rapid rise in Reform Judaism. "Demographic studies suggest that . . . [the Reform] movement is growing more rapidly than any other and at the expense of its competitors."[50]

Where Jews do affiliate, especially in suburbia, they wrestle with some common questions. How much time do we actively invest in our tradition, and to what extent do we participate in the more general and homogenized life of "Middle America"—the athletic club; soccer, little league and ballet for the children; or sports on TV? How do we spend our leisure time, and where do we spend our discretionary dollars? For the Jewish community this question is further subdivided into competing demands by the "secular" arm of the Jewish community: the local "Federation" or other groups such as B'nai B'rith; the Anti-Defamation League; the American Jewish Committee; the American

Jewish Congress; or the Jewish Community Center. All of these groups are competing with the synagogues for the time and financial support of the members of the Jewish community.

Furthermore there is a continuing power struggle between the leadership of the synagogue and the leadership of the Federation. Rabbis today are not the "superstars" in terms of wielding political power as were the giants of the 1940s and 1950s, a Rabbi Abba Hillel Silver or Rabbi Stephen S. Wise. Describing life in the mid 1970s, Murray Polner suggests that "rabbis tend to be ignored as ineffectual and irrelevant by the more influential Jewish federations that collect and disperse funds and by the national secular agencies, all of which help shape national policies for the many different Jewish communities in America."[51] There is little evidence that the situation has changed in the decades since that evaluation.

Indeed an ongoing complaint is that rabbis have little or no real influence at the federation level, and that power is exercised by the few enormously wealthy lay leaders, oftentimes people who lack any substantial knowledge about Jewish history, religious practice, theology, Bible, Talmud, culture, or Hebrew. Indeed this complaint about rabbinical influence has been ongoing, true in one form or another, since 17th century in America.

For all that, the synagogue and the rabbi are important institutions, as at least, grudgingly, federations do acknowledge. Indeed, in recent years, there have been attempts to seek new partnerships between synagogues and federations.[52] As sociologist Jonathan S. Woocher points out, the "synagogue remains the place where most Jews gather to give ritual and symbolic expression to their Jewishness, to educate their children, and to find a Jewish context in which to share the joys and cope with the sorrows of human existence." While that is so, the synagogue is "no longer the exclusive venue for any of these activities, and the rabbi is no longer the [sole and] unquestioned leader of the Jewish community."[53]

> Though the rabbi may not be sole and unquestioned leader in the Jewish community, the rabbi can play a pivotal role in the life of his or her congregants. Arkady Leokum suggests that all congregants establish some kind of relationship with their rabbi, whether deep or distant. "Whatever the degree of involvement with religion and the Temple, it becomes neces-

> sary for every group in the congregation to establish some kind of relationship with their Rabbi. It is one of the miracles of Judaism. We are what we are, but let Rabbi know us. He is our Rabbi, let us know him. The relationship may become close and deep, or it may remain so distant that it has no meaning for either side, but the effort must be made. It's as if two parts of an organism that function independently still sense an underlying unity."[54]

A further observation is necessary in regard to Woocher's comment that "the rabbi is no longer the [sole and] unquestioned leader of the Jewish community." This matter centers on the whole issue of "Rabbinic Authority." When, in times past, the rabbi was "the unquestioned leader of the Jewish community" his was, in many ways, the final word. Today, the rabbi clearly does not have this power or authority.[55]

Indeed, writing on the subject of rabbinic authority, Eli Turkel (1993) has suggested that in "our contemporary setting, it is clear that no rabbi or [rabbinic] court has any power to impose their halakhic [halakhah—Jewish law, traditional practice] opinions on other individuals or communities. The authority of a rabbi extends only to the immediate congregation that has accepted him as its *posek*" [interpreter of Jewish law]. He goes on to say that the "opinion of any individual, no matter how learned he may be, carries no halakhic force except that of persuasion."[56]

This question of the rabbi's authority, and likewise the issue of *mara d'atra*, the local rabbi serving as the ultimate halakhic authority, has been a vexing problem in recent years within the Conservative movement. There are deep divisions on this matter between the rabbinical association, the Rabbinical Assembly, and Conservative Judaism's lay organization, the United Synagogue of America.[57]

Rabbi Emanuel Feldman, editor of the journal *Tradition*, which is published by the ("Centrist" Orthodox) Rabbinical Council of America, is also the Rabbi Emeritus of Congregation Beth Jacob in Atlanta. In 1993, he editorialized on the subject of Rabbinic Authority. While his editorial concluded with comments that much had changed, and that the Atlanta community is now more serious, learned, and more Jewish sophisticated, he did present an amazing picture of rabbinical life. His editorial is titled: "I Could Have Used Some Rabbinic Authority."

> No one sat me down before I came to Atlanta as a young rabbi and said "Remember, you have rabbinic authority. What you say about God, Torah, and life in general is going to be listened to, because you are the living embodiment of Torah, and you represent the holy Jewish tradition. What you say is *da'at Torah*, the Torah position. Your community will have *emunat hakhamim* ['faith in the sages'] in you, trusting you as they trust the words of the Sages. Your opinion on any subject is, in a way, the word of God filtered through our wise men. . . . And while you do not have literal *ruah ha-kodesh* [the holy spirit], what you say is a distillation of the divine will."
>
> No one told me these things, nor even hinted at them. Perhaps it's just as well they didn't. For one thing, my community, thoughtful and kind as they were, never heard of *da'at Torah* or *emunat hakhamim*. (Uncannily, however, they had an instinctive understanding of the concept of personal autonomy. One Federation leader, upon being informed by me that a certain contemplated action was against Torah law, responded, "Listen, rabbi, we need to do our own thing, so let's keep the Torah out of this. No one understands it anyway.")
>
> I did have rabbinic authority when I answered questions about the time for Yizkor, or the date for next year's Seder, which answers they accepted fully and unreservedly, no doubt sensing that I represented four thousand years of Jewish tradition. And when they wanted to know the Jewish names for Clete and Rosemarie and Butch and JoAnn, and I unhesitatingly replied Kalman and Rivka and Barukh and Yocheved Chana, they knew that this brilliance was not only the culmination of a superb rabbinic education, but were convinced that I was reflecting the divine will.

He goes on to say, that once,

> when a fine lady told me that she "didn't practice ritual but only lived by the Ten Commandments," and I made bold to inform her that Shabbat was the fourth of the ten, she was mildly surprised and said politely but firmly, "Are you absolutely sure?"
>
> No one really suspected that I had *ruah ha-kodesh* except Joe the chronic gambler, who called me one Erev Yom Kippur with his own awesome concern: the World Series was approaching and would I please pick the winner for him? "But Joe," I would protest, "you're risking hundreds of dollars on the word of someone who is not an expert in these things." Joe, overcome by genuine *emunat hakhamim* and convinced that I had a direct line, would insist, "Listen rabbi, whatever you pick, I'm ready to lay money on it." For four years running, in an amazing display of rabbinic *mazal*, I picked winners,

> and Joe would happily give ten percent of his earnings to the Shul, informing one and all that his rabbi truly possessed the divine spirit . . . .
>
> At births, bar mitzvahs, weddings, and funerals, mine was the unquestioned *da'at Torah*. In sickness and domestic crisis I was their pipeline to the Holy One. But when it came to life's major decisions—how to raise the children, how much tzedakah to give and where to give it, where to send a child to school, how to live life as a Jew—it was, "Rabbi, we love you, but the Torah was for then, and this is now."
>
> When I spoke about anti-Semitism, I was their halakhic decisor, but when I asked why black athletes are called Isaiah and Jewish children are called Lucas, I was their very young rabbi who would some day mature.
>
> When I taught about our glorious past, they had faith in my every word, but when I suggested that without Torah living we may not have a future, I was out of touch with the present.
>
> When I supported the State of Israel in its tribulations, I was the voice of Jewish authority, but when, one Pesach, I inquired from the pulpit why the church across the street was overflowing on that Easter Sunday while we had fifteen people for our Yom Tov davening, I was being impractical and Utopian.[58]

While the examples might differ in Conservative, Reconstructionist, and Reform congregations, the role of the rabbi and his or her authority as a religious leader is also a concern for those movements. The tension between rabbis and laity indeed is not a new phenomenon. In an article on "The Origin and Authority of the Rabbi," Harold I. Saperstein (1982) makes it clear that these tensions have a venerable history.[59]

Rabbis in America generally serve within one of the major denominational movements. In the next chapter, I shall explore both the Mainstream Judaic traditions within America and what I term Sectarian Judaism.

NOTES

1. Fishman, P. (1973). *The Jews of the United States*, ed. Priscilla Fishman (New York: Quadrangle/New York Times Book), pp. 12, 17.

2. Fishman, P., pp. 11, 26. See also Sachar, H. M. (1992). *A History of the Jews in America* (New York: Alfred A. Knopf), pp. 104 ff; Raphael, M. L. (1984). *Profiles in American Judaism: The Reform, Conservative, Orthodox and Reconstructionist Traditions in Historical Perspective* (San Francisco: Harper and Row), pp. 14 ff; Marcus, J. R. (1989–1993). United States Jewry: 1776–1985. 4 vols. (Detroit: Wayne State University Press.)

3. Rosenthal, G. S. (1986). *Contemporary Judaism: Patterns of Survival*, 2d ed. (New York: Human Sciences Press), p. 15. See also Davis, M. (1965). *The Emergence of Conservative Judaism* (Philadelphia: Jewish Publication Society), pp. 55 ff.

4. Ahlstrom, S. E. (1972). *A Religious History of the American People* (New Haven and London: Yale University Press), p. 581. Ahlstrom's point, however, has been challenged.

5. Fishman, P., p. 49.

6. Ahlstrom, p. 976. See also Sachar, pp. 386 ff.

7. Gurock, J. S. (1996)."The Winnowing of American Orthodoxy," in *American Jewish Orthodoxy in Historical Perspective* (New York: Ktav Publishing), p. 306. This article originally appeared in *Approaches to Modern Judaism II* (Chico, CA, 1984), pp. 41–54.

8. Gurock, J. S. (1996)."Resisters and Accommodators: Varieties of Orthodox Rabbis in America, 1886–1983," in *American Jewish Orthodoxy in Historical Perspective* (New York: Ktav Publishing), p. 40. This article originally appeared in *American Jewish Archives* (Cincinnati, November 1983), pp. 100–187.

9. Rosenthal, p. 40. Coincidentally, the outstanding novel about the European Yeshiva experience is probably Chaim Grade's *The Yeshiva*.

10. Helmreich, W. B. (1982). *The World of the Yeshiva: An Intimate Portrait of Orthodox Jewry* (New York: Free Press), p. xii.

11. Kane, A. (1995). *Rabbi, Rabbi* (New York: Saint Martin's), p. 127. A much earlier novel which features a yeshiva-trained rabbi who does not pursue the rabbinate is the classic work by Abraham Cahan, *The Rise of David Levinsky* (1917).

12. See Davis, M. *The Emergence of Conservative Judaism*; as well as Sklare, M. (1985). *Conservative Judaism: An American Religious Movement* (Lanham, MD, New York, London: University Press of America), pp. 66 ff.

13. Alpert, R. T. and J. J. Staub (1988). *Exploring Judaism: A Reconstructionist Approach* (Wyncotte, PA: Reconstructionist Press), p. 5.

14. As the twentieth century comes to a close there are other rabbinic institutions which train rabbis for mainstream Judaism in addition to the seminaries mentioned: Orthdoxy's Rabbi Isaac Elchanan Rabbinical Theological Seminary at Yeshiva University, and the Hebrew Theological College in Chicago; the Conservative movement's Jewish Theological Seminary; the

Reconstructionist Rabbinical College; and the Reform movement's Hebrew Union College-Jewish Institute of Religion. In the mid-1990s the Conservative movement's University of Judaism in Los Angeles opened the Ziegler School of Rabbinic Studies (see Chapter 3, Rabbinic Training). Other institutions include the Institute of Traditional Judaism, based in Teaneck, New Jersey; ALEPH, Alliance for Jewish Renewal, associated with Rabbi Zalman Schachter-Shalomi; and the Academy for Jewish Religion, based in New York. For a brief overview of these institutions and their philosophies, see *Sh'ma: A Journal of Jewish Responsibility*, ed. Eugene Borowitz, 27:527 and 27:528 (February 7 and 21, 1997), and relevant articles by Zevulun Charlop (Rabbi Isaac Elchanan Theological Seminary at Yeshiva University); William H. Lebeau (Jewish Theological Seminary); Norman J. Cohen (Hebrew Union College-Jewish Institute of Religion); Daniel Gordis (Ziegler School of Rabbinic Studies, University of Judaism); David Teutsch (Reconstructionist Rabbinical College); Ronald D. Price (Institute of Traditional Judaism); Zalman Schachter-Shalomi (ALEPH, Alliance for Jewish Renewal); and Shohama Wiener (Academy for Jewish Religion).

15. Rosenthal, p. 16. See Chapter 4, Congregational Rabbis and Their Communities and in particular Rabbi Eugene Lipman's description of the varied dominant "self-images" of many mainstream rabbis.

16. Tarr, H. (1963). *The Conversion of Chaplain Cohen* (New York: Avon), pp. 309–310. In the novel itself, Chaplain Cohen's remarks are part of a eulogy for five airmen who have died in a plane crash. At least one of the bodies, the good friend of Chaplain Cohen, was totally incinerated. On one level he is addressing that specific situation, but I feel that Tarr intends a wider context for his remarks. The fact that the body was burned totally, if you will, a "holocaust," and the fact that Chaplain Cohen's fiancée is herself a Holocaust survivor suggests that the rabbi's remarks are also addressing the question of divine responsibility concerning the Holocaust.

17. Twersky, J. (1968). *A Marked House* (New York: Thomas Yoseloff), p. 226.

18. Woocher, J. S. (1986). *Sacred Survival: The Civil Religion of American Jews* (Bloomington and Indianapolis: Indiana University Press) p. 77.

19. Sachar, p. 565. See also Ellenson, D. (1995)."Zion in the Mind of the American Rabbinate during the 1940s," in *The Americanization of the Jews*, ed. Robert M. Seltzer and Norman J. Cohen (New York and London: New York University Press), pp. 193–212.

20. Woocher, p. 77.

21. See Woocher, p. 66, ad. loc.; Sachar, pp. 735 ff.; Silberman, C. E. (1985). *A Certain People: American Jews and Their Lives Today* (New York: Summit), pp. 194 ff.

22. Kemelman, H. (1973[1972]). *Monday the Rabbi Took Off* (Greenwich, CT: Fawcett Crest), p. 39.

23. Silberman, pp. 176–177.

24. Silberman, p. 177.

25. Karp, A. J. (1987). "Overview: The Synagogue in America—A Historical Typology," in *The American Synagogue: A Sanctuary Transformed*, ed. Jack Wertheimer (Cambridge, England and New York: Cambridge University Press), p. 25. On page 26, Karp quotes statistics which suggest that *fewer than* 2 percent had cited "I am religious" as their reason for synagogue affiliation. This point echoes Howard Singer's comment that most of "the post-World War II generation of Jewish suburbanites, were motivated in their community activities less by religious feeling than by the desire to establish a discreet presence in what was then a totally non-Jewish environment." Singer, H. (1985). "Rabbis & Their Discontents." *Commentary* 79:5 (May): p. 56.

26. Roth, P. (1959) "Eli the Fanatic," in *Goodbye Columbus and Five Short Stories*. (Boston: Houghton Mifflin), pp. 263 ff. Leokum, A. (1969). *The Temple* (New York and Cleveland: NAL/World Publishing); Weidman, J. (1975). *The Temple* (New York: Simon and Schuster); Fast, H. (1984). *The Outsider* (Boston: Houghton Mifflin). In Weidman's novel, while the community is quick to build a synagogue, it is not done for the purpose of finding "approval" from their neighbors.

27. Wertheimer, J. (1989)."Recent Trends in American Judaism," in *American Jewish Year Book 1989*, ed. David Singer and Ruth R. Seldin, vol. 89 (New York: American Jewish Committee and Philadelphia: Jewish Publication Society), p. 65. For more details concerning the growth of Orthodox congregations, see Liebman, C. S. (1974). "Orthodoxy in American Jewish Life," *Aspects of the Religious Behavior of American Jews* (New York: Ktav), pp. 111–187. [This article originally appeared in the *American Jewish Year Book 1965*, ed. Morris Fine and Milton Himmelfarb, vol. 66 (New York: American Jewish Committee and Philadelphia: Jewish Publication Society, 1965)]. For details about Conservative growth, see Wertheimer, "Recent Trends," p. 65, note 8. For growth in Reform Judaism, see Raphael, pp. 71, 198; and for the growth of Reconstructionist Judaism, see Raphael, p. 191.

28. Wertheimer, "Recent Trends," pp. 64–65.

29. Goldman, A. J. (1987). *The Rabbi Is a Lady* (New York: Hippocrene), p. 1.

30. Falk, H. (1972). *Days of Judgment* (New York: Shengold), p. 16.

31. Telushkin, J. (1992 [1991]). *An Eye for an Eye* (New York: Bantam), p. 85.

32. Segal, E. (1992). *Acts of Faith* (New York: Bantam), pp. 352–353.

33. Fruchter, N. (1987 [1962]). *Coat Upon A Stick* (Philadelphia: Jewish Publication Society), pp. 34, 42.

34. Appel, A. (1986). *The Rabbi of Casino Boulevard* (New York: Saint Martin's), pp. 5–6.

35. Fast, p. 5.

36. Longstreet, S. (1969). *Pedlock Saint, Pedlock Sinner* (New York: Delacorte), p. 25. See Levin, M. (1965 [1963]). *The Fanatic* (New York: Pocket), p. 82.

37. Schreiber, M. (1991). *The Rabbi and the Nun* (New York: Shengold), p. 13.

38. Fast, pp. 207 ff. The issue of rabbis involved in working toward the full civil and social rights for African-Americans is also taken up in novels by Tarr, *The Conversion of Chaplain Cohen* pp. 121 ff.; Gordon, N. (1965). *The Rabbi* (New York: McGraw-Hill), pp. 253 ff.; Leokum, pp. 210 ff.; and Tennenbaum, S. (1978). *Rachel, the Rabbi's Wife* (New York: William Morrow), pp. 72, 371 f.

39. Wertheimer, "Recent Trends," p. 75 (for a further development of this theme see Wertheimer, "Recent Trends," pp. 75–96—materials which includes tables and other data).

40. Gurock, "Resisters and Accommodators," p. 60.

41. Dresner, S. H. (1963). *The Jew in American Life* (New York: Crown), pp. 262, 264. See also Kohn, D. B. (1994). "Modern Congregants: Jewish by Proxy?" *Jewish Spectator* 59:1 (Summer): 26–28.

42. Siegel, M. (1971). *Amen: The Diary of Rabbi Martin Siegel*, ed. Mel Ziegler (New York and Cleveland: World), p. 82.

43. Berenbaum, M. G. (1995)."The Situation of the American Jew," in *Events and Movements in Modern Judaism*, ed. Raphael Patai and Emanuel S. Goldsmith (New York: Paragon House), p. 237.

44. Meyer, M. (1988). *Response to Modernity: A History of the Reform Movement in Judaism* (New York and Oxford: Oxford University Press), p. 381.

45. Bershtel, S. and Graubard, A. (1992). *Saving Remnants: Feeling Jewish in America* (New York: Free Press), p. 142.

46. Sklare, M. (1971). *America's Jews* (New York: Random House), pp. 122, 124, 126.

47. Schnall, D. J. (1993). "The Way (They Say) We Are: Using Quantitative Data to Explore the Parameters of Orthodoxy." *Tradition* 27:2 (Winter), p. 72. Schnall points out that "one need not travel far to see the figure dwindle . . . the size and strength of New York's Orthodox communities varies with only small change of venue." Thus, in suburban Westchester, Nassau, and Suffolk counties, or in nearby Metrowest, New Jersey, the figures drop precipitously.

48. Wertheimer, "Recent Trends," p. 80.

49. Wertheimer, "Recent Trends," pp. 80–81. Wertheimer refers to the studies by Barry Kosmin, director of the North American Jewish Data Bank, and figures published in 1987.

50. Wertheimer, "Recent Trends," p. 107.

51. Polner, M. (1977). *Rabbi: The American Experience* (New York: Holt, Rinehart and Winston), p. 26.

52. Dresner, S. (1994)."From Jewish Inadequacy to a Sacred Community," in *Federation and Synagogue: Towards a New Partnership* (Los Angeles: The Susan and David Wilstine Institute of Jewish Policy Studies, The University of Judaism), p. 41. See also the other essays in this pamphlet, Arnold Eisen's "Working Towards Cooperation and Pluralism," and Barry Shrage's "Bringing Federations Closer to Synagogues."

53. Woocher, pp. 162 f.

54. Leokum, p. 328.

55. For recent discussions about "Rabbinic Authority" from both Orthodox, and Reform viewpoints, see the following works. The Summer 1993 issue of *Tradition* (27:4), the publication of the Rabbinical Council of America, is devoted to the subject of "Rabbinic Authority." A decade earlier the Central Conference of American Rabbis published *Rabbinic Authority*, ed. Elliot L. Stevens, Vol. 90, Part 2 (New York: Central Conference of American Rabbis, 1982.)

56. Turkel, E. 1993."The Nature and Limitations of Rabbinic Authority." *Tradition* 27:4 (Summer), p. 86.

57. Zelizer, G. L. 1995."Conservative Rabbis, Their Movement, and American Judaism." *Judaism* 44:3 (Summer), pp. 298–300. See also the responses by Jonathan D. Sarna, Jenna Weissman Joselit, and Henry Feingold.

58. Feldman, E. 1993. "I Could Have Used Some Rabbinic Authority." *Tradition* 27:4 (Summer), p. 1 f. See also Feldman's *Tales out of Shul: The unorthodox journal of an Orthodox rabbi* (New York: Shaar Press/Mesorah Publications, 1996), pp. 40 ff.

59. Saperstein, H. I. (1982)."The Origin and Authority of the Rabbi," in *Rabbinic Authority*, ed. Elliot L. Stevens, Vol. 90, Part 2 (New York: Central Conference of American Rabbis), pp. 16 ff.

2

Mainstream Rabbis and Sectarian Orthodox Rabbis

THE MAINSTREAM RELIGIOUS COMMUNITIES

Within the mainstream religious communities, the majority of rabbis, factual as well as fictional, serve within a congregational setting in North America. Nearly all of these synagogues are affiliated with one of four movements: Orthodox, Conservative, Reconstructionist or Reform. There often are distances or differences in personal belief and observance between the rabbis themselves within those movements, as there are distances and differences in personal belief and observance between the rabbis and their congregants, as well as between congregants and congregants. Nonetheless, each of the movements in its own way has a certain cohesiveness and history.

Though it was mentioned in the previous chapter, it is worthwhile to iterate that while about a quarter of American Jews define themselves in terms such as "just Jewish," fewer than 10 percent are affiliated with Orthodox congregations; about 35 percent regard themselves as Conservative; and nearly 30 percent self-define as Reform Jews. The numbers associated with Reconstructionist Judaism are about two percent. Among these religious movements, the Reform group is growing more quickly than, and at the expense of, its competitors. All this, even though it appears that overall synagogue membership is in decline.

Bershtel and Graubard offer the thought that in recent decades, the differences between Reform and Conservative Judaism, though still articulated by the scholars and leaders of each movement, are not significant to the great majority of those who belong to the respective groups. They suggest that there is hardly any serious difference between the movements, practically speaking, at least for the average laity.[1] While many congregants may be as happy in one environment as the other, I feel that Bershtel and Graubard overstate their case, perhaps to be deliberately provocative. Further, while there is cooperation between the Reform and Conservative movements locally and nationally on various sociopolitical issues, as well as advancing the cause of religious pluralism in Israel, there also has been considerable strain resulting from the Reform movement's decision in 1983 to endorse formally the concept of "patrilineality." Jews agree that a child born of a Jewish mother, whether or not the father is Jewish, is Jewish ("matrilineality"). Patrilineality expands the definition to include the child of a Jewish father whether or not the mother is Jewish. As the resolution adopted by the (Reform) Central Conference of American Rabbis explains, "the child of one Jewish parent is under the presumption of Jewish descent. This presumption of the Jewish status of the offspring of any mixed marriage is to be established through appropriate and timely public and formal acts of identification with the Jewish faith and people."[2]

When it comes to a definition of Orthodox Judaism, one of the difficulties is that there are no universally accepted descriptions. Inasmuch as there is a continuum of beliefs and practices from strict observance to a more liberal approach to the place of Jewish law and tradition, it is impossible to offer hard and fast categories.[3] Further, Orthodoxy is much more institutionally fragmented than its counterparts to the religious left. Some use the term "fundamentalist,"[4] or "Ultra Orthodox"[5] when referring to the very traditionally minded, conservatively committed, section of Orthodoxy. I like neither the terms fundamentalist nor ultra-Orthodox. "Fundamentalist" is a term that has a specific meaning within the Christian community. It refers to a series of tracts that were published between 1912–1914 titled *The Fundamentals.* These tracts sought to define and defend certain "fundamental" aspects of Protestant doctrine. Among these fundamentals are the inerrancy of the Bible, the doctrine of the Trinity, and the virgin birth.[6] "Ultra-Orthodoxy" in my mind carries a pejorative meaning which suggests that those who support such beliefs are reactionaries and "beyond the fringe." I would hope that the term that I employ for the very traditionally minded, conservatively committed group, "Sectarian" Orthodox, is understood to be value-neutral.

I divide the Orthodox movement initially into two broad categories: "Centrist" Orthodox and "Sectarian" Orthodox. I place "Centrist" Orthodoxy among the mainstream movements and shall deal with this movement presently. Following the descriptions of Mainstream Judaism, I shall then consider two aspects of "Sectarian" Orthodoxy, the heirs of the "Hasidic Orthodox" tradition and the heirs of the (non-Hasidic, Mitnagged [Misnagged]) "Litvishe (Russian-Lithuanian) Yeshiva Orthodox" tradition. As a leading Orthodox thinker, Rabbi Walter S. Wurzburger has observed, "the mere fact that the term 'Modern Orthodoxy' is no longer in vogue and has been replaced by an expression ['Centrist Orthodoxy'] that deliberately avoids any reference to modernity speaks volumes."[7]

> Without doubt, in the vast majority of cases, fiction which features rabbis as characters have these rabbis serving mainstream congregations. Certainly exceptions exist, including novels by Chaim Potok, Jacob Twersky, Rhoda Lerman and Faye Kellerman which feature rabbis from the "Sectarian" Orthodox (Hasidic and "Litvishe" Yeshiva [Mitnagged] groups—these terms shall be explained, below).

"Centrist" Orthodox Judaism

Historian Jack Wertheimer has observed that since the mid-twentieth century, Orthodoxy of all stripes generally "has achieved an unprecedented degree of respectability, in the eyes of both non-Orthodox Jews and non-Jews." Further, as a movement, it has shifted considerably to the religious right in the thinking and behavior of Orthodox Jews.[8]

Illustrative of the acceptance of Orthodoxy is the fact that male Orthodox professionals have taken to wearing *kipot* (plural of *kipah*, *yarmulkes*, head coverings) whether in university settings, law offices, or in hospitals. The Orthodox women are less obvious in their distinct dress, but they tend to be more conservatively dressed and some may be wearing wigs. The widespread availability of kosher foods, often prepackaged and/or frozen, at supermarkets throughout the land is another sign of the sensitivity to a more traditional clientele.

Wertheimer also points out that since the 1970s

> Orthodox Jews have assumed positions of power and influence in the organized Jewish community in an unprecedented manner . . . individual Orthodox Jews have risen to leading administrative posts in the Council of Jewish Federations, the American Jewish Committee, the American Jewish Congress, the Conference of Presidents of Major Jewish Organizations, the World Jewish Congress, and a range of local federations and other Jewish agencies.[9]

At the same time, however, there also is a feeling among some Orthodox leaders that they should be even further separated from the general Jewish community. As Orthodoxy has become more self-confident, there is, especially among those who are sympathetic to the goals of the religious right, a call for Orthodoxy to "go it alone" and not be tainted by association with Reform, Conservative, or Reconstructionist Judaism. Observers of the Orthodox scene have noted the shrill and strident criticism of non-Orthodox viewpoints and indeed of Orthodox leaders who are perceived as being *too liberal*. A review of the year 1989 highlighted the internecine "conflict between the moderate Orthodox-associated primarily with Yeshiva University and the Rabbinical Council of America (RCA)—and those with a more stringent approach to Orthodoxy. . . . The key issue of debate remained how the Orthodox should relate to non-Orthodox expressions of Judaism." Later in that same article there was a discussion about a proposed interdenominational rabbinic panel that would deal with the issue of conversion, as well as look at the thorny issue of "Who is a Jew?" It was clear that even within Yeshiva University there was internal dissent. "Senior Talmud professor Aaron Soloveitchik compared cooperation with non-Orthodox bodies to the biblical sin of the golden calf, declaring that such a step would 'mislead many of the innocent, ignorant Jewish masses to worship the idol of Reform and Reconstructionist Judaism.'"[10]

> In a novel set in the mid-1980s, (*Rabbi, Rabbi*) a character attends some services at the Lincoln Square Synagogue in the Upper West Side of Manhattan. The rabbi, a successful "Cen-

trist" Orthodox, is wearing a *kipah*, which bears "a colorful, hand-crocheted design—a symbol of the modern-Orthodox."[11] The rabbi devotes part of his sermon to the recent decision of the Jewish Theological Seminary to ordain women. In heaping scorn on this ruling which embraces egalitarianism in gender roles, fictional Rabbi Roth explains that the Conservative movement has started down a road that will lead to a line of reasoning where they will decide eventually to accept the notion that either the father or the mother can determine the Jewish status of a child. He explains that the Reform movement already has reached this decision on *patrilineality*, to allow fathers to play an equal role in determining the religion of children.

"And what will this do to the Jewish people? . . . In years to come, there will be people who believe they are Jewish even though their mothers were not. And *we* will not regard them as Jews, we cannot. For to us the mother determines the religion of the child! So, in the end there will be two separate Jewish people who *really* cannot marry one another or pray together."[12]

As an Orthodox rabbi, whether "Centrist" or "Sectarian," one might not expect any other argument from Rabbi Roth. Yet what makes Rabbi Roth's criticism so important is that among his colleagues, he is a relative liberal. As the novel explains, Rabbi Roth

had developed a reputation in the community for being a proponent of expanding women's roles within traditional Jewish life. At times, it even appeared that he was stretching *Halacha*, Jewish law, and pursuing far-reaching conclusions to accommodate the needs of those egalitarian-minded types who attended his synagogue. One such decision, for example, was to establish a women's *minyan*, a service exclusively for women. In this setting, women would conduct and lead every aspect of the prayers. The catch? No men were allowed. For this, Roth was vociferously denounced by most of his Orthodox colleagues.[13]

To further complicate matters, even within "Centrist" Orthodoxy there are deep divisions between the philosophically or ideologically "Centrist" and the behaviorally "Centrist." Sociologist Chaim I. Waxman (1993) has written of these divisions.[14] He defines *philosophically* ["Centrist"] Orthodox as

> those who are meticulously observant of Halakhah [Jewish law, traditional practice] but are, nevertheless, philosophically modern. Within this context, being modern means, at minimum, having a positive perspective on general education and knowledge; viewing oneself, from a religious perspective, as being a part of, and having responsibility for, both the larger Jewish community as well as society in general; and being positively disposed to Israel and religious Zionism.[15]

As shall be discussed presently, the "Sectarian" Orthodox community is much more inward-looking and is not concerned with issues outside of the Jewish community unless it affects them personally.[16]

The *behaviorally* ["Centrist"] Orthodox "are not deeply concerned with philosophical ideas about either modernity or religious Zionism . . . [nor are they] meticulously observant." They are ["Centrist"] "in the sense that those who see themselves as part of it are committed to the tradition, in general, but feel free to pick and choose in their observance of rituals."[17]

Though there are some clear differences in the liturgies of the four American movements, the "Centrist" Orthodox congregational rabbi functions in a very similar way to his non-Orthodox counterpart. "Unlike his European predecessor who preached only several times a year and spent the rest of his time answering *shealot* (ritual questions) and studying or teaching the Talmud, the American Orthodox [congregational] rabbi is virtually a carbon copy of his Reform and Conservative colleague: he preaches, teaches, administrates, serves as a pastor, acts as a counselor, and in general, fills a wide variety of roles."[18]

In recent years, the "Centrists" have moved to the religious right. One manifestation of this is that many "Centrist" Orthodox rabbis are committed to the practice of daily Talmud study.

Conservative Judaism

Though Conservative Judaism is, in terms of statistics, arguably the largest movement, it also has been racked by many internal disputations which some would argue threaten its future strength. A double tension exists within the Conservative movement. There is a "considerable distance between the [Jewish Theological] Seminary 'schoolmen' and the rabbis in the field."[19] Further, there is a wide discrepancy between the personal beliefs and ritual observances of Conservative rabbis and their congregants. Marshall Sklare (1985) writes of the discontinuities and conflicts between the professors at the Jewish Theological Seminary, the "Schoolmen," and the rabbis in the field, the "Practitioners."[20] Sklare quotes a prominent rabbi who explains that (many of) the faculty at the Seminary have a low regard for congregational rabbis. They "laugh at us as ignoramuses . . . [and imply] that we have been graduated as social workers and not as Rabbis for humanity."[21]

Rabbi Richard L. Rubenstein in his autobiography explains that when he studied at the Jewish Theological Seminary in the late 1940s and early 1950s, the prevailing mood was that many of the professors, including the great Talmudic scholars, had little regard for their students. "Our rabbinic superegos were shaped by the conviction that we would never be as wise or as learned as our teachers. . . . When in doubt, we were expected to turn for guidance to the fountainhead of Jewish wisdom, the faculty of the Jewish Theological Seminary."[22] Coincidentally, a generation later, little seems to have changed. Rabbi Jay Rosenbaum, who studied in the late 1960s and mid-1970s, is quoted as having a similar experience.

> JTS prided itself on teaching Torah as it would be taught at Harvard. . . . People were humiliated in class if they even uttered something like "I feel." "You feel! Who in hell cares what you feel! What do you think?" . . . . Prayer? Observance? Forget it. Not part of the curriculum. JTS wanted scholars, not practicing Jews. "Rabbi" was no longer the highest approbation; it was "doctor," and the better the school your Ph.D. came from, the more respected you were.[23]

The faculty at the Seminary, by and large, is much less open to progressive changes than the rabbis in the field. Though virtually every Conservative congregation had mixed seating for decades, where men and women prayed alongside each other, at the Seminary's own synagogue there was separate seating until the 1980s. This was indicative of the mind-set of many of the "Schoolmen."

On the whole, Conservative rabbis are disappointed with the low level of ritual observance of their congregants. Very few congregants who belong to Conservative congregations follow the traditions of being *Shomer Shabbat* ("Observing the Shabbat," i.e., refraining from working on the Sabbath) and likewise very few follow the laws of *kashrut* (ritual dietary laws) beyond the confines of their homes, if there at all. Nonetheless, these self-same congregants often expect just such behavior from their rabbis (see Chapters 4 and 5, Congregational Rabbis and Their Communities.)

For a time in the 1970s, Conservative congregations were affected by declining membership, and even more by an aging of their congregational population. Yet by the mid-1980s, greater numbers of young families were reportedly joining Conservative congregations. This was particularly true of new congregations in the Sunbelt states and recently constructed suburban subdivisions. Nonetheless, suggests Jack Wertheimer, this vitality could not "entirely forestall the numerical decline of Conservative synagogues during the last decades of the twentieth century."[24]

The most divisive issue for the Conservative movement in the last fifty years has been the decision which led to the ordination of women. At least initially, it caused rifts between various rabbis at the Jewish Theological Seminary, between Seminary rabbis and rabbis in the field, between rabbis and rabbis serving congregations, between rabbis and laity and between congregants and congregants.

The decision to ordain women was an important innovation for the Conservative movement, but it was and remains a contentious and controversial issue for many Conservative rabbis. It was openly debated within the movement for a decade, from the early 1970s until the 1980s when, finally, in 1985, the first Conservative woman rabbi was ordained. Naturally it did not happen in a vacuum. Women were first permitted to be counted as members of the congregation, then they were accorded equal honors, and finally came ordination. The movement as a whole is moving toward gender equality, but it is not without its naysayers. In 1983, those who were "opposed to egalitarianism and other recent changes in Conservatism . . . organized the Union for Traditional Conservative Judaism . . . as a lobby within the movement."[25]

> Probably the most famous fictional rabbi, and unquestionably the most famous fictional Conservative rabbi, is Rabbi David Small, of the Weekday *Rabbi* detective series by Harry Kemelman (*Friday the Rabbi Slept Late, Saturday the Rabbi Went Hungry, Sunday the Rabbi Stayed Home*, and others[26]). In his synagogue, at least as late as 1978 (when *Thursday the Rabbi Walked Out* was published), women were not counted among the *minyan*, the minimum of adults to form a prayer quorum,

though they were by then members of the Board. Giving full equality to women was an issue of contention for some of his members.[27] Other fictional Conservative rabbis include Rabbi Seymour Sonnshein in a novel by Sylvia Tennenbaum, *Rachel, the Rabbi's Wife*[28]; Rabbi Arthur Bloom, the protagonist of Allan Appel's *The Rabbi of Casino Boulevard*[29]; and Rabbi Daniel Winter, in fact another rabbi-detective who made his debut in Joseph Telushkin's *The Unorthodox Murder of Rabbi Wahl*.[30]

"Many people, both Jews and non-Jews, learn about Judaism in general and about Conservative Judaism in particular from Rabbi David Small," writes Elliot B. Gertel, himself a real-life Conservative rabbi, in an article titled "A Novel Approach to Conservative Judaism" (1981). For Rabbi Small's creator, Harry Kemelman, "Conservative Judaism *is* Judaism, pure and simple. . . . As far as Kemelman is concerned, the authenticity of Conservative Judaism is a given: a sociological opportunity, a theological necessity and an historical fact."[31]

Gertel goes on to praise Kemelman/Small for his fine interpretation of the Jewish tradition. For example, in *Tuesday the Rabbi Saw Red*, Rabbi Small defends the concept of the "Chosen People" to a college class. The rabbi explains that while other nations, including England, the United States, Russia, and China all have, in their own way, felt that they were "chosen," in most cases the doctrine of chosenness calls upon the country to do "something to someone else, usually by force. The Jewish doctrine alone calls for Jews to live up to a high standard so that they might be an example to others."[32]

Earlier, in *Monday the Rabbi Took Off*, in a wonderfully illustrative point, Rabbi Small infers that Judaism places more emphasis on our deeds than our particular faith, or the nature of that faith, at any given moment. When asked if he believes in God, Rabbi Small replies that this is a difficult question to answer, because it depends on a number of variables when you ask if "I believe in God"? These variables include, do you mean the "I" of today, or yesterday, or of several years ago? The word "believe" is another variable: is it the same kind of belief as in "two and two make four? Or the way that I believe that light travels a certain number of miles per second, which I myself have never seen demonstrated but which has been demonstrated by people whose competence and integrity I have been taught to trust?" Furthermore, there is the variable of God. Do you mean God, as an ineffable presence, or a God who is aware of our being, and responsive to our call, or a God who is far beyond human knowledge? The rabbi concludes with this statement: "I suppose I have the feeling of belief and certainty some times and lack it at others."[33]

In *Sunday the Rabbi Stayed Home*, Rabbi Small, in a conversation with a Roman Catholic priest, mentioned that faith is not required of Jews. Rabbi Small alludes to the teaching of the prophet Micah, who suggested that what God expects of humans is to walk in God's ways (Micah 6:8). Rabbi Small explains that people can walk in God's ways and still have doubts about God's existence. "After all, you can't always control your thoughts." Further, he says, faith "is not a requirement of our religion . . . I suspect it's a kind of special talent that some have to a greater degree than others."[34]

Though Rabbi Winter (*The Unorthodox Murder of Rabbi Wahl, The Final Analysis of Dr. Stark, An Eye for an Eye*), Rabbi Sonnshein (*Rachel, the Rabbi's Wife*) and Rabbi Bloom (*The Rabbi of Casino Boulevard*) serve Conservative congregations, there are only occasional references which would indicate that particular affiliation.

Reconstructionist Judaism

Though the Reconstructionist movement was several decades old at the time,[35] it made a quantum leap forward when, in 1968, it opened its seminary in Philadelphia through a special relationship with the department of religion at Temple University. The movement has grown considerably. Through 1996, it had ordained 185 rabbis: 110 men and 75 women. Ninety-one are pulpit rabbis: 39 in Reconstructionist congregations, seven in Reform, 24 in Conservative, and 21 in "unaffiliated" congregations. Another 23 serve either as Chaplains with Hillel on the college campus or in hospitals or the military.[36]

The Reconstructionist movement has taken a very liberal view on the issues of intermarriage and patrilineality. A number of Reconstructionist rabbis do officiate at intermarriages and, in terms of patrilineality, "since 1968, [the movement] has recognized the Jewishness of the child of a Jewish father and a non-Jewish mother when that child is raised and educated as a Jew."[37] Their decision on the Jewishness of children came fifteen years *before* the Reform movement took a similar stance.

Likewise, in terms of the position of women, the Reconstructionist movement has been a leader in this area. Women not only have full equality in terms of ritual and leadership roles, but the Reconstructionist Rabbinical College has been in the forefront of offering administrative and full-time faculty posts to women.

> To my knowledge, there has yet to be any fictional material that deals with Reconstructionist rabbis. In discussing this phenomenon with several Reconstructionist rabbis, their common comment was that the movement is yet too young to have been the object of fictional consideration. This certainly is a matter which will change in years to come.

Reform Judaism

Of the major movements, it is probably Reform Judaism that has changed the most in the past 30-plus years. Beginning in the 1970s, the Hebrew Union College-Jewish Institute of Religion (HUC-JIR), the Reform seminary, required that all rabbinic students spend their first year studying at the HUC-JIR campus in Jerusalem. In 1977, the Association of Reform Zionists (ARZA) was established with the express purpose of strengthening ties between Reform Judaism in Israel and America. "Reform leaders have participated in a deep change in the meaning of the word *Zionism* and its implications. As do most American Jews, Reform Jews equate Zionism with pro-Israel convictions and actions aimed at the preservation and enhancement of the life of the Jewish people."[38] Virtually without exception, Reform synagogues and Reform rabbis encourage their members to visit Israel and actively to participate in programs in support of Israel.

Items of social action have continued to be of importance for Reform Jews and the American Reform rabbinate. Concerns with such issues as Civil Rights, Human Rights, the Equal Rights Amendment, drug and alcohol abuse, people with AIDS and who are HIV-positive, and matters surrounding homosexuality have received major attention in resolutions passed by the Central Conference of American Rabbis, the Reform rabbinic professional association. In 1960, the Reform movement set up the Religious Action Center in Washington, DC, and this has been a leading light in the area of social action.

> Rabbi David Benjamin (Morton Levine's *The Congregation*) is invited to join Detroit's Social Action Committee when he is chosen to lead the large Reform congregation in that city. Rabbi Benjamin has a longstanding commitment to social action and social justice issues and at one point is called upon to testify at a Senate investigation in Washington. His Reform colleagues, Michael Kind (Noah Gordon's *The Rabbi*) and David Hartman (Howard Fast's *The Outsider*), are each in their own way concerned with Civil Rights activities.[39]
>
> In his first sermon at his new congregation, Rabbi Gideon Abel (*Heaven Help Us!*) outlines his "social action program to aid Jews abroad (support of Israel and combat of Russian anti-Semitism), Negroes at home (new housing, improved schools, guaranteed jobs) and other fellow Americans (a preschool for disadvantaged children, a two-dollar minimum wage)."[40]
>
> Rabbi Joshua Kaye (*The Rabbi and the Nun*) studies at the Quincy Rabbinical Seminary (a thinly veiled reference to the Hebrew Union College-Jewish Institute of Religion in Cincinnati, the Reform seminary) because of its commitment to a platform of social action. As he explains it to his father, at that "school each student is free to pursue his own ideas and beliefs within . . . Liberal Judaism, . . . the students and the professors [share a] . . . commitment to . . . the renewal of Judaism as a prophetic faith."[41]

The Reform movement has reintroduced many ritual practices that had been discarded in years past. Further, there is a reassessment of the potential importance and contribution of religious observance to spiritual deepening. In many, many Reform congregations one will now see a fair amount of men—and, increasingly, women (!)—wearing *kipot* and *tallitot* (prayer shawls). The amount of Hebrew found in services also has increased significantly, though it is far from the average amount found in Conservative congregations. At the same time, the Reform movement has introduced measures that are a radical departure from past Judaic practice, namely the ordination of women, and as mentioned earlier, a recognition of "patrilineality." Women's ordination in the Reform movement was initiated in 1972, but as a principle it had been discussed and affirmed for many decades. I shall return to the issue of ordination in the Reform movement in Chapter 7 (Women Rabbis). Patrilineality had been followed by Reform Jews for decades. It was only in 1983 that this practice became formally adopted. This topic shall be discussed further in Chapter 9 (Assimilation, Intermarriage, and Patrilineality).

There have been other changes in the Reform movement. Since 1970, there have been two major revisions of the earlier *Union Prayer Book* which had last been revised in 1940. The *Gates of Prayer* and its High Holiday companion, the *Gates of Repentance*, contain considerably more Hebrew, as well as direct references to the State of Israel and the Holocaust. In the 1990s, a prayerbook where the liturgy is gender-neutral was introduced.

A continuing hallmark of Reform Judaism is its commitment to religious diversity and pluralism. In the 1976 statement on the philosophy, principles, and practices of current Reform Judaism, "A Centenary Perspective," it was clearly explained that "Reform Jews respond to change in various ways, according to the Reform principle of the autonomy of the individual. However, Reform Judaism does more than tolerate diversity; it engenders it."[42] Reform's commitment to autonomy, including rabbinic autonomy, has a vexing side to it. A question that continues to be a divisive issue within the Reform movement is the issue of rabbinic officiation at marriages where one of the couple *at the time of the marriage* is not Jewish.[43] In the 1980s, Reform congregations were fairly stable. While they did not experience rapid growth, neither did they lose members.

While Reform Judaism maintains its support of religious diversity and pluralism, there has been a definite change in terms of its former openness to the concept of universalism in specific contrast to particularism. Eugene B. Borowitz, a leading theologian within Reform Judaism, explains that universalistic concerns are ". . . not the most pressing question of Jewish life today. Survival is." Borowitz explains that the battles to achieve acceptance from the larger society have been largely won. Jews are experts at modern living, he says. Yet, he criticizes Reform Jews as being "amateurs at being Jewish, inept in religious practice, childlike in knowledge, at best fluctuating in our commitment."[44]

Nonetheless, Reform rabbis continue to stress a message which addresses all humanity. Rabbi Samuels (in *Rabbi, Rabbi*) not only heads up a very large and distinguished congregation, he also serves as a professor at the Reform seminary in New York. In his Rosh Hashanah sermon he "did not speak of parochial and exclusive Jewish interests, but rather of universal and inclusive ones." He suggested that the message of Rosh Hashanah is to call all humanity to awaken to its moral responsibilities and obligations.[45]

Another prestigious congregational head, Rabbi Alvin Blumenfeld (*The Rabbi and the Nun*), a man described as "the rising leader of American Jewry, heir to Stephen Wise and Abba Hillel Silver" proclaims from his "pulpit that the purpose of Liberal Judaism was to perfect the world in the image of the kingship of God."[46]

Rabbi David Hartman (*The Outsider*) is characterized as a prophet who thunders and rages against injustice, denouncing war, and evil in high places.[47]

THE "SECTARIAN" ORTHODOX COMMUNITIES

This book draws primarily on examples from the Mainstream Jewish community, factual and fictional. Consequently, in this chapter, more material, proportionately, will be devoted to the "Sectarian" Orthodox community.

The Hasidic Community

In contrast to rabbis who serve mainstream congregations either in urban or more often suburban settings, the Hasidic community is usually located in a very densely Jewish-populated area. It is not only that the locale itself features a high percentage of Jews: These are Jews who associate with that particular Hasidic sect. For example, in New York City, the Crown Heights section of Brooklyn is the center of Lubavitch Hasidim, while Williamsburg, and lately Borough Park, is a Satmar Hasidic neighborhood. As William B. Helmreich (1982) notes, other important Hasidic "sects with substantial communities in Brooklyn and Israel are Ger, Bobov, Belz, Tzelem, Stoln and Papa, all of whom . . .

derive their names from the European towns in which they originated."[48] The devoted relationship of a Hasidic community to its specific, often charismatic leader,

> "the Rebbe, offers a clear contrast to the status of congregational rabbis, even those most beloved." Each [Hasidic] Rebbe is believed by his followers to possess remarkable powers because of his holiness, his devotion to the law and to prayer, and his lineage linking him to the great Rebbes of past generations.
>
> . . . The Rebbes are thought to move in spheres not understood by ordinary men. It is believed that the Rebbes can, in dire circumstances, intercede on behalf of their followers with the Heavenly Court. Their prayers, unhampered by the gross sins of lesser men, fly upward and are received on high,

explains Jerome R. Mintz in his book *Hasidic People: A Place in the New World* (1992).[49]

Though the Hasidic movement is now well over 200 years old and, as a result of the Holocaust, is no longer centered in Europe, both the dynamic of deepest reverence for the Rebbe and the dynastic element are still present.

> In Chaim Potok's novel *The Chosen*, one of the major characters offers some historic perspective.
>
> The Hasidim [plural of Hasid] had great leaders—tzaddikim, they were called, righteous ones. Each Hasidic community had its own tzaddik, and his people would go to him with all their problems, and he would give them advice. They followed these leaders blindly. The Hasidim believed that the tzaddik was a superhuman link between themselves and God. Every act of his and every word he spoke was holy. Even the food he touched became holy. . . . Many of the positions of tzaddik became inherited posts, going automatically from father to son, even if the son was not a great leader. . . . Their customs and beliefs are also the same as they were hundreds of years ago.[50]

Most Hasidic groups are insular. Generally they do not associate with communities other than their own. Often members do not attend secular colleges. Many are involved in trades and business. "With the exception of the Lubavitcher, whose dress and demeanor are somewhat more modern, the [Hasidim] . . . are characterized by a distinctive garb and physical appearance that includes long black coats, large black hats, and full beards, all of which make them noticeable to even the most casual observer."[51]

The Lubavitch Hasidim provide a great exception to the general rule. Not only are they more modern in their dress, but they have a tremendous "outreach" program, especially to influence non-observant Jews to turn to a ritually more observant life.

> The Lubavitcher *Rebbe*, it sometimes seems, commands the largest Jewish army outside of Israel. His followers regard him as their commander in chief and obey all his orders. Hasidim routinely uproot their families and move to whatever city the *Rebbe* directs them, in order to establish or strengthen a Lubavitch presence there. There are Lubavitcher representatives in hundreds of cities throughout the United States and the world.

Indeed it is reported that a prominent Israeli Orthodox rabbi once remarked, "I have found two things in every city I have ever visited, Coca-Cola and Lubavitcher Hasidim."[52]

> The phenomenon of a Rebbe of a Hasidic dynasty making special demands on his followers is reflected in a novel by Chaim Potok. At the Ladover Rebbe's request in the book *My Name is Asher Lev*, people earn advanced degrees, travel all over the world, and set up Hasidic communities. Others move thousands of miles to be near their Rebbe. As one character explains, "My father traveled for the Rebbe's father . . . I travel for the Rebbe. It is a great honor to be able to travel for the Rebbe."[53]

Though founded in the late eighteenth century in Eastern Europe, the headquarters and main synagogue of the Lubavitch Hasidic movement today is located at 770 Eastern Parkway in Brooklyn. Most often it is referred to simply as "770." In a personal vignette titled "Growing up Lubavitch," Shoshana Gelerenter-Liebowitz (1992) explains that

> Part of the focal point of going to 770 is to see "The Rebbe." That is special in Lubavitch life. The people want to get a glimpse of "The Rebbe." Women daven [pray] quietly because, if there is any noise,

> they can't hear the Torah reading or the *ba'al tefilah* (prayer leader). It is a gigantic place, 770. The downstairs (men's) section is very large. The women's section is built over it. There is a dark-tinted glass partition. The women can see through, but the men can't see in. . . .
>
> "The Rebbe" is a role model for both men and women. There are special *farbrengen* (gatherings to hear "The Rebbe" teach) for women several times a year. . . .
>
> "The Rebbe" is a transcendental figure, very elevated and spiritually capable of guiding his followers in their personal decisions. Men and women share a respectful reverence toward him. . . . He activates everybody.[54]

> In the specific case of Hasidic, though not Lubavitch Hasidic, Reb Saunders (*The Chosen*) we are told of the "zealousness with which he ruled his people and settled questions of Jewish law." We meet his son, Danny, who is to succeed his father. Danny explains, "Once I'm a rabbi . . . I'll be sort of like God to" my people.[55]

Messianism, and the coming of the Messiah, has a long history within Jewish thought. There is quite a debate whether one can, or should, do anything to hasten the coming of the Messiah. Likewise there are varying views about how one will know when the Messiah, or Messianic age, is about to come. Within Orthodoxy there are those who wait impatiently for the arrival of the Messiah. More specifically within Hasidism there is a tradition that in each generation a Messiah is born, and periodically there are those who claim to know the name of the Messiah.[56] In the 1980s and 1990s, as the health of the Lubavitcher Rebbe, Rabbi Menahem Mendel Schneerson, began to wane, there developed suggestions that he might actually be the Messiah. Mintz quoted a Lubavitcher Hasid, who offered these statistics: 35 percent would say that the Rebbe was the Messiah, 35 percent believed inside that the Rebbe was the Messiah but would not say it, and 20 percent believed that what was important was the idea, but not the person. Mintz also quoted Rabbi Yehuda Krinsky, a frequent spokesman for the Lubavitcher movement, a man associated with its educational programs. Krinsky explained that there were students who said that the Rebbe was the Messiah, and there were people who did not believe this. We believe, he attested, "And the Rebbe could be the Messiah."[57]

> Allegra Goodman takes up this question in a story found in her collection *Total Immersion: Stories:*
>
> "Let me tell you something that the Rebbi [sic] said," Moshe begins.
>
> But Mark cuts him off. "Hey, do you think your Rebbi is the Messiah? Is he going to like save the world—headquarters in Borough Park?"
>
> Moshe answers in a lilting Talmudic voice. "No one says the Rebbi is the Messiah. We think only that in every generation there is one man who could be the Messiah. And our Rebbi is a good candidate for the job."[58]

Though the Hasidic communities are limited in population, they exert an influence on Jewish life greater than their small numbers would suggest. The breadth of their appeal is not so much ideological or doctrinal as emotional. Earlier reference was made to the fact that the Lubavitcher "Rebbe" seems to command the largest Jewish army outside of Israel and that his followers regard him as their commander in chief and obey his orders. The military analogy is very apt. Though men and women would seem to lead separate lives, Gelerenter-Liebowitz explains that "Lubavitch women don't ever feel secondary or deprived. Their lives are as busy as the men's. There is always so much activity. An equal responsibility for performing *mitzvot* [commandments] rests with the males and females. *All children are soldiers in* HaShem's [*God's*] *army* [my emphasis.]"[59]

With their unquestionably strong group-feeling and loyalty to their movement, they appear to have sure and solid answers in a world which is beset by problems which range from assimilation and intermarriage to potential nuclear destruction and unjust wars; from a widening gulf between the haves and have-nots to drug-abuse and general despair. In fact the Lubavitch movement's concerns are not restricted purely to ritual observance. Some Lubavitch centers run drug-rehabilitation programs, "and more than a few wealthy donors to Chabad [Lubavitch] are nonreligious Jews whose children were broken from drug habits by Lubavitcher rabbis. Non-Jews as well have been treated in these drug-rehabilitation programs."[60]

Historian Wertheimer notes that part of the appeal of the religious right is that "the waning decades of the twentieth century have been a time of declining confidence in the viability of modern cultural norms.

This mood has strengthened the hand of fundamentalists through the world, including traditionalists in the yeshivah world who reject the values of secular America."[61]

The 150,000 "friends and sympathizers" of the Lubavitcher Rebbe "far outnumber the immediate coterie of followers. The overwhelming majority [of his supporters] are said to be non-Orthodox. Many Jews seek the Rebbe's advice on personal matters and accept him as a religious guide, and he sees an estimated 3,000 people a year for personal interviews averaging 10 to 15 minutes in length."[62]

Visiting the Rebbe, whether he is the Lubavitcher, Satmar, Skverer, Bobover, or whichever dynasty, at least once a year and seeking his advice is a phenomenon common to the Hasidic community. The Rebbe is frequently asked for advice or aid in difficult situations, perhaps economic, health, or reproductive issues.

> When Rebbetzin Tamar Finegold (*The Sacrifice of Tamar*), recently pregnant, visits the Hasidic Kovnitzer Rebbe, she seeks his advice as well as his blessing. In her mind, the "Rebbe had that sixth sense, that ability to know the past and the future that came from being so close to G-d. He would know everything just by looking at her!"[63]
>
> A person may be the member of one synagogue and even hold a prominent position in it (for instance [in "The Old System" fictional] Isaac Braun is the President of his local congregation), and still seek out the advice of his "Rebbe." "Isaac had a rabbi in Williamsburg . . . He waited in the anteroom, where the rabbi's bearded followers went in and out in long coats . . ."[64]

The Hasidic communities are complex organizations and not infrequently there are challenges in the power structure.

> Novels by Chaim Potok, Jacob Twersky, Erich Segal, and Rhoda Lerman focus on Hasidic communities. They present the inner strength of the movements, their strong feeling of love and support for their respective "Rebbes." At the same time these authors raise questions about the Hasidim. In their novels we read of sons who would have naturally inherited the position of tzaddik yet choose to bypass it in favor of other studies.[65]

> Coincidentally, the same issue of a son not wishing to inherit the mantle of his father's leadership comes up in the novel by Andrew Kane, *Rabbi, Rabbi*, but there the rabbi is Mitnagged, not Hasidic.[66]

These novels do not in themselves indicate a trend, but they do highlight the fact that Orthodoxy, even close-knit Hasidic Orthodoxy, is not devoid of internal problems.

> Erich Segal offers an interesting variation to the son who decides to reject the inherited mantle of his father's Hasidic dynastic group. First Danny Luria (*Acts of Faith*) opts not to follow in his father's footsteps. The title goes to Danny's uncle. Then, "fate" intervenes. Some years later Danny's uncle is shot by a dissident congregant (!) and so, as Danny explains, "I could avoid my destiny no longer.
>
> " . . . At last I was my father's son. Rav Daniel Luria—the Silzcer Rebbe."[67] The central character of Rhoda Lerman's *God's Ear* would probably voice a similar thought—he too could avoid his destiny no longer.

The question of succession notwithstanding, these novels often convey a believable view of Hasidic life. The tzaddik not only settles questions of Jewish law, he is his people's cherished leader.

> Leadership, however, is not without burdens. "Everyone imposes on him. But he is always patient," explains one of Rabbi Aaron's (*A Marked House*) followers, "always kind. A *tzaddik* . . . a true saint."[68] Likewise Reb Saunders (*The Chosen*) explains, "of all people a tzaddik especially must know of pain. A tzaddik must know how to suffer for his people. . . . He must take their pain from them and carry it on his own shoulders."[69] Yet at the same time there are great compensations, not the least being the respect which the Rebbe is accorded. In a few lines, Twersky conveys both the respect of a tzaddik's followers and the great power that is inherent in the natural dynasty. One of Rabbi Aaron's coterie says to the Rabbi's son: "The question is: are you willing to help your father? We can't help him. He doesn't listen to us, and we're powerless to act against his wishes. You

are the son. You have rights. You have powers. It is up to you. There is no one else"[70]

Part of the appeal, perhaps part of the romanticism, of Hasidic life is the Shabbat afternoon meal with the Rebbe which also includes festive singing and a discourse by the rabbi. As I point out in an earlier section, Hasidic life is male-oriented and in the passage which follows, this is strictly a man's activity, including the dancing:

> At the synagogue meal, *Shalosh Sudis* [the third meal], that began in the late sabbath afternoon, his father sat at the long table with the *Chassidim* [Hasidim] most devoted to him. They ate potato *kugel* and fish prepared by women members of the congregation. They sang and his father preached and then they sang again. Sometimes, in response to one of them snapping his fingers rhythmically, all rose and danced.[71]

The Russian-Lithuanian ("Litvishe") Yeshiva Community

The "Litvishe" (Russian-Lithuanian) Yeshiva "Sectarian" Orthodox community, sometimes referred to as the Mitnagged [Misnagged] community, also is to the religious right of the "Centrist" Orthodox. It is parallel to the Hasidic community in terms of religious observance. While many of the heirs of the "Litvishe" community are often associated with the "Yeshiva world" culture, this is somewhat misleading in that today there also are Hasidic yeshivas.[72] Nonetheless, in common parlance, when referring to the term "Yeshiva world," people generally mean the "Litvishe" Yeshiva community, and this is the focus of the previously mentioned work by William B. Helmreich, *The World of the Yeshiva*.

While the hundreds of "Litvishe" yeshivas will differ in individual ways, they share certain characteristics. They have programs where their students concentrate on Talmudic study. A "*Rosh yeshiva*" [literally the "head of the yeshiva"] serves as the dean of the institution. The orientation and philosophical approach of the yeshiva is based on a European model. For the most part, with the exception of the more modern Yeshiva University and Hebrew Theological College in Chicago, those associated with the yeshiva share a common set of values and move in the same social circles. Those social circles and values are clearly "right-wing,"—religiously as well as politically conservative—in their thinking. Just as the Hasidic Orthodox community is largely inward-looking and consciously separates itself from other forms of Judaism, so the "Litvishe" yeshiva world is insular in its own way.

> Representative of this "Litvishe" Yeshiva "Sectarian" Orthodox outlook within the fictional world is Rabbi David Eisen, an important character in Andrew Kane's novel, *Rabbi, Rabbi*. Rabbi Eisen, we are told, has a strong antipathy for anyone who is not of his particular group. His son explains:
>
> "At the top were non-Orthodox Jews, whether Reform, Conservative, or unaffiliated. He despised them all and referred to them with the same degrading Yiddish euphemisms that he used for Gentiles: *goyim* or *shkotzim* [shkotzim: literally abomination, detestable thing]. . . .
>
> "Also on my father's list; though not as high up, were some groups of Orthodox Jews; namely those who disagreed with his particular leanings. There were, on one end, the more liberal types [i.e. "Centrist" Orthodox] . . . And on the other end, there were the Hasidic Jews."[73]

The tensions between the Hasidim and the "Litvishe" yeshiva world go back to the middle of the eighteenth century. It was at that period that two men thrived, both Orthodox rabbis, both great religious leaders, but with very different approaches as how best to serve God and the Jewish people. Israel Baal Shem Tov (1700–1760) was the founder of Hasidism. He was born in Poland, though he lived in the Ukrainian regions of Podolia and Volhynia. He was a healer and wonder worker. The Baal Shem Tov's view was that in addition to reaching God through learning, people could approach God through prayer, through song and joy. He emphasized the emotional senses. The ideas and teachings of the Baal Shem Tov were in direct opposition to the second great Orthodox leader of that period, Elijah the Gaon ("genius") of Vilna, sometimes referred to as the Vilna Gaon. Born in 1720 in Selets, Lithuania, he was an intellectual giant and a child prodigy. The Vilna Gaon argued that all learning, whether of the past, present, or future, could be found in the Torah. He urged his students to study both traditional Jewish texts and various secular works because the secular works would help in comprehending both the Written and Oral teachings, the Torah and the Talmud. The Vilna Gaon was unalterably opposed to the ways and the teachings of the Hasidic movement. He was appalled at their emotionalism and the hero-worship of the Hasidic "Rebbes." Whereas the Hasidim stressed the spiritual and emotional direction to reach God, the Vilna Gaon urged the way of the intellect: that the common man become an uncommon scholar. Through his influence, on two occasions the Jewish community of Vilna sought both to excommunicate the Hasidim and to burn their books.

> In Andrew Kane's novel, one of the major characters discusses the dispute between those who followed the path of Hasidic Jewry and those who did not. He explains that while the initial events took place well over 200 years ago, that the legacy reaches to this very time. The original Hasidim were followers of the Baal Shem Tov, and they rebelled against the religious rigidity [Kane uses the term "fundamentalism"] that dominated so much of East European Jewry. These Hasidim placed great emphasis on the powers of their Rebbes and stressed a belief that "devotion itself is greater than studying Talmud and observing laws." With this kind of an approach, the Hasidim "incurred the wrath of the Jewish establishment, the Lithuanian rabbis of the renowned Talmudic academies in cities like Vilna and Velozhin, who waged their opposition with a vengeance. . . . And now their descendants lived in America, side by side with their former adversaries." Rabbi David Eisen, though born in America, nonetheless was "a proud bearer of the Lithuanian tradition" and he "was committed to the old grievances."[74] He teaches in Borough Park, at the Mirrer Yeshiva on Ocean Parkway in Brooklyn, a Talmudic academy named after the Polish/Lithuanian town of Mir, where it had originated. Rabbi Eisen teaches there, as his father had done before him, and as Yaakov Eisen, Rabbi Eisen's son, will be expected to do. Like the Hasidim, the Lithuanians also have a tradition of dynastic succession.

Though there will be individual differences between yeshivas, certain structures are constant. There will be a multipurpose room where yeshiva students spend their days studying Talmud and related works. Students will work in pairs or occasionally in groups of threes in order to study, understand, and explicate the texts. These "study groups" are called "havrusas." The three daily prayers also will be often recited in this room. A student will spend about 10 hours a day at this study hall. Resident halls which house both students who live in the city and those who come from other places will be found in most of the major yeshivas and even some of the smaller ones. Yeshivas will vary on the question of going home on weekends or at other times during the year. A major library is part and parcel of the yeshiva.

The *Rosh yeshiva* will certainly teach a class, perhaps once a week or so, depending on his other responsibilities. These classes are usually for the most advanced of the students.

Some *Rosh yeshivas* are very personable and engaged with their students while others are clearly more distant. Helmreich notes that the *Rosh yeshiva* walks a difficult path between being approachable and warm, and being too friendly with the students, and thereby eroding some of his power and authority. He must have the students' trust and yet maintain his standing as a scholar and leader.[75]

> In a series of novels by Faye Kellerman, the Rita Lazarus/Peter Decker mysteries, an important character is the Rosh Yeshiva (the "dean" of the school) of a yeshiva located in the metropolitan Los Angeles area. He is the "Sectarian" Orthodox, "Litvishe" Yeshiva Rabbi Aaron Schulman who is first introduced in *The Ritual Bath*.[76] Rabbi Schulman is European-born, he studied in Minsk, a major city in Lithuania, he is a Holocaust survivor, and as is not *un*common with the Mitnagged, "Litvishe" Yeshiva attitude, he has also studied secular subjects, notably American law, philosophy, psychology, economics and political science.[77]
>
> Rita Lazarus, the widow of a yeshiva prodigy, explains to Peter Decker that the Mitnaggedim and the Hasidim are like the Hatfields and the McCoys. They are poles apart. She explains that "the Chasidim [Hasidim] think that the Misnagdim [Mitnaggedim, "Litvishe" (Russian-Lithuanian) Yeshiva] lack human emotion, and the Misnagdim think the Chasidim are a bunch of ignoramuses." She goes on to suggest that, at least originally, Hasidim took the position that "Judaism is primarily in the heart, not the brain."[78]

An important part of the yeshiva experience in America is the *Kollel* experience. The *Kollel* is somewhat akin to doing graduate work. Married men come to the yeshiva to do further study. Some yeshivas have stringent "undergraduate" requirements; others are more flexible. There is no "graduation" from the *Kollel*, and students often study between 2 and 5 years. The students may receive a stipend, but this is rarely adequate to cover expenses. Oftentimes their wives will work to support their husbands.

> Most of the residents of Yeshivas Ohavei Torah (in the novel *Sacred and Profane*) are of college age. They are studying religious subjects, but the yeshiva also has a high school and elementary school where both secular and religious subjects are taught. The elementary school is for the children of the married men who are studying in the *Kollel*. Private homes are provided for the *Kollel* families, as well as "the two dozen rabbis who serve as full-time teachers, and the head-master—the Rosh Yeshiva . . . Rav [Rabbi] Aaron Schulman.
>
> ". . . The women who lived on the grounds simply came along with their husbands or fathers. The school catered exclusively to men."[79]

Though study-for-its-own-sake as well as scholarship are important values within Jewish life, one of the great concerns—even complaints of congregational rabbis—is that they do not have time for these activities.

NOTES

1. Bershtel, S. and Graubard, A. (1992). *Saving Remnants: Feeling Jewish in America* (New York: Free Press), pp. 141–142.

2. Lipman, E. J. (1990)."*Tanu Rabbanan*: Our Masters Have Taught Us," in *Tanu Rabbanan: Our Rabbis Taught CCAR Yearbook 1989*, vol. 2, ed. Joseph B. Glaser, vol. 2 (New York: Central Conference of American Rabbis), p. 48.

3. See Wertheimer, J. (1989)."Recent Trends in American Judaism" in *American Jewish Year Book 1989*, ed. David Singer and Ruth R. Seldin, vol. 89 (New York: American Jewish Committee and Philadelphia: Jewish Publication Society), pp. 108 f. For a discussion of this phenomenon, see also Helmreich, W. B. (1982). *The World of the Yeshiva: An Intimate Portrait of Orthodox Jewry* (New York: Free Press), pp. 52 ff.

4. In contrast to "Centrist" Orthodoxy, such as that associated with Yeshiva University, Charles Selengut refers to two groups which "insist on separatism and fundamentalism as essential to Jewish piety." These two groups are those of the "right-wing Yeshivah and Hasidic communities." Selengut, C. (1995). "Themes in Modern Orthodox Theology," in *Events and Movements in Modern Judaism*, ed. Raphael Patai and Emanuel S. Goldsmith (New York: Paragon House), pp. 125, 126. See also Silberman, C. E. (1985). *A Certain People: American Jews and Their Lives Today* (New York: Summit), pp. 38, 39. Rosenthal writes of "the right-wing, fundamentalist groups . . . in Orthodoxy" today (Rosenthal, G. S. (1986). *Contemporary Judaism: Patterns of Survival*. 2d ed. (New York: Human Sciences Press), p. 312). Likewise, in Andrew Kane's novel *Rabbi, Rabbi* the author refers to the "fundamentalism" of Yeshiva Orthodoxy. Kane, A. (1995). *Rabbi, Rabbi* (New York: Saint Martin's), p. 21.

5. Helmreich, p. 52 ff.

6. Harvey, V. A. (1964)."Fundamentalism," in *A Handbook of Theological Terms* (New York: Macmillan), p. 103.

7. Wurzburger, W. S. "Centrist Orthodoxy—Ideology or Atmosphere." *Journal of Jewish Thought*, 1:1985, p. 67 f. Wertheimer quotes this line in "Recent Trends," p. 118. A further division exists. Some Orthodox synagogues and rabbis define themselves as "Traditional." These "Traditionalist" Orthodox would be religiously to the *left* of the "Centrist" Orthodox. See Wertheimer, "Recent Trends," p. 145, n. 237.

8. Wertheimer, "Recent Trends," pp. 107 f.

9. Wertheimer, "Recent Trends," p. 113.

10. Grossman, L. (1991)."Jewish Communal Affairs," in *American Jewish Year Book 1991*, ed. David Singer, vol. 91 (New York: American Jewish Committee and Philadelphia: Jewish Publication Society), pp. 199–200. See also Wertheimer, "Recent Trends," pp. 107 ff.

11. Kane, p. 121.

12. Kane, p. 123.

13. Kane, p. 122. See Wertheimer, "Recent Trends," p. 122.

14. Waxman, C. I. (1993). "Dilemmas of Modern Orthodoxy: Sociological and Philosophical." *Judaism* 42:1 (Winter): 59–70. For reasons of consistency, though Waxman utilizes the term "modern" I shall substitute the word "Centrist".

15. Waxman, p. 59.

16. Wertheimer, "Recent Trends," p. 111.

17. Waxman, pp. 59–60.

18. Rosenthal, p. 74.

19. Wertheimer, "Recent Trends," p. 125.

20. Sklare, M. (1985). *Conservative Judaism: An American Religious Movement* (Lanham, MD, New York, London: University Press of America), pp. 185–190.

21. Sklare, *Conservative Judaism*, p. 190.

22. Rubenstein, R. L. (1974). *Power Struggle* (New York: Charles Scribner's Sons), p. 129.

23. Wilkes, P. (1994). *And They Shall Be My People: An American Rabbi and His Congregation* (New York: Atlantic Monthly), p. 115. This kind of mentality, of humiliating the students, certainly was prevalent likewise during the 1960s at the Hebrew Union College-Jewish Institute of Religion, Cincinnati when I studied there.

24. Wertheimer, J. (1987)."The Conservative Synagogue" in *The American Synagogue: A Sanctuary Transformed*, ed. Jack Wertheimer (Cambridge, England and New York: Cambridge University Press), p. 134.

25. Wertheimer, "Recent Trends," p. 136 f.

26. Kemelman, H. (*Friday the Rabbi Slept Late* (New York, Crown, 1964); *Saturday the Rabbi Went Hungry* (New York: Crown, 1966); *Sunday the Rabbi Stayed Home* (New York: G. P. Putnam's Sons, 1969); *Monday the Rabbi Took Off* (Greenwich, CT: Fawcett Crest, 1973 [1972]); *Tuesday the Rabbi Saw Red* (New York: Arthur Fields Books, 1973); *Wednesday the Rabbi Got Wet* (New York: William Morrow, 1976); *Thursday the Rabbi Walked Out* (New York: William Morrow, 1978); *Someday the Rabbi Will Leave* (New York: William Morrow, 1985); *One Fine Day the Rabbi Bought a Cross* (New York: William Morrow, 1987); *The Day the Rabbi Resigned* (New York: Fawcett Columbine, 1992); *That Day the Rabbi Left Town* (New York: Fawcett Columbine, 1996). Another fictional book that centers on Rabbi Small, but is not a murder mystery, is Kemelman's *Conversations with Rabbi Small* (New York: William Morrow, 1981).

27. Kemelman, *Thursday the Rabbi Walked Out*, p. 14.

28. Tennenbaum, S. (1978). *Rachel, the Rabbi's Wife* (New York: William Morrow), p. 24.

29. The congregation in this novel is not specifically designated as Conservative, but it is clear that Rabbi Bloom is a Conservative rabbi. His mother explains that he is an ordained Conservative rabbi. Allan Appel, *The Rabbi of Casino Boulevard* (New York: Saint Martin's, 1986), p. 82. Further, at one point he is "invited" by his rabbinic association to come to New York to defend his actions. Appel terms this professional body the "Rabbinical Association" and it is located at the "Theological Seminary, New York" (p. 177). Earlier in the novel, reference was made to the the seminary being located "not a half dozen blocks from . . . Columbia University" (p. 8). It is quite clear that this is a thinly veiled reference to the Conservative rabbi's Rabbinical Assembly, and to the Jewish Theological Seminary, both located in New York.

30. Telushkin, J. (1987). *The Unorthodox Murder of Rabbi Wahl* (Toronto and New York: Bantam). Other novels by Telushkin featuring Rabbi Winter are: *The Final Analysis of Dr. Stark* (Toronto and New York: Bantam, 1988) and *An Eye for an Eye* (New York: Bantam, 1992 [1991]).

31. Gertel, E. B. (1981)."A Novel Approach to Conservative Judaism." *United Synagogue Review* (Winter).

32. Kemelman, *Tuesday the Rabbi Saw Red*, p. 139.

33. Kemelman, *Monday the Rabbi Took Off*, p. 186.

34. Kemelman, *Sunday the Rabbi Stayed Home*, p. 58.

35. Raphael, M. L. (1984). *Profiles in American Judaism: The Reform, Conservative, Orthodox and Reconstructionist Traditions in Historical Perspective* (San Francisco: Harper and Row), p. 180. Raphael explains that there is some dispute among historians when the Reconstructionist movement actually began. Some date it to 1922 when Mordecai Kaplan began, programmatically, to "reconstruct" Judaism. Others argue that the "founding date" should be 1940 with the establishment of the Jewish Reconstructionist Foundation; and disciples of Kaplan argue for the date 1934 when he published *Judaism As a Civilization: Toward a Reconstruction of American Jewish Life*. Kaplan, himself suggested the date 1935, when he and some of his friends first published their official magazine, "The Reconstructionist".

36. "Reconstructionist Rabbinical College 1996–97 Fact Sheet." Wyncotte, PA: Reconstructionist Rabbinical College, 1996.

37. Alpert, R. T. and Staub, J. J. (1988). *Exploring Judaism: A Reconstructionist Approach* (Wyncotte, PA: Reconstructionist Press), pp. 58, 61.

38. Lipman, E. J. (1990)."*Tanu Rabbanan*: Our Masters Have Taught Us," in *Tanu Rabbanan: Our Rabbis Taught*, ed. Joseph B. Glaser, (see p. 94, n. 18) (New York: Central Conference of American Rabbis), p. 62.

39. Levine, M. with the Kantor (1985). *The Congregation* (New York: G. P. Putnam's Sons), pp. 68, 102; Gordon, N. (1965). *The Rabbi* (New York: McGraw-Hill), pp. 254 ff.; Fast, H. (1984). *The Outsider* (Boston: Houghton Mifflin), p. 207 ff.

40. Tarr, H. (1968). *Heaven Help Us!* (New York: Random House), p. 41.

41. Schreiber, M. (1991). *The Rabbi and the Nun* (New York: Shengold), p. 33.

42. Borowitz, E. B. (1978). *Reform Judaism Today* (New York: Behrman House) p. xxi; see Book One "Reform in the Process of Change," pp. 114 ff.

43. See Lipman, section on "Officiating at Mixed Marriages," in "*Tanu Rabbanan: Our Masters*," pp. 45–47.

44. Borowitz, Book One, p. 84.

45. Kane, p. 162. See Ullman, A. M."The Rabbi in American Jewish Fiction." Unpublished rabbinic thesis, Hebrew Union College-Jewish Institute of Religion, Cincinnati, 1985, chapter two, for a discussion of Reform theological positions in some recent fiction.

46. Schreiber, p. 13.

47. Fast, pp. 305, 309.

48. Helmreich, p. 53.

49. Mintz, J. R. (1992). *Hasidic People: A Place in the New World* (Cambridge, MA and London: Harvard University Press), p. 3.

50. Potok, C. (1967). *The Chosen* (New York: Simon and Schuster), pp. 111–112.

51. Helmreich, p. 53.

52. Telushkin, J. (1991). *Jewish Literacy* (New York: William Morrow), p. 431. See also Sachar, p. 696. Rabbi Menachem Mendel Schneerson, the "Lubavitcher Rebbe" referred to here served in that position for well over four decades, from the early 1950s until his death in 1995.

53. Potok, C. (1972). *My Name is Asher Lev* (New York: Alfred A. Knopf), p. 9 f., see also pp. 24, 91 f.

54. Gelerenter-Liebowitz, S. (1992)."Growing up Lubavitch," in *Daughters of the King: Women and the Synagogue*, ed. Susan Grossman and Rivka Haut (Philadelphia and Jerusalem: Jewish Publication Society), pp. 240–242.

55. Potok, *The Chosen*, pp. 19, 86–87.

56. Mintz, p. 348. For further information, see Mintz's chapter titled: "Lubavitch: The Messiah Issue," pp. 348–364.

57. Mintz, p. 353.

58. Goodman, A. (1989)."And Also Much Cattle," in *Total Immersion: Stories* (New York: Harper and Row), pp. 145–146. Even though the text reads "Borough Park," presumably it should be "Crown Heights," which is the headquarters of the Lubavitch movement.

59. Gelerenter-Liebowitz, p. 239.

60. Telushkin, *Jewish Literacy*, p. 431.

61. Wertheimer, "Recent Trends," p. 121.

62. Liebman, C. S. (1974)."Orthodoxy in American Jewish Life" in *Aspects of the Religious Behavior of American Jews* (New York: Ktav Publishing), p. 170. [This article originally appeared in the *American Jewish Year Book 1965* ed. Morris Fine and Milton Himmelfarb, vol. 66 (New York: American Jewish Committee and Philadelphia: Jewish Publication Society, 1965.)] Liebman's figure of 150,000 "friends and supporters" was written in the 1960s. Undoubtedly that number would be larger today.

63. Ragen, N. (1994). *The Sacrifice of Tamar* (New York: Crown), p. 233.

64. Bellow, S. (1968)."The Old System," in *Mosby's Memoirs and other stories* (New York: Viking Press), pp. 60, 73–74.

65. Potok, *The Chosen*, p. 276; Twersky, J. (1968). *A Marked House* (New York: Thomas Yoseloff), pp. 97, 114; Segal, E. (1992). *Acts of Faith* (New York: Bantam), pp. 230 ff. Rhoda Lerman's (1989) novel, *God's Ear* (New York: Henry Holt), is set largely in Kansas and Colorado, but again the heir apparent of a hasidic line chooses not to follow in his father's footsteps. Lerman, pp. 1 ff.

66. Kane, pp. 70 ff.

67. Segal, pp. 495, 496. Fact follows fiction. In this novel, the rabbinic uncle is assassinated by a Jew, a member of his own congregation, because he [the uncle] supports dialogue between Jews and Palestinians (p. 493). Some years later, in 1995, Prime Minister Yitzhak Rabin was assassinated by a Jew because Rabin favored a peace settlement with the Palestinians. Coincidentally, in 1966 Rabbi Morris Adler of Detroit was killed while conducting services. See Chapter 6 ("Congregants View Their Rabbis").

68. Twersky, p. 80.

69. Potok, *The Chosen*, p. 278. This issue of carrying the "pain" of his followers also is dealt with in Lerman, p. 114.

70. Twersky, p. 81.

71. Twersky, p. 106. See also Potok, *The Chosen*, pp. 131 ff.

72. Helmreich, p. 49. Helmreich mentions "numerous hasidic institutions" with many, many students. Technically, the Hebrew plural of "yeshiva" is "yeshivot," but in popular parlance many people Anglicize the plural to "yeshivas." In this study "yeshivas" and "yeshivot" will be used interchangeably.

73. Kane, p. 20.

74. Kane, p. 21.

75. Helmreich, p. 74.

76. Kellerman, F. (1986). *The Ritual Bath* (New York: Arbor House) pp. 25 ff.

77. Kellerman, *The Ritual Bath*, pp. 119, 281. See also *Milk and Honey* (New York: William Morrow, 1990), p. 354.

78. Kellerman, *The Ritual Bath*, pp. 118 f..

79. Kellerman, F. (1987). *Sacred and Profane* (New York: Arbor House), p. 15.

3

Rabbinic Training

The Rabbi Isaac Elchanan Theological Seminary (RIETS) at Yeshiva University ("Centrist" Orthodoxy); the Jewish Theological Seminary (JTS, Conservative); the Reconstructionist Rabbinical College (RRC, Reconstructionist); and the Hebrew Union College-Jewish Institute of Religion (HUC-JIR, Reform) together are the foremost schools in North America for the preparation of rabbis for the mainstream Jewish community. In addition, a number of rabbis serving Mainstream communities are graduates of the Hebrew Theological College (Traditional Orthodox.)[1] A brief historical sketch of these institutions was noted in Chapter 1 (The American Rabbi).

The Rabbi Isaac Elchanan Theological Seminary. The Rabbi Isaac Elchanan Theological Seminary at Yeshiva University was formed late in the nineteenth century. Originally, it was a transplanted East European Yeshiva which provided immigrant students and scholars alike a place to continue their studies. In time, this would become first part of Yeshiva College and then Yeshiva University. RIETS' founding purpose as an East European Yeshiva was consciously changed through the efforts of Americanized Orthodox East European lay leaders. Rabbi Bernard Revel took over the stewardship of RIETS, and through his influence the school began to produce rabbis who were knowledgeable in American ways. They also preached in English and served as a countervailing force to the successes of the Jewish Theological Seminary.

At RIETS, unlike the Jewish Theological Seminary, the Reconstructionist Rabbinical College, and the Hebrew Union College-Jewish Institute of Religion, the *primary* focus of studies is the Talmud and related literature. Not only is the Talmud the center of study but again, unlike the other seminaries, very little effort is made to understand the historical or social context in which the Talmud came into existence and was later edited. As Charles Liebman explains, no serious effort is made "to explore whether the received text is accurate." A critical examination of the text is not at issue at Yeshiva University's RIETS, because the extant text of the Talmud has been the accepted version for hundreds of years. The assumption is that "the Talmud and its traditional commentaries are authoritative, that the material in its essence is transcendent in origin, and that the commentaries . . . are independent of time and place." Students are expected to understand the text, and are required to resolve any seeming contradictions within the text or the interpretations of the traditional commentators.[2]

> In Chapter 10 (God, Israel, and Tradition), there will be a reference to Rav Kalman, an important character in Chaim Potok's *The Promise*. Rav Kalman is a prominent professor of Talmud at the Orthodox seminary. His approach to the Talmud text is that it is all revealed from God, and that the Talmud text and its traditional commentaries are authoritative.[3]

There is an important reason why RIETS has such a different focus from the other seminaries. It is based on the model of a European yeshiva as opposed to a rabbinical seminary. At the yeshivot, Talmud was virtually the exclusive subject that was studied, though ethical tracts ("musar") also were taught. The Talmud text and its commentaries were regarded as authoritative. Many students would literally memorize the text. Men who opted to become communal rabbis—usually one really did not serve one single congregation—obtained *semikhah* (ordination) when they were competent in certain portions of the *Shulhan Arukh*, the sixteenth century Code of Jewish Law. "Some young men sought *semikhah* from a number of rabbis.

Others, though eminent as *talmide hakhamim* [scholars], might never bother to obtain the *semikhah*. The European yeshivah was a place where one studied to become a master of Talmud. At best, ordination was secondary."[4]

By way of contrast, rabbinical seminaries were instituted in Europe in the mid-nineteenth century; they were created to train rabbis in skills different from the narrow focus on Talmud study. Among the most prominent of the European rabbinical seminaries were the Jewish Theological Seminary of Breslau (1854) founded by Zechariah Frankel, and the *Hochschule fur die Wissenschaft des Judentums*, which was centered in Berlin (1872), where one of the prominent faculty members was Abraham Geiger, a leading Reform thinker. Though there were other seminaries as well, Breslau in time would become the ideological model for Conservative Judaism's Jewish Theological Seminary in New York, and the curriculum of the *Hochschule* would influence the Reform movement's Hebrew Union College in Cincinnati.

Rabbinical seminaries, as opposed to the traditional yeshivot, "sought to give the rabbinical student familiarity with Jewish culture in a broad sense—Bible, Talmud, Midrash, history, rabbinical literature. They also undertook to train him in the scientific methods of study, the dispassionate examination and understanding of Jewish texts in a manner no different from the examination of other texts."[5]

In an overview of the studies offered at RIETS, it is suggested that the approach is "hardly distinguishable from the classical yeshivot." The students at RIETS, certainly those who enter the *semikhah* program, typically have been engaged in intensive Jewish studies for at least 8 years, and some have taken additional advanced Talmud studies in Israel. In recent years the yeshiva core at RIETS has been intensified, as well as offering a post-*semikhah* program for additional and advanced *semikhah* studies. Yet having said this, RIETS is different in that there is an acceptance of secular learning; there is a clear connection to the outside Jewish world, and in particular to Zionism and the State of Israel; and there is, by and large, in place of insularity, a commitment to work with the totality of the Jewish people.[6] Talmud, moreover, is not the only area of study. Rabbi Norman Lamm, the President of Yeshiva University has stressed that "secular studies were not merely to be tolerated but were part of the totality of being a Jew, particularly in this rapidly changing age and that with these studies one can function better as a rabbi."[7]

> In Chaim Potok's *The Chosen* and *The Promise*, as well as Andrew Kane's *Rabbi, Rabbi*, readers are introduced to the world of the Orthodox rabbinical yeshivot. Knowledge of Talmud is absolutely essential, and reading certain parts of those novels is similar to reading a fictionalized account of Charles Liebman's and Zevulun Charop's comments about Yeshiva University. The Rabbi Isaac Elchanan Theological Seminary is a division of Yeshiva University, which earlier had been called Yeshiva College. In *The Promise*, Reuven Malter attends Hirsch University, which had formerly been known as the Samson Raphael Hirsch Seminary and College.[8] Samson Raphael Hirsch (Germany, 1808–1888) is the spiritual forebear of an Orthodoxy that saw some value in secular studies, albeit a limited one. As Chaim Waxman has noted, there is in fact some disagreement about linking Samson Raphael Hirsch's name with Yeshiva University.[9] In *The Promise*, the Jewish Theological Seminary is called the Zechariah Frankel Seminary.[10] Frankel (Germany, 1801–1875) was the ideological forebear of Conservative Judaism. As noted earlier, Frankel founded the Jewish Theological Seminary in Breslau in 1854.

The Talmud program at RIETS is very intense. Students study on their own as well as in a classroom setting from 9:00 in the morning until 3:00 in the afternoon. Liebman reported that students learn sections of *Yoreh De'ah*, which is part of the *Shulhan Arukh*, specifically the "laws of *shehitah* (slaughtering), although the growth of large slaughtering and kosher packing houses makes it unlikely that most rabbis will ever be called upon to decide such questions." He goes on to say that the "Sabbath laws, marriage and divorce laws, and laws of family life and family purity are largely neglected."[11] Some would suggest that the purpose of studying the laws of slaughtering is not for the practical knowledge but because of the intellectual demands required to master such a text. As Charlop mentions, "at RIETS *lomdus*—the analytical mastery of the text, the intellectual stock-in-trade of the yeshivah—is of the highest standard."[12]

In recent years, there have been some changes. Now there are additional courses in *Orach Hayyim*, another section of the *Shulhan Arukh* where laws concerning prayer and everyday conduct are studied. In addition, for quite a long period the ordination program was three years, but then in the mid-1980s, it was increased to 4 years. The new 4-year curriculum has a vital component that consciously stresses "Contemporary Halakhah" [Jewish law, traditional practice]. According to Charlop, suggested topics for study include, for example in the area of "The Family" such areas as contraception, abortion, adoption, the aged, mental illness, and so forth. In the area of "Medicine," suggested study topics include genetic engineering, withdrawal of treatment, transplants, and euthanasia.[13]

The need for a wider curriculum, yet one which is also traditional in nature, is addressed in the following statement. It is true for graduates of Yeshiva University as well as for those rabbis serving congregations who have earned their *semikhah* from the more sectarian Orthodox yeshivas.

> A striking paradox underlies Jewish reality today, posing an awesome challenge to the Orthodox rabbi. On the one hand, the community he serves directly is apt to be more learned and punctiliously observant than in the preceding generation. Congregants ask questions of far broader range and complexity than their parents asked and expect their rabbis to be able to answer them. On the other hand, the largest part of the community is fast slipping away from its Jewish moorings, so that the rabbi has to be a greater *talmid hakham* [scholar] and have the necessary credibility and be no less knowledgeable than the people he is trying to reach "out there," beyond his congregation.[14]

In Chaim Potok's *The Promise*, we read that Reuven Malter studies the Talmud tractate *Chullin*, which "deals with the laws of ritual slaughter and with the dietary laws. A thorough knowledge of this tractate is one of the requirements for Orthodox ordination." He also studies the laws found in the medieval code *Yoreh De'ah*, a part of the *Shulhan Arukh*.[15]

A similar description of rabbinic studies is found in Andrew Kane's *Rabbi, Rabbi*. Rabbi Eliezer Trachtenberg (the irascible Talmudist who will be described in Chapter 11, Non-Congregational Rabbis) teaches this class. Trachtenberg

> was called "the *shoichet*," or slaughterer, a title bestowed upon him because of his fame for failing students. It was also a pun on the subject matter he chose to teach; namely, a detailed analysis of the rules pertaining to the slaughtering of animals and proper prepara-

tion of kosher meat. For him and others of his mind-set it was the most relevant area of Jewish law for rabbinical students to study. Matters such as medical or business ethics, family counseling, and the like seemed of little importance.

In the course of the introduction to his class, Trachtenberg refers directly to Rabbi Joseph Caro, the author of the sixteenth-century *Shulhan Arukh*.[16]

In both of these novels, as in Chaim Potok's *The Chosen*, we learn how very thoroughly these students need to prepare for their classes, learning both the text itself and appropriate commentaries. As shall be seen in Chapter 11 (Non-Congregational Rabbis) at the fictional Samson Raphael Hirsch Seminary (i.e., the Rabbi Isaac Elchanan Theological Seminary) textual emendations, which would be part of a scientific study of Talmud, are not an acceptable form of study at that school.[17] This conforms with the description of Yeshiva University found above, namely "the Talmud and its traditional commentaries are authoritative, that the material in its essence is transcendent in origin, and that the commentaries . . . are independent of time and place."[18]

Hebrew Theological College. Though the Hebrew Theological College (HTC), located in Skokie, Illinois, is considerably smaller than Yeshiva University's Rabbi Isaac Elchanan Theological Seminary, its program is similar to that of RIETS. According to Charles Liebman, with the exception of RIETS, it is the only yeshiva for the training of rabbis that is not under "Sectarian" Orthodox auspices. Some of the "Sectarian" Orthodox yeshivot were mentioned in Chapter 1. These include Brooklyn's Torah Vadaat, Chaim Berlin, and Lubavitcher Yeshivah; Manhattan's Jacob Joseph and Tifereth Yerushalayim; Baltimore's Ner Israel; Cleveland's Telshe Yeshivah; Lakewood, New Jersey's Beth Midrash Gavoha; and Spring Valley, New York's Beth Midrash Elyon as well as many other smaller institutions. The Hebrew Theological College appeals to students who "believe that a rabbi must be firmly rooted in all aspects of Jewish culture and civilization, besides having a comprehensive knowledge of Talmud." Yet, Liebman points out, most students really concentrate on their Talmudic studies, which is at the core of the HTC curriculum. There is some tension between the instructors of Talmud and those teaching in the area outside of Talmud. The Hebrew Theological College was founded in 1922, and in its first four decades produced many rabbis who went on to serve congregations. In more recent years, the percentage of rabbis who go on to pulpit work has steadily declined.[19] Though it is not a section of their regular curriculum, HTC does now offer courses in pastoral education as part of their graduate program.

The Jewish Theological Seminary. Liebman explains that study of Talmud is stressed at the Graduate Rabbinical School at the Jewish Theological Seminary. In terms of Talmud study, a number of approaches are taken. JTS employs the scientific method—including such concepts as a textual-philological method, a comparative-law or comparative institutions method, and, thirdly, a text-critical method.[20] Other course areas include Hebrew language, Bible, Jewish history, Jewish literature, and philosophies of Judaism. The professional aspect of training is also recognized. There are courses in practical rabbinics, homiletics, education, pastoral psychology, as well as clinical training for chaplaincy and an internship program in the rabbinate. In recent times, a year in Israel program has been established as part of the curriculum. The Jewish Theological Seminary is consciously more than a professional school. "On the contrary, it always viewed pure scholarship as a major part of its training." Yet as Reuven Hammer points out, from early on "there existed a tension between professional training and scholarship among those whose goal was the congregational rabbinate."[21] It is just this tension that was the subject of Sklare's observations found in Chapter 2 (Mainstream Rabbis and Sectarian Orthodox Rabbis.) A recent description (1992) of the Seminary's Rabbinical School Curriculum suggests that throughout its more than century-long history, it has been committed to certain ideas and ideals which include the development of a "viable American Judaism; a dedication to critical, *wissenschaft*-style scholarship; an emphasis on the 'fact' of history, especially as illustrated by the historical development of Judaism; . . . the concept of *k'lal yisrael* [the unity of the Jewish people]" and other matters such as the importance of "Hebrew language and the textual content of rabbinical education; and an underlying religious conservatism expressed in terms of a commitment to *halakhah* and its centrality in Jewish life."[22]

The Jewish Theological Seminary ordained the first Conservative woman rabbi in 1985.

> While most of Chaim Potok's descriptions in *The Chosen* and *The Promise* focus on the Samson Raphael Hirsch Theological Seminary (i.e., RIETS), he does spend some time in describing life and studies at the Zechariah Frankel Seminary (i.e., JTS). The Frankel Seminary has many distinguished faculty on its staff, world renowned scholars, a fine rare-manuscript room, and the course of study includes an approach which is in line with scientific criticism. Once on a visit there, Reuven Malter overhears a couple students discussing "a passage . . . in Martin Buber's *I and Thou*." He also refers to "a heated discussion about the relevance of traditional Jewish law to the modern world, another discussion about the way a professor had rearranged a chapter of Hosea . . . a third discussion about the advantages and disadvantages of small-town pulpits." Some of the people wore skullcaps, and some did not.[23]

While the Jewish Theological Seminary is Conservative Judaism's time-honored rabbinic institution, in the mid-1990s the University of Judaism, located in Los Angeles, opened its own Conservative rabbinical school, the Ziegler School of Rabbinic Studies. In 1997, Daniel Gordis, the Dean of the Ziegler School, explained that the School intended to incorporate the best of the *yeshiva*, graduate school, and professional school models in forming its curriculum and vision.[24]

The Reconstructionist Rabbinical College. As noted in Chapter 1, the Reconstructionist Rabbinical College (RRC) was founded in 1968, and for a number of years it augmented its courses with Judaica offerings at Temple University. Within a few years, however, the College could depend on its own Judaica resources. While in more traditional models, rabbis were authority figures, entrusted with decision-making in the community, "Reconstructionist rabbis do not seek to possess that kind of authority. They understand themselves as part of a community which must decide issues of Jewish life together," explains Rebecca T. Alpert. "From this perspective the rabbi is a guide, not the final arbiter."[25]

The Reconstructionist Rabbinical College differs from the other seminaries in that the latter offer courses in history and texts of various periods in Jewish life. At the RRC "a five-year core curriculum [is] organized around each period of Jewish civilization. Judaism is studied, extensively and intensively, by the strata through which it evolved."[26] The five-year rabbinic program centers on the biblical civilization, followed by the rabbinic civilization, and then in turn the medieval, modern, and contemporary periods.

The Reconstructionist Rabbinical College ordained its first woman in 1974.

As mentioned earlier, I am unaware of any novels or short stories that feature Reconstructionist rabbis, and so likewise there are no fictional examples of life at the Reconstructionist Rabbinical College.

The Hebrew Union College-Jewish Institute of Religion. The Hebrew Union College-Jewish Institute of Religion, located in Cincinnati, New York, and Los Angeles, are Reform Judaism's seminaries in America. From Liebman we learn that there are courses in Bible, Mishna, Talmud, Midrash, modern Hebrew, and the commentaries, as well as courses in philosophy, theology, and history. These courses are supplemented by others in practical rabbinics which include human relations, education, speech, and homiletics. There is a scholarly approach to the academic studies. Yet there is no fixed method of study. Liebman gives the example of a faculty member who suggests, for example, that there are two ways to study the Bible. The first is to "stress the scientific method—biblical criticism and philology—to help in the scholarly understanding of the Bible. Alternately, you can study Bible with the traditional Jewish commentaries and thereby achieve the traditional Jewish perspective and understanding of the Bible. In fact, the method used actually depends on the proclivities of the instructor."[27] The Hebrew Union College-Jewish Institute of Religion was the first institution of higher Jewish learning to require a year in Israel for their first-year students. This allows them to participate in an intensive Hebrew language program as well as deepen the students' knowledge about the land and the people of Israel. Another part of the curriculum has a very practical side: field training and supervision. "Students in the rabbinic program are required to serve part-time in small congregations or as interns to rabbis in larger congregations. There are also opportunities for students to serve as rabbinic chaplains in hospitals, homes for the aged, and other communal institutions."[28]

The Hebrew Union College-Jewish Institute of Religion ordained the first Reform woman rabbi in the United States in 1972.

Reform Rabbi Gideon Abel (in Herbert Tarr's *Heaven Help Us!*) mentions the courses that he took at the Rabbinical Seminary (a school based on the Hebrew Union College-Jewish Institute of Religion): "Bible, Talmud, Midrash, theology, philosophy, education, homiletics, history, archeology, comparative religion, Hebrew literature, the Code of Laws, pastoral psychology."[29] It is a virtual blueprint of Liebman's list of classes at the Hebrew Union College-Jewish Institute of Religion.

Drew Baron (in Herbert Tarr's *So Help Me God!*) is a student at the Rabbinical Institute of America (a school, again based on the Hebrew Union College-Jewish Institute of Religion) situated in New York. As part of his training, he serves as the part-time assistant to Rabbi Brownmiller at Temple Shalom on Long Island. He explains that "the freshman class was appointed to serve as adjunct rabbis on the High Holidays." Later in the novel, he helps Rabbi Brownmiller set up *havurot* at the synagogue, regular meetings of six to ten families who band together to do some kind of Jewish activities together.[30]

In a description of HUC-JIR, recently retired President Alfred Gottschalk explained that the

> College-Institute requires that the rabbi it ordains be an educated person. He/she must, of course, know Judaica and Hebraica but is also expected to be on the frontiers of new knowledge in the humanities. The College is defined as being: "A liberal institution of higher learning in Judaism. The College shares in the spirit of free inquiry and study which marks American colleges and universities."

He also speaks of the different demands placed on rabbis, and further of the "demands which in our age are close to the very center of prophetic Judaism and religious actions."[31]

Rabbi Joshua Kaye (*The Rabbi and the Nun*, quoted in part in Chapter 2) describes the Quincy seminary located in Ohio (i.e., the Hebrew Union College-Jewish Institute of Religion) in terms that are reflective of Gottschalk's description: "At that school each student is free to pursue his own ideas and beliefs within the broad philosophical spectrum of Liberal Judaism, yet all the students and the professors are bound by a common purpose, which is a total commitment to Jewish survival and the renewal of Judaism as a prophetic faith."[32]

In his study *Rabbi and Synagogue in Reform Judaism* (1972), Theodore Lenn reports that many students at the Hebrew Union College-Jewish Institute of Religion consider themselves agnostics. One seminarian explains that being "an agnostic is not being an atheist . . . and it is not contrary to Judaism to search one's soul. Agnosticism means searching. . . . Incidentally I don't intend to be a pulpit rabbi, at least not for the present."[33]

> The voice of that real-life seminarian is echoed by Maury Finkelstein (in Meyer Levin's *The Fanatic*). He has an opportunity to study at the Reform seminary. Yet "he could not say he believed in the Lord. He considered himself an agnostic. How could an agnostic become a rabbi and preach about God?" Later, when he does begin his studies, "Maury discovered that many of the students shared his doubts."[34] Coincidentally, Finkelstein does not enter the congregational rabbinate. Michael Kind (Noah Gordon's *The Rabbi*) at one point also claims that he is an agnostic. Yet as his mentor, Orthodox Rabbi Max Gross, replies to him "Do you think I have scientific knowledge of God? Can I go back in time and be there when God speaks to Isaac or delivers the Commandments? If this could be done there would be only one religion in the world; we would all know which group is right." He then goes on to say, "About God, you don't *know* and I don't *know*. But I have made a decision in favor of God."[35] In time Rabbi Kind does overcome his doubts and serves several congregations.

Real-life Rabbi Dan Cohn-Sherbok recalls his life at the Hebrew Union College-Jewish Institute of Religion. In the second year of the rabbinic program, he took a required course in synagogue administration. "In one session, the most prominent rabbi in the city came to speak to us." After covering a number of practical subjects such as synagogue finance, curriculum planning, and general management skills, he went on to some other areas. In this later discussion the rabbi says: "A rabbi is basically an actor." When queried about this by one of the students, the rabbi says, "Yes. That's the essence of the job. He plays a part in the Jewish drama of ritual observance. When you take a funeral you're there to comfort the mourners. At a wedding your job is to make people happy. At a bar mitzvah your responsibility is to make sure the spotty adolescent gets through the service. When confronted by a Jewish boy and a Gentile girl, you've got to look disapproving. In all this you've got to play the role."[36]

> Fiction follows/reflects fact. Cohn-Sherbok was ordained in 1971. The first section of Mordecai Schreiber's novel *The Rabbi and the Nun* is set in Quincy, Ohio, in 1969. The main figure, Rabbi Joshua Kaye, is a recent graduate of the Quincy Rabbinical Seminary (i.e., Cincinnati's Hebrew Union College-Jewish Institute of Religion). He is serving as the Assistant Rabbi in the most prominent synagogue in the city. His senior rabbi, previously described as "the rising leader of American Jewry, heir to Stephen Wise and Abba Hillel Silver," tells him: "You have to *do* like a rabbi. . . . What do I mean by that? A rabbi is basically an actor. The better you play the part the more effective you become. . . . We have to minister to the needs of these people. . . . You've got what it takes, m'boy. Learn how to play the part. You will go far if you do."[37]

Why has there not been a greater amount of depiction within the fictional world of life in the seminaries? The simple answer is that in many cases, life there was not a happy time. Lenn reports that rabbis who are satisfied with their careers and rabbis who are not are equally critical of the Hebrew Union College-Jewish Institute of Religion.[38] Rabbi Martin Siegel explains that he hated his classes at Hebrew Union and he found the school a bore. He berates both the teaching and intellectual level. He remembers a Hebrew grammar course taught by a man "who seemed to consider proper Hebrew conjugation at least one level holier than Godliness. He terrified me. He reduced me to a memorizing mummy."[39] The experience of rabbis who were students at RIETS, as reflected in the fictional works of Chaim Potok and Andrew Kane, or rabbis who were students at JTS, as indicated in previous quotations (in Chapter 2) by Richard Rubenstein or Jay Rosenbaum, show that they, too, were filled with less than sanguine memories.

Is the atmosphere different today? Though not a scientific example by any means, in conversations with a number of rabbis who were ordained in the 1980s and 1990s, I sense that much *has* changed. A considerably larger number of the faculty at the seminaries are American-born, American-trained, and, on the whole, younger than the average age of the faculties at these schools 30 and 40 and more years ago. In addition, as shall be mentioned in a later chapter, the rabbinate in a number of cases is the second career choice of rabbinic students. This means that the disparity in age between the students and the faculty is much smaller, and sometimes nonexistent. This allows for a much more respectful dynamic between faculty and students.

In an article addressing the "changing face of rabbinic education" the Provost of the Hebrew Union College-Jewish Institute of Religion in New York, Norman J. Cohen (1997) suggests that "the mandate of a seminary is to maximize not only the academic growth of its students, but their spiritual growth as well." He writes that the faculty are "expected to serve as models for our students." Indeed he states quite clearly, "Faculty have to be models of empowerment. The classroom cannot be a place of power, but rather one of dialogue."[40] This sort of thinking certainly is a change from what had been the practice years earlier.

As the twentieth century comes to a close, other rabbinic institutions have been established which train rabbis for mainstream Judaism, in addition to the seminaries mentioned: Orthdoxy's Rabbi Isaac Elchanan Rabbinical Theological Seminary at Yeshiva University, and the Hebrew Theological College in Chicago; the Conservative movement's Jewish Theological Seminary, and the Ziegler School of Rabbinic Studies at the University of Judaism; the Reconstructionist Rabbinical College; and the Reform movement's Hebrew Union College-Jewish Institute of Religion. These institutions of rabbinic training include the Institute of Traditional Judaism, based in Teaneck, New Jersey; ALEPH, Alliance for Jewish Renewal, associated with Rabbi Zalman Schachter-Shalomi; and the Academy for Jewish Religion, based in New York.[41]

NOTES

1. See Wertheimer, J. (1989). "Recent Trends in American Judaism," in *American Jewish Year Book 1989*, ed. David Singer and Ruth R. Seldin, vol. 89 (New York: American Jewish Committee and Philadelphia: Jewish Publication Society), pp. 145, n. 237.

2. Liebman, C. S. (1974). "The Training of American Rabbis," in *Aspects of the Religious Behavior of American Jews* (New York: Ktav Publishing), p. 8.

[This article originally appeared in the *American Jewish Year Book 1968*, ed. Morris Fine and Morris Himmelfarb, vol. 69 (New York: American Jewish Committee and Philadelphia: Jewish Publication Society).

3. Potok, C. (1969). *The Promise* (New York: Alfred A. Knopf), p. 167.

4. Liebman, "The Training of American Rabbis," p. 5. See also Charlop, Z. (1985). "Orthodox Rabbis" [a section of] "The Making of American Rabbis" in *Encyclopedia Judaica Yearbook 1983/5* (Jerusalem: Keter), pp. 84–85.

5. Liebman, "The Training of American Rabbis," p. 5. See also Hammer, R. (1985). "Conservative Rabbis" [a section of] "The Making of American Rabbis" in *Encyclopedia Judaica Yearbook 1983/5*, (Jerusalem: Keter) p. 91.

6. Charlop, p. 85. In 1997, Rabbi Charlop iterated the uniqueness of Yeshiva University, and RIETS, mentioning again the "acceptance of secular learning"; its "relation to the outside world, and particularly to Zionism and the State of Israel"; as well as its "aggressive commitment to the totality of the Jewish people." "Rabbinic education: then, now and tomorrow." *Sh'ma* 27:527 (February 7), p. 1.

7. Charlop, p. 86.

8. Potok, C. (1967). *The Chosen* (New York: Simon and Schuster), p. 207, *The Promise*, p. 2.

9. Waxman, C. I. (1993). "Dilemmas of Modern Orthodoxy: Sociological and Philosophical," *Judaism* 42:1 (Winter), p. 61.

10. Potok, *The Promise*, p. 3.

11. Liebman, "The Training of American Rabbis," p. 26.

12. Charlop, p. 86.

13. Charlop, p. 89.

14. Charlop, p. 87.

15. Potok, *The Promise*, pp. 104, 326.

16. Kane, pp. 167, 169.

17. Potok, *The Chosen*, pp. 250–251.

18. While textual emendations as part of a scientific study of Talmud may not be taught at RIETS, at the Bernard Revel Graduate School (BRGS), the graduate school for Jewish and Semitic studies at Yeshiva University, one finds a serious consideration of textual variants and the redaction process of Talmudic/Rabbinic texts as part of the regular curriculum.

The program leading to ordination at Yeshiva University requires that students be enrolled in both RIETS and the BRGS. Liebman, "The Training of American Rabbis," p. 25.

19. Liebman, "The Training of American Rabbis," p. 22.

20. Liebman, "The Training of American Rabbis," pp. 42–44.

21. Hammer, p. 92.

22. Ackerman, D. M. (1992). "A Not Too Distant Mirror: The Seminary Rabbinical School Curriculum." *Conservative Judaism* 44:4 (summer), p. 48.

23. Potok, *The Promise*, pp. 229, 230.

24. Gordis, D. (1997). "Visions From a New Rabbinical School." *Sh'ma* 27:527 (February 7), p. 5.

25. Alpert, R. T. (1985). "Reconstructionist Rabbis" [a section of] "The Making of American Rabbis" in *Encyclopedia Judaica Yearbook 1983/5*, (Jerusalem: Keter) p. 101.

26. Alpert, "Reconstructionist Rabbis," p. 102.

27. Liebman, "The Training of American Rabbis," pp. 55–56.

28. Gottschalk, A. (1985). "Reform Rabbis" [a section of] "The Making of American Rabbis" in *Encyclopedia Judaica Yearbook 1983/5*, (Jerusalem: Keter), p. 98.

29. Tarr, H. (1968). *Heaven Help Us!* (New York: Random House), p. 16.

30. Tarr, H. (1979). *So Help Me God!* (New York: Times Books), pp. 37 f., 233. See also Gordon, N. (1965). *The Rabbi* (New York: McGraw-Hill), p. 144.

31. Gottschalk, pp. 97, 100.

32. Schreiber, M. (1991). *The Rabbi and the Nun* (New York: Shengold), p. 33.

33. Lenn, T. (1972). *Rabbi and Synagogue in Reform Judaism* (New York: Central Conference of American Rabbis), p. 324.

34. Levin, M. (1965 [1963]). *The Fanatic* (New York: Pocket), pp. 35, 36.

35. Gordon, p. 134.

36. Cohn-Sherbok, D. (1993). *Not a Job for a Nice Jewish Boy*, (London: Bellew Publishing), p. 33 f. In the book, he calls the seminary the "Progressive Rabbinical Seminary" (p. 22) but he is a graduate of the Hebrew Union College-Jewish Institute of Religion in Cincinnati.

37. Schreiber, pp. 13, 23.

38. Lenn, p. 161.

39. Siegel, M. (1971). *Amen: The Diary of Rabbi Martin Siegel*, ed., Mel Ziegler (New York and Cleveland: World), pp. 172, 229.

40. Cohen, N. J. (1997). "The Changing Face of Rabbinic Education." *Sh'ma* 27:527 (February 7): p. 4.

41. See *Sh'ma* ed. Eugene Borowitz, 27:527 and 27:528 (February 7 and 21, 1997), and the relevant articles by Ronald D. Price (Institute of Traditional Judaism); Zalman Schachter-Shalomi (ALEPH, Alliance for Jewish Renewal); and Shohama Wiener (Academy for Jewish Religion); as well as Jacob, "Private Ordination—Need We Be Concerned?" *CCAR Journal* 44 (Winter): 3–8.

4

Congregational Rabbis and Their Communities

The predominance of rabbis *who serve professionally as rabbis* (as opposed to having rabbinic ordination and then serving in some other occupation) do so—in fact, and in fiction—in a congregational setting. The subject of the *congregational* rabbi is the focus of the next two chapters. Chapter 4 looks at several issues. It commences with some observations on the rabbi "as religious leader"; then considers the rabbi and the Synagogue Board (of Trustees); then the ubiquitous committees; and the chapter concludes with a section on rabbis and the predominance of women in their congregations.

Chapter 5 addresses the rabbi as the synagogue's representative; the rabbi and the non-Jewish world; anti-Semitism; and concludes with the issue of rabbinic loneliness/isolation. Congregants' views of their rabbis and how they evaluate them shall be taken up in Chapter 6 (Congregants View Their Rabbis). Material dealing with how rabbis view their rabbinate and their role in the modern world is found in Chapter 12 (Rabbis View the Rabbinate).

Rabbis are primary Jewish role models: leaders at religious services, preachers, teachers, and pastoral counselors. Their satisfactions and frustrations come from working with people.

Most rabbis who are graduates of the Reform and Reconstructionist movements serve congregations. The percentage of graduates who serve as congregational rabbis rapidly declines when we consider the graduates of the Conservative and Orthodox seminaries.

Theodore Lenn, in *Rabbi and Synagogue in Reform Judaism* (1972), reports that 85 percent of full-time, employed Reform rabbis are associated with "ministerial" work. Of these, nearly four out of five are congregational rabbis; the remainder serve as chaplains or Hillel (the Jewish group on the university campus) directors. An additional eight percent teach or are involved in administrative work with the Hebrew Union College-Jewish Institute of Religion (the Reform Seminary); the Central Conference of American Rabbis (the Reform rabbi's professional organization) or the Union of American Hebrew Congregations (the lay organization of the Reform movement).[1] As the twentieth century draws to a close, most Reform rabbis continue to serve in a congregational setting, whether as a full or part-time position. In the past quarter-century, however, those who are serving in rabbinic, non-congregational positions are increasing both in real numbers as well as a percentage of those who are ordained.[2] Charles S. Liebman (1968) reports that of the graduates of the Conservative Jewish Theological Seminary, 61 percent of those who are active are congregational rabbis; and of those who are graduates of Orthodox Yeshiva University, about 50 percent serve congregations.[3] Nearly 20 years later, those figures seem to remain constant. In a study on "The Making of American Rabbis" (1985), it was reported that while a large majority of the men ordained by Yeshiva University serve the Jewish community, at present 400 serve pulpits, 350 serve as educators, and 100 are involved in communal organizations. Seventy-five head up yeshivot and day schools, and another 30 are in key executive positions in Israel's educational system.[4]

Though pulpit rabbis are still plentiful and probably shall continue to be so, since the beginning of the 1970s (with attendant inflation and its economic problems), fewer new congregations are being formed, some are merging, and large congregations are finding it more financially difficult to support "assistant" or "associate" rabbis. As a consequence, rabbis increasingly are entering the fields of teaching, administration, and community work in greater numbers, as well as choosing non-rabbinic occupations.[5] I shall consider non-congregational rabbis in Chapter 11 (Non-Congregational rabbis).

Among the fictional rabbis, the representation is fairly similar. The congregational rabbis (including Hillel rabbis and chaplains) far outnumber their colleagues involved in other matters, and the majority of non-congregational rabbis are teachers and administrators.[6]

AS RELIGIOUS LEADER

What does it mean to be the "religious leader" of the congregation? Jack H. Bloom (1981) succinctly explains that "the most distinguishing factor of the pulpit rabbi . . . is that he is, most of all, a symbolic exemplar. The rabbi is the symbol of something other than himself and the pulpit rabbi is a symbolic leader who is set apart to function within his community as a symbol of that community and as an exemplar of that community's desire for moral perfection."[7]

Congregational rabbis fill a number of roles. Rabbi Eugene Lipman suggests that, for at least the mainstream rabbinate, there are nine major dominant self-images. These are: the Preacher; the Priest; the Prophet; the Pastor; the Symbolic Jew; the Technician; the Administrator; the Teacher; and the Scholar. These categories are presented with the caveat that "no rabbi is only, solely, and totally one or another of these in his [her] own eyes."[8] Rabbis often see themselves as a blend of several of these positions. When we view the rabbinate, factual as well as fictional, most if not all these images can be found, even though certain roles predominate over others.

In real life most congregants come into contact with their rabbis when he or she functions in one or more of three or four limited roles. Using Lipman's criteria these are the rabbi as Priest, Preacher, Teacher, or Pastor. *The most frequent situation where Jews interact with a rabbi is when congregants attend a religious service where the rabbi is leading prayers on the High Holidays, Rosh Hashanah, or Yom Kippur, or at Shabbat (the Sabbath) services*. Next would be where the rabbi is involved in a life-cycle ceremony: often a Bar or Bat Mitzvah, a wedding, or a funeral. In addition, parents may interact with the rabbi as the teacher (or often Hebrew language tutor) of *children*, or the rabbi as pastor, visiting someone in hospital or seeking the rabbi's advice on some issue.

Finding rabbis in these roles conforms well with Bershtel and Graubard's observation that statistically "synagogue membership is closely tied to Hebrew school, bar and bat mitzvah, and for Reform congregations, confirmation. Families of school-age children show much higher membership levels than families without children or families whose children have passed the relevant ages."[9] For many Jews living in America, the rabbi is a peripheral figure. Often rabbis are specialists called in to perform a specific duty.

The description of a real-life contemporary rabbi touches on this very notion.

> Like his counterparts in the Catholic and Protestant clergy . . . [the modern rabbi] is called upon to mark and individualize life-cycle events for members of his congregation . . . [members] who, for the most part, do not attend a synagogue with much regularity. Thus the rabbi often officiates at ritual circumcisions, weddings, and funerals for people whose faces he might recognize and can match with a name, but whose lives and souls are unknown to him.[10]

Many rabbis are frustrated by the fact that they are regarded as only tangential to the lives of their congregants. Rabbi Martin Siegel describes this phenomenon of the rabbi-as-specialist in his work *Amen: The Diary of Rabbi Martin Siegel* (1971). There we read: "Slowly, I am beginning to recognize my position. I am only their public property. They pay me to be instantly available; they pay me to lead them in acting out their abstract sense of religion; they pay me to bar mitzvah their sons, marry their children and conduct their funerals. I'm not a human being. I'm an institution. A symbol. A walking, talking, superhuman neo-divine reality."[11] One of the major ideas in Siegel's book deals with the problem of not having an on-going relationship with his congregants. This thought shall be considered further in the next chapter, in the section on rabbinic isolation and loneliness.

It should not be surprising that rabbis are resentful when they are "used" purely as a religious functionary. At a symposium, rabbis' views were solicited on their greatest and least satisfactions. Among their complaints we find "the response of people who say 'Rabbi, I enjoy your services whenever I go . . . but I don't go unless I have to for a bar mitzvah or *yahrzeit* [year's anniversary of a death];'" ". . .Least satisfactory is the need to officiate as a priest . . . officiating at unveilings and weddings"; "the 'formal' occasions when my presence and sometimes my words are necessary but are nevertheless considered a formality." In this same symposium, rabbi after rabbi speaks of the great satisfaction of teaching—some specifically mentioned adult education, while others were more general. Clearly, however, these rabbis meant that they found joy in teaching as education, as opposed to tutoring children mechanically, as for their Bar Mitzvah.[12]

Many rabbis do not find satisfaction when they are required to "officiate as a priest" and they do not consider themselves the priests' successors. Writing on the role of "The Rabbi as Religious Figure," Rabbi Samuel E. Karff (1990) explains that if "pressed, we crisply disavow any special praying power. Our words, we insist, carry no distinct weight with the Eternal. Younger colleagues seem even more anxious to disclaim any priestly prerogative. Unlike their rabbinic elders, they will not raise their hands when dismissing the congregation in prayer even if they use the traditional formula." Yet, having said this, he goes on to note that especially at life-cycle ceremonies the rabbi's "words of prayer or blessing . . . have a resonance which the layperson's words lack."[13] His evaluation is not self-serving. Laymen would readily acknowledge that the rabbi's words have a special resonance, as does the rabbi's very presence. This point shall be considered in the following chapter in the section on the rabbi as congregational "representative."

> As we would expect, when rabbis are central or major figures in the fictional literature, we see them in several roles. What, however, is the case where the rabbi is only a tangential figure; is there any pattern? Fiction presents an accurate picture on this point. In general, the lesser the rabbi's role in the story, the greater the chances that he or she will be shown as the Priest, the Preacher, or the Teacher, in short, the religious specialist. To mention but a few examples among many (for other instances see the list in this note), there is the rabbi who gives a eulogy for Morris Bober in Bernard Malamud's *The Assistant*; the rabbi giving a sermon in Paul Goodman's short story "A Prayer for Dew" and the Rabbi who is involved in the religious school in Philip Roth's short story, "The Conversion of the Jews."[14]

THE SYNAGOGUE BOARD

Call it the Synagogue Board, the Council, or the Trustees—their role is the same throughout. They are the elected representatives, the lay administrators of the synagogue. Elected (and probably reelected) yearly at an annual meeting, they are men and women whose time is freely volunteered. The rabbi (and sometimes in the board's eyes, "their" rabbi) is the paid professional. Boards—in conjunction with the rabbi—decide policy and administer synagogue affairs. That, at least, is the theory. Not lightly did the Lenn Report entitle its section on rabbinical-board relations "The Pulpit Rabbi and his Establishment." More than 75 percent of rabbis mention their board as playing the major role in synagogue politics, but less than 50 percent feel the board as a board makes the greatest contribution to the synagogue. The difference between synagogue *politics* and synagogue *affairs*, that is the difference between maintaining the *power status* (synagogue politics) and *serving the needs* of the congregation (synagogue affairs), is over 30 percent. The slack is taken up in two areas: the *Sisterhood* and "*individual members* rather than groups as strong contributing agents to synagogue growth."[15]

The relationship between rabbi and congregation is sometimes described as being analogous to a marriage. There are two partners, and each must meet the needs of the other. Constant and open communication is required. Respect, if not actual love, are essential ingredients for an ongoing association. Congregants as well as rabbis refer to this arrangement as a *shiddach* (Hebrew for "marriage"). As most analogies, it has certain limitations. For instance, it raises questions about traditional gender roles, all the more so with the addition of women rabbis.[16]

Even though marriage is an imperfect analogy, the concept may be helpful. Rabbis and congregations, like married spouses, differ at times and must find grounds for reconciliation. When this proves impossible, when "irretrievable breakdown" takes place, the partners do go their own way. Inasmuch as a congregation cannot speak as a unified group, the Board becomes the synagogue's representative body.

> The description of Rabbi Charles Pedlock (*Pedlock Saint, Pedlock Sinner*) sums up the situation somewhat crudely, albeit succinctly. "He was alert to the world of the *shul*, the temple. The vast modern fields of Judaism he knew as mine fields where

> the unwary careerist could be flung in fragments to the winds by a hostile board of directors."[17] Alternately, consider this advice given to Rabbi David Benjamin (*The Congregation*) about the Board of Trustees: "Don't let yourself think of them as people. . . . Think of them as votes for or against you."[18]
>
> In the fictional literature, synagogue boards vary in size from a handful to over forty people in number.[19] The Cabinet of the President of the United States, or the Prime Minister of Canada, is probably smaller than many synagogue boards.

According to Lenn, most Reform rabbis are pleased with their boards because they and the general membership are willing to accept changes in synagogue policy. He concludes that most Reform rabbis are relatively free from shackling restraints. Certainly self-respecting rabbis will not "take orders" from their board, nor will they be compromised on matters of morality.[20]

Paul Wilkes describes the factual rabbinate of Rabbi Jay Rosenbaum of Worcester, Massachusetts, in his work *And They Shall Be My People: An American Rabbi and His Congregation* (1994), a book that was on the *New York Times* "best seller" list for many weeks. There he writes directly about the issue of rabbinic autonomy. "The search committee [for a new rabbi] said that while they wanted a rabbi who was reasonable and open to suggestions, they did not want one they could push around. Rabbi Rosenbaum assured them he would not be so moved."[21]

Even so, rabbi and synagogue must complement one another and if there is too wide a chasm in opinion or style, they will part ways.

> Michael Kind (*The Rabbi*) leaves Cypress, Georgia, because he cannot reconcile his conscience with racial segregation, and he resigns from his post in Wyndham, Pennsylvania, because he does not feel he can serve as a rabbi and be part of synagogue fund raising. David Mendoza (*Pedlock Saint, Pedlock Sinner*) resigns over a question of "free speech."[22]

The rate of factual rabbinic/congregational "divorce" is difficult to evaluate in the Lenn Report. This is not to suggest that there are not a fair number of changes of position. Rabbis may simply choose to move away because they wish to do so. It need not be differences in rabbinic/ congregational issues that motivates them. In principle it may mean that the rabbis wish to serve a larger (smaller) congregation; in a more (less) metropolitan area with greater (fewer) opportunities for study. More realistically, a fair number of these changes were because the rabbi was forced out of the congregation. Lenn does not present any data as to "why" rabbis have left one congregation to serve another. While over 20 percent of the rabbis were still serving in their first congregation, some three out of four rabbis have served more than one congregation, and 45 percent have served in three or more pulpits. Only a small percent have served seven or more congregations. Lenn suggests that these figures do not necessarily suggest an abnormal turnover rate. "In fact . . . there appear to be no differences in satisfaction between those who have held their positions a long time and those who have recently changed posts."[23]

There is a general correlation between the Lenn findings and the fictional rabbinate: in most cases in the fiction, rabbis have served more than one pulpit. What is more stark in the fiction, however, is that in a fair amount of cases either the rabbi is forced to resign or the rabbi's contract is not renewed. When there are difficulties between rabbi and board, the conflict often revolves around differences in role expectation. In Chapter 6 (Congregants View Their Rabbis), we shall look at this phenomenon in greater depth. Gideon Able's (*Heaven Help Us!*) and Ed Gordon's (*Thy Daughter's Nakedness*) contracts are not renewed because they have offended too many people in the congregation. Rabbi Myra Wahl (*The Unorthodox Murder of Rabbi Wahl*) is in very serious trouble with her Board because she has been too outspoken.[24] Rabbi Joshua Levi (*The Firing of Rabbi Levi*) is told that the congregation appreciates what he has done for them, that the children like him and that they have learned a great deal, that he is honest, forthright, and sincere in his religious beliefs, but that he is much too inflexible in his attitudes and opinions and that he is too old-fashioned. In addition, he is in trouble for his sermon topics. "We are all greatly impressed by your scholarship, but many are frankly bored by your topics. We are tired of hearing what Judaism stands for, what problems we Jews face."[25]

Though the preceding remarks are blatantly stupid and inane, in terms of the fictional Boards of Trustees, there are

> few which can match the sustained pettiness and maliciousness of the congregational Boards depicted in Barnard's Crossing, Massachusetts, and their twenty-five year relationship with Rabbi David Small of Harry Kemelman's Weekday *Rabbi* series. With rare exceptions, the Barnard's Crossing Boards, and their successive congregational presidents, are boorish, manipulative, under-handed, irascible, and mean-spirited. While in any given novel they do have some competition with the Board or presidential exploits found in the fictional works by Marilyn Greenberg, Israel Jacobs, Arkady Leokum, and Richard Rubenstein, as a group they are truly something to behold. As I point out elsewhere, that Rabbi Small is able to "survive" working with these people is one of the mysteries of the detective series itself.

Unquestionably, oftentimes in the past, Boards of Trustees were made up of the wealthy elders of the synagogue. As shall be discussed in Chapter 6 (Congregants View Their Rabbis) in the section on "Expectations," these Board members, past and present, are more interested in the "profits" than the "prophets." Times do change. Some suggest that the image of the Boards made up of the wealthy elders has given way to include men and women of a younger age and who do not have the same financial resources. Furthermore, given the synagogues' "competition" with federations and other Jewish organizations, there are many places where people can serve in leadership positions. As in the past, so in the present, good, wise, committed, and Judaically knowledgeable leaders are far and few between. As shall be explained in Chapter 6, there often are significant differences in the expectations that Boards have of rabbis, and how rabbis see themselves as religious leaders.

COMMITTEES, COMMITTEES

> "The only one who doesn't get a rest one day in seven is the rabbi. On the Sabbath, when we get off, he works. And on the days we work he works, too . . . he's at his studies. And when he's not studying, he's called different places to speak, or he goes to committees."[26] "We have . . . a sisterhood, men's club, youth group, some twenty committees, and an expansion fund. We are, you see, a very active temple."[27]

How do people gauge a rabbi's effectiveness within a community? Surely it is not by the number of meetings he can (and is expected) to attend in a given week. Yet a real-life rabbi is quoted as saying: "I know of no other profession or skill . . . where one man is called upon to be so many things to so many different people. Success in the rabbinate will often depend upon the number of meetings a rabbi can attend . . . the number of people he can see . . . the number of phone calls he can make . . . and the number of congregational activities he can juggle in one week. Such frenzied activity can only tend in the direction of shallowness. . . ."[28] Though this "complaint" appeared in a journal several decades ago, there is reason to believe that little has changed in the intervening years.

Describing the life and activities of Rabbi Jay Rosenbaum of Worcester, Massachusetts, Paul Wilkes writes of a "plethora of religious and community responsibilities [which] adds up to considerably more than a full-time job."[29] These activities include "social action," "ritual," "youth," and "administration." In addition there are the duties of visits to the sick and bereaved congregational families, others whom he has not seen in a while, and still others who he has heard might need his attention. "[He is] not only the spiritual leader of his congregation; he must also be a principal representative of the Jewish community in the secular world. Toward this end, Rosenbaum is involved in a cornucopia of causes. . . . Then of course, there are the community-wide functions of the Worcester Jewish Federation, ranging from the celebration of certain Jewish holidays and Israel-oriented events to assisting Russian Jews arriving in the area."[30]

> Fictional Rabbi Lynda Klein (*A Place of Light*) had just skipped her lunch. "She'd missed breakfast too, for there had been no time. The Religious School board had scheduled a coffee meeting in the morning. . . . After it broke up, the singles-group president came in, and it took her half an hour to talk him out of resigning. Then . . . she'd dashed off to the hospital, where Nita Gold was undergoing emergency surgery. She'd gotten back in time for Abe Katz's funeral . . . she still had correspondence to do, not to mention the two boys coming in for bar mitzvah training."[31]

In a symposium on life in the congregational rabbinate conducted by the American Conservative movement, rabbis wrote of "endless meetings" that they were "required to attend," meetings that were "frequently monotonous and repetitive." There is nothing new under the sun. As with any situation, however, there is at least another side to consider. Meetings for the sake of meetings are intrinsically boring, and there are few meetings which we attend that are not monotonous or repetitive. Yet as most congregational rabbis know, meetings can be, and frequently are, a real indication of the vitality and activity of a synagogue. Meetings are democracy at work, meetings can mean involvement on a score of issues related to Judaism.[32]

> In one novel alone, we read of programs organized by an "adult education committee" for "Sabbath Eve lectures," a "sisterhood, which runs the preschool kindergarten; the youth group, which tutors disadvantaged kids," and a "social-action committee"[33] which all suggest a synagogue whose members are committed to Judaism. Naturally, activity by itself does not mean commitment to Jewish ideals. In another novel, Rabbi David Small (*Friday the Rabbi Slept Late*) explains that synagogues need leaders who will guide their congregations so their activities will be *Jewish*, not merely "ostensibly Jewish," such as when the dance group works up an interpretive dance based on an Israeli theme or the choral group adds White Christmas to its repertoire so they can sing it at Christian churches during Brotherhood Week.[34]

It is also through the synagogue's committees, however, that rabbis can meet with congregants and influence them. Meetings might well be boring and time-consuming, but they also can be the vehicle for Jewish programming of real value. At its best, when congregants are involved, they put their Judaism into practice by privately studying their tradition in order to incorporate it into a public presentation.

It is frustrating for rabbis when they are leading services on a Friday night or Saturday morning, and the attendance is limited, to know that many congregants are to be found at social events or at the local football or baseball stadium. One factual rabbi, in planning out a congregational trip to Israel, hopes that upon their return the congregants will be imbued with "creating a Jewishly observant community . . . a community that honored the Sabbath not only by coming together for services, but . . . forgoing travel, work [. . . all this] within a society where Saturday more typically meant Little League, lawn mowing, and trips to beach, ski slope, or shopping mall."[35]

Low attendance at services, however, has been part of the American Jewish scene for decades. As noted earlier in Chapter 1, The American Rabbi, beginning in the mid-twentieth century there had been a large increase in synagogue affiliation. This "was not matched by a rise in synagogue attendance." Polls conducted in the mid-1960s and early 1970s showed that Jews were far behind Roman Catholics and Protestants in their attendance at weekly services.[36] Surveys since that time show that there has been little, if any, improvement in synagogue attendance among Jews.[37]

> Fictional Rabbi Michael Kind (*The Rabbi*) is unhappy in his knowledge "that at least a *minyan* [quorum of ten people] could be collected in a bowling alley within driving distance . . . that tent theaters, supper clubs, and several Chinese restaurants no doubt held more of his congregation than the temple did."[38]
>
> Low attendance *is* a matter of concern, but this is not the only way to gauge effectiveness. The rabbi who quipped that all "Jewish life naturally centered round the synagogue—round it rather than in it" was missing the point. For in his very next sentence we read, "If prayers in the synagogue attracted scores, meetings in the synagogue hall could attract hundreds."[39]

A much more realistic consideration than mere attendance at services would be the amount and level of Jewish programming which takes place in a given year and the number of people who are affected, directly or indirectly, as planners, participants, or audience.

RABBIS AND THE PREDOMINANCE OF WOMEN

Sisterhood

The "most active" lay leaders in Reform congregations, says Lenn, are men. He is quick to note, however, that women are not far behind. Women are a force with which to be reckoned. When considering the combined total of "most active" and "reasonably active" in Lenn's lay leadership index, women out-poll men considerably, sixty-two percent to forty-eight percent.[40] In a study of the "Impact of Feminism on American Jewish Life," it was reported that though "Jewish women are substantially less likely to volunteer for a church or synagogue group than are non-Jewish women (59 percent of Jewish women compared to 69 percent of non-Jewish women), the synagogue group remains the single activity most likely to attract Jewish women."[41]

It should come as no surprise that Lenn reports that one of the most significant committees for getting work *done* in the synagogue is the Sisterhood.[42] In an analysis contrasting British and American Jewry, Charles Angoff (1961) notes it is the women who rank high on the list of doers, this especially in contrast to their British counterparts, vis-à-vis the synagogue community. "In America, in a very important sense, it's the women who form the pillars of the *shulen* [synagogues], the various drives, the cultural activities. A synagogue . . . in America, without a sisterhood is almost unthinkable. . . . It's really a *mechaye* [a wonderful thing] to see Jewish-American women in action. But in England they seem to be in the background."[43] The Sisterhoods of the American religious movements are organized nationally and have annual conferences.

> Novelists often know the importance of Sisterhood. When the authors wish to indicate that the rabbi has given offense, Sisterhood is a good place to begin. Sisterhood meetings, not infrequently, are places where angels, never-mind rabbis, should fear to tread. Comments we read include the criticism of the rabbi who suggested that a "kosher home was more important for Jewish women than campaigning for gifts for the temple"[44]; the rabbi whose talk was not geared for the ladies' interests[45]; and the rabbi whose "dogmatism threatens to destroy everything. That man is too much of a Jew, and he runs too tight a temple. Sisterhood simply isn't big enough for the both of us."[46] Rabbi Daniel Winter (*The Final Analysis of Dr. Stark*) is in trouble with his Sisterhood committee when he suggests that a Jewish gossip columnist is not a proper model to receive the Jewish "Woman of the Year" award.[47]

Women's Status

In mainstream secular American Jewish life, women are very prominent in all aspects. They are often board members, they serve on or chair local, regional, and national committees. Women's equal or near-equal role in the synagogue, however, is true only in terms of non-Orthodox Judaism in America. When we combine role with status, we see that the further we move toward "religious-traditionalists," the lesser the position women play in synagogue politics (such as board members) and certainly their role is diminished in the sanctuary itself.

In the American Conservative Movement, the United Synagogue of America, women's role and status is in an intermediate position. It is only recently that women have been considered eligible to participate fully in religious activities, and this equality is not universal. It appears that women have made progress more rapidly in the political realm (Board) than on the religious side (leading services, given honors) though this certainly is changing toward *greater* egalitarianism.[48]

In a study conducted in the late 1970s, polling synagogues throughout the United States, it became clear that mixed seating, men and women praying together, was a universal phenomenon for Conservative and Reform Judaism. Nearly all Reform congregations counted women as part of the *minyan* (the required prayer quorum of ten people) and about half of the Conservative congregations did so, though none of the Orthodox counted women. These figures remained constant when the question concerned honoring women by asking them to bless the Torah in a service. Women gave sermons in nearly all Reform congregations, in more than three-quarters of the Conservative, and seven percent of the Orthodox congregations. Women participated ritually in services in most Reform congregations, in about two-thirds of Conservative, and in only two percent of the Orthodox.[49] In recent years, the percentage of congregations which feature women's ritual participation in Conservative congregations has increased enormously, in no small measure due to the fact that since 1985, the Conservative movement has been ordaining women.[50]

In Orthodox synagogues, at least until the advent of the feminist movement, the place of women has been in support services. Their contribution to synagogue life is largely in terms of welfare and catering, not religious services. An Orthodox synagogue may have a women's group. Their role is to cater, raise money on behalf of the synagogue, give assistance where needed, often to organize educational programming, yet they have no status concerning public prayer. They are not counted as part of the *minyan* for services, and certainly they are not to be called to the Torah to recite blessings. In Orthodoxy, this is yet a male prerogative. The women who are elected to Orthodox synagogue Boards are limited in number, rarities and not the rule. As one moves further away from the more progressive wings of Judaism, political status for women becomes a non-issue. Women rabbis are (as yet) unthinkable for Orthodoxy.[51]

> In fiction, as in fact, as we move toward the religious traditionalists, the public role of women becomes more diminished. They may or may not attend religious services on a regular basis. "You are a man. She is only a woman," a Hasidic rabbi explains in a short story by Saul Bellow.[52] In the Hasidic novels of Jacob Twersky and Chaim Potok, we encounter a wall of men, and in another novel dealing with Orthodoxy, we read "few women had ever ventured into the synagogue."[53]

In the section dealing with the Hasidic community, we met Shoshana Gelerenter-Liebowitz. In her article "Growing Up Lubavitch," she explains that when she was very young, she "loved to go to *shul* [synagogue] with [her] father. . . . [She] was allowed to enter the men's section. . . . Nobody had to explain why girls cannot sit with their fathers in *shul* past age ten. . . . The separation of the sexes is accepted throughout the [Hasidic] society." Gelerenter-Liebowitz also mentions that "Mothers don't usually go to *shul* on Friday night because they are home with their children."[54] Orthodox Jews would not carry or wheel baby carriages outside on the Sabbath, since this would violate the laws of work on the Sabbath.

Unique Problems

As mentioned above, it is in the more progressive and moderate wings of Judaism that women play a correspondingly larger role and have a correspondingly higher status. They sit on synagogue, regional, and national boards, they do more than cater and fund-raise, they lead services and take their full place in synagogue life, and this too is reflected in the literature.[55] It is, in fact, because of the increasing role of women in what was once a Jewish man's world that causes other, somewhat unique problems for the modern rabbi. As Mirsky (1974) explains, the modern rabbi spends "a large portion of his time with women and children. He is expected to keep the children Jewish and to provide 'inspiration' to Jewish wives so that their days might be filled with meaning. He must be able to counsel them, and increasingly, to convert them from non-Jews into Jewish women." He also observes that Judaism is influenced by many of the same sociological and societal factors that affect Christianity.

> Christianity in America has become a religion primarily for women. Every survey of church attendance, participation in church activities, and devotion to the church has indicated that women are far more "religious" than are men. The portrayal of Christian clergymen in novels, cartoons and other manifestations of pop culture indicate that he is regarded by males virtually as being part of the world of women. He is expected to work with them, get along with them, and one might conjecture, to make certain that they do not deviate from the moral code of the church which discourages them from doing violence to the double-standard. Like a woman, a Christian clergyman has a "house" to look after and a "flock" ("of children") to guide . . . he is expected to maintain a woman's naiveté in matters sexual."[56]

As the Christian clergyman oftentimes is "neutered" by his congregants, so the male rabbi can be psychologically emasculated by his congregants.

> Consider: "A healthy man needs a woman. You being a rabbi wouldn't understand." The rabbi replies tersely: "Rabbis aren't castrated."[57] Single men have difficulties dating. A young lady explains, "Well, you being a rabbi, it would be sort of like dating God."[58] Women rabbis face similar problems. In a briefly portrayed episode, it appears that the man at the art gallery who is interested in speaking to Rabbi Diane Warburg ("Love hurts") beats a hasty retreat when he finds out that she is a rabbi.[59] In Rhonda Shapiro-Rieser's novel *A Place of Light*, Lynda Klein has had difficulties finding someone to date who does not assume that her primary interest in conversation is theology.[60] On the other hand, Rabbi Arnold Gold (John Haase's *The Nup-*

tials) finds that there was "no doubt that choosing the rabbinate made him more popular with the opposite sex." To put that in perspective, however, the author goes on to explain that "all the mothers in the neighborhood blessed with an unattractive daughter saw their salvation in Arnold Gold. Any boy so shrewd as to choose a career with the Lord would be able to overlook a few minor impediments like a couple extra pounds, a crossed eye . . . and would see the *true* measure of their offspring. . . ."[61]

For male rabbis, the rabbi as a "man among men" can be questioned in other ways. There is a certain camaraderie that exists between men which allows them to tell off-color jokes which they would consider tasteless to tell in front of women or in polite company. Rabbis—and clergy in general—fall into some sort of middle category: They can hear the remark or joke, but with due apologies—another example of neutering the rabbi. In real life a student rabbi relates the following typical incident:

> After dinner, the men went into the den, and the women went into the living room. No sooner had cigars been distributed than the men began to regale me with every joke involving a clergyman that has been told throughout history. It was bad enough that I had to laugh at a thousand jokes which I had already heard. Then the final blow was struck. Anytime anything to do with sex occurred as a theme in any of the stories, either about clergymen or in general, one of the men would say, "You'd better cover your ears for this one, Rabbi," or another man would say, "Oops, pardon me, Rabbi." My first temptation, which, thankfully, I resisted, was to tell them the raunchiest joke I knew.[62]

Fiction reflects reality. On a given occasion, one of the three most important politicos in the synagogue comes late to a luncheon meeting. In his brief apology he explains, "We had a fashion show this noon at our Vine Street bank. Marvelous tiddies—pardon me, rabbi,—and I had to say a few words to the reporters."[63] To show that their rabbi-characters are neither asexual nor indifferent to sex, some authors dwell on their rabbi's sexual life or interest in sex, suggesting that either through fecundity or frequency that these are "real men."[64]

An interesting variation of this is in a novel where the rabbi admits that for a while he was impotent.[65]

Sensuality and sexuality is also raised in another context. One of the images of a rabbi is as the person who comforts the lonely. Some novelists, therefore, write about a real problem in the rabbinate: the rabbi as object of seduction (usually by a lonely or frustrated woman). Remarkable tact is required in these situations so as not to give offense. As William Congreve observed, "Heaven has no rage . . . Nor Hell a fury, like a woman scorned." In the fiction both single and married rabbis are the objects of seduction. While to be sought is very flattering to be sure ("Everybody says you're really too good-looking to be a rabbi," one man is told), most rabbis politely but firmly decline to get involved.[66]

Given the limited *fictional* examples of women rabbis, to my knowledge there are—thus far—no instances of *fictional* women rabbis as objects of seduction. Regrettably, in real life, women rabbis have faced a great deal of unwanted and unwarranted sexual advances, as well as many examples of sexual harassment.[67]

A related problem in the modern rabbinate is the whole issue of "sexual boundary violations." There have been several non-fiction articles dealing with this issue.[68]

While there are some novels which portray rabbis, or rebbetzins [rabbi's wives], having extra-marital affairs,[69] the issue itself of a rabbi who has had an affair and is then confronted by the congregation, and therefore losing his/her position, much less doing some form of redemptive acts, has yet to appear in fiction. There is, nonetheless, one novel where a rabbi, on his own, burdened by the guilt he carries, chooses to resign from his post because, among other sins, he has committed adultery. In this novel, he indicates that he shall perform acts of atonement to repent for his wrongdoing. Since this literally comes at the close of the work, we do not know how this repentance will be realized.[70]

> There is one novel where a rabbi is falsely accused of adultery, and though he is patently innocent, the net result is that at the conclusion of the book he is forced to resign his position.[71]

Though the issue of sexuality can "separate" rabbis from their congregations, sexuality as such is only one category among many. In my experience, congregants are reluctant to socialize with rabbis. The whole matter of rabbinic loneliness and isolation shall be dealt with in the next chapter.

Is there a way that rabbis can be seen and treated as human beings, and not "categorized," "protected," or "neutered" by their congregants? The answer clearly is yes. It probably does take, however, a conscious, active intervention on the part of the rabbi. One can explain that rabbis are people, with the same desires and the same virtues and failings as others. I am a rabbi and I am also a man (woman), a father (mother), a husband (wife). I exercise, I socialize, I wear many different hats. Is this always effective? Probably not. Rabbis often *are* regarded as persons apart. As a rabbi you are a role model. Rabbis may not always see themselves as standing on pedestals, but oftentimes they are placed there by congregants. My experience tells me that on occasions, rabbis can step out of their roles. I exercise on a regular basis. When I am in a fitness center, or jogging along in my shorts and a T-shirt, or wearing my sweats, huffing and puffing alongside someone else who is similarly dressed and equally winded, we are just a couple of amateur athletes. After we put on our clothes, however, more likely than not we return to our "roles."

NOTES

1. Lenn, T. (1972). *Rabbi and Synagogue in Reform Judaism* (New York: Central Conference of American Rabbis), p. 22.

2. Rabbi Elliot L. Stevens, Executive Secretary, Central Conference of American Rabbis in a personal communication to David J. Zucker, December 11, 1995.

3. Liebman, C. S. (1974). "The Training of American Rabbis," in *Aspects of the Religious Behavior of American Jews* (New York: Ktav Publishing), pp. 22, 25. [This article originally appeared in the *American Jewish Year Book 1968*, ed.

Morris Fine and Morris Himmelfarb, vol. 69 (New York: American Jewish Committee and Philadelphia: Jewish Publication Society, 1968.)] While the numbers for JTS are explicitly stated, the numbers for YU had to be extrapolated from the statistics offered.

4. Charlop, Z. (1985). "Orthodox Rabbis" [a section of] "The Making of American Rabbis" in *Encyclopedia Judaica Yearbook 1983/5* (Jerusalem: Keter), p. 86. In the article it was unclear if the 75 rabbis who headed up yeshivot and day schools, as well as the 30 in Israel's educational system, were or were not part of the figure of 350 educators.

5.Meyer, M. (1988). *Response to Modernity: A History of the Reform Movement in Judaism* (New York, Oxford: Oxford University Press), pp. 369–370.

6. A few examples of non-congregational rabbis (or non-teaching, non-administrative) are Finklestein, a writer: Levin, M. (1965 [1963]). *The Fanatic* (New York: Pocket), p. 13; Lifschitz, a "wonder rabbi": Malamud, B. (1973). "The Silver Crown," in *Rembrandt's Hat* (New York: Farrar, Straus & Giroux), p. 10; and Getzelles a retired editor: Singer, I. B. (1974 [1973]). "The Bishop's Robe," in *A Crown of Feathers and other stories* (Greenwich, CT: Fawcett), p.137.

7. Bloom, J. H. (1981). "The Inner Dynamics of the Rabbinate," *Proceedings of the Rabbinical Assembly 42*, p. 132. The article is quoted in *The Rabbinate in America: Reshaping An Ancient Calling*, ed. Jacob Neusner (New York and London: Garland, 1993), pp. 2–7.

8. Lipman, E. J. (1970). "The Changing Self-Image of the Rabbi." *Dimensions* (New York: Union of American Hebrew Congregations), (Spring), pp. 28–29. In his article, Lipman briefly described the various styles of rabbi which I paraphrase below:

1. *The preacher* prepares sermons carefully, they are serious and have reasoned content.
2. *The priest* concentrates on life cycle events, making Bar Mitzvahs, weddings, and funerals personal statements. Symbolically, the priest is always robed, no matter where he is.
3. *The prophet* battles for causes. His public speeches and his sermons are often belligerent polemics and he is a social activist.
4. *The pastor* often has undergone special training, academic and clinical. He counsels and regularly does hospital visitation. He knows his people—and thinks of them as his people, the flock he shepherds.
5. *The symbolic Jew* represents Jewry and Judaism. He is the Jew on all community boards, on all ecumenical committees, in all civic enterprises.
6. *The technician* believes that his employers have a right to expect specific actions of him, and efficient smoothness in their performance is his aim.
7. *The administrator* knows more about the synagogue's budget than the executive director. He holds staff meetings, and everyone reports to him.

8. *The teacher* teaches Judaism to anyone who will listen—children of all ages, adults, prospective converts, patients in hospitals, social groups at dinner parties.
9. *The scholar* reads constantly. He writes articles and books, in his chosen area of Judaica. He is respected by other rabbis as their teacher.

9. Bershtel, S. and Graubard, A. (1992). *Saving Remnants: Feeling Jewish in America* (New York: Free Press), p. 142.

10. Wilkes, P. (1994). *And They Shall Be My People: An American Rabbi and His Congregation* (New York: Atlantic Monthly), p. 36.

11. Siegel, M. (1971). *Amen: The Diary of Rabbi Martin Siegel*, ed., Mel Ziegler (New York and Cleveland: World), pp. 185–186.

12. Agus, J. B., Brief, N., and Charry, E. (1975). "The Congregational Rabbi and the Conservative Synagogue: A Symposium." *Conservative Judaism* 29:2 (Winter): *Least satisfactions*: pp. 52–53, 55, 94; *Teacher*: pp. 19, 33, 45, 49, and so on.

13. Karff, S. E. (1990). "The Rabbi as Religious Figure," in *Tanu Rabbanan: Our Rabbis Taught CCAR Yearbook 1989, vol. 2*, ed. Joseph B. Glaser, (New York: Central Conference of American Rabbis), p. 86.

14. Malamud, B. (1957). *The Assistant* (New York: Farrar, Straus & Giroux), pp. 228 ff.; Goodman, P. (1965). "A Prayer for Dew," in *Breakthrough: A Treasury of Contemporary American-Jewish Literature*, ed. Irving Malin and Irwin Stark (Philadelphia: Jewish Publication Society), p. 116; Roth, P. (1959). "The Conversion of the Jews," in *Goodbye, Columbus and Five Short Stories* (Boston: Houghton Mifflin), pp. 151 ff.

Rabbi at life-cycle events (B'rith Milah, Bar Mitzvah, Wedding, Funeral) or at Services: Friedman, B. J. (1974). *About Harry Towns* (New York: Alfred A. Knopf), pp. 124 ff.; Goldman, W. (1965 [1964]). *Boys and Girls Together* (New York: Bantam), pp. 175 ff.; Green, G. (1959 [1957]). *The Last Angry Man* (New York: Pocket Books), pp. 592 f..; Harris, M. (1970). *The Goy* (New York: Dial), p. 243; Gold, H. (1966). *Fathers* (New York: Arbor House), pp. 266; Leahy, S. R. (1974). *A Book of Ruth* (New York: Simon and Schuster), p. 266 f.; Longstreet, S. (1966). *Pedlock & Sons* (New York: Delacorte), pp. 116, 349; Markfield, W. (1964). *To An Early Grave* (New York: Simon and Schuster), pp. 142–160; Richler, M. (1971). *Saint Urbain's Horseman* (New York: Alfred A. Knopf), p. 388; Roth, P. (1959). "Defender of the Faith," in *Goodbye, Columbus and Five Short Stories* (Boston: Houghton Mifflin), pp. 185–186; Singer, I. B. (1970). "The Joke," in *A Friend of Kafka* (New York: Farrar, Straus & Giroux), p. 179; Singer, I. B. (1975). "A Pair," in *Passions* (New York: Farrar, Straus & Giroux), p. 215; Tarr, H. (1989). *A Woman of Spirit* (New York: Donald I. Fine), p. 303; Wouk, H. (1955). *Marjorie Morningstar* (Garden City, New York: Doubleday and Co.), p. 84; Goodman, A. (1996). "The Art Biz" in *The Family Markowitz*

(New York: Farrar, Straus & Giroux), p. 41; "One Down" in *The Family Markowitz* (New York: Farrar, Straus & Giroux, 1996), p. 258.

Rabbi as teacher of children: Bellow, S. (1964). *Herzog* (New York: Viking Press), p. 131; Weidman, J. (1971). *Last Respects* (New York: Random House), pp. 87–96.

15. Lenn, pp. 110–111. Not all rabbis are members of the board. See Kemelman, H. (1985). *Someday the Rabbi Will Leave* (New York: William Morrow), p. 81; Telushkin, J. (1992 [1991]). *An Eye for an Eye*, (New York: Bantam), p. 99.

16. There are precedents for the concept of *shiddach* [marriage] in Jewish tradition. Many people see the Biblical book, the Song of Songs as a love song about the *shiddach* between God and Israel. Likewise the Kabbalists often use the image of the *shiddach* between God and the Jewish people. See also Hosea 2:21–22 H [2:19–20.]

Though he does not use the term *shiddach*, Paul J. Menitoff describes the connections between rabbis and congregants and suggests ways to enhance those relationships. His ideas are equally applicable to a marriage. "A Formula for Successful Rabbinical-Congregational Relationships." *CCAR Journal* 40:1 (Winter 1993), pp. 35–43.

17. Longstreet, S. (1969). *Pedlock Saint, Pedlock Sinner* (New York: Delacorte), p. 6. See Siegel, M. (1971). *Amen: The Diary of Rabbi Martin Siegel*, ed., Mel Ziegler (New York and Cleveland: World), pp. 131, 204–205.

18. Levine, M. with Hal Kantor (1985), *The Congregation* (New York: G. P. Putnam's Sons), p. 10.

19. Tarr, H. (1968). *Heaven Help Us!* (New York: Random House), p. 3 (eighteen); Longstreet, *Pedlock Saint, Pedlock Sinner*, p. 144 (fifteen); Kemelman, H. (1964). *Friday the Rabbi Slept Late* (New York: Crown), pp. 56, 58 (forty-five!). But by Kemelman, H. (1976). *Wednesday the Rabbi Got Wet* (New York: William Morrow), p. 211 there are (only) eighteen plus officers and past presidents, and then a decade later it was down to fifteen members, Kemelman, *Someday the Rabbi Will Leave*, pp. 22–23.

20. Lenn, pp. 110–111.

21. Wilkes, pp. 18–19.

22. "Michael Kind": Gordon, N. (1965). *The Rabbi* (New York: McGraw-Hill), pp. 256, 354; "David Mendoza": Longstreet, *Pedlock Saint, Pedlock Sinner*, pp. 243–249. David Small of Kemelman's "Weekday" *Rabbi* series is either almost voted out or almost resigns in each of the stories. That he continues to serve that congregation is one of the mysteries of these detective novels, Harry Kemelman, *Friday the Rabbi Slept Late*, p. 128 ff., *Saturday the Rabbi Went Hungry*, (New York: Crown, 1966) p. 200, *Sunday the Rabbi Stayed Home*, (New York: G. P. Putnam's Sons, 1969) p. 223, *Thursday the Rabbi Walked*

Out, (New York: William Morrow, 1978) p. 217; Charles Pedlock retains his position because he has enough material to blackmail his trustees. Longstreet, *Pedlock Saint, Pedlock Sinner*, pp. 448 ff.

23. Lenn, pp. 25, 21.

24. "Gideon Able": Tarr, *Heaven Help Us!*, pp. 249 ff.; "Ed Gordon": M. S. Kaufmann, (1968). *Thy Daughter's Nakedness* (Philadelphia and New York: J. B. Lippincott, pp. 552 ff.; "Myra Wahl": Telushkin, J. (1987). *The Unorthodox Murder of Rabbi Wahl* (Toronto and New York: Bantam), pp. 16 ff. Other rabbis forced from their congregations include David Gordon, who has lost his congregation's support when he is too critical of their lack of commitment to Jewish values, Leokum, A. (1969). *The Temple* (New York and Cleveland: NAL/World Publishing), p. 362 ff.; Joshua Rosenstock when he is the victim of a cabal of discontents, Greenberg, M. (1983). *The Rabbi's Life Contract* (Garden City, NY: Doubleday and Co.), p. 26; Morris Kleinman's congregation terminates his contract when he alienates certain board members by publicly taking certain unpopular stances including when he writes a letter to the local paper criticizing the school board for scheduling classes or other special programs on the Jewish High Holidays, or his refusal to back down in his protest to allow a well-known anti-Semite to speak in the local high school. Jacobs, I. (1972). *Ten For Kaddish* (New York: W. W. Norton), pp. 104 ff., 192, 214. In a British novel we find that the rabbi is let go after a six month leave-of-absence because he has suffered a mental breakdown and is unable to function as a rabbi. Jamie Arnatt: Benedictus, D. (1976). *The Rabbi's Wife* (London: Blond and Briggs), p. 147.

25. Agress, H. and F. (1978). *The Firing of Rabbi Levi* (New York: Manor Books), p. 11.

26. Kemelman, *Sunday the Rabbi Stayed Home*, p. 253; in a British novel we read: "His Sundays, winter and summer, were usually packed with meetings he had to attend. . . ." "In the morning there had been a meeting of one of the innumerable Synagogue Committees. . . ." Charles, G. (1961 [1960]). *The Crossing Point* (New York: Alfred A. Knopf), p. 242, 272.

27. Tarr, *Heaven Help Us!*, p. 6.

28. Albert M. Lewis quoted in Shudofsky, M. M. (1954). "Portrait of the Inauthentic Rabbi," *Reconstructionist* 20:5 (April 23), p. 24.

29. Wilkes, p. 18.

30. Wilkes, p. 17.

31. Shapiro-Rieser, R. (1983). *A Place of Light* (New York: Pocket), p. 271.

32. Agus, Brief, Charry, pp. 20, 29. Rabbis grudgingly concede that meetings can be worthwhile, pp. 20, 45, 57.

33. Tarr, *Heaven Help Us!*, p. 247.

34. Kemelman, *Friday the Rabbi Slept Late*, p. 77.

35. Wilkes, pp. 5–6.

36. Wertheimer, J. (1989). "Recent Trends in American Judaism," in *American Jewish Year Book 1989*, ed. David Singer and Ruth R. Seldin, vol. 89 (New York: American Jewish Committee and Philadelphia: Jewish Publication Society), p. 75.

37. Wertheimer, "Recent Trends," p. 85.

38. Gordon, pp. 14–15.

39. The quotation actually comes from a British novel by Bermant, C. (1966 [1965]). *Ben Preserve Us* (New York: Holt, Rinehart and Winston), p. 39. It does, however, have the ring of truth.

40. Lenn, p. 282.

41. Fishman, S. B. (1989). "The Impact of Feminism on American Jewish Life," in *American Jewish Year Book 1989*, ed. David Singer and Ruth R. Seldin, vol. 89 (New York: American Jewish Committee and Philadelphia: Jewish Publication Society), p. 36.

42. Lenn, pp. 110, 281–282. On a "Lay Leadership Index" the following statistics emerge: "Most active" Men, 13 percent, Women, 8 percent, of total congregants. But when we add "reasonably active" then the total combined figures changes the picture. Combined "most-and reasonably active" Men, 48 percent, Combined "most-and reasonably active" Women, 62 percent.

43. Angoff, C. (1961). "The Future of European Jewry: The Need for an Enquiry" *The Jewish Quarterly*, 8:4 (Autumn), p. 8.

44. Kemelman, *Friday the Rabbi Slept Late*, p. 32.

45. Kaufmann, *Thy Daughter's Nakedness*, pp. 313–318.

46. Tarr, *Heaven Help Us!*, p. 104.

47. Telushkin, J. (1988). *The Final Analysis of Dr. Stark* (Toronto and New York: Bantam), p. 32.

48. Agus, Brief, Charry, pp. 16, 36–37, 39, 46, 54, 59, 84. In the Conservative congregation of fictional Barnard's Crossing, initially women do not vote, Kemelman, *Sunday the Rabbi Stayed Home*, p. 117. In time, this changes and women become members of the Board of Trustees, Kemelman, *Thursday the Rabbi Walked Out*, p. 14.

49. Fishman, "Impact of Feminism," pp. 45–46.

50. Wertheimer, "Recent Trends," p. 136.

51. The same divisions between genders obtains in Great Britain, at least as of some years ago. In response to written questions Moshe Davis, Executive Director of the office of the Chief Rabbi, London, writes: "Increasing numbers of women [are] sitting on Boards of Management. The whole question at the moment is whether this can be by election and *how* they can be elected. The Chief Rabbi has pressed for women to be on Boards of Management. I repeat, however, that there are some halachic [halachah-Jewish law] problems regarding election and this is now being discussed and considered." There are no women members on the U. S. [United Synagogue of Great Britain] Council and I am

reasonably sure that this is the situation in other orthodox bodies." Personal correspondence, Moshe Davis to David J. Zucker, June 2, 1976.

52. Bellow, "The Old System," in *Mosby's Memoirs and other stories* (New York: Viking Press, 1968), p. 76.

53. Fruchter, N. (1987 [1962]). *Coat Upon A Stick* (Philadelphia: Jewish Publication Society), p. 34.

54. Gelerenter-Liebowitz, S. (1992). "Growing up Lubavitch," in *Daughters of the King: Women and the Synagogue*, ed. Susan Grossman and Rivka Haut (Philadelphia and Jerusalem: Jewish Publication Society), pp. 238–239.

55. Tarr, *Heaven Help Us!* p. 10; Kemelman, *Thursday the Rabbi Went Out*, p. 14; Longstreet, *Pedlock Saint, Pedlock Sinner*, p. 204, Appel, A. (1986). *The Rabbi of Casino Boulevard* (New York: Saint Martin's), p. 25.

56. Mirsky, N. (1974). "Rabbinic Dilemmas." *The Jewish Spectator* 39:1 (Spring): 33–34, 36.

57. Kemelman, *Friday the Rabbi Slept Late*, p. 157. See also *Tuesday the Rabbi Saw Red*, p. 242.

58. Tarr, *Heaven Help Us!*, p. 200. See also Tarr, H. (1963). *The Conversion of Chaplain Cohen* (New York: Avon), p. 71; Longstreet, *Pedlock Saint, Pedlock Sinner*, p. 124. In Britain see Charles, p. 40. The neutered clergyman: In British television or cinema, even more so than America, the vicar is oftentimes portrayed in programs or in advertisements as effeminate or ineffectual.

59. Marks, L. and Gran, M. (1992–1993). (Allan McKeown and Joanna Willett Executive Producers), "Love hurts" (London: Alomo Productions, SelecTV), Series 2, Episode 5, "Band of Gold."

60. Shapiro-Rieser, p. 237.

61. Haase, J. (1969). *The Nuptials* (New York: Simon and Schuster), p. 42.

62. Mirsky, "Dilemmas," p. 34.

63. Longstreet, *Pedlock Saint, Pedlock Sinner*, p. 44; in one novel a rabbi explains that he is irritated that people do not act naturally when he is around. "I'll be in a group and somebody will use a four-letter word and then stammer, 'Oh, excuse me, Rabbi.' It drives me crazy." Telushkin, *The Unorthodox Murder of Rabbi Wahl*, p. 11.

64. "Rabbi's sexuality": Longstreet, *Pedlock Saint, Pedlock Sinner*, pp. 81, 298; Ashe, P. (1975 [1969[). *Naked Came the Stranger* (New York: Dell), pp. 62–63; Kaufmann, *Thy Daughter's Nakedness*, pp. 70, 216; Ozick, C. (1983). "The Pagan Rabbi" in *The Pagan Rabbi and Other Stories* (New York: E. P. Dutton), p. 9; Welles, P. (1967). *Babyhip* (New York: E. P. Dutton), p. 92. Note: Is it purely coincidental that the most fecund men, Rabbi Kokenholtz (Longstreet's *Pedlock Saint, Pedlock Sinner*) and Rabbi Kornfeld (Ozick's "The Pagan Rabbi") have six and seven daughters respectively. Is there some unspoken comment that they are unable to produce *male* heirs?

65. Telushkin, *The Final Analysis of Dr. Stark*, p. 181 ff.

66. Kaufmann, *Thy Daughter's Nakedness*, p. 70; See Tarr, *Heaven Help Us!*, pp. 104–106, *The Conversion of Chaplain Cohen*, p. 159 ff.; Gordon, pp. 344–345; Ashe, pp. 61 ff.; Longstreet, *Pedlock Saint, Pedlock Sinner*, pp. 191, 304.

67. Cowan, J. R. (1993). "Survey Finds 70% of Women Rabbis Sexually Harassed," *Moment* 18:5 (October), pp. 34–37.

68. Adler, R. (1993). "A Stumbling Block Before the Blind: Sexual Exploitation in Pastoral Counseling." *CCAR Journal* 40:2 (Spring): 13–43. Responses by Rabbi Jeffrey K. Salkin and Rabbi Julie R. Spitzer, pp. 43–54; Papers presented at a symposium at the Pacific Association of Reform Rabbis titled "Rabbi's Sexual Misconduct: Collegial Response and Methodology of Teshuvah [Repentance] and Communal Healing," January 1994; Karen L. Fox. "Hearing the voice of survivors of sexual misconduct"; Patricia Karlin-Neumann. "Dealing with Rabbis who have committed acts of sexual misconduct"; Martin S. Lawson. "Duty of Rabbi to disclose knowledge of sexual misconduct of a colleague"; Jeffrey A. Marx. "Healing the congregation in the aftermath of clergy sexual misconduct"; Arthur Gross Schaefer, "Breaking the Silence: rabbinic sexual misconduct," *Sh'ma* 24:473, pp. 5–7; "Teshuvah and Rabbinic Sexual Misconduct." *CCAR Journal* 42:2 (Summer/Fall 1995), pp. 75–80; Jacobs, P. (1994). "What's Behind Rabbi's Touch?: When a kiss results in a violation of trust," [Detroit] *The Jewish News* (July 8), pp. 1 ff.; Kosovske, H. (1994). "Sexual Exploitation: A Jewish Response" *CCAR Journal* 41:3 (Summer): 5–20; Marder, J. (1994). Sexual misconduct: How vulnerable are synagogues? *Reform Judaism* 23:2 (Winter): 16–20, 81–82.

69. Tennenbaum, S. (1978). *Rachel, the Rabbi's Wife* (New York: William Morrow), pp. 260, 280; Longstreet, *Pedlock Saint, Pedlock Sinner*, pp. 50 ff.; 222 ff.; Weidman, J. (1975). *The Temple* (New York: Simon and Schuster), p. 299 f.; Ashe, pp. 61 ff.; Haase, p. 113 f. A variation of the rabbi or rabbi's spouse having an extra-marital affair is the suggestion that a rabbi's fiancée has had an affair: Schisgal, M. (1984). "The Rabbi and the Toyota Dealer." [A play.] In *Closet Madness And Other Plays* (New York: Samuel French).

70. Levine, pp. 266 ff.

71. Leokum, pp. 52, 362.

5

Congregational Rabbis and Their Communities Continued

THE SYNAGOGUE'S REPRESENTATIVE

Plus ça change, plus c'est la même chose. Samuel Butler, in his classic novel, *The Way of All Flesh*, explains:

> The clergyman is expected to be a kind of human Sunday. Things must not be done in him which are venial in the week-day classes. He is paid for this business of leading a stricter life than other people. It is his *raison d'être*. If his parishioners feel that he does this, they approve of him, for they look upon him as their own contribution towards what they deem a holy life. This is why the clergyman is so often called a vicar—he being the person whose vicarious goodness is to stand for that of those entrusted to his charge.[1]

Should you think that this does not have direct application to the rabbinate, consider this description by a former congregational rabbi. "The community wanted to be on the safe side. They required a representative figure who would observe the law for them, in the remote possibility that the law might really turn out to be God's law. The rabbi was their representative."[2] Rabbi Daniel B. Kohn (1994) writes that he has "heard many congregational rabbis express their secret suspicions that they are actually being paid to observe Shabbat, Kashrut and daven [pray] regularly in the synagogue *instead* of their congregants . . . many American rabbis today have been recast in the role of 'substitute Jew,' expected to fill in and observe Shabbat, Kashrut and attend Shabbat and holiday services when their congregants (frequently) can't or choose not to."[3]

> Rabbi Gideon Abel (*Heaven Help Us!*) is told quite directly, *"Rabbi, you are our representative."*[4] Rabbi David Small (*Thursday the Rabbi Walked Out*) is very resentful of his congregation's expectation that he is to be their "representative." "While the commandment to visit and comfort the sick was enjoined on all Jews, the congregation expected its rabbi to perform this function for them, quite content to have him gain the credit for the mitzvah."[5] Rabbi Brownmiller (*So Help Me God!*) says that is the "trouble now with congregants. They turn over Judaism for safekeeping to the rabbi. . . ."[6]

In Jewish religious tradition, rabbis are not classified as "separate" and "holy." They have no status in Jewish law different from a layperson when it comes to leading services or performing ritual duties. The unique position of the Hasidic "Rebbe," his special and revered place as tzaddik, is based on Hasidism's own internal traditions, not on the concepts of mainstream Judaism. The major exception in contemporary life, where a rabbi is necessarily placed in a role different from a layperson, is in the matter of conducting a wedding. Here the operative factor is not Jewish law (for traditional Jewish law states any adult male Jew who is conversant with the laws of marriage and divorce can conduct a wedding), but the law of the land which in most cases recognizes as "religious" weddings only those performed by an ordained or recognized minister of a religious group. Jewish law notwithstanding, rabbis nonetheless are seen by their congregants as being special, as being separate and apart.

Matters of theology shall be considered elsewhere (Chapter 10, God, Israel and Tradition), yet the following interchange is important because it shows how the rabbi is often—again incorrectly according to Jewish law—seen as the link between the congregation and God. It also shows how rabbis' acceptance by their congregants as their spiritual leader may depend on the rabbis publicly maintaining certain stances. In Jewish law and custom, rabbis often, but not necessarily, lead the congregation at prayer. In more religiously traditional congregations, laypersons often lead the prayers. Yet the common expectation is that the rabbi is fit to lead services. Being fit to do so is a matter of morality and literacy, not a question of belief systems. Nonetheless, congregants expect that the rabbi will "believe."[7]

> Rabbi Ed Gordon (*Thy Daughter's Nakedness*) explains that he does not personally believe that people return from the dead. He goes on to say that he does not believe in life after death. This comes as a shock to his congregants. He asks a woman, "Do you believe it?" She answers, "Well, I don't know. . . . It seems to me that's what we pay the rabbi to believe. If the rabbi doesn't believe it what are we here for?" "That's right" another lady says. "If the rabbi doesn't believe I can't even believe in the rabbi."[8]

Though the preceding example is perhaps an overstatement of the case, there is a mood conveyed which shows how rabbis are often placed in a special position by their congregants. Jacob Neusner, in his work *American Judaism: Adventure in Modernity* (1974), suggests that modern rabbis have become, in the eyes of their congregants, more religious figures than in the past. While they have less power in the community as a whole, rabbis stand behind the community leaders who invariably belong to synagogues. These lay leaders are under the spell of the rabbi as a "holy" person. They depend on the rabbis to interpret Judaism for them.[9]

Rabbi Richard L. Rubenstein (1974) echoes this same thought in his autobiographical book *Power Struggle*. He pointedly titles his chapter "Holy Man In Israel" and then writes: "Officially, rabbis are not priests. The hereditary priesthood lost its religious authority two thousand years ago. Yet, the holy man in Israel remains indelibly a priest. Rabbis are, in fact if not in law, the priestly order which supplanted the old priesthood after the fall of Jerusalem."[10] Describing his place within congregational life, he says that they had not hired him to be an intellectual leader, rather "basically they required a priest. . . . I was really needed for weddings, funerals, circumcisions, and bar mitzvahs."[11]

Yet rabbis have mixed feelings about their role as "priest," as was mentioned in the previous chapter. Rabbis do not feel that they are performing arcane rituals on behalf of their congregations. As was noted above, Judaism does not place any special sacerdotal status upon the rabbi. Lay people can lead all religious services in Judaism, and they can perform most ceremonies. Most rabbis would say that they are not inherently more "holy" or necessarily, or even potentially, more "in touch with God" than those congregants who take their religion seriously. Yet the fact is that the words and the prayers of the rabbi do carry more weight. I am reminded of the phrase "perception *is* reality." It really does not matter that rabbis do not regard themselves as closer to God, most of their congregants regard them as being in this position. That is why a prayer offered by a rabbi *does* carry a special meaning. This is why, in my experience, when making hospital visits or spending time with those who are feeling unwell, it is the rare person who says that he or she does not want that I offer a prayer of well-being on their behalf. It is not merely the recitation of the prayer, it is who is reciting the prayer that counts. In the minds of many congregants, on some level it is not just *someone* praying, it is "God's representative"—the rabbi!

Another factor that lends authority to the rabbi, and at the same time enhances and amplifies the perception of the rabbi as someone who is "holy," is that rabbis by their very training are familiar with the sacred texts and the sacred symbols of Judaism. The Torah scroll is one of Judaism's most revered and hallowed objects. Sabbath after Sabbath, it is the rabbi who holds the Torah, who in many cases reads from the Torah, who bases her or his sermon on the weekly Torah portion, or gives an explanation based on the Torah. On a psychological level, there is a natural association with the holy object and the person who is so familiar with it. While rabbis are not priests, they nonetheless are, as has been explained earlier, exemplars of Judaism; and as people closely associated with the rites and rituals of Judaism, they are perceived as somehow priest-like. It follows then that many congregants assume that the rabbi is closer and more familiar with God and God-language than the average layperson. *Rabbis stand for an ideal: not the least part of which is as the voice of tradition and the person who has specialized knowledge in interpreting God's will.*

Congregational rabbis, however, are not merely judged on their theology (as long as they do "believe") but on what impression they present to their congregation and to the outside community. In many cases, it is congregational rabbis who serve as the spokesperson, the "representative" of their congregants to the wider Jewish community and even more often to the non-Jewish world. This is especially true in smaller Jewish communities, where there may be but one or two synagogues.

Though they often serve as their synagogue's spokesperson, congregants have ambivalent feelings about the rabbi's extracurricular activities. On one hand, they are proud when a non-congregant, and especially a non-Jew, says, "I met or heard your rabbi at such-and-such a meeting. She made an excellent impression on all who saw and heard her." At the same time, there is a certain resentment, for the congregant feels "*We* are paying her salary . . . she should spend her time on activities within, not outside of the synagogue."

Like it or not (and many rabbis do not like it), the rabbi is considered to be the "model Jew."[12] This being so, congregants are deeply concerned with what the rabbi says or does, especially in the outside world.

One recurring theme, certainly throughout the 1960s and 1970s which concerned many congregants, was the rabbi who was involved in Civil Rights activities. This was a major issue in the Southern section of the United States, where segregation was an accepted way of life and part of the educational system until 1964. In Murray Polner's work *Rabbi: the American Experience* (1977), the chapter titled "Mississippi" focuses on the lives and experiences of several Southern rabbis. When these rabbis dared to speak out, much less be involved in Civil Rights activities, time and again they were fired by their congregations. More often the rabbis were silent or even supportive of the existing order. Many of these Jews had lived in the South for generations. They had accepted the life-values and lifestyle of their non-Jewish neighbors. Most did not want their rabbis "making trouble"—involving themselves in challenges to the status quo. They certainly did not want their rabbis involved in the Civil Rights movement, for they understood that activity as a threat to their own security and well-being. It is reported that in the early 1960s, Rabbi Charles Mantinband was fired by his congregation in Hattiesberg, Mississippi, essentially because of his activities and public stands in the area of Civil Rights. They felt and feared that his "religious honesty endangered their business interests." Mantinband himself noted that with the exception of too few places, "'rabbis played it safe.' 'I wish,' he said toward the end of his life, 'the record had been better.'"[13] One prominent exception was Rabbi Jack Rothschild, of Atlanta, who was outspoken on the issue of civil rights.[14]

> In several novels, rabbis are in trouble because they hold more liberal political views than their congregants. Rabbi Michael Kind (*The Rabbi*) is forced to leave his small congregation in the South when he delivers a sermon excoriating the membership for their practices. Among the more memorable lines of his sermon:
>
> > Three members of this congregation own businesses which refuse to sell food or drink to a man, woman, or child whose skin is not whiter than was the skin of Moses' wife.
> >
> > Two members of this congregation own businesses which refuse shelter and lodging to a person of color . . .
> >
> > The entire congregation patronizes a bus line which forces Negroes to sit in the rear or stand while there are empty seats in forward sections.[15]
>
> Chaplain David Cohen (*The Conversion of Chaplain Cohen*) is in trouble when he makes it clear he intends to bring a Jewish "Negro to a white Southern Seder."[16] Rabbi Seymour Sonnshein (*Rachel, the Rabbi's Wife*) is fired by his congregation in part because of his work toward racial integration.[17]

In other cases the rabbi is criticized for being . . . too Jewish. Real-life Rabbi Steven Lerner irritated some of his congregants. While someone at the Jewish Theological Seminary had described Lerner as a "rabbi's rabbi," a former congregant dismissed him as being too ambitious, too innovative. "Too Jewish, "added the ex-member's wife." Too radical" added another voice.[18] Elsewhere we learn of a rabbi who is fired by his congregation. "He was too outspoken."[19]

Congregational life can be very political. Many, if not most, rabbis enjoy serving in leadership positions. Yet rabbis find that they have to walk a fine line between being the direction-setter and yet at the same time having the support of the centrist majority. There were moments while I was serving as a congregational rabbi when I had to decide whether or not to speak out on what I perceived to be crucial issues. When I did speak, I fully realized that there would be negative consequences to my being forthright. For example, in 1982, during the Begin government when Israel took the Lebanese incursion to the outskirts of Beirut, I criticized the extent of the war effort. Many of my congregants were considerably more "hawkish" than I was. I had to make a decision about which was more precious to me, my congregational position, or my conscience.

> In the fiction, there are a number of examples where rabbis are in trouble because they speak their mind. When Rabbi Ed Gordon (*Thy Daughter's Nakedness*) stresses Judaism's message as being distinct from that of Christianity, he is criticized by members of his Executive Board that he is being "too controversial" and "too sectarian." He is told, "For one thing . . . I wish you were a little less narrow, not quite so sectarian. . . . I don't like your attitude that our religion is the best, you know. I don't approve of that." Someone else remarks that all religions are equal. The rabbi responds and suggests that if all religions are equal, it is all rather pointless. "If after four thousand years we're only saying the same thing as everyone else, it's time to quit. Who needs one more people? Aren't there enough already?" In response he is told, "Well that's a hell of a God damn attitude!"[20]
>
> When Rabbi Gideon Able (*Heaven Help Us!*) criticizes congregants for having Christmas trees, he is castigated by one of the members, who writes, "Rabbi Able's dogmatism threatens to destroy everything. That man is too much of a Jew, and he runs too tight a temple."[21]

It is not only by what rabbis say that they are judged by congregants. Rabbis' actions also are scrutinized. In some cases rabbis do not look or act the part expected of them. At a specially called meeting, a Conservative rabbi is seriously and solemnly chastised by the chair of his ritual committee. "'Rabbi,' he said with the utmost gravity, 'you were seen entering the kosher butcher shop without a hat. You're supposed to set an example. I hope this never happens again.'"[22]

> The fictional rabbinic world reflects the experience of rabbis in the factual one. Rabbi Ed Gordon is told: "A Clergyman has to play the part. You're our spokesman. . . . I'd like to see a little more of a saintly demeanor. . . ." "Some people say you don't seem like a clergyman. . . ." "It's a matter of dignity."[23]

> In one novel a rabbi speaks of being hounded by his more liberal colleagues because he is too traditional for them.[24] In Telushkin's novel *An Eye for an Eye*, Rabbi Daniel Winter is criticized in a newspaper letter to the editor, sent by a rabbinic colleague. At issue is a stand that Rabbi Winter has taken publicly, a stand which, to use a current phrase, is not "politically correct."[25] The opposite situation can also take place. A rabbi is criticized by a Christian clergyman for eating non-Kosher food in public.[26] Finally, Samuel Butler's vicar, "whose vicarious goodness is to stand for that of those entrusted to his charge," has his revenge through the immorality of Rabbi Charles Shaphan Pedlock (*Pedlock Saint, Pedlock Sinner*). When confronted with his moral turpitude, Rabbi Pedlock accuses his interlocutors with their immoral business practices. One man replies, "Things I do in business—we all do—is a *shondeh* [a highly improper act] in a temple of God. We're not rabbis." Pedlock then blackmails them with the fact that should they dismiss him, he will reveal publicly that these men, ("the most important of the temple's rulers" including the President of the synagogue) have betrayed their public trust and have also awarded contracts for the new synagogue building to relations and friends. Rather than face scandal, the three men agree to suppress the evidence against the rabbi.[27]

Being the synagogue's representative is a two-edged sword. On the one hand, rabbis are always expected to be "on duty." This makes the rabbinate a very difficult profession. Yet at the same time, being the synagogue's representative, and in a way God's representative, can serve to empower rabbis. When they have the support of their centrist majority, rabbis can serve as community leaders who will effectively change the future of American Judaism.

THE NON-JEWISH WORLD

If being the "model Jew" means rabbis are relegated to a different status, then likewise being the "model Jew" means they are delegated to the position of spokespeople to the non-Jewish world.

Depending somewhat on their inclination, rabbis might spend a greater or lesser amount of time on (non-Jewish) community relations. Certainly most of their week is spent on affairs directly associated with the synagogue: in no special order, conducting services, telephoning, preaching, teaching, writing, committee work, sermon preparation, pastoral or hospital visits, counseling. Often, they are also committed to working with the Jewish community at large: speaking at or attending a rally protesting the treatment of Jews in the former Soviet Union, or pro-Israel rallies; perhaps being the guest speaker at the monthly luncheon meeting of the local Hadassah (women's Zionist) chapter; maybe attending the local Jewish Federation or community representative board meeting, or supporting a local or regional Jewish historical group. Though rabbis' weeks must be centered primarily around their congregation, and secondarily around the Jewish community, generally speaking, they do not "ignore" the wider community, nor does it ignore them. Modern rabbis are heavily committed to communal activities, both Jewish and non-Jewish. Though not exclusively so, rabbis often are expected to be a public relations worker on behalf of their fellow Jews.

Not unexpectedly the degree of non-Jewish community participation is strongly influenced by several factors: The individual rabbi's interest in this area is one determinant, but another factor is the demands placed upon rabbis by virtue of where their congregations are located. In mainstream congregations in New York, Los Angeles, Chicago, Boston, Saint Louis, Denver, Toronto, or Philadelphia, when one goes into the suburbs and the hundreds of smaller cities and towns, where Jews live alongside their non-Jewish neighbors, there one finds the rabbi "in dialogue" and often involved in various civic programs.

To offer a personal example, in the past few years I have served on the Executive Committee of the Rocky Mountain Rabbinic Council. I also have served on the Executive Committee of the Denver Interfaith Clergy Council; I have been involved in Jewish-Roman Catholic dialogue, sponsored by the local Anti-Defamation League regional office, and the Jewish-Muslim dialogue, sponsored by the local American Jewish Committee regional office; for several years I sat on the Inter-group Relations Committee of the local Anti-Defamation League; I have served on the Boards of the Colorado Council of International Organizations, the Hospice of Metro Denver, and the Colorado Interfaith Chaplains. In addition, I belong to various Jewish organizations. In recent years, I have attended and presented papers at the National Workshop on Christian-Jewish Relations.

Though there are exceptions, in general, the further one moves away from Orthodoxy, the greater the amount of congregational and rabbinic interest and participation in interreligious dialogue or interfaith activity. The issues may be civic in nature, political, or social justice issues. In many communities throughout the United States, rabbis regularly join their Christian colleagues on interfaith discussion committees, programs which stress ecumenicity and shared religious values. Whether it is a meeting about teen suicide, violence in the inner city, the proliferation of drugs, the ongoing debates about physician-assisted suicide, prayer in the public schools, school vouchers, or matters of civil rights or liberties, on many a platform one will find rabbis alongside Protestant ministers, Catholic priests, and, increasingly, leaders from the Muslim community. While in principle the rabbi may have been ordained at an Orthodox, Conservative, Reconstructionist, or Reform seminary, in all likelihood, the more one moves toward exponents of religious traditionalism, the lesser the interest in interreligious dialogue or general civic participation. Indeed, the closer we get to the more conservative religious traditionalists, the less at ease and the less likely the case for friendships between Jews and non-Jews.[28]

> A comparison between two fictional rabbis illustrates the differences in approaches to working with clergy in the non-Jewish world. Technically, the settings are London and Los Angeles, respectively, but in reality, London, England, could be New London, Connecticut. When visiting the home of the well-known and respected Church of England ecclesiastic, Dean Mitchell, Orthodox Rabbi Leo Norberg was off-put by a certain alien odor. "Perhaps it was the faint ghost of fried bacon and larded Sunday joint, which, together with the aroma of furniture polish and fresh roses, had combined into a curiously Gentile smell—rather like waiting rooms in Harley Street." How different the reaction of Progressive Conservative Rabbi Charles Shaphan Pedlock, who is frequently involved in interfaith activities. When he visits his "good friend," the Archbishop of Los Angeles, Cardinal O'Drood, we learn about the rabbi's impressions. "As he walked in he admired the clean

> smell of the halls of the Cardinal's house, the faint odor of peppermint candy, candle wax and furniture polish. . . .
>
> "Charles Pedlock often felt the cardinal's faith was second only to his own."
>
> Both Rabbi Pedlock and the Cardinal are publicly political and social conservatives, both are powerful within their respective "dioceses" and both have high aspirations, though someone who disliked the cleric said of him, "Cardinal O'Drood has no ambition to become Pope, he is waiting for a vacancy in the Trinity." No doubt, if there were a comparable position in Jewish life, Rabbi Pedlock would have sought it.[29]

Members of the "Sectarian" Orthodox community rarely are interested in promoting interfaith understanding or interfaith dialogue.

> Reb Saunders is the leader of a Hasidic community (*The Promise*). He lives in "the Williamsburg section of Brooklyn." Hasidim are seen everywhere. As the narrator indicates, "the neighborhood seemed dark with their presence." Many are refugees from the horrors of the Holocaust. They are
>
> > somber figures in long black coats and black hats and long beards, earlocks hanging alongside gaunt faces. . . . Lee Avenue, the main street of the neighborhood, was filled with their bookstores and bookbinderies, butcher shops and restaurants, beeswax candle stores . . . and hardware stores—the signs in Yiddish and English, the storekeepers bearded and in skullcaps, the gentiles gone now from behind the counters, the Italians and Irish and Germans and the few Spanish Civil War refugee families all gone now too from the neighborhood.[30]

Such a congregation of Hasidic Orthodox Jews does not lend itself to a Christian-Jewish dialogue. It hardly lends itself to a Hasidic-Hasidic dialogue, much less Hasidic to non-Hasidic dialogue.

Brotherhood services, exchange of pulpits with Christian clergy, and synagogue–church dialogue groups are common in North America. On the whole, these activities do promote a great deal of understanding between Judaism and Christianity. At its international headquarters in New York, the Anti-Defamation League of B'nai B'rith has a Department of Interfaith Affairs, with Rabbi Leon Klenicki as its Director. Likewise, the American Jewish Committee features a National Director of

Inter-Religious Affairs, Rabbi A. James Rudin. The American Jewish Congress and other organizations have similar programs. While some of the rabbinic staff in these organizations are Orthodox-trained, their personal interest in matters of interfaith dialogue generally does not translate to the Orthodox communities. The biennial conferences of the National Workshop on Christian-Jewish Relations regularly features some of the best "dialogue" that is currently taking place worldwide, and most, though clearly not all, of the rabbis who participate are from the more progressive wing of Judaism.

> Jewish-Christian dialogue between rabbis and Christian clergy, or between Jewish and Christian groups, as well as rabbis and ministers' exchange of pulpits is featured in the fiction.[31] On the whole, however, though in principle much good can take place, more often than not the authors highlight the pitfalls of such activities, such as when a minister gives a sermon wherein he tells the Jewish congregation why they bring anti-Semitism upon themselves,[32] or where a minister speaks of the superiority of the church over Judaism.[33] Triumphalism, the message that "my" religion is better than "yours," regrettably is not a one-way street. On several occasions, Rabbi David Small (of the Weekday *Rabbi* series) sounds a note of triumphalism when comparing Judaism to Christianity.[34]
>
> As one Protestant minister wryly remarks to a rabbi, "What a mess! We each learned just enough to prove to ourselves why the other's denomination was inferior to our own."[35]

In 1967, leading up to the Six Day War, Israel was increasingly threatened by her Arab neighbors. The United Nations had pulled out its forces, which had served as a kind of buffer between Israel and Egypt. Israeli shipping from the port of Eilat was seriously threatened. Many of Israel's Arab neighbors were threatening to attack, to drive the Israelis into the sea. There was a real fear that less than 20 years after Israel's declaration of independence as a sovereign nation, that her very national security was at stake. Whatever successes had been achieved in terms of Christian-Jewish dialogue nearly foundered fatally on the shoals of what was perceived by the Jewish community as a pro-Arab stance by many Christian clergy. In many cases, Christian clergy either were antagonistic toward Israel or simply remained silent on this issue of Israeli freedom and sovereignty, which was—and remains—so important to American Jews. "The silence of the churches which preceded the war, and the subsequent unfriendly, even hostile, declarations of the Protestant leadership concerning Israel and her post-war policies was disillusioning, and indicated the limitations of the dialogue, as conducted previously."[36] While there was a clear anti-Israel bias among Christian clergy, and this did set back dialogue, there also were voices within the Christian community that did speak out in opposition to that position. In the summer and fall of 1967, A. Roy and Alice L. Eckardt were very clear in their condemnation of the churches' stand. At the time, A. Roy Eckardt served as professor of religion at Lehigh University and was a prominent member of the World Council of Churches' Committee on the Church and the Jewish People. In an article published originally in *The Christian Century* in August, 1967, and then reprinted in *Midstream*, the Eckardts wrote: if "the world Jewish community has been shocked and disillusioned by the new Christian silence before Israel's plight, it must be driven to the very verge of despair by the readiness of some Christian leaders to call black 'white,' to label as 'aggressors' the targets of aggression, to identify as 'annihilationists' those who barely escaped being annihilated. . . ."[37]

> In the novels, we find several realistic portrayals of rabbinic-clergy relations through the local "ministerial" group where the rabbi is one of the members. In several cases, the tensions which separated Jewish and Christian leaders during the Six Day War are described. When Rabbi Morris Kleinman (*Ten For Kaddish*) asks his fellow members of the Blueport ministerial group to protest the unjust condemnation of Israel, he is told that while they understand that Israel has a special place in his heart, the rabbi needs to see the other side of the coin, that people were made homeless by the Jewish occupation of Palestine.[38] Likewise, when Rabbi Joshua Levi (*The Firing of Rabbi Levi*) attempts to get his local ministerial association to take a stand, he hears his Christian colleagues suggest that it would be impolitic of them to pass such a resolution. "I was astonished. Where was the same sense of fair play and justice [Lutheran pastor] Paul Jorgensen called for when he talked of the Mexican grape pickers in southern California or the Puerto

> Ricans in southern Harlem? Why couldn't Jews be considered an oppressed minority? Why didn't Israel have the right to live?"[39]

David Biale, in his book *Power and Powerlessness in Jewish History* (1986), explains that only with the 1967 "Six Day War did American Jews begin to confront the Holocaust. The real fear that Israel might be annihilated opened up a floodgate of associations with the Holocaust and a much greater sense of identification with the Jewish state than had been true in the period since the establishment of Israel in 1948." He suggests that by 1967, Jews were able—or to use his term, prepared—"to express their sense of collective trauma." Israel and the Holocaust are inextricably intertwined. "The often exaggerated sense of guilt that American Jews today feel over their failure to save the European Jews reflects their fear for Israel, just as their fear for Israel feeds their consciousness of the Holocaust. In their association of the Holocaust with the state of Israel, American Jews have come to see Israel as a second chance to defend what they failed to save" earlier.[40] With this mentality, rightly or wrongly, the "silence of the churches" was understood, at best, as indifference to Jewish suffering and, at worst, as proof positive of the lingering anti-Semitism of the Christian church.

Another area where the factual and fictional worlds overlap is the issue of the congregation's expectations of the "rabbi-and-the-non-Jewish-community." It matters little if the synagogue has been there for decades or is just developing. Relations with the non-Jewish world is a very important question in the mind of congregants. "Getting along" with "them"—at the very least having their respect, if not outward friendship—is often an unspoken but very real concern of Jews. "What will the *goyim* [non-Jews] think?" has been and continues to be a factor in American Jewish life. Bershtel and Graubard (1992) report that despite the fact that, statistically speaking, anti-Semitism is actually in decline, Jews continue to worry about it as an issue.[41] I shall look at the question of anti-Semitism presently. Congregants both are pleased and sometimes nervous about the fact that their rabbis are friendly with their non-Jewish clergy counterparts.

> "We're trying to build good relations," a congregant tells Rabbi Gordon (*Thy Daughter's Nakedness*). "That's the purpose of

> these meetings. . . ." "We all have to live together."[42] "You're our spokesman."[43]

Rabbis throughout North America teach courses about Judaism at both secular and Christian-sponsored universities. They are featured on radio and television and write regular articles for newspapers and magazines. The Reform movement's Jewish Chautauqua Society actively promotes university courses taught by rabbis.

> Fictional Rabbi Abraham Cohen (*Days of Judgment*) teaches courses in philosophy at a local university. Rabbi David Small (The Weekday *Rabbi* series) first teaches an occasional course at a local college; in time he accepts a full-time position at the school. Rabbi Daniel Winter (*An Eye for an Eye*) hosts a regular radio talk-show.[44] While Lenn reports that over 40 percent of Reform rabbis teach part time as secondary employment, nowhere near this figure is reflected in the fiction.[45]

ANTI-SEMITISM

By most accounts, anti-Semitism is at a very low level in the United States in the 1990s. It has been moving that way for several decades. Overt incidents of anti-Semitism, such as painting swastikas on synagogues or other Jewish communal buildings, or the desecration of Jewish cemeteries, are relatively speaking, far and few between.[46] More subtle anti-Semitism in the "Board room" or the "Country club," or having "restricted neighborhoods" is for all intents and purposes a matter of the past. It is true that there have been anti-Semitic pronouncements or writings by radical militia or racial groups such the Posse Comitatus or the Aryan Nations or demonstrations for a white, Aryan country by various forms of skinheads. Yet, with the exception of occasional outbursts by such prominent figures as the owner of the Cincinnati Reds baseball team, anti-Semitism is a thing of the past. Certainly, compared to 50 years ago, Jews face very little in the way of overt discrimination. An exception to this general trend has been the amount of anti-Semitism among African-Americans in recent years. Notable among the modern demagogues has been the Nation of Islam's Minister Louis Farrakhan. Charles S. Liebman (1995) has suggested that there will be an increase in anti-Semitism among African-Americans, and that this will in its own way legitimize hostility toward Jews among other Americans.[47] Another writer, Charles E. Silberman (1985), has taken just the opposite view. He writes of the diminution of discrimination and prejudice toward Jews and the acceptance of Jews in almost every stratum of society. He says Jews do not face the disabilities that they did in the past. In Silberman's view, America is a different place, different in kind and degree from any other society in which Jews have lived.[48] This view is reflected by Leonard Dinnerstein in his work *Anti-Semitism in America* (1994), wherein he concludes that "antisemitism in the United States is neither virulent nor growing. It is not a powerful social or political force. Moreover, prejudicial comments are now beyond the bounds of respectable discourse and existing societal restraints prevent any overt antisemitic conduct except among small groups of disturbed adolescents, extremists, and powerless African Americans."[49]

Though neither a powerful social or political force, anti-Semitism clearly does exist. At times, it takes on overt manifestations, such as threats to Jews or Jewish property; at times, it is more subtle. A disturbing aspect of anti-Semitism that continues to linger is found on a number of college campuses, where it often takes the form of anti-Zionism or anti-Israel demonstrations.

As noted earlier, despite the general decrease in anti-Semitism and clear acceptance of Jews in nearly all sectors of society, many Jews do worry that things may change. Jews need to be ever on guard, this argument goes, because anti-Semitism does not really go away, it just becomes dormant. Not so, Alan M. Dershowitz argues in his book *Chutzpah* (1991). Jews need to be more assertive, America *is* different. There is no need for Jews to consider themselves second-class citizens. There is nothing that Jews cannot accomplish in the United States if they set their minds to it. Indeed, he argues that the best antidote to anti-Semitism is more Jews, and more active Jews. He argues that Jews have no need to apologize for their successes.[50]

Of course, there are also Jews who worry that life is *too good* in North America. With acceptance comes assimilation; and, certainly, as shall be discussed in a later chapter, assimilation and intermarriage are real concerns in the Jewish community.

In the fiction which portrays rabbis over several decades, there are several examples of anti-Semitism. Some of it is clearly manifest—for it takes the forms of swastikas on synagogues—and other examples are more subtle.

When vandals paint swastikas on the synagogue in Leighton Ridge, Connecticut, Rabbi David Hartman (*The Outsider*) calls a meeting of his Board to solicit their reaction. The reaction is mixed: There are those who want to keep the information within the community; those who want to call the *New York Times* to show that it can happen here too; and those who take a more middle ground and want to go public, and consciously to involve the non-Jewish community. The desecration is viewed as an attack on the local community because the synagogue had originally been a Congregational Church. Consequently, the vandalism is understood to be an attack on the democratic values of the town itself. In any event, a town meeting is held and both Rabbi Hartman and the local Congregational minister address the well-attended meeting. Repairing the damage becomes a community event.[51]

It is not a swastika painted on a synagogue but a dead rat mailed in a box alongside a card inscribed with the words "DROP DEAD, JEW-BASTARD!" that is sent to Rabbi David Gordon (*The Temple*) as well as a half-dozen members of the Jewish community in Greenlake, New York. One of the recipients, while Jewish, does not belong to any, much less the local, synagogue. He is a real estate developer, brash, rich, ["chutzpah-dic" in the image of Dershowitz' book]. In his anger, he phones the local newspaper and complains loudly about this anti-Semitic incident. A meeting is called at the newspaper office. In attendance are not only the editor, the First Selectman from the town, the rabbi, and members of the synagogue's Executive Committee (though, pointedly, not the real estate developer), but, to the surprise of the Jews, the local Roman Catholic priest and a very prominent Protestant clergyman. As with the incident in Leighton Ridge, the Jews are divided as how best to deal with the situation. The President especially wants to downplay the event, fearing that to publicize it would increase the possibility of more anti-Semitism. Rabbi Gordon, however, takes the position that "this particular act of anti-Semitism should receive the widest publicity possible . . . [for] it is a dangerous precedent. And as such, it must be condemned.

Openly, unequivocally, forcefully."[52] While Rabbi Gordon's advice is shared by the non-Jews present, it is clear that he is opposed by his laymen. In any event, the consensus is to print an editorial and run a news story about the incident.

Anti-Semitism need not take the more outward forms such as painting a swastika on a synagogue or Jewish cemetery. Good examples of covert or latent anti-Semitism are found in two novels by Herbert Tarr, *The Conversion of Chaplain Cohen* and *Heaven Help Us!* In both cases, the anti-Semitic remarks are made in sermons by Christian ministers while the rabbi himself is seated as part of the congregation. In the second novel (*Heaven Help Us!*), a somewhat less credible situation arises, for the rabbi is then invited to reply, and he selectively quotes Scripture for Scripture to show that Christianity can be interpreted as a very dogmatic, unloving religion. In the first novel (*The Conversion of Chaplain Cohen*), a rabbi hears his good friend, the Protestant Chaplain, deliver a sermon about the legend of "the Wandering Jew" ("an unlovely medieval fictional justification of anti-Semitism," remembers the rabbi). The Protestant Chaplain "reminded the people of the legend of Ahasuerus the Jew refusing to let Jesus, on the way to Calvary, rest for a moment against the wall of his house, consequently being condemned to wander eternally over the earth without rest or death, like another Cain." The preacher then concluded, "And the wandering Jews are *still* with us, still *cursed* to wander the earth forever, like Cain before them, still serving as the living witnesses of the consequences of sin. . . ."[53] In Tarr's book, the two men finally sit and discuss the sermon, and this enables the novelist to look at the problem of anti-Semitism more closely. What becomes clear is that the minister never questioned the implications of the legend, never stopped to realize what his words really said.

The Conversion of Chaplain Cohen was written in 1963. Four years later, as noted earlier, in real life, Christian-Jewish dialogue was severely set back by the controversy surrounding the pro-Arab, or supposedly "neutral" stance, of Christian clergy during the 1967 Six Day War. Nonetheless, in the view of Rabbi Leon Klenicki of the Anti-Defamation League of B'nai B'rith, in the mid-1990s, there are new bonds of friendship and covenental relationship which are healing some of the alienation that has taken place over the centuries. Jews and Christians are recognizing each other as children of God.[54]

LONELINESS/ISOLATION

Another corollary of being the synagogue's "representative" is that the rabbi is necessarily the person apart. A rabbi explains: "No matter how much I seek out personal relationships, people only view me as an object."[55] Rabbi David Wortman, executive director of the Board of Rabbis of Greater Philadelphia, is quoted in an article titled "Rabbis Under Stress" (1986). "The rabbinate is a very lonely profession. . . . Rabbis have a hard time making friends. They can't be friends with congregants because that destroys the rabbi-congregant relationship. As much as you become friendly, to the congregant you're still always the rabbi. The reality is that wherever the rabbi goes, the rabbi is always the rabbi."[56] Rabbis have few peer relationships that allow for shared confidences. Rabbis, likewise, are called upon to both counsel and then socialize with congregants—something that would be considered outside of the bounds of traditional psychotherapeutic norms. "Also, unlike therapists who can confront their dysfunctional clients and refer them to another professional if the chemistry is not working, a clergy person knows that a particular difficult congregant may always remain part of the congregation and be a constant source of irritation."[57] That irritation is true for rabbi and congregants alike. Not only does the rabbi know some unsettling facts about particular persons, or about their family life, but the congregants know that the rabbi is aware of these personal failures and resents that knowledge. Coincidentally, while a client in therapy has the ultimate veto—he or she need not return to the therapist—the only possible choices to not see the rabbi are to cease from participating in activities in the synagogue, leave the congregation, or do what one can to have the rabbi's contract terminated.

A rabbi, now no longer serving a congregation, mentions that congregations expect their rabbis to be family men and women, yet they set the rabbis apart. "No seminary course in pastoral psychology can prepare [a rabbi] . . . for what experience alone must teach—the experience of being utterly isolated . . . in short, the experience of being a holy [person]."[58] A rebbetzin [rabbi's wife] is quoted: "A Rabbi and his wife cannot have friends inside the congregation—it must be friendly but impersonal."[59]

> Her lament is reflected in the fiction in a number of ways. Rabbis and rabbis' families are singularly bereft of people with whom they can easily converse. Time and time again, we find that rabbis will speak openly only with their wives, friends of very long standing, or fellow colleagues—either rabbis or ministers.[60]
>
> None of the fictional rabbis are able to shake the congregational concept of a mystique associated with the rabbi. The theme of rabbinic loneliness is a recurring refrain in the fiction. The matter is put very clearly in Howard Fast's novel *The Outsider*. Rabbi David Hartman is ever conscious of his being an outsider. "He felt that he had come into this room as an outsider; he felt that he came into the Jewish homes of his congregants as an outsider; and he even felt at times that he stood in the synagogue as an outsider."[61]

In the real world, sociologist-Rabbi Norman Mirsky has written of the rabbis who seek to disabuse their congregants of their awe of the sacred. "He may give lectures on the human provenance of the Scriptures, he may espouse a non-theistic ideology, or he may simply choose to dress in an ultra-mod fashion, unconsciously to prove to his congregation that he is one of them."[62] A rabbi openly shares his dilemma. There are certain congregational expectations. "The other day I wanted to buy a pair of bell-bottom trousers. I didn't. Why? Because a congregation does not *expect* its rabbi to wear bell-bottom trousers."[63]

> In one of the novels, we read of Rabbi Kuntz, "who wore sport jackets and tartan bowties whenever not actually in the Temple."[64]

The distance between rabbi and congregant is especially noticeable when it comes to moments of crisis. While the rabbi serves as a comforter, who comforts the rabbi? Earlier, I questioned the validity of the analogy of a "marriage" between a rabbi and the congregation. It is frequently at times of difficulty that the caring and comforting partner (ostensibly the congregants for the rabbi) simply *cannot* be found.

The loneliness of rabbinic life, and especially the pressures it places on the rebbetzin, is discussed with candor in Martin Siegel's autobiographical work, *Amen: the Diary of Martin Siegel*. "Since Judith's illness, I have become sensitive to the fact that neither of us has any close friends—only official acquaintances. This had made the events of the last several weeks more sad, more lonely. . . . A little kindness, a little warmth from anybody—if anybody would bother to take the trouble—would certainly go a long way toward helping her to recover. And yet she has not had the courtesy of even a single telephone call from anyone."[65]

In one case, the loneliness of the rabbinate seems to be a serious factor in the mental breakdown of a rebbetzin, Leslie Kind, the wife of Rabbi Michael Kind (*The Rabbi*). The psychiatric report indicates her problems stem in part to the stress inherent in the role of being the rabbi's wife. At one point in the novel, Rabbi Kind asks his wife if she minds working with the women at the congregation, the *yentehs* [busybodies]. She replies, "Damn the *yentehs*. . . . There'll always be people to whom you and I are freaks."[66]

An even starker fictional example is found in a British novel, David Benedictus' *The Rabbi's Wife*. Though the plot centers on the rabbi's wife, who is kidnapped by Arab terrorists, it is the rabbi who has a mental breakdown. While Rabbi Jamie Arnatt receives some initial sympathy, it takes the synagogue board nearly six months to delegate someone to see if anything can be done for him. Apparently, Jamie's colleagues show even less interest. This indifference contributes to Jamie's mental breakdown. It is not that the congregants are unsympathetic. They will do "the right thing" initially, but there seems to be none of the ongoing comfort that is required.[67]

The issue of rabbinic isolation permeates the novel by Marilyn Greenberg, *The Rabbi's Life Contract*. Rabbi Joshua Rosenstock returns from a Sabbatical in Israel to find that a small cabal in his congregation has voted to fire him, this despite his 20 years of service and the fact that he holds a "life contract" with the congregation. Most of the congregants display a callous indifference to the cabal's immoral behavior.[68]

The rabbi's, or the rabbinical-family's, loneliness is not entirely a making of the congregation. To be sure, the congregation does set the rabbi and the rabbi's family apart. Yet rabbis to some extent consciously, or subconsciously, set themselves apart. In a brutally honest self-description, Rabbi Martin Siegel shares this insight:

> I am not considered a *Jew*, but *Judaism* itself. I am not expected to be a human being. I am not allowed to be a human being.
>
> And who most of all does not allow me to be a human being? Me. I don't allow it. I am a rabbi, and I must live with the reality that unless people have confidence in me on the pulpit I cannot be effective. Therefore, in everything I want to do, I must first assess whether in doing it I will be destroying the confidence my congregation has in me.[69]

In Chapter 8 (The Rabbi's Family), which centers on rabbis and their families, we see how this isolation and loneliness effects their family relationships.

NOTES

1. Butler, S. (1944 [1903]). *The Way of All Flesh* (Garden City, NY: Doubleday and Co.), p 114.

2. Rubenstein, R. L. (1974). *Power Struggle* (New York: Charles Scribner's Sons), p. 138.

3. Kohn, D. B. (1994). "Modern Congregants: Jewish by Proxy?" *Jewish Spectator* 59:1 (Summer): 26.

4. Tarr, H. (1968). *Heaven Help Us!* (New York: Random House), p. 94. See also Jacobs, I. (1972). *Ten for Kaddish* (New York: W. W. Norton), p. 106; Agress, H. and F. (1978). *The Firing of Rabbi Levi* (New York; Manor Books), p. 46. Alan M. Ullman (1985) suggests that in "no less than seven different novels such words as 'Rabbi, you are our representative' underscore the congregants' understanding of the rabbis' role." Alan M. Ullman. "The Rabbi in American Jewish Fiction." Unpublished rabbinic thesis, Hebrew Union College-Jewish Institute of Religion, Cincinnati, p. 56, see also pp. 71 ff. in his thesis.

5. Kemelman, H. (1978). *Thursday the Rabbi Walked Out* (New York: William Morrow), p. 113.

6. Tarr, H. (1979). *So Help Me God!* (New York: Times Books), p. 234.

7. While the congregation's expectations of the rabbi's "belief in God" certainly is the norm, exceptions do exist. In the early 1960s, American Jews were shocked to learn of "a self-confessed and outspokenly candid 'atheist' rabbi at the head of a congregation of like-minded Jews in suburban Detroit." Mirsky,

N. B. (1978). "The Vision of Man Triumphant," in *Unorthodox Judaism* (Columbus: Ohio State University Press), p. 112. See also the discussion about Cincinnati, Ohio's Congregation Beth Adam, a congregation led by an HUC-JIR ordained rabbi but which describes itself as practicing Judaism from a humanistic perspective. Congregation Beth Adam had applied for membership to the Reform movement's Union of American Hebrew Congregations, but the UAHC Board of Trustees overwhelmingly voted not to accept it because it excludes God from its liturgy. Bush, L. (1994). "Can We Accept a Congregation That Does Not Worship God?" *Reform Judaism* 23:2 (Winter): 25–27, and accompanying articles.

8. Kaufmann, M. S. (1968). *Thy Daughter's Nakedness* (Philadelphia and New York: J. B. Lippincott), p. 315. Note: in Kaufmann's novels women are frequently portrayed as ignorant, almost incapable of learning. They are seen as inferior to men. On page 494 we read: "To teach a woman . . . was to write your name on water." An additional factor in the Kaufmann novel is that this is a new congregation with its first rabbi. He has been there less than a year and clearly has been unable to make his congregants understand that he is neither "God's representative" to the Synagogue nor the "synagogue's representative" to God.

9. Neusner, J. (1972). *American Judaism: Adventure in Modernity* (Englewood Cliffs, NJ: Prentice-Hall), pp. 45–46.

10. Rubenstein, p. 144.

11. Rubenstein, p. 145.

12. Cohen, A. A. (1967). *The Carpenter Years* (New York: New American Library), p. 139. See also Gary A. Tobin's statement: "The rabbi is . . . a modern role model." Tobin, G. A. (1987). "Eating up the rabbi." *The Jerusalem Post*, April 13, p. 5.

13. Polner, M. (1977). *Rabbi: The American Experience* (New York: Holt, Rinehart and Winston), p. 91.

14. Greene, M. F. (1996). *The Temple Bombing* (Reading, MA: Addison-Wesley), p. 11.

15. Gordon, N. (1965). *The Rabbi* (New York: McGraw-Hill), p. 254.

16. Tarr, H. (1963). *The Conversion of Chaplain Cohen* (New York: Avon), p. 122.

17. Tennenbaum, S. (1978). *Rachel, the Rabbi's Wife* (New York: William Morrow), p. 371.

18. Polner, p. 150.

19. Siegel, M. (1971). *Amen: The Diary of Rabbi Martin Siegel*, ed., Mel Ziegler (New York and Cleveland: World), p. 34.

20. Kaufmann, *Thy Daughter's Nakedness*, p. 536–537. Cf.. Tarr, *Heaven Help Us!*, pp. 75, 253; David Small is criticized for stressing scholarship over athletics, Kemelman, H. (1964). *Friday the Rabbi Slept Late*, (New York: Crown, 1967) p. 32.

21. Tarr, *Heaven Help Us!*, p. 104.

22. Rubenstein, p. 137.

23. Kaufmann, *Thy Daughter's Nakedness*, pp. 539–540. Cf. Kemelman, *Friday the Rabbi Slept Late*, p. 66 ff.

24. Longstreet, S. (1969). *Pedlock Saint, Pedlock Sinner* (New York: Delacorte), p. 69. See also pp. 85, 200–201.

25. Telushkin, J. (1992 [1991]). *An Eye for an Eye* (New York: Bantam), pp. 223 f.

26. Kaufmann, M. S. (1957). *Remember Me To God* (Philadelphia and New York: J. B. Lippincott), p. 248.

27. Longstreet, *Pedlock Saint, Pedlock Sinner*, pp. 449, 446.

28. Heilman, S. C. (1987). "Orthodox Jews: An Open or Closed Group?" in *Uncivil Religion: Interreligious Hostility in America*, ed. Robert N. Bellah and Frederick E. Greenspahn (New York: Crossroads), pp. 122–126.

29. "London": Charles, G. (1961 [1960]). *The Crossing Point* (New York: Alfred A. Knopf), p. 158; "Los Angeles": Longstreet, *Pedlock Saint, Pedlock Sinner*, p. 195. Note: "the cardinal's faith." Longstreet is ambiguous as to whether Pedlock means faith as belief or faith as Roman Catholicism.

In another novel, Rabbi Everett Siegel is praised for his interfaith activities in the Honolulu area. Goodman, A. (1989). "The Succession," in *Total Immersion: Stories*, (New York: Harper and Row), p. 29.

30. Potok, C. (1969). *The Promise* (New York: Alfred A. Knopf), p. 1.

31. Kemelman, H. (1969). *Sunday the Rabbi Stayed Home* (New York: G. P. Putnam's Sons), pp. 53 ff..; Longstreet, *Pedlock Saint, Pedlock Sinner*, pp. 31, 131, 306; Kaufmann, *Thy Daughter's Nakedness*, pp. 509–510; Leokum, A. (1969). *The Temple* (New York and Cleveland: NAL World Publishing), p. 162 ff.

32. Leokum, p. 167 ff.

33. Tarr, *The Conversion of Chaplain Cohen*, pp. 83 ff.; *Heaven Help Us!*, pp. 82 ff.

34. Kemelman, *Sunday the Rabbi Stayed Home*, pp. 53–55; Kemelman, H. (1973 [1972]). *Monday the Rabbi Took Off* (Greenwich, CT: Fawcett Crest), pp. 201 ff.

35. Tarr, *The Conversion of Chaplain Cohen*, p. 77.

36. Fishman, P. (1973). *The Jews of the United States*, ed. Priscilla Fishman (New York: Quadrangle, New York Times Book), p. 271. See Silberman, C. E. (1985). *A Certain People: American Jews and Their Lives Today* (New York: Summit), p. 202; Jacob, W. (1991). "Dialogue in the Twentieth Century," in *Toward a Theological Encounter*, ed. Leon Klenicki, (New York, Mahwah: Paulist Press), p. 76. One could argue that "Church Silence" concerning Israel is not anti-Semitism and that Dr. Larrabie's address "Swelling Revelation" (in Tarr's *Heaven Help Us!*, pp. 82 ff.) was merely bad theology. In Jewish eyes, nonetheless, the Silence was taken as anti-Semitism and Dr. Larrabie's

sermon on "Swelling Revelation" at the very least contains the seeds of anti-Semitism.

37. Eckardt, A. R. and A. L. (1967). "Silence in the Churches." *Midstream*, (October): 28; see also their statement "Again, Silence in the Churches," Appendix in Eckardt, A. R. (1967). *Elder and Younger Brothers: The Encounter of Jews and Christians* (New York: Charles Scribner's Sons) pp. 163–177.

38. Jacobs, I. pp. 39–41.

39. Agress, p. 135.

40. Biale, D. (1986). *Power and Powerlessness in Jewish History* (New York: Schocken), p. 200.

41. Bershtel, S. and Graubard, A. (1992). *Saving Remnants: Feeling Jewish in America* (New York: Free Press), p. 68.

42. Kaufmann, *Thy Daughter's Nakedness*, p. 511. Cf. Tarr, *Heaven Help Us!*, p. 109.

43. Kaufmann, *Thy Daughter's Nakedness*, p. 539.

44. Falk, H. (1972). *Days of Judgment* (New York: Shengold), p. 125; Kemelman, H. (1992). *The Day the Rabbi Resigned* (New York: Fawcett Columbine), p. 265; Telushkin, *An Eye for an Eye*, pp. 126 ff. See also Longstreet, *Pedlock Saint, Pedlock Sinner*, pp. 10, 39; Richler, M. (1963). *The Incomparable Atuk* (London: Andre Deutsch) pp. 102, 146.

45. Lenn, T. (1972). *Rabbi and Synagogue in Reform Judaism* (New York: Central Conference of American Rabbis), p. 22.

46. Dinnerstein, L. (1994). *Anti-Semitism in America* (New York, Oxford: Oxford University Press), p. 228 f.; see also Lunin-Pack, J. (1996). "1995 Audit of Anti-Semitic Incidents." [Prepared by Jesse Lunin-Pack] (New York: Anti-Defamation League), pp. 1–2.

47. Liebman, C. S. (1995). "Jewish Survival, Antisemitism, and Negotiation with the Tradition" in Robert M. Seltzer and Norman J. Cohen, *The Americanization of the Jews* (New York: New York University Press), p. 437 f.

48. Silberman, p. 22 ff.

49. Dinnerstein, p. 243.

50. Dershowitz, A. M. (1991). *Chutzpah* (Boston: Little, Brown and Co.), pp. 3, 8–9.

51. Fast, H. (1984). *The Outsider* (Boston: Houghton Mifflin), p. 73 ff..

52. Leokum, p. 106.

53. Tarr, *The Conversion of Chaplain Cohen*, p. 84. In the latter novel (*Heaven Help Us!*), the Protestant minister preaches on "Swelling Revelation." "Swelling Revelation shows how, beginning at low ebb with the Old Testament's fierce tribal deity of primitive justice, Jesus force-marches humankind via the New Testament to the heights of apprehending the God who is Love." *Heaven Help Us!*, p. 82.

54. Klenicki, L. (1995). "Jewish-Christian Dialogue" in *A Dictionary of*

the Jewish-Christian Dialogue, Expanded Edition, ed. Leon Klenicki and Geofferey Wigoder (New York, Mahwah, New Jersey: Paulist), p. 107. See also relevant articles in *Toward A Theological Encounter: Jewish Understandings of Christianity*, ed. Leon Klenicki (New York, Mahwah, New Jersey: Paulist, 1991).

55. Siegel, p. 189.

56. Reisner, N. (1986). "Rabbis Under Stress," the [Philadelphia] *Jewish Exponent* (September 26): 31.

57. Gross-Schaefer, A. G. and Weiss, E. (1994). "The Endangered Rabbi." *Jewish Spectator* 59:2 (fall): 28.

58. Rubenstein, p. 144.

59. Lenn, p. 374.

60. Kemelman, *Sunday the Rabbi Stayed Home*, p. 17 ff.; Kemelman, H. (1987). *One Fine Day the Rabbi Bought A Cross* (New York: William Morrow), p. 46 f.; Kemelman, H. (1996). *That Day the Rabbi Left Town* (New York: Fawcett Columbine), pp. 191, 220; Kaufmann, *Thy Daughter's Nakedness*, p. 287 ff.; Tarr, *Heaven Help Us!*, p. 89 ff.

61. Fast, p. 91. See Leokum, pp. 245–254.

62. Mirsky, N. (1974). "Rabbinic Dilemmas," *The Jewish Spectator* 39:1 (Spring): 32.

63. Siegel, p. 189.

64. Kaufmann, *Remember Me To God*, p. 248. Cf. Ashe, P. (1975 [1969]). *Naked Came the Stranger* (New York: Dell), p. 55.

65. Siegel, p. 179, cf. 185, 186.

66. Gordon, pp. 104, 317.

67. Benedictus, D. (1976). *The Rabbi's Wife* (London: Blond and Briggs), p. 147.

68. Greenberg, M. (1983). *The Rabbi's Life Contract* (Garden City, NY: Doubleday and Co.), pp. 26, 49, 75 ff.

69. Siegel, p. 189.

6

Congregants View Their Rabbis

Though, as noted earlier, rabbis are found in a number of places outside of the congregational setting—for some are in business and others are in education, social work, organizational life, and the various kinds of chaplaincies—the fact is that most rabbis who serve *professionally as rabbis* do so within a congregational setting. That being so, this chapter considers how congregants view their rabbis. It begins with the question often asked of congregational rabbis: What motivated you to enter the rabbinate? Then the chapter continues with two major areas: congregational "expectations" and congregational "attitudes."

What do congregants want, or expect *from* their rabbis? What are congregants' attitudes *toward* their rabbis? These congregational "expectations" and "attitudes" are very different matters. "Expectations" are defined as the areas with which congregants *want* their rabbis to be involved. "Attitudes" are the congregants' *feelings about* their rabbis.

"WHY DID YOU BECOME A RABBI?"

The rabbinate is a lonely profession. As a very experienced Denver rabbi, the late Manuel Laderman wrote in a letter "To A Future Rabbi," the sad but realistic fact is that the "rabbinate is a hard profession." Furthermore, the "best laity in the world will never fully understand all that you stand for as a rabbi." He continued, explaining that "Your rabbinical status is always disturbing, because you are an unsatisfied person. You want more than they are willing to do and be. . . . That is why I warn you about the separation between you and them. In a very definite sense you are a man apart."[1] Many people have written about the "distance," indeed the *necessary* distance, between rabbis and their congregants. If rabbis are too close to their congregants, they cannot be effective as leaders. Though it is true that the laity "will never fully understand all that [one stands] for as a rabbi," time and again in one form or another, rabbis are asked by their congregants, "Why did you become a rabbi?"

What is the reason that this query is raised with such frequency? Generally speaking, people do not ask their physicians why they chose medicine or their lawyers why they opted for the law much less their auto mechanic why he or she went into that field. Sociologist-Rabbi Norman B. Mirsky (1974) suggests that the question stems from increased secularization in America. As "Jews become Americanized and secularized, they increasingly regard religion as apart from life. Anyone who is 'religious' as a rabbi is presumed to be, is regarded as someone with a calling who has had an experience with the 'other world.'" This idea is frightening to both Jews and non-Jews. The fact is, however, that someone who enters the rabbinate because he or she has identified with "an older rabbi, through interest in Jewish learning, or through a desire to serve" the Jewish people does not view going into the rabbinate "as a 'calling.'" Nor does the rabbi "feel 'apart.'"[2]

Though it does not come up as a subject in all of the rabbi-centered novels, certainly a recurring theme, nonetheless, is the congregant who asks, "Why did you become a rabbi?" When Leo Berdick (*The Strong Hand*) is asked that question, he first explains that it is not because he received a "call" or because something dramatic happened in his life. He rather gives this explanation:

> Most of us become rabbis, I think, because we like to teach. . . . We rabbis don't have a special Grace or position. We are not intermedi-

aries between man and God. We may feel a sense of mission but it is to teach. Actually, a rabbi is merely one among equals. . . . At any rate, we like to think we're at least the equals of our fellow men. . . . I love to teach and I chose this form of teaching because it gave me a chance to explore the field of my people and my religion as a full-time task."[3]

Mirsky's point that oftentimes anyone "who is 'religious' as a rabbi is presumed to be, is regarded as someone with a calling who has had an experience with the 'other world'" is admirably captured in the following example, taken from Bernard Malamud's poignant short story "The Magic Barrel." A few months before he will be ordained at Yeshiva University, Leo Finkle takes a young woman on an arranged date. She asks him, "How was it that you came to your calling? I mean was it a sudden passionate inspiration?" He pauses and then explains that he was always interested in the Law. Finkle then is asked, "You saw revealed in it the presence of the Highest?" He nods his assent. His date will not be put off. "'When,' she asked in a trembly voice, 'did you become enamored of God?'"[4]

EXPECTATIONS

Congregational rabbis need to meet the expectations of two different groups: that of the Board of Directors, and then, more generally, of the congregants themselves. It is the Board of Directors, explain Arthur Gross Schaeffer and Eric Weiss (1994), "that usually interacts most directly and powerfully with the rabbi. The board ratifies the hire/fire decisions, evaluates performance and decides salary, benefits, convention allowances and other matters that dramatically affect time and focus." They go on to point out that

> the directors may feel that they can only judge the rabbi's effectiveness based on the smooth running of the temple as a business organization. Issues of budget, membership numbers, fundraising, employee procedures can be their primary focus. Priorities that may be central to clergy such as prayer, study, observance, social action and covenant with God are too frequently not shared by board members or even considered relevant to the board's function.[5]

When there are difficulties between rabbis and their congregations, it often centers around the differences in role expectation.

From a Board's point of view, one of the primary expectations of rabbis is that they will attract and retain members, who in turn will provide the wherewithal to support the congregation. This means that the rabbi, above all, must be "popular." Being popular means avoiding issues that could lose members—and their financial support.

> The rabbi may be forced to focus time and energy on those least committed, often least appreciative and least understanding of the role of a congregation and a religious movement. Such members may leave if the wrong thing is said, if someone else is given a desired honor, or if the rabbi does not cater to their whims. Rather than strengthening the core of committed members, a rabbi must often devote an inordinate amount of attention to the periphery of the congregation. And yet, the board expects the rabbi to do what is necessary to keep them as members. If they leave, it is often viewed as the rabbi's failure.[6]

In *Heaven Help Us!* Rabbi Abel is told that one of his members is quitting the synagogue, and that from what she said, it apparently "sounded like a personal matter . . . as if she had a fight with you." Without even looking further into the situation, his synagogue president suggests that "maybe an apology from you would help."[7]

The president of Rabbi Small's congregation (*Thursday the Rabbi Walked Out*) wants to bring an unaffiliated, very wealthy industrialist into the congregation. Apparently the man never went through a formal Bar Mitzvah ceremony when he was 13 and feels somewhat diffident about joining because of this. The president then approaches Rabbi Small and suggests that the synagogue arrange a Bar Mitzvah ceremony for the man, thereby ensuring his membership and financial support. The president is appalled when Rabbi Small tells him that such an adult Bar Mitzvah ceremony is not only not necessary but that he will not permit such a charade to take place. The president turns to Rabbi Small and says, "We'll see about that, Rabbi." He loses no time. That very evening at a dinner party, the synagogue president initiates a plan to force the rabbi out of the pulpit.[8]

When Rabbi Daniel Winter (*An Eye for an Eye*) takes a public stand which infuriates his synagogue president and vice president, the two suspend their very substantial gifts to the building fund until such time that the congregation can reconsider its options. The clear message is that they want to force the rabbi to leave. In the president's words, "The rabbi has, in my . . . opinion, been obstinate, selfish, totally unwilling to be a team player. . . ."[9] Another board member, a strong supporter of the rabbi, challenges the president and his remarks. He says that what the president really wants is a rabbi who will do what the president says, and never argue back. "But that's not a rabbi, that's a hired hand. And Daniel Winter is nobody's hired hand. He answers to one boss, God—or at least God as he understands Him." He then continues, "Over the past few days, it's occurred to me that all this is really a fight about the Golden Rule. Rabbi Winter's golden rule is the one he always likes to quote from the Talmud: 'What's hateful unto you, don't do unto your neighbor' . . . Russell's [the synagogue president, Russell Kahn's] golden rule is a little different. 'He who has the gold makes the rules.'"[10]

In another analysis of synagogue life in modern America, a rabbi suggests that

> many congregational board members are confused as how to view their rabbi. Is he or she a run-of-the-mill employee or a respected and even holy figure? The traditional role of a rabbi has undergone such radical transformations over the past century that today there is an absence of any clear social or religious guidelines. In generations past, the rabbi was frequently the *dayan* and *posek*, that is, the final judge and religious arbiter of any and all social and religious disputes and his ruling was final. This model of rabbinical authority no longer applies . . . but one result is that the rabbi of a congregation is expected to fulfill a host of often conflicting expectations.[11]

At a meeting with his Executive Board (of Directors), Rabbi Ed Gordon rather unceremoniously is told that they understand his status to be one of an employee: "Ed, the trouble with you is, you don't want a religion, you want a way of life." When he dares to rebut this inane statement, Rabbi Gordon is told,

> "You lose sight of one thing. . . . You're an employee of the congregation." Another board member chimes in, "That's right. . . . You work for us."[12]

A different, and less definable, group of expectations come from the congregation as a whole. "The rabbi is expected to be a teacher, sermonizer, officiant, counselor, healer, advisor, visionary, ambassador, fundraiser and all around fix-it person."[13] On top of this, congregants frequently draw on (imperfect) memories from the past, expectations which are formed by their earlier experiences. If their previous, or childhood rabbi gave good sermons, then by definition, to be a "good" rabbi, this rabbi should give good sermons. If they carry a fond memory of a rabbi who was particularly good at working with the youth group, then this becomes part of their present expectations.

To further complicate rabbinic-congregational relations, Rabbi Martin Siegel notes that people often transfer their personal expectations to the rabbi. "People tend to see the rabbi as a symbol for whatever they themselves are working toward, psychologically, emotionally, and intellectually. He is a scale on which they measure what they are, against what they would like to be. To the extent they fall short in their own self-esteem, they are likely to resent the rabbi. Conversely, if they think well of themselves, they think well of him."[14]

Rabbis, a congregant quipped, are something like "Democracy." If all is going well, we take rabbis for granted. If all is not going well, then we blame them. Though democracy as a political system has its faults, it remains humankind's best defense against totalitarianism. She then concluded, the rabbis, for all their human faults, remain as the Jews' best defense for survival *as Jews.*

In a study of what congregants want or expect from rabbis, what is very clear is that their number one expectation, *"far beyond any other responsibility, is to 'solve' the 'youth problem,'* to transmit the heritage to the young." When posed with the question what they would want from a rabbi if their congregation was seeking a new leader, congregants in that study set their priorities in this manner: 1) a capacity to relate to young people; 2) Jewish education, family counseling, and sermons; 3) interfaith activities, prayer, study, social action or social reform; and finally, at a much, much lower level, 4) socializing with members of the congregation.[15]

> The focus on "youth" is admirably captured in a short story by Allegra Goodman. At a meeting of the synagogue, the president says: "I think right now we need to get back to the bottom-line issues. What was the rabbi *hired* for? The young people. This is his forte, and I think we all agree that he's made the new confirmation class the best-attended in years."[16]

Broadly speaking, suggests Lenn, rabbis fill three roles for their congregants. The first is the "pastoral role"—counselor on personal problems; visiting the ill or bereaved; and officiating at life cycle ceremonies: weddings, bar or bat mitzvah, and funerals. Second is the role of "community leader"—as representative to the wider Jewish community; as representative of the Jewish to the non-Jewish community; as social action leader; and then as the rabbi in the world of media. Finally, a third role is the rabbi as "scholar"—specifically, rabbinical scholarly achievement, and then writer of books and or articles primarily on Jewish subjects. Those are the expectations. When it comes to the realizations of those expectations, there is a serious shortfall in the pastoral component. While 65% of the congregants have "high expectations" of the rabbi to be active in pastoral matters, somewhat less than 50% have their high expectations met. In the other two areas, "community leader" and "scholar," the high expectations and the high performance ratings are comparatively close, within two or three percentage points.[17]

Rabbi as Pastor

While American Reform congregants are unsatisfied with their rabbis as pastors, Stephen Sharot (1975) reports that actually a fair amount of time is spent by Reform rabbis in pastoral work and that this is true likewise of Conservative and "Centrist" Orthodox rabbis. The vast amount of these rabbis, right across the denominational spectrum, were engaged in pastoral visiting. Well over half in each movement explained that they had specialized training to prepare them as counselors, and very high percentages of these rabbis (77 percent Reform, 74 percent Conservative, and 87 percent of the Orthodox) regarded their counseling work as "either 'more important' or 'as important' as preaching."[18]

Coincidentally, that rabbis in all of the mainstream movements are involved in counseling bears out an observation made earlier, that many American Orthodox congregational rabbis are virtually carbon copies of their Reform and Conservative colleagues: they preach, teach, administrate, serve as pastors, act as counselors, and, in general, fill a wide variety of roles.

Wherever the rabbi stands along the religious continuum, how can one explain the apparent contrast in rabbinical self-image and congregational evaluation? Patently, the phenomenon of "dissatisfaction" with rabbi-as-pastor is not limited to Reform congregations, as Reconstructionist, Conservative, and Orthodox rabbis would be quick to point out. The key to satisfaction, or lack thereof, of rabbi-as-pastor is probably *the amount of time that the rabbi takes with a particular individual*, and, to some extent, whether the rabbi can offer some solution to the problem at hand. The solution, however, is secondary. Merely taking the time to listen is an important act in and of itself. People with problems, however, frequently want more of the rabbi's time than he or she can give.

> Oftentimes, merely the rabbi's physical presence coming to someone's home to offer congratulations or condolences means a great deal. A congregant praises Rabbi David Gordon (in *The Temple*) for his presence following her child's death. "He was here with me every day. For whole days he sat with me, giving me the only thing I could hold on to. An understanding. A faith. An *acceptance*. . . . Only Rabbi gave me the strength to live with it."[19]
>
> When Rina Lazarus (in Faye Kellerman's *Grievous Sin*) has a serious operation, she is visited in the hospital by Rav Schulman. She tells him, "Thank you for coming down, Rav Schulman. You have always been a rock of support for me and my family."[20]
>
> At times congregants turn on a rabbi when the answer that they sought is not what they thought they wanted. Rabbi Ed Gordon is criticized when the Weiler's daughter-in-law makes religious demands upon her husband. "The elder Mr. Weiler at last phoned Ed angrily." His comment? "'You did a fine job converting her and we appreciate it,' Mr. Weiler said, 'but enough's enough. You know? You're gonna bust up the

> marriage—the kid can't even get cream in his coffee. He didn't marry a fanatic. So lay off the food business, will you? Nobody keeps that stuff. I don't know, a rabbi's always unrealistic.'"[21]
>
> Then there is the congregant who complained (in *Heaven Help Us!*, and quoted in an earlier chapter): "It took me four years of analysis to work through my conflicts with an authoritarian father—and now Rabbi Abel's dogmatism threatens to destroy everything. That man is too much of a Jew, and he runs too tight a temple."[22]

Rabbi as Community Leader, to Jews and Non-Jews; Rabbi as Scholar

Chapter 5 (Congregational Rabbis and Their Communities Continued) looked at the phenomenon of how the rabbi is oftentimes seen as the community *representative*, both to the Jewish and the non-Jewish communities. There are rabbis who attain regional or national prominence and have the support of their congregations, and there are those whose stand is seen as a threat to the local community. Mention was made in an earlier chapter of a rabbi who irritated some of his congregants. While colleagues had praised him as a "rabbi's rabbi," a former congregant saw the matter differently. He dismissed the rabbi as being too ambitious and too innovative. Other comments were that the rabbi was too Jewish and too radical. In another case, a rabbi was fired by his congregation because he was perceived as being too vocal on political/social matters. Lenn quotes a congregant who suggested, "I think a Rabbi should preach and run the [synagogue] . . . and let the President run the country."[23] What is unclear is whether this congregant objected to the rabbi's busy schedule organizationally or whether the rabbi was preaching on issues of national policy. On the whole, however, as noted above, there is a close correlation between congregational expectations and performance ratings when it comes to the rabbi as community leader.

> Fictional as well as real-life rabbis are both praised (or perhaps, tolerated) as well as criticized for their stands on such issues as Civil Rights, Civil Liberties, and Labor issues. Yet there are many occasions where congregants want the rabbi's presence

> at a function—even if the program is of a purely social nature—and the only "Jewish" component is that the participants themselves are Jewish. One of the board members of Rabbi Gordon's congregation (*The Temple*) is organizing a get-together at the local golf club. He wants his rabbi to be present. "Your presence, the Rabbi himself being there, participating, it already gives it a different touch, y'know? A meaning. . . . To see the rabbi involved, participating. It makes it *Jewish* somehow."[24]

Rabbis regularly complain that they do not have—or cannot find—the time to study. Nonetheless, when it comes to their congregants' expectations and performance ratings in the area of rabbi/scholar, there seems to be a very close correlation.

> The issue of "rabbi as scholar" or the rabbi who is too scholarly does appear in the fiction. Rabbi Levi (*The Firing of Rabbi Levi*), who probably is in his late twenties or early thirties (as mentioned in Chapter 4), is told, "You're too old fashioned. You're unwilling to try new ideas. . . . Your emphasis has been on the past, not the future." Rabbi Levi's sermons are also criticized: "We are all greatly impressed by your scholarship, but many are frankly bored by your topics. We are tired of hearing what Judaism stands for, what problems we Jews face."[25] In *Thy Daughter's Nakedness*, a congregant expresses these comments about Rabbi Gordon's sermons: "When a man talks about . . . building a hospital in Boston for all races and creeds, I know what he's talking about. But when a man starts talking about God, and all that kind of stuff, I don't know what he's talking about."[26]
>
> In the Weekday *Rabbi* series, Rabbi David Small is portrayed as having scholarly interests. He writes occasional articles for learned journals, and in the last novel he is on the faculty of a local college.[27]

ATTITUDES

Just as congregational "expectations" refer to those areas with which congregants *want* their rabbis to be involved, so "attitudes" are the congregants' *feelings about* their rabbis.

Congregants View Their Rabbis

There is a psychological dimension to the relationship between rabbis and their congregants. Rabbis are oftentimes seen as fulfilling one or more of three images: Rabbi as one's parent; Rabbi as Judaism incarnate; and, finally, Rabbi as God's representative. This last point is particularly true, because rabbis, like other clergy, but typically *unlike the situation with lay therapists*, often are asked questions about ultimate meaning: "Why do people suffer?" and "What is the good life?" Rabbis stand for an ideal, not the least part of which is as the voice of tradition and the person who has specialized knowledge in interpreting God's will.

The image of rabbi as Parent-Judaism-God certainly can have positive associations. These might be such terms as love, goodness, approval, protection, compassion, forgiveness, concern, and the like. The presence of the rabbi, being there, counseling, comforting, consoling, congratulating, potentially carries with it emotions much wider, much more important, and much further-reaching than the specific occasion would seem to warrant. Rabbi Susan Grossman writes: "I do find I am particularly effective in ministering to the sick and bereaved, serving not only as the representative of a comforting God (as Rabbi Harold Kushner articulates it) but also as the paradigmatic Mother who comforts her children when they are hurt or fearful."[28]

Likewise, the image of rabbi as Parent-Judaism-God clearly can have negative associations. There are congregants who are burdened by their own authoritarian parent(s); or by an oppressive religious upbringing; or contradictory feelings about God's traditional attributes about justice and mercy—this latter point especially following the Holocaust. Subconsciously, they may associate the rabbi with a parent, or with a former rabbi, or they may transfer negative feelings onto the rabbi, holding the rabbi responsible for what euphemistically are called "Acts of God," for the rabbi is the "representative of God": At the very least the rabbi is the person who has specialized knowledge in interpreting God's will—the same God who "allowed" the Holocaust to take place. These images of rabbi as Parent-Judaism-God often manifest themselves in attitudes toward the rabbi.

> Though the phenomenon of associating rabbis with Parent-Judaism-God shall be explored shortly, a couple of fictional examples are illustrative. In *The Launching of Barbara Fabrikant*, the rabbi's daughter puts the matter quite plainly when she

> says, ". . . no one hates rabbis like Jews. The only other Being . . . that Jews hate as much as the rabbi is God. For hating God they have the best reasons . . . what [was] God . . . doing during Auschwitz? . . . And do you think none of this . . . bitterness doesn't spill over onto the rabbi?"[29]
>
> In *Heaven Help Us!* a congregant asks Rabbi Abel, "who can explain some people's reactions to father figures and God images?"[30]

Though she was addressing the role of rabbi-as-counselor, Rachel Adler's comments about rabbinical-congregant relations is very applicable. She writes,

> the rabbinical role evokes its own powerful transference: attitudes congregants transfer to the rabbi, not only from feelings toward influential persons in their own pasts but also from earlier experiences of God and religious teaching. The greater the discrepancy between rabbis' and congregants' liturgical roles, access to sacred objects such as the Torah, and perceived familiarity with sacred texts, with the Hebrew language, and with Jewish tradition, the greater the likelihood that congregants will endow the rabbi with a numinous [holy, religious] aura and unique hieratic [priestly] powers, and that they will base upon these ascriptions distorted or inflated expectations of the rabbi.[31]

> The aforementioned congregant (in *Heaven Help Us!*) who links in one sentence the prior conflicts with her "authoritarian father" and the perceived "dogmatism" of her rabbi on some level sees the rabbi as a "parent"—though clearly not a "good" parent.
>
> In *Friday the Rabbi Slept Late* Rabbi David Small, though in his late twenties, reminds one of his earliest supporters of the man's own youth. There "was something about his [Rabbi Small's] gestures and tone vaguely reminiscent of the bearded patriarch from whom he himself had learned the Talmud when a lad in the old country."[32] There is some transference here, but it is a positive memory.

Many congregants regard their rabbi as their spiritual representative to God. Rabbis (and often people in the ministry in general) are teased about their "direct line to God."

Clearly meant in jest, a sympathetic congregant (in *The Rabbi's Life Contract*) turns to the rabbi's wife and says: "But I didn't make the world. That's your hubby's department."[33]

In *The Conversion of Chaplain Cohen*, the main character falls in love with a young woman who is a Holocaust survivor. When he proposes marriage to her, she refuses him. She sees the rabbi as God's representative—or, again at least as the person who has specialized knowledge in interpreting God's will.

She says, "As a rabbi you talk about love and peace and the Messianic hope and God. . . . You pray, and you ask God to forgive you for your sins. But I *never* pray, David, because I can never forgive God for *His* sins. . . . I no longer believe in *God* . . . *How* then can you expect me to believe in *you*?"[34]

Earlier in this chapter I had quoted a few lines from *The Launching of Barbara Fabrikant*. She suggests that the anger that some congregants feel with God, or their perception of God's "absence" during the Holocaust, is projected onto the rabbi. "And do you think none of this (very justifiable, in my opinion) bitterness doesn't spill over onto the rabbi?"

She then continues her monologue.

> They came to him for comfort, and they go away angry. Because if you're the parents of a little boy, say, who died in a car accident, and the rabbi says to you, "Trust in God. His goodness and mercy surpass our understanding," you tell me how you'd feel. You'd like to get your hands on this God of such tremendous Understanding and wring his neck. Instead, his flock complain about the rabbi—God not having the courage to show Himself to them recently—his sermons aren't long enough, they're too long, he only likes his rich members, not his poor, his children are snobs. . . .
>
> The rabbi is at a terrific disadvantage, having to be the spiritual emissary of so bad a Supreme Being, and his flock lose faith easily, which is completely understandable. The mystery is that they have any faith at all.[35]

The rabbi who visits Joe Berman (in Edward Lewis Wallant's *The Human Season*) likewise is the recipient of an anger that is really directed at God. The rabbi, however, lacks empathy when he tries to comfort this mourner with words about God, such as "He is with you always, there is no denying Him . . . you are not doing yourself any good being bitter

> at God. He has reasons. We are but made in His image, not in His wisdom. . . ."[36]

One reply is that if rabbis only tell a grieving family to "trust in God, for God's goodness and mercy surpass our understanding," or that God "has reasons. We are but made in His image, not in His wisdom," then those rabbis are counseling in an ineffective manner. Clearly we do not have God's wisdom. Likewise being bitter with God *can* be harmful. Yet, trying to console a mourner in this fashion is not helpful. In addition, I would certainly argue that these rabbis are doing bad theology. The real point, however, is that the narrator in *The Launching of Barbara Fabrikant* is right on the mark: too often congregants *do* take out their grievances on the rabbi, because rabbis are, in the popular imagination, God's representatives.

> In what must be one of the most poignant short stories involving a rabbi, Lee Brian's "With Tenderness," a rabbi counsels a young man named Everett off and on for a period of about 10 years. Everett's parents constantly fight with each other, and in the course of the story, Everett's father commits suicide. It is clear that Everett is suffering from chronic depression. In the story, at the very least, Rabbi Tellerman represents Judaism, or perhaps a combination of Judaism, good parent, and God. Throughout the narrative, the rabbi continues to have a strong emotional effect on Everett, but time and again Rabbi Tellerman is an appalling counselor. In place of any kind of empathy, he mouths platitudes and harkens back to the example of the boy's grandfather. Rabbi Tellerman also utters such trite and hackneyed phrases as "Providence moves in mysterious ways. It was all for some purpose," "No matter how bad things are, you must believe they'll get better," and "Experience is what counts." Toward the end of the narrative, Everett starts to take illegal drugs, and it is plain that he is in the midst of a mental breakdown. At the conclusion of the story, Everett phones Rabbi Tellerman and asks to see him. The rabbi regrets that he cannot make time that day, but he invites Everett to Shabbat services that very evening. He tells Everett that ". . . well, tonight the sermon might tell you something . . . that'll prove important." The story concludes that

evening when Everett, sitting in the third row of the synagogue, stands up in the middle of the rabbi's sermon, takes a gun, fires, and kills the rabbi.[37]

Though there are examples of appalling rabbinic counseling and rabbis doing bad theology, this is not the whole story. Earlier in this chapter, reference was made to the time when Rina Lazarus expressed her appreciation to Rav Schulman for his pastoral visit immediately following her hysterectomy. Rav Schulman does a wonderful job of counseling and comforting.

Rina sighs, grimaces, and finally says: "It isn't the Holocaust."

Rav Schulman gently replies: "No, it is not the *Shoah* [the Holocaust]. But that does not mean you aren't entitled to your grief, Rina Miriam. I lived through the *Shoah*; I lost my only son. Yet I still become frustrated when I misplace my wallet. So what does that say about human nature?"

Rina replies . . . "I feel petty for being so . . . bitter."

"Your operation was far from petty. Your bitterness is very understandable," says Rav Schulman. He then goes on: "You needn't reproach yourself for showing human emotion. Nowhere in the Torah does it say we cannot feel sadness or happiness or anger or even *doubt*."

A few moments later Rina whispers to Rav Schulman, "I'm angry at God." His reply is appropriate and absolutely filled with comfort—It also is a superb example of good theology: "I, too, have been angry at God. He is strong. He can take your anger without feeling personally affronted."

Were he to have left the matter there, he would have accomplished a great deal. In fact, he goes on and offers her some further thoughts. Again, his counseling, comfort, and compassion shine through his words. "In reality, how much control do we actually have over our lives? Life is a loan from *Hashem* [God]. We are put here by His design; so shall we leave by His design. So if death, like life, is part of the Eternal's plan, why do we say *tehilim* [psalms] for the sick? Do we really think that our prayers will alter *Hashem*'s design?"

The rabbi continues. "The answer for me is yes, they can. We believe in a personal God—a God who at least *listens* to our prayers. We don't understand *Hashem*'s ultimate design. But that doesn't mean we can't *ask*."

He then goes on with some additional advice. "Our prayers are not empty words, Rina Miriam. Though the world may seem very dark now, *Hashem* has an open ear for you. You may ask. You may not get, but you may *ask*." [38]

Unlike some of the other rabbis who utter platitudes or suggest merely that God's plan is beyond our ken, Rav Schulman *allows* Rina to grieve, he affirms her pain, making no attempt to deny it. He allows her to doubt, to feel angry, to express her hurt. He also gives Rina hope.

NOTES

1. Laderman, M. (1991). "To A Future Rabbi," in *Letters of Faith* (Denver: Hebrew Educational Alliance), pp. 114, 116.

2. Mirsky, N. (1974). "Rabbinic Dilemmas." *The Jewish Spectator* 39:1 (Spring): 36.

3. Blankfort, M. (1956). *The Strong Hand*, (Boston, Toronto: Little Brown and Co.), pp. 12 f. See also Longstreet, S. (1969). *Pedlock Saint, Pedlock Sinner* (New York: Delacorte), p. 286; Kaufmann, M. S. (1968). *Thy Daughter's Nakedness* (Philadelphia and New York: J. B. Lippincott), p. 71.

4. Malamud, B. (1958). "The Magic Barrel," in *The Magic Barrel* (New York: Farrar, Straus and Cudahy), p. 203.

5. Schaeffer, A. G. and Weiss, E. (1994). "The Endangered Rabbi." *Jewish Spectator* 59:2 (Fall): 26. See also Menitoff, P. J. (1993). "A Formula for Successful Rabbinical-Congregational Relationships." *CCAR Journal* 40:1 (Winter): 35–43.

6. Gross-Schaefer and Weiss, p. 27.

7. Tarr, H. (1968). *Heaven Help Us!* (New York: Random House), p. 106.

8. Kemelman, H. (1978). *Thursday the Rabbi Walked Out* (New York: William Morrow), p. 74 ff. The issue of "rabbinic authority" was touched on in Chapter 1 (The Rabbi in America). Is the rabbi, or the Board of Trustees, or the United Synagogue of America, Conservative Judaism's lay body, the final authority on religious matters in individual congregations? This problem has been especially troublesome for the Conservative movement, and is still unresolved. See Zelizer, G. L. (1995). "Conservative Rabbis, Their Movement, and American Judaism." *Judaism* 44:3 (Summer): 299.

9. Telushkin, J. (1992 [1991]). *An Eye for an Eye* (New York: Bantam), p. 252.

10. Telushkin, *An Eye for an Eye*, pp. 252–253.

11. Kohn, D. B. (1994). "Modern Congregants: Jewish by Proxy?" *Jewish Spectator* 59:1 (Summer): 26–27.

12. Kaufmann, *Thy Daughter's Nakedness*, p. 538.

13. Gross-Schaefer and Weiss, p. 27. As Rabbi Paul J. Menitoff has written, "congregants do not know what to expect from their rabbis. The many constituent groups within each congregation have diverse expectations of what the rabbi should be; each has its own definition of the rabbi's role . . . [congregants] expect their rabbis to function ubiquitously as preacher, teacher, pastor, leader, friend, parent, youth worker and social worker. The list seems endless." Menitoff, P. J. (1987). "Diverse Expectations in Congregational-Rabbinic Relations." *Journal of Reform Judaism* 34:4 (Fall): 1.

14. Siegel, M. (1971). *Amen: The Diary of Rabbi Martin Siegel*, ed., Mel Ziegler (New York and Cleveland: World), p. 90.

15. Fein, L. J. (1972). et. al., *Reform Is A Verb: Notes on Reform and Reforming Jews.* (New York: Union of American Hebrew Congregations), p. 90.

16. Goodman, A. (1989). "The Succession," in *Total Immersion: Stories* (New York: Harper and Row), p. 48.

17. Lenn, T. (1972). *Rabbi and Synagogue in Reform Judaism* (New York: Central Conference of American Rabbis), pp. 302 ff.

18. Sharot, S. (1995). "The British and American Rabbinate: A Comparison of Authority Structures, Role Definitions and Role Conflicts," *A Sociological Yearbook of Religion in Britain 8*, ed. Michael Hill (London: SCM Press), p. 151 f. The term that Sharot uses is "modern" Orthodox, but as noted earlier in this study, "Centrist" today is the preferred term.

19. Leokum, A. (1969). *The Temple* (New York and Cleveland: NAL/World Publishing), p. 115. See also Telushkin, *An Eye for an Eye*, p. 271.

20. Kellerman, F. (1993). *Grievous Sin* (New York: William Morrow), p. 79.

21. Kaufmann, *Thy Daughter's Nakedness*, pp. 236.

22. Tarr, *Heaven Help Us!*, p. 104.

23. Lenn, p. 316.

24. Leokum, pp. 120–121.

25. Agress, H. and F. (1978). *The Firing of Rabbi Levi* (New York: Manor Books), p. 11.

26. Kaufmann, *Thy Daughter's Nakedness*, p. 554.

27. Kemelman, *The Day the Rabbi Resigned*, p. 143; *That Day the Rabbi Left Town*.

28. Grossman, S. (1995). "The Dual Nature of Rabbinic Leadership." *Conservative Judaism* 48:1 (Fall): 45.

29. Rose, L. B. (1974). *The Launching of Barbara Fabrikant* (New York: David McKay Company), pp. 8–9.

30. Tarr, *Heaven Help Us!*, p. 234.

31. Adler, R. (1993). "A Stumbling Block Before the Blind: Sexual Exploitation in Pastoral Counseling." *CCAR Journal* 40:2 (Spring): 21–22.

32. Kemelman, H. (1964). *Friday the Rabbi Slept Late* (New York: Crown), p. 63.

33. Greenberg, M. (1983). *The Rabbi's Life Contract* (Garden City, NY: Doubleday and Co.), p. 46.

34. Tarr, H. (1963). *The Conversion of Chaplain Cohen* (New York: Avon), pp. 267–268.

35. Rose, p. 9.

36. Wallant, E. L. (1960).*The Human Season* (New York: Harcourt Brace Jovanovich), p. 161.

37. Brian, L. (1980). "With Tenderness." *Reconstructionist* 46:8 (December): 24, 27. Coincidentally, in 1966, Rabbi Morris Adler of Detroit was shot during services by a young man suffering from mental illness.

38. Kellerman, *Grievous Sin*, pp. 78–80.

7
Women Rabbis

The year 1997 marked 25 years since the first woman rabbi was ordained in the United States. The idea, at least in principle, was not a new one.

According to a study by Pamela S. Nadell (1995),[1] women had sought to be ordained as rabbis by the Reform movement since the 1890s. A major debate over women's ordination erupted within the Reform movement in the early 1920s. While the Central Conference of American Rabbis concluded that "in keeping with the spirit of our age and traditions of our conference . . . women cannot justly be denied the privilege of ordination," nonetheless, storms of protest developed among the laity—and probably many rabbis as well. The matter came to a negative conclusion. According to Livia Bitton-Jackson (1995), "Thirty-three years later a committee formed to investigate the issue urged the Reform rabbinical college to admit women to ordination. However, it took another sixteen years for the first woman to become a Reform rabbi."[2]

About that same time, there were stirrings in the Conservative movement regarding a larger ritual role for women. In 1955, the Conservative movement had mandated that women could be called to bless the Torah. While this had been adopted by some Conservative congregations, it was far from universally followed. The year 1971 saw the formation of a women's "consciousness-raising group called Ezrat Nashim, meaning 'succor for women.'"[3] The term Ezrat Nashim was carefully chosen, explains Judith Hauptman in "The Ethical Challenge of Feminist Change" (1995). It "is intended as a play on words: the literal meaning is 'help for women.' But *azarah* also means 'gallery' and this term is usually used to refer to the women's gallery in an Orthodox synagogue. It was also the name of the gallery in the Temple in Jerusalem into which everyone entered, but beyond which women were not permitted to go."[4]

In 1972, a group of women who were part of Ezrat Nashim decided to bring up their concerns publicly at the annual convention of the Rabbinic Assembly, the Conservative movement's professional rabbinic body. In short order, women were permitted to be counted in the prayer quorum (*minyan*) and in other ritual matters.[5] The acceptance of women did not, however, come overnight. While by 1990 about "two-thirds of the Conservative congregations were giving women *aliyot* [reciting the blessings and/or reading from the Torah] and approximately one-half were counting them in the *minyan*," many of these changes had only come about in the last few years,[6] *after* the Jewish Theological Seminary actually had begun to ordain women in 1985.

Hauptman traces the more than decade-long debate over women's ordination among the laity and rabbis of the Conservative movement.

> A fact-finding commission was established, testimony was collected in Conservative synagogues across the United States. . . . The majority of those consulted . . . favored the ordination of women. . . .
>
> Both the advocates and opponents of women's ordination agreed that most contemporary rabbinic functions, such as religious role model, teacher, preacher, and pastoral counselor, could be filled without making any halakhic [Jewish law and traditional practice] adjustments. . . .
>
> A number of JTS [Jewish Theological Seminary] faculty members prepared position papers, some arguing in favor of ordination and others arguing against it. . . .
>
> [T]he faculty approved the admissions of women by a substantial majority. . . .
>
> By the time JTS ordained its first female rabbi in May 1985, much of the Conservative community was ready to embrace this change.[7]

The Orthodox movement could not but take notice of what was taking place regarding women's ordination. While some in the more moderate to "Centrist" wings made encouraging noises, the fact is that "most Orthodox Jews reject feminist ideology." Indeed most "Orthodox rabbis have reacted with apologetics, scorn or vituperation to the feminist critique of Judaism and its assertion of women's need for, and right to, equal access to Jewish learning, public religious expression, and leadership."[8] Blu Greenberg, a leading Orthodox feminist, at one point was optimistic about the ordination of women rabbis within an Orthodox context.[9] With Orthodoxy's general drift to the religious right, her optimism remains unrealized.

> In Andrew Kane's novel *Rabbi, Rabbi*, a "Centrist" Orthodox rabbi[10] lambastes the Conservative movement for its decision to ordain women. He notes that in the past, when the Conservative movement faced an issue where there were conflicts between modern and traditional values, the Conservatives attempted resolutions that respected both positions yet "put the integrity of Jewish law first and foremost, above all other considerations." Now, he suggests, the Conservative movement has achieved resolution "by dispensing with Jewish law altogether, just as the Reform Movement has done from the onset."[11]

CURRENT STATISTICS

In his book *A Concise History of the Rabbinate* (1993), Simon Schwartzfuchs notes that the female rabbinate is only a couple of decades old. He suggests that "the full impact of the female rabbinate on synagogue life cannot be gauged." He ponders whether women rabbis "will develop alongside the traditional male rabbinate or slowly replace it."[12] Such a "radical" statement in a very serious and well-researched book highlights how much has changed since 1972, when the first woman rabbi was ordained. From the point of no women rabbis to graduating classes where they number about a third to a half of the ordination group in a given year is quite a change in a very short period of time.

As of the mid-1990s, there were well close to 250 women rabbis ordained at the Hebrew Union College-Jewish Institute of Religion, the

Reform branch of Judaism. Alongside these women stood 75 graduates of the Reconstructionist Rabbinical College and likewise well over 50 from the Conservative branch of Judaism, the Jewish Theological Seminary.[13] Coincidentally, in Great Britain, as of 1994 there were 19 women ordainees.[14]

These real-life women serve as pulpit rabbis, as professors, chaplains, professional educators, administrators, and Hillel Directors (the Jewish group on the university campus), and in other forms of organizational life.[15]

Within the Reform movement, well over a third of these women serve as full-time congregational rabbis in pulpits of the Union of American Hebrew Congregations, and it is estimated that another 25% serve on a part-time basis. Of the full-time congregational rabbis, more than half head up solo pulpits, and the others were either associate or assistant rabbis.[16]

The Reconstructionist Rabbinical College has been ordaining rabbis since 1974. To date, over 40 percent of their ordainees are women.[17] Their President, Rabbi David A. Teutsch, notes that women tend to work part-time during their child-rearing years. He goes on to point out, however, that this is only "relevant if they are married or coupled and have children. We do not have enough experience to know whether they return to full-time work when their children are older."[18]

WOMEN RABBIS HAVE CHANGED THE FACE OF JUDAISM

As Rabbi Laura Geller (1995) reminds us, "Women rabbis have changed the face of Judaism."[19] Rabbi Nina Beth Cardin (1995), a Conservative Rabbi, argues further: "*Women rabbis are creating the rabbinate anew*. . . . If all goes well, women rabbis will create paradigms of the rabbinate that [will] . . . offer guidance to both women and men."[20] Addressing just that issue from the perspective of a woman rabbi, Elizabeth Weiss Stern (1993) notes that women can refer to many examples in their rabbinates where they

> have transformed the Rabbinic model. Many of us can point to successes for which we can take credit: gender sensitive worship experiences [where God is addressed as neither "he" nor "she"]; women in positions of leadership; Rosh Hodesh [services acknowledging the

> new lunar month] celebrations; empowerment of lay people; a growing appreciation among Jews—Rabbis and congregants alike—of the benefits of smaller, more intimate congregations and of the Rabbi's need for a personal life.

Rabbi Stern, however, does continue, "But I do not believe that we have come up with a convincing model for success."[21]

While women rabbis *have* changed the face of Judaism, this is less clear in the world of fiction. There are literally dozens of novels which portray rabbis in contemporary American Jewish fiction. Examples where the rabbi is a "central" character, naturally, are more limited. Though women have been ordained in the United States since 1972, there are almost no examples of "women-rabbi-centered" novels. Women rabbis are even hard to find as more minor characters in a novel.[22]

To date, only four novels have been published in North America which feature women rabbis as central figures. They are, in order of publication: Rhonda Shapiro-Rieser's *A Place of Light* (1983); Alex J. Goldman's *The Rabbi Is a Lady* (1987); Joseph Telushkin's *The Unorthodox Murder of Rabbi Wahl* (1987); and Erich Segal's *Acts of Faith* (1992).[23] In addition, I am aware of only two short stories which feature women rabbis as important figures: "The Rabbi in the Attic" in Eileen Pollack's *The Rabbi in the Attic and Other Stories* (1991)[24] and "Here and Now," by Glenn and Jeanne Gillette and David J. Zucker (1996).[25] Though neither a character in a novel nor a short story nor even set in North America, we can add to this list another "fictional" woman rabbi. This is the major role featured in a British television series created by Laurence Marks and Maurice Gran, a series titled "Love hurts," which aired in 1992 and 1993.[26] While a television series stretches the conventional use of the term "fiction," the experiences of fictional Rabbi Diane Warburg so clearly parallel those of her American counterparts that I have taken the liberty of including her story in this study. In addition, given the dearth of examples of fictional women rabbis, her very presence significantly increases our sample from six to seven women rabbis, thereby adding enormously to the available literature in this field.[27]

Undoubtedly, women rabbis have different goals and priorities than do their male counterparts. Women challenge the "conventional view that the rabbinate must be an all-consuming calling. In the past, male rabbis have often tended to take pride in how many hours they devote to their work." Women, however, emphasize "the ways they have made room in their life for other priorities and have been willing to limit the hours spent in work. Some have chosen to work part time, or serve smaller synagogues or in rabbinic positions that require fewer evening or weekend commitments; others have accepted a lower salary for lighter responsibilities."[28] Now that there are several hundred women rabbis, it is clear that they are found in a variety of situations.

> The fictional women rabbis are wonderfully diverse,[29] but given the paucity of their numbers, they are found in limited situations. All seven women serve congregations, four as the solo rabbi, and three as assistants. Most of these fictional rabbis are articulate, intelligent, and very capable.[30] Yet as women in congregational life, they both bring and face certain gender-specific issues. In these matters, they certainly reflect the stresses and strains of congregational life. Among the issues they face are: will—and if they will, how will—congregants, male and female, accept them; likewise will (how will) their male colleagues accept them; if they already have, or opt to have, children, will their dual roles as mother and rabbi be too large a burden; what of their own spiritual needs?

BALANCE, INTIMACY, AND EMPOWERMENT

Rabbi Janet Marder has addressed the difference between men's and women's goals. In a seminal article (1991) published in the journal "Reform Judaism," Marder explains that women rabbis are striving to achieve "balance," "intimacy," and "empowerment"[31] in their professional lives.

"Balance"

Women rabbis seek a proper "balance" between the demands of their professional life and their personal family life. In an analysis of Marder's article, Professor Ellen M. Umansky (1995) confirms that Rabbi Marder's point is absolutely correct. While not all of the women ordained as rabbis would characterize themselves as feminists, nonetheless "the feminist emphasis on balance has proved to be appealing not just to the vast majority of women rabbis but to a small, but growing number of male rabbis as well."[32] In the public's eye, "*Women rabbis symbolize Western feminism's successful challenge to Judaism.*" Further, whether or not they themselves are comfortable with the mantle of feminism, people do link feminism with women rabbis. "*All women rabbis are seen as advocates for and champions of the external feminist challenge*"[33]

The need for balance is not in itself an inherently "gender-related" issue, and it has much wider implications and applications then merely the rabbinate. That some male rabbis are *also* seeking "balance" between their professional and personal family lives is not in dispute. In terms of the rabbinate, however, it was women rabbis who raised that question first and this is part of their enduring legacy to the profession.

> It is the issue of "balance"—finding time for a reasonable blend between the demands of their professional life and their personal family life—that is most clearly addressed in the women-rabbi fiction. Balance is also related to the questions of how accepting are congregants of women rabbis, generally, and those who get pregnant or who already have children as well as how these women rabbis cope with their dual roles as mother and rabbi; and it is also connected with how these women rabbis deal with their own spirituality.
>
> As with many male rabbis, the incessant time demands of synagogue life likewise are a burden for Rabbi Lynda Klein (*A Place of Light*). She had moved from Talmud student in Jerusalem to rabbinical student in America. From there she moves on to become Rabbi Aaron Stern's assistant. Whatever dreams she had in her mind were quickly dispelled.
>
> Like many of her real-life counterparts, male and female, serving as full-time rabbis of medium and larger congregations, Rabbi Klein struggles unsuccessfully to establish the goal of balance between her professional and personal family lives. Her fictional colleague, Rabbi Deborah Luria (*Acts of Faith*) fares no better. "Almost by definition, a rabbi's duties are performed at abnormal hours. This was doubly difficult for a young single

mother like herself. . . . Deborah was conscientious and compassionate. She was dedicated. And while these qualities were also necessary for the exercise of motherhood, she seemed invariably to fulfill the rabbi's duties, not the parent's."[34]

Rabbis Lynda Klein and Deborah Luria strive to find their place as rabbis as well as women and as mothers. A similar question is faced by Rabbi Sara Weintraub. In the novel, we see her at committee meetings; as a counselor; teacher; making pastoral visits; and leading services.[35] Technically, we only see her over the span of a year, but in that time, Rabbi Weintraub manages to face and comment on many of the major issues facing Jewish life in North America. In alphabetical order they include abortion, AIDS, Black-Jewish relations, cults, homosexuality/lesbianism, Jews-for-Jesus, nursing home abuses, women's liberation, women's ordination, and Zionism. While it is an impressive list, she herself comes to the realization that there is a serious lack of balance in her life.

"Intimacy"

Marder's second point, "intimacy," has resulted in women rabbis choosing smaller pulpits where they can form a close relation with their congregants—and where it is easier to form a sense of community. Whether or not this is directly connected to the fact that almost no women occupy the large American pulpits (defined as 1,000-member families and larger) is still open to question.[36] Surely, it is instructive, however, that in planning a symposium for the tenth anniversary of the Conservative movement's decision to ordain women, "issues of placement emerged as uppermost in the minds of most of those in attendance."[37]

It would seem, however, that at least at this point, women have chosen *not* to aim for the more conventional definition of "upward mobility." Yet the issue is more complicated still. If the larger pulpits do not seem to be available to women, it does not necessarily follow that they will have an easier time to obtain a smaller congregation. Small congregations at times have balked at hiring women rabbis because of the cost of providing for maternity leave.[38]

A fair question to consider is if women serve smaller pulpits because that is their preference or because this *factually* is their only realistic choice?

Indeed, other issues sometimes come into play. One woman rabbi explained that she decided to allow herself a transition period where she would continue her chaplaincy work, teaching and serving a part-time pulpit. Yet it was not an easy decision. "Watching many of my peers go off to various pulpits around the country I did feel pangs. They were the real rabbis. I was choosing to remain on the sidelines."[39] In other situations, a spouse's professional commitments are a factor, or it may be that there are practical family considerations which impact the woman's decision not to seek placement.

> Some [women rabbis] are committed to staying in a particular location because of a husband's well-established career, child custody arrangements, other family ties, or a strong affection for the area. . . . Some do not experience the financial pressure to move to a better paying job because theirs is not the primary income in the family. And some women with young children prefer to remain in a less demanding congregation.[40]

> The issue of "staying in a particular location because of a husband's well-established career" takes an interesting twist in the British television series "Love hurts." Rabbi Diane Warburg is in the process of divorcing her husband, who, in fact, has left London to move to the Provinces. She meets a charismatic Russian Jewish concert pianist and they are clearly mutually attracted. In the event, however, she decides not to follow him on his worldwide tours, and he is unwilling or unable to be based in London.[41]

"Empowerment"

Finally, "empowerment" is defined by most women rabbis as a conscious desire to replace the more traditional hierarchical structures with much greater emphasis on "shared responsibilities, privileges and power."[42] Julie Goss (1990), writing on the "Reworking [of] the Rabbi's Role," explains that women rabbis are consciously reinterpreting the relationship between rabbi and congregant. No longer is it "omnipotent patriarchal leader and humble follower," for the rabbi's role is being redefined. Goss quotes Rabbi Nina Beth Cardin: "It's no longer the distant holy man, but rather that of a hand-holder, an educator to inspire and teach. . . . The idea is to empower the congregant to be a more active member of the Jewish community."[43]

Real-life Rabbi Sally Priesand has expressed her commitment to "establishing what she calls 'creative partnership' with her congregation—and with the board she reports to."[44]

This form of empowerment without sacrificing one's own self in the process is part and parcel of the feminist critique. How male rabbis react to these goals of "intimacy" and "empowerment" will remain to be seen. It is too early to reach clear conclusions, but anecdotal material suggests that a number of male rabbis are consciously opting out of the traditional pattern of upward mobility.

> "Empowerment," the conscious desire to replace the more traditional hierarchical structures with much greater emphasis on "shared responsibilities, privileges and power," is often connected to "intimacy"—choosing smaller pulpits where one can form close relations with congregants and where it is easier to form a sense of community. In large congregations, the power structures are set fairly clearly. These matters have not been dealt with as issues in the seven fictional examples available to us. Of the seven women rabbis, Rabbis Lynda Klein (Shapiro-Rieser's *A Place of Light*), Myra Wahl (Telushkin's *The Unorthodox Murder of Rabbi Wahl*) and Sarah Pollock (Gillette and Zucker's "Here and Now") are assistant rabbis; so these are by definition larger congregations. Rabbi Sara Weintraub (Goldman's *The Rabbi Is a Lady*) serves a congregation described as "one of the most impressive synagogues on the East Coast."[45] It probably has well over 700 or more member families, clearly a substantial entity. The membership of Rabbi Diane Warburg's (Marks and Gran's "Love hurts") congregation is not defined. Using the size of the sanctuary as a gauge, as an educated guess I would place it at least at 300 families. Rabbi Deborah Luria (Segal's *Acts of Faith*) sets her sights as rabbi of a "relatively young and growing community" which has a sanctuary which holds "nine hundred worshippers."[46]

So we might assume that there are at least 500-member families. These are not modestly sized congregations which allow for intimacy. Only Rabbi Marion Bloomgarten (Pollack's "The Rabbi in the Attic") serves a small congregation.

NON-CONGREGATIONAL RABBINIC POSITIONS

Many women choose to explore rabbinic positions outside of the traditional congregational structure. Some move from the pulpit to religious administration, Hillel or chaplaincy, others go directly into those fields. Jessica R. Davidson (1991) suggests that while most male ordainees head straight to congregations and remain as pulpit rabbis for the rest of their careers, about two-thirds of the women rabbis opt to work part-time or in non-congregational jobs.[47] Women turn away from congregational life because it just becomes too difficult to find a way to achieve a true balance between their professional and private lives. As we have seen above, this problem is true in the factual world of the women's rabbinate, and it is also reflected in the fictional rabbinate.

> Rabbi Deborah Luria, in Erich Segal's novel *Acts of Faith*, finds that the incessant time demands of the rabbinate and specifically the toll it takes on her son prove too great a difficulty. Though outwardly successful, after serving for a few years, she relinquishes her position as a congregational rabbi and becomes a teacher.[48] Likewise, Rabbi Diane Warburg ("Love hurts") chooses to take an extended leave of absence from the rabbinate. She speaks of going into social work or perhaps turning to the academic world.[49]

ACCEPTANCE OF THE WOMEN RABBIS

Clearly women rabbis are being *more* accepted as rabbis as time goes by. Yet, having said this, with some few exceptions where they serve as the solo rabbi of a sizable congregation (though as yet not among the largest), women generally serve either as associate and assistant rabbis, as rabbis in smaller congregations, or oftentimes in non-congregational posts such as professors, chaplains, professional educators, administrators,

Hillel Directors (the Jewish group on the university campus), and in other forms of organizational life. Judith Hauptman writes of the instance of smaller, outlying synagogues which "find themselves faced with the choice of a qualified man and *a more qualified woman* who will not be employed by a larger or better-located congregation because of residual prejudice [my emphasis]."[50]

In the fictional examples available, we find both supporters and detractors among the congregants on the very issue of women rabbis serving congregations. Rabbi Sara Weintraub's board of trustees has very mixed feelings about offering her the position, though the women's group, the "Sisterhood generally liked the idea of a woman rabbi."[51] When Rabbi Diane Warburg meets someone who is surprised that she is serving a congregation, she explains that her synagogue is "very progressive."[52] Rabbi Myra Wahl is in serious trouble with her congregational board, not because she is female, but rather because she is perceived as having such politically extreme viewpoints and her tendency to express her ideas in a caustic and acerbic manner. She has expended the necessary goodwill to succeed in her post.[53]

Rabbi Marion Bloomgarten's congregation hires her out of desperation. They are an Orthodox congregation but have had such a bad name that the Orthodox seminary will not deal with them. When the search committee seeks a candidate from that Orthodox institution, they are told: "Ten rabbis in twelve years! . . . you pay less and treat worse than any congregation in New York—in United States, perhaps!"[54] Their reputation is also known to the Conservative movement, and they will not offer them the name of a candidate either. Since they have no choice they turn to the Reform rabbinate. Nonetheless, at the end of the story, she does win over the hearts and minds of most of her congregation.

Turning to the question of acceptance by male rabbinic colleagues, this question appears only briefly in the literature. That Lynda Klein, Myra Wahl, and Sarah Pollock are featured as assistant rabbis to male colleagues indicates the tacit approval of their rabbinate, at least in the Reform movement. In *The Rabbi Is a Lady*, Rabbi Sara Weintraub discusses her pos-

> sible rabbinate with a colleague who is described as "one of a new breed of Orthodox rabbis." Rabbi David Hollens, however, explains to her that he cannot have any "*official*" association with her.[55] In that same novel, we also find some of the arguments that were debated among the Conservative movement before they voted to ordain women.[56]
>
> As noted earlier in the novel *Rabbi, Rabbi*, reference is made to an Orthodox rabbi who lambastes the Conservative movement for choosing to ordain women.[57] Reform Rabbi Bloomgarten, at least initially, is rejected by her Orthodox predecessor. He calls her "an a-bom-in-a-tion" [sic].[58] At the end of the story, however, they achieve a reasonable relationship.

Even when women have succeeded in achieving leadership positions within the Jewish community, they find that their competence and/or their executive methods and are frequently challenged. Sylvia Barack Fishman (1993) reports that both "female rabbis and female federation executives have found that their fiduciary skills, especially, are the subject of skepticism from male congregants or colleagues. Female rabbis report ongoing paternalism from some congregants, which sometimes expresses itself in a kind of avuncular, protective stance. . . . Additionally, female rabbis seem to experience fairly high rates of divorce."[59]

Paternalism and high rates of divorce are only a couple aspects of the difficulties with which women rabbis have to deal in terms of their acceptance. Sexual harassment appears to be rife. Janet Marder refers to a 1993 study of women rabbis conducted by the American Jewish Congress. It suggests that "73% of the respondents said that they had been sexually harassed at least once or twice in the course of their work; 24% reported being harassed once a month or more. Of those reporting harassment, 60% said it was by laypeople; 25% said it came from other rabbis." Marder goes on to explain that women rabbis have reported that they are the recipients of unwelcome letters, of unwelcome phone calls, and inappropriate gifts from male congregants. Some female rabbinic students "report offensive and demeaning remarks as well as unwelcome physical contact of a sexual nature." Even allowing for the difficulty in properly defining "sexual harassment," and the complexity of power dynamics in the synagogue, where rabbis are both spiritual leaders and employees who "may on occasion feel quite vulnerable in relation to their congregational leadership,"[60] it is clear that women rabbis—and male rabbis as well—are subject to sexual harassment and even to false accusations of sexual harassment.

THE DUAL ROLES OF RABBI AND MOTHER

The "burden" of motherhood frequently is discussed in the literature dealing with women rabbis. "But now, Rabbi B . . . is leaving her . . . congregation. The pressures of the pulpit, coupled with those of motherhood, have proved too much of a strain, at least for the time being."[61] A number of women colleagues, however, are critical of their counterparts who limit their work to spend more time with their children.

> "A lot of women are on the 'mommy track,'" says one woman rabbi, herself single and childless. "They've opted not to kill themselves professionally. They've accepted a lower salary in exchange for a lighter schedule. I understand why, but I don't think it's good for women. As long as women rabbis stay on the 'mommy track,' they'll never set the world on fire."[62]
>
> *A Place of Light* is set mostly in the late 1970s. It highlights a problem that women rabbis faced and continue to face. What will happen to their careers if they become pregnant? What would the congregation do? Certainly this is a fear of Rabbi Lynda Klein. She assumes that pregnancy is incompatible with the time constraints of the congregation. While a real concern,[63] the difficulty is overcome. At the close of the novel, we learn that Lynda is pregnant, and further she has been elected to succeed Rabbi Stern when he opts for early retirement.[64]

One would hope that she has a better experience than that reported about real-life Rabbi Elise Goldstein. "When . . . Rabbi Goldstein went on maternity leave—which had been written into her contract—she was surprised to discover that the synagogue expected her to officiate at funerals and answer her mail during the eight-week leave. When she refused, synagogue members were furious."[65] Coincidentally, Rabbi Goldstein no longer serves as the rabbi of that congregation. She opted to leave the congregational rabbinate and move to an administrative post in Jewish studies.

In an article published in 1995, it is noted that the Reform movement has taken a proactive stance on this issue of maternity leave. "The most recent guidebook for Rabbinic Congregational Relations includes a recommendation of two months paid maternity leave plus accrued vacation. It is far from perfect, *and often congregations ignore it* [my emphasis]."[66]

The question of how the woman rabbi will deal with her dual roles of rabbi and mother is an issue that congregational Boards also need to face. When the Board of Trustees is debating whether to offer the position to Rabbi Sara Weintraub (*The Rabbi Is a Lady*), one of her supporters muses that the rabbinate requires great stamina. "The job of a rabbi is a killing one. And Sara, if she's offered the position and accepts, *will* give herself. It's in her nature. But she has two children to raise . . . can she be a good rabbi and a good mother at the same time? Isn't it asking too much of a human being?"[67]

This same question "Isn't it asking too much of a human being"—to be a full-time parent and a full-time rabbi—is never raised in terms of a male rabbi. That surely is a telling point in its own right.

In the novel, Rabbi Sara Weintraub asks herself if she can be both rabbi and mother. At one point we read the following description: "Sara stopped. Felt a twinge. She was alone. A single. Career? Yes. But she . . . felt the bitterness of her private reality. . . . She struggled with her inner self."[68] "Sara's mind was . . . tumultuous. . . . Woman or career?"[69]

That lack of balance is underscored by her children. Her teenage daughter says to her: "You're never home anymore. You go from one meeting to another. You're not like a mother anymore. . . .

"You've cared more about everybody and everything else."

Rabbi Weintraub openly admits to her children, "I've let things run away with me."[70]

In the British series "Love hurts," Rabbi Diane Warburg concedes that she works unsociable hours, mostly evenings and weekends.[71] It is quite clear that she is struggling with her role as rabbi, wife, and mother. This becomes even more exacerbated after she and her husband separate and she has to

> function as a single mother. There is little balance in her life. She says at one point, "I'm only on a twenty four hour day."[72]

In the factual—as opposed to the fictional—world, some women rabbis find a different solution to the problem. Though it was a difficult choice, real-life "Rabbi [Sally] Priesand realized she couldn't handle family and pulpit, so she decided to do without the family. . . . 'I realized I couldn't handle both. I devote 24 hours a day to this congregation. It wouldn't be fair otherwise.'"[73]

SPIRITUALITY

Women rabbis—no less than their male counterparts—find themselves working many long hours. There is a great deal of anecdotal material which suggests that two areas which were highly valued when they were in rabbinical school—time for study as well as time for personal meditation and prayer (as opposed to the "official" moments when the rabbi is leading services)—too often simply get squeezed aside. This problem of finding, or making, time for one's own spiritual life is dealt with in the fiction.

> Rabbi Lynda Klein (*A Place of Light*) believed that in becoming a rabbi, she would be free to pursue her sense of her own destiny. "She'd sought to take the sparks of Jerusalem, gather them and make them flame. She'd exile herself from the ancient city to free herself of its walls. But here, in this modern city, she had found new walls: the walls of the rabbinate."[74] In the early days, she had found time to pray, even if it was late at night in the synagogue. Yet the real demands of the rabbinate have interfered in her plans.
>
> As the novel relates, "there was no time. The congregation waited, a jealous lover. Hundreds of people wanted her to inspire them, to lead them to God, or prayer, or to their own souls."[75]

As noted earlier, there are now hundreds of women rabbis. There are dozens and dozens of articles written by and about women rabbis.

With but seven characters there is a limited group from which to offer fictional examples.

These fictional accounts, however, do share similar visions in their focus on the joys and satisfactions as well as the burdens and demands of the congregational rabbinate. They also suggest that women rabbis can serve the Jewish community in an effective manner. In addition to portraying the rabbinate as a difficult profession, they also suggest that the rabbi (female or male) fills a very important place in her (or his) community. She can fulfill many roles: a spiritual leader, a teacher, pastor, and a voice of conscience. These fictional works also reflect the reality that the rabbi has to make difficult choices. How does one "balance" the real needs of family life with professional demands? When and how does one say "no" to the ongoing call of a congregation?

In the coming years, we probably shall see more fictional examples which depict women rabbis. With this additional material, we might be able to offer examples where women take part-time positions; are portrayed in non-congregational positions; introduce new rituals; and at least question how successfully they deal with the issues of "balance," "intimacy" and "empowerment" in a congregational setting.

NOTES

1. Nadell, P. S. (1995). "The Women Who Would Be Rabbis," in *Gender and Judaism: The Transformation of Tradition*, ed. T. M. Rudavsky (New York and London: New York University Press), p. 126. See also Umansky, E. M. (1996). "Women's Journey toward Rabbinic Ordination," in *Women Rabbis: Exploration and Celebration*, ed. Gary P. Zola (Cincinnati: HUC-JIR Rabbinic Alumni Association Press), pp. 27–41.

2. Bitton-Jackson, L. (1995). "New Roles for Jewish Women," in *Events and Movements in Modern Judaism*, ed. Raphael Patai and Emanuel S. Goldsmith (New York: Paragon House), pp. 291–292. The first woman rabbi ordained in the United States was Sally Priesand (1972), ordained by the Reform movement's Hebrew Union College-Jewish Institute of Religion. Sandy Sasso (1974) was the first woman ordained by the Reconstructionist movement's Reconstructionist Rabbinical College, and Amy Eilberg (1985) was the first woman ordained by the Conservative movement's Jewish Theological Seminary. Regina Jonas, technically the first woman rabbi was privately ordained in Germany in 1935 and practiced primarily in homes for the elderly.

3. Hauptman, J. (1995). "Conservative Judaism: The Ethical Challenge of Feminist Change," in *The Americanization of the Jews*, ed. Robert M. Seltzer and Norman J. Cohen (New York and London: New York University Press), p. 298.

4. Hauptman, p. 306, n. 6. For more information on Ezrat Nashim see the article by Hyman, P. E. (1995). "Ezrat Nashim and the Emergence of a New Jewish Feminism," as well as the references in Hyman's article in *The Americanization of the Jews*, ed. Robert M. Seltzer and Norman J. Cohen (New York and London: New York University Press), pp. 284–295.

5. Hauptman, p. 299; See also Hyman, pp. 285–286.

6. Hauptman, p. 307 n. 13.

7. Hauptman, pp. 300, 302. See also the articles by Fishman, S. B. (1989). "The Impact of Feminism on American Jewish Life" (especially pp. 50–54,) in *American Jewish Year Book 1989*, ed. David Singer and Ruth R. Seldin, vol. 89 (New York: American Jewish Committee and Philadelphia: Jewish Publication Society); and Wertheimer, J. (1989). "Recent Trends in American Judaism" in *American Jewish Year Book 1989*, ed. David Singer and Ruth R. Seldin, vol. 89 (New York: American Jewish Committee and Philadelphia: Jewish Publication Society, especially pp. 130–134). Further information is found in Simon Greenberg, ed. *The Ordination of Women as Rabbis: Studies and Responsa* (New York: Jewish Theological Seminary, 1988).

8. Hyman, p. 290. See also Fishman, S. B. (1993). *A Breath of Life: Feminism in the American Jewish Community* (New York: Free Press), pp. 215–216.

9. Greenberg, B. (1984). "Will There Be Orthodox Women Rabbis?" *Judaism* 33:1 (Winter): 23–33. Greenberg's article appeared alongside a variety of viewpoints. This particular issue of *Judaism* was devoted to the question of "Women As Rabbis." Even a decade later, Greenberg remained hopeful that Orthodoxy would ordain women. "Is Now the Time for Orthodox Women Rabbis?" *Moment* 18:6 (December 1993), pp. 50–53, 74.

10. Kane actually uses the word "modern-Orthodox." Kane, A. (1995). *Rabbi, Rabbi* (New York: Saint Martin's), p. 121.

11. Kane, pp. 122–123.

12. Schwartzfuchs, S. (1993). *A Concise History of the Rabbinate* (Oxford, UK and Cambridge, USA: Blackwell), p. 129.

13. Geller, L. (1995). "From Equality to Transformation: the Challenge of Women's Rabbinic Leadership" in *Gender and Judaism: The Transformation of Tradition*, ed. T. M. Rudavsky, (New York and London: New York University Press), p. 244. In a footnote in Umansky's article "Women's Journey toward Rabbinic Ordination" it states that as of June 1995, 239 women have been ordained by HUC-JIR, p. 36.

14. Sarah, E. (1994). "Introduction" in *Hear Our Voice*, ed. Sybil Sheridan (London: SCM Press), p. 1.

15. Fishman, S. B., "Impact of Feminism," p. 50.

16. Marder, J. (1991). "How Women are Changing the Rabbinate." *Reform Judaism* (Summer): 5.

17. "Reconstructionist Rabbinical College 1996–97 Fact Sheet." The actual figures are 185: 110 men, 75 women.

18. David A. Teutsch, personal communication to David J. Zucker, December 12, 1995.

19. Geller, p. 244.

20. Cardin, N. B. (1995). "The First Generation of the Women's Rabbinate." *Conservative Judaism* 48:1 (Fall): 19.

21. Stern, E. W. (1993). "Practical Realities of the Rabbinate" (paper presented at the Women's Rabbinic Network Conference, Oakland, Calif., March 21–24), 26.

22. In Tarr's *So Help Me God!* Isaca Zion is a rabbinical student at the Reform seminary, and at the end of the novel she is ordained, but she is a minor character. Tarr, H. (1979). *So Help Me God!* (New York: Times Books), p. 237. In Appel's *The Rabbi of Casino Boulevard*, a minor character is a woman who is studying for the rabbinate, Appel, A. (1986). *The Rabbi of Casino Boulevard* (New York: Saint Martin's), p. 209.

23. Shapiro-Rieser, R. (1983). *A Place of Light* (New York: Pocket); Goldman, A. J. (1987). *The Rabbi Is a Lady* (New York: Hippocrene); Telushkin, J. (1987). *The Unorthodox Murder of Rabbi Wahl* (New York: Bantam); Segal, E. (1992). *Acts of Faith* (New York: Bantam). [I have referred to these books earlier, but I list them here for easier reference.]

24. Pollack, E. (1991). "The Rabbi in the Attic," in *The Rabbi in the Attic and Other Stories* (Harrison, New York and Encino, California: Delphinium Books), pp. 85–120.

25. Gillette, G. and J. and Zucker, D. J. (1996). "Here and Now." *Jewish Spectator* 61:2 (Fall): 43–49.

26. Marks, L. and Gran, M. (1992–1993). (Allan McKeown and Joanna Willett Executive Producers), "Love hurts" (London: Alomo Productions, SelecTV). My special thanks to Joanna Willett for sending me copies of all 20 of the videos where Rabbi Diane Warburg appeared as a character.

27. It is noteworthy that among the four novels, three of the authors are male. Whatever else, this means that we are reading a male's view of a female rabbi. Coincidentally, two of these novelists, Goldman and Telushkin, are rabbis, and Shapiro-Rieser is a rabbi's wife. In terms of the short stories, Zucker, the co-author with the Gillettes, is a rabbi. While none can claim to be a woman rabbi writing about women rabbis, these particular stories are being written with, and certainly reflect, an "insider's" experience. The British series, created by Marks and Gran, did feature both male and female script writers. The scripts were written by various authors.

Series 1, episodes 1, 2: Lawrence Marks and Maurice Gran, "Crawling From The Wreckage," "Take It To The Limit."
episodes 3, 4: Sam Lawrence, "Walk Right Back," "Relative Values."
episode 5: Richard LeParmentier and Paddy Fletcher, "Cured.."
episode 6: David Humphries, "Stormy Weather."
episode 7: Sam Lawrence, "A Day In The Life."
episode 8: Richard LeParmentier and Paddy Fletcher, "Charity Begins At Home."
episodes 9 and 10: Alan Clews, "Who's Sorry Now?," "Let's Do It.."
Series 2, episode 1: Lawrence Marks and Maurice Gran, "Strictly Business."
episode 2: Alan Clews, "Cold Comfort."
episode 3 and 4: Sam Lawrence, "The Max Factor," "Your Money Or Your Life."
episode 5: Catherine Johnson, "Band Of Gold."
episode 6: Sam Lawrence, "Face The Music."
episode 7: Catherine Johnson, "If The Cap Fits."
episode 8: Sam Lawrence, "Just A Bit Of Business."
episode 9: Lawrence Marks and Maurice Gran, "For A Few Dollars More."
episode 10: Sam Lawrence, "Love For Sale."

Though none of the writers were rabbis, a woman rabbi was consulted about the authenticity of the scripts. The rabbi was Rabbi Jacqueline Tabick of the West London Synagogue. (Verbal communication from Joanna Willett to the David J. Zucker, August 1995.) Likewise the figure of Rabbi Diane Warburg—particularly her academic background and her being a popular figure on British radio and TV—reflected a real person, Rabbi Julia Neuberger.

28. Geller, p. 247.

29. Rabbi Lynda Klein (Shapiro-Rieser, *A Place of Light*) comes from a secular background, has been married for a few years, and is recently pregnant. Rabbi Sara Weintraub (Goldman, *The Rabbi Is a Lady*) is a rabbi's daughter, is the mother of two adolescent children, and is recently widowed. Rabbi Myra Wahl (Telushkin, *The Unorthodox Murder of Rabbi Wahl*) and Rabbi Marion Bloomgarten (Pollack, "The Rabbi in the Attic") are from secular backgrounds and are single. Rabbi Sarah Pollock (Gillettes and Zucker, "Here and Now") is married; she comes from a secular background. Rabbi Deborah Luria (Segal, *Acts of Faith*) also is a rabbi's daughter, and she is a single mother. Finally, Rabbi Diane Warburg (Marks and Gran, "Love hurts") presumably comes from a secular background, is a mother of three adolescent/pre-adolescent children, and is in the process of divorcing her husband.

30. Rabbi Marion Bloomgarten, however, is described by the placement

director as having "a good heart, not brainless . . . but no head for study." Pollack, p. 98.

31. Marder, "How Women are Changing the Rabbinate," p. 5.

32. Umansky, p. 272. This point is also brought out by Peter J. Rubinstein, (1990) where he states that some "recent graduates have sought part-time positions, or positions that will allow more private time, affording them the opportunity to stay home with children." Peter J. Rubinstein, "The Next Century," in *Tanu Rabbanan: Our Rabbis Taught CCAR Yearbook 1989, vol. 2* ed. Joseph B. Glaser, (New York: Central Conference of American Rabbis, 1990), p. 150.

33. Cardin, pp. 16–17.

34. Segal, pp. 385–386.

35. Goldman, Committee meetings: p. 79; counseling: p. 198 ff.; teacher: p. 105 ff.; pastoral visit, p. 229 ff.; services, p. 85 ff..

36. Umansky, p. 273. See also Geller, p. 247.

37. Kensky, A. (1985). "Women in the Rabbinate: The First Ten Years." *Conservative Judaism* 48:1 (Fall): 4.

38. Goss, J. (1990). "Women In The Pulpit: Reworking the Rabbi's Role." *Lilith* 15:4 (Fall): 19.

39. Springer, M. (1995). "A Rabbinate on the Fringe." *Conservative Judaism* 48:1 (Fall): 85.

40. Marder, "How Women are Changing the Rabbinate," p. 7.

41. Laurence Marks and Maurice Gran, "Love hurts," Series 2, Episode 10, "Love for Sale."

42. Umansky, p. 274.

43. Goss, pp. 16–17. See also Christine Stutz, "Natural Wonder: Gila Ruskin redefines the role of the rabbi." "Baltimore Jewish Times" 227:8 (Feb. 23, 1996), pp. 52–56.

44. Sally Priesand quoted in Goss, p. 17.

45. Goldman, p. 47.

46. Segal, pp. 352, 383.

47. Jessica R. Davidson, "When the Rabbi is a Woman." *Congress Monthly* 58:6 (September/October 1991), pp. 12, 11.

48. Segal, p. 520.

49. Marks and Gran, "Love hurts," Series 2, Episode 10, "Love For Sale."

50. Hauptman, p. 302.

51. Goldman, pp. 18 ff., 75.

52. Marks and Gran, "Love hurts," Series 1, Episode 1, "Crawling From The Wreckage."

53. Telushkin, *The Unorthodox Murder of Rabbi Wahl*, pp. 16 ff.

54. Pollack, p. 96.

55. Goldman, pp. 51–52.

56. Goldman, pp. 38 ff., 186 ff.

57. Kane, pp. 121 ff., 216.

58. Pollack, p. 109.

59. Fishman, S. B. *A Breath of Life*, p. 218.

60. Marder, "Sexual Misconduct: How Vulnerable Are Synagogues?" p. 20. See Cowan, J. R. (1993) "Survey Finds 70% of Women Rabbis Sexually Harrassed," *Moment* 18:5 (October), pp. 34–37.

61. Davidson, p. 10. Marder likewise explains, "Some women rabbis have found it impossible to arrive at a satisfying balance between work and family demands. Their solution has been to leave the congregational rabbinate, at least until their children are older." Marder, "How Women are Changing the Rabbinate," p. 6.

62. Marder, "How Women are Changing the Rabbinate," p. 6.

63. Shapiro-Rieser, p. 266.

64. Shapiro-Rieser, pp. 242 ff.; 294.

65. Davidson, p. 12.

66. Geller, p. 248.

67. Goldman, p. 21. The phrase, the "job of a rabbi is a killing one" is not lightly stated. Sara's late husband, Rabbi Sam Weintraub "had died after a brief illness. His heart gave way," p. 1. See the discussion in Chapter 12 (Rabbis on the Rabbinate) about congregations "eating up their rabbis."

68. Goldman, p. 264.

69. Goldman, p. 267.

70. Goldman, p. 272.

71. Marks and Gran, "Love hurts," Series 1, Episode 1 "Crawling From The Wreckage."

72. Marks and Gran, "Love hurts," Series 2, Episode 1 "Strictly Business." Later on, Diane states quite clearly that she is struggling as a single mother, that she does not have sufficient time for her children, "Love hurts," Series 2, Episode 4 "Your Money Or Your Life."

73. Quoted in Davidson, p. 12.

74. Shapiro-Rieser, p. 242.

75. Shapiro-Rieser, p. 243.

8

The Rabbi's Family

PARENTS

In his study of rabbinical students of the three major "mainstream" rabbinical seminaries, Yeshiva University (Orthodox), the Jewish Theological Seminary (Conservative), and the Hebrew Union College-Jewish Institute of Religion (Reform), Charles S. Liebman (1968) suggested that students clearly follow in the religious pattern set by their families. When asked about the religious affiliation of their fathers in the year before they entered the seminary, 85 percent of the fathers of Yeshiva University students belonged to Orthodox synagogues. At the Jewish Theological Seminary, close to 70 percent were affiliated with Conservative congregations, and at the two campuses of the Hebrew Union College-Jewish Institute of Religion, a clear majority were associated with the Reform movement. Liebman further suggests that these findings bear out the tendency of seminaries to recruit from amongst their own groupings. This reflects a nearly full acculturation of mainstream varieties of American Judaism.[1] Though most Conservative and Reform rabbis today are products of their own movements, the pattern for both

JTS and HUC-JIR is to attract students who come from homes where the families are more to the left (less religiously observant) than to the right on the religious spectrum. A high number (70 percent) of these students described themselves as *more* religiously observant then their fathers.[2]

Nearly 30 years later, Liebman's findings are borne out by the recent study of a typical American Jewish community, Dan and Lavinia Cohn-Sherbok's *The American Jew: Voices from an American Jewish Community* (1994). Here we see that wherever the rabbis sit on the continuum of Orthodoxy, from "Sectarian" to "Centrist" to "Traditional" Orthodox, the more likely he will come from an Orthodox background. By the same token, the more progressive the rabbis are, the more likely that they will be more religiously observant than the practice of their parents' home. The right-of-"Centrist" Orthodox Rabbi comes from a strictly Orthodox family; so does the Hasidic Rabbi, and in fact his father was the local Hasidic Rabbi before him; the "Traditional" Orthodox Rabbi's father was a "modern Orthodox" rabbi; the Conservative Rabbi came from a fairly non-religious household; the Reform rabbi's family were active in the Reform movement, as was the family of his Associate, but their fathers were not rabbis. The woman rabbi interviewed mentioned that her parents belonged to a Conservative synagogue, but they were secularists.[3]

> Among the fictional rabbis, in general, similar trends can be found. On the whole, Orthodox rabbis come from Orthodox homes. Conservative and Reform rabbis vary in the standard of religiosity found in their parents' homes. Orthodox Rabbi Leo Berdick (*The Strong Hand*) studied at the Rabbi Isaac Elchanan Rabbinical Seminary at Yeshiva University; his father is a rabbi. The father of Orthodox Rabbi Abraham Cohen (*Days of Judgment*), while not a rabbi himself, does attend Talmud classes at the Rivington Street Synagogue.[4] Exceptions can be found. Orthodox Rabbi Jerry Goldkorn (*The Rabbi of Lud*) speaks of his coming from a secular family.[5] That the father of Hasidic Rabbi Yussel Fetner (*God's Ear*) is himself a rabbi is absolutely central to the novel.[6] Though he serves a Conservative congregation and studied at the Conservative seminary, Rabbi David Small (the Weekday *Rabbi* series) explains that his roots are in traditional Judaism and that both

his father and grandfather were rabbis.[7] Conservative Rabbi Arthur Bloom (*The Rabbi of Casino Boulevard*) does not come from a rabbinic home nor does Conservative rabbi Seymour Sonnshein (*Rachel, the Rabbi's Wife*).[8] Conservative Rabbi Dana Selig (*That Day the Rabbi Left Town*) mentions that his parents were not the least bit religious and did not even go to synagogue on the High Holidays.[9] In Chapter 7 (Women Rabbis), it was noted that the father of Conservative Rabbi Sara Weintraub (*The Rabbi Is a Lady*) was himself a rabbi, as was the father of Reform Rabbi Deborah Luria (*Acts of Faith*). Of the other five women rabbis, four are Reform Jews and coincidentally come from non-rabbinic homes, and Rabbi Warburg in England, a Progressive Jew, also is from a non-rabbinic home. Reform Rabbis Joshua Kaye (*The Rabbi and the Nun*), Gideon Abel (*Heaven Help Us!*), David Gordon (*The Temple*), and Michael Kind (*The Rabbi*) all come from non-rabbinic homes.[10]

A recent study of the Rabbinical School at the Jewish Theological Seminary shows some interesting trends. While in 1967 only 55 percent of the students were the sons of American-born fathers, now students are the grandchildren of immigrants. Furthermore, while 85 percent of the students' parents were professionals today (as opposed to 34 percent in the 1940s), there has been a radical decline in the number of students whose fathers are employed as professionals serving the Jewish community. In 1967, close to one-fifth of the students came from a home where the father was a Jewish professional. In the late 1980s, that figure had dropped to seven percent. The authors of the report explained "that the tradition of service to the Jewish community that characterized many rabbinic families in the past is disappearing in the Conservative movement."[11]

In his study in the 1970s, Lenn noticed that while the number of Reform rabbinical students who were themselves the children of rabbis had increased in recent years from 10 percent to 13 percent, it was quite clear that the overwhelming majority of students came from non-rabbinic homes. Parents are often ambivalent, or even hostile, to a child's entering the rabbinate. Not without a touch of irony did Dan Cohn-Sherbok title his autobiography *Not a Job For a Nice Jewish Boy*. His father, a prosperous doctor, was concerned about his son's decision to enter the rabbinate. "It was simply unthinkable that the son of a successful surgeon should become a rabbi. This was a career for the less advantaged." In a conversation with his wife, the doctor said: "A rabbi! What kind of a job is that? You can't make a living being a rabbi!"[12] A woman rabbi is quoted as having a similar reaction from her parents. She explained it this way: "Becoming a rabbi had very little to do with my parents, that's for sure. I grew up in a Conservative congregation in Phoenix, Arizona. My family is entirely secular and for my parents any form of religious observance is a waste of time. My father thinks the best thing a rabbi can do is to get a proper job."[13]

In the fiction we find that parents have a variety of reactions to their children entering the rabbinate. Some are opposed, others are more resigned to their child's decision, and still others are delighted. When Joshua Kaye (*The Rabbi and the Nun*) tells his father that he intends to become a rabbi, his father is appalled. "'You want to help the Jewish people?' his father said rhetorically, 'There's only one way to do it—Israel. Religion? We Jews today have only one true religion—Zionism. A rabbi? Liberal, Orthodox, it makes no different. It's all an anachronism.'"[14] Seymour Sonnshein's father in *Rachel, The Rabbi's Wife* is no more encouraging. "You become a rabbi, you have to learn to beg."[15] Rabbi Gideon Able (*Heaven Help Us!*) explains that on the night before his ordination, his father came up to him to ask: "Gideon, you're actually going through with this?" Rabbi Able goes on to explain that he did not have a more sympathetic reaction from his mother. "When I announced my plans to enter the rabbinate, she said nothing at first, and then, 'If I seem shocked, Gideon, it isn't because I'm not happy with your choice; I am if you are. It's just that people we know—well, they don't *do* that sort of thing.' Which, of course, is the curtain line in *Hedda Gabler* after the woman has committed suicide."[16]

Reuven Malter's father (*The Chosen*) would have preferred him to go into university teaching but acknowledges that he will be a good rabbi.[17] Rabbi Leo Berdick (*The Strong Hand*) comes from a line of rabbis. His rabbi-father wonders aloud if he had not been too much of an influence on his son.[18] On the other hand, the parents of Rabbis David Gordon (Arkady Leokum's *The Temple*) and David Hartman (Howard Fast's *The Outsider*) are thrilled that their sons have chosen this profession.[19]

SPOUSE

Until fairly recently, when one would speak of the rabbi's spouse, it clearly meant the *rebbetzin*, the "rabbi's wife." The term often was used as a compliment. She was, to use the Biblical phrase (Genesis 2:18), his "*ezer k'negdo*"—his helping hands (literally his "helper opposite him"). The rabbi's wife was often idealized. She was thought of as a person who was knowledgeable in the ways of the world of human beings as well as having a reasonable knowledge of the details of religious life. Naturally, she managed the rabbi's home, handled the family budget, reared their children, and was a model hostess. In America it was "expected" that the *rebbetzin* would be a member—and an active member at that—of Sisterhood, the women's auxiliary group of the synagogue. More often than not, it was also expected that she would be an officer of Sisterhood. Variations of these expectations included the ideas that she would be a teacher in the religious school and/or active in the Jewish community.

By the same token, just as the rabbinate elicited reactions from the Jewish community which ranged from respect to disdain, from honor to mockery, so this also was true of the role of the rabbi's wife. On the whole, however, just as the rabbinate was considered a very honorable profession, so likewise was the *rebbetzin* viewed in a positive light.

"The ideal *rebbetzin* was dramatized in *Awakened*, a novel published in [1954] . . ." explains Shuly Rubin Schwartz in her insightful article on "The *Rebbetzin* in Twentieth-Century America" (1995).

> *Rebbetzin* Ellen Rosen is depicted as a respectful, caring helpmate deeply involved in the lives of the congregants, though always in a secondary, supportive way. She makes pastoral calls with her husband, enhances a wartime wedding with song and refreshment, and befriends a beleaguered convert. In the final climatic scene, when the son of an influential congregant disappears just before his bar mitzvah, it is Ellen who knows where to find him, who speaks to him, understands him, and gives him the courage to return. The *rebbetzin* makes things right.[20]

A typical description of Rebbetzin Ellen Rosen (*Awakened*) in action shows her at the synagogue on a wintry cold Friday evening just before the services are to start at eight. One of the congregants, Mr. Jacobson,

> feeling even more crotchety than usual, stepped in from the cold darkness. . . . At ten minutes to eight, Ellen Rosen came through the door of the rabbi's study and, when she saw Mr. Jacobson, a look of welcome and pleasure kindled her face. She came to him and shook hands. She asked about his rheumatism, about his daughter, Gussie, in Kansas City, and she chided him for not wearing a scarf against the winter cold.[21]

Yet, by the 1970s, Schwartz continues, in

> the wake of the women's movement, and as part of the general anti-establishment sentiment of the age, the term *rebbetzin* lost its distinguished status. The demythologizing of leaders characteristic of the era affected rabbis and *rebbetzins* as well. The term *rebbetzin* began to be replaced first with the more neutral "rabbi's wife," a term that carried less baggage but also less honor, and then, soon after, with the politically correct and more accurate "rabbi's spouse" (though one male rabbinic spouse suggested the term "rebbitz").[22]

Call her (or him) what you like, the fact was that oftentimes congregations certainly had clear expectations of what they wanted from the rebbetzin. Said simply, in many, many congregations the rabbi's wife was considered to be an extension of her husband. As was iterated by a rebbetzin at a recent convocation (1996) on the "Changing Role of Clergy Spouses"—a program which was part of the wider series, "The Feminization of the Rabbinate and the Cantorate" sponsored by the Denver Institute of Jewish Studies—congregations often assume that when they hire the rabbi they have in fact hired two religious leaders at one salary. Details may differ from congregation to congregation, and with the size of the congregation (the smaller the congregation, the larger the expectations), but the role of the rebbetzin often was (is) seen as inextricably linked to that of the rabbi.

In his 1972 study of the Reform rabbinate, Lenn suggested that rebbetzins are clearly ambivalent about the rabbinical world. Nearly half of the wives polled (there were only rabbinic-wives then) said that if they had the choice, they would *not* have their husbands become rabbis if they could have done it all over again. By the same token, well over 90 percent felt their husbands were appreciated by most who knew him, and nearly 90 percent felt that he enjoyed his work as a rabbi.[23]

Seventy-five percent of rebbetzins in that study almost always attended Sabbath, Festival and special services, and a mere four percent said they rarely attended. When he reported that 90 percent of the wives accompanied their husbands to social affairs, the author quipped: "And why not? Would many have much opportunity to go out with their husbands otherwise?" Some 84 percent claim to be "reasonably active" in synagogue affairs, and virtually all (94 percent) held membership in Sisterhood.[24]

Being the rabbi's spouse, however, is a lonely life. Lenn quotes three "overview comments" from rebbetzins. "A Rabbi and his wife cannot have friends inside the congregation—it must be friendly, but impersonal." "My experience has taught me to be nice to everyone, but not too close to anyone." "No confidants—never!"[25] In real life, this means that the rabbinate is, for rabbi and spouse, a very lonely existence.

> The previous set of quotations are neatly summed up in a dialogue between a retired rabbi, a man who was deemed successful in his position, and his wife. She explains: "As the *rebbitzin* [sic], I had to be careful and circumspect. My behavior might affect your job. I had to trim my friendships to the politics in the synagogue. Arlene Rudman would call me practically every morning . . . and I listened and never cut her off, because her husband was the big moneyman in the congregation and one of your strongest backers." She goes on to say, "Whenever they came to visit us, I always had the feeling that she was making an inspection of the premises." She then says to her husband, "I never had any real friends; friendships that you cultivate on the basis of the importance of their husbands to the congregation don't mean much."[26]

One of the phenomena that Lenn considered was the "advisory" role of the rebbetzin—does she have a say in what her husband is doing? More than half volunteered their advice whenever they felt it was necessary, and 43 percent offered their advice when asked. Lenn states that "the rebbetzin, in order to be able to comment, must know a lot about what is going on, but she usually tries to keep herself in the background. Safely effective."[27]

Several years ago, in the Senior Seminar for students and spouses at the Hebrew Union College-Jewish Institute of Religion, it was strongly suggested that rabbis listen carefully to their spouses, who will tell the truth, even if it is not what the rabbis want to hear. For example, if, when you (the rabbi) are at home after services, you have a little moan that your sermon was not really appreciated, or that you did not seem to get through in what you wanted to say, and your spouse says, "It was a great sermon"—then believe your spouse. Conversely, if you are full of self-congratulation, and you remark how many people offered you praise on your sermon or Torah explanation, and your spouse says "Frankly, it was not that good!"—again, believe your spouse. ("They are your most honest critics.") As an aside, what is clear is that the speaker evidently *assumed* that the rabbi's spouse would be there at the synagouge to hear her/his spouse's talk!

Earlier, I referred to the rebbetzin as the rabbi's *ezer k'negdo*, literally the "helper opposite him." In a very insightful essay, Ellyn Hutt (1997) explains how wives help *to complete* their husband's visions. She suggests that oftentimes help is defined as "assisting someone with their efforts, standing side-by-side, sharing the same work." Yet, as the "helper opposite him," she sees wives taking on a different task.

> Most of us, in spiritual or relationship issues, rely on our own perspective of things. Although we think that we can see the whole picture, the reality is that we tend to see things only from our point of view. . . . Our physical vision . . . is restricted to what is in front of us. We only have eyes in front of our heads. Our field of vision is 180 degrees at the most. We can only see what we can see. And, we know that if someone else stands in front of us, opposite us, that person can tell us what is behind us, what we cannot see. . . .
>
> To this day, it is the spiritual function of the woman to help her husband in this way. Of course, it is ideal if the help flows both ways between both partners. But according to our tradition, woman was created with an intuitive gift of insight that made her especially valuable in this role. To be an *ezer k'negdo* is to be a helper of the highest level as it takes insight, integrity, and courage to stand opposite the one you love and speak the wisdom that you know.[28]

Just as Rabbi David Small of the Weekday *Rabbi* series is the best known fictional rabbi, so, by extension, Miriam Small, his wife, is probably the best known rebbetzin.[29] In some of the various novels where she appears, she is described as "vivacious," "forceful," "open"[30] and likable.[31] She is not afraid to criticize her husband, but she does this in the privacy of their home. Her comments are usually of a constructive manner.

> She has the insight, integrity, and courage to stand opposite her husband and speak the wisdom that she knows. At one point, Rabbi Small is complaining about the lack of respect shown to him by his congregants. He feels that he has not been an effective leader. Miriam will not allow him to wallow in his self-pity. "'You're talking nonsense!' She exploded. 'You're an excellent rabbi and an excellent teacher, too. You have trouble with your congregation *because* you are a good rabbi.'" She goes on to explain, "If you want to get along well with your congregation, if you want to be popular, David, you go along with them, instead of directing them and leading them. You don't ever make them face hard truths. And if a teacher wants to be popular with his class he doesn't try to make them learn anything."[32] In a later novel, coming home from a social evening at a congregant's home, she "coldly" tells her husband that he was not very sociable. "In fact, you were positively hostile." She says that he has been antagonistic and short-tempered with his congregants as of late. She suggests to him that he needs a vacation![33]

Not all rebbetzins are happy in their role. Murray Polner, in his book *Rabbi: the American Experience*, quotes Harriet. Her husband is a rabbi in the Midwest. "I rarely go to temple. I'd rather play tennis or sculpt. As far as I'm concerned, Al is a professional with his job. I've got my own interests." He also tells the story of Barbara, a rabbi's wife who earned her MBA and now does a fair amount of traveling. "He wants me home. Wants me to go to those damned sisterhood meetings. I won't. We'll just have to work it out, or there'll be no marriage."[34] Anne Lapidus Lerner is a scholar in her own right. She is married to a congregational rabbi, she has a strong Jewish background, and she appreciates the work of her congregational-rabbi husband. Yet, she "says with some heat," "Don't call me rebbetzin."[35]

Another rabbi's wife says, "I do not share my life with a rabbi. I share my life with a man whose profession is the rabbinate. I do not love a rabbi. I love a man who is a rabbi. The distinctions have not been easily achieved." She goes on to explain: "Privacy—a precious commodity for rabbinic families but very hard to find." What does this mean? She offers an example that *virtually every rabbinic family can affirm as true*. "How *can* you have a personal life when your evenings are spent teaching or attending meetings, and weekends are your busiest times? You plan on taking off a day every week, but inevitably something comes up. A doctor's answering service tells patients that the doctor is not on call today, but I cannot tell a troubled congregant that their rabbi is not 'on call.'"[36]

Shuly Rubin Schwartz explains that there are also are wives who lack Jewish knowledge or professional interests and merely tolerate their husband's calling. She refers to the example of a prominent rabbi in New York whose wife "had no interest in religion and no desire to fill the traditional *rebbetzin's* role. Her attitude greatly complicated" the rabbi's life, and made congregational life difficult for him.[37]

"It is not easy to be a *rebbetzin*," explains Rabbi Emanuel Feldman in his recent work *Tales out of Shul: the unorthodox journal of an Orthodox rabbi* (1996):

> . . . she shares center stage with her husband and is viewed as an extension of him. She is watched, admired, criticized, talked about, because she lives her life in the same glass house as her husband.
>
> But there is a difference: the rabbi is trained for the rabbinate . . . the rabbi's wife becomes a *rebbetzin* by virtue of her marriage to the rabbi. To be suddenly thrust out on the stage in a starring role is a frightening experience. That certain women do it so well is remarkable.[38]

Many fictional rebbetzins are, in many ways, supportive in their conduct and certainly are appreciated by their husbands. Speaking of his wife, Minna, Rabbi Charles Pedlock (*Pedlock Saint, Pedlock Sinner*) describes her as a "paragon among women. The kind of wife every rabbi needs. Social . . . a born leader of women's groups."[39] Surely it is noteworthy that he praises his wife for her social and leadership roles, not her commitment to Jewish values. Madeleine Stern (*A Place of Light*) is described as "an exemplary rebbetzin." "She was good at it, talking of doctors, pregnancies and rumors spicy enough to be interesting, but never hot enough to be gossip. She knew the right people, and for thirty years had kept the powers in balance."[40] Nonetheless, there are other portrayals as well. Lucinda Gordon (*Thy Daughter's Nakedness*) is supportive of her husband, Ed. He "knew she was loyal . . . and did what was necessary for his success." Yet at the same time, often "she had seemed to feel he was a nut, and his life's work a fraud. . . . She can no more comprehend religion than she can comprehend science, he thought. . . . To Lucinda, religion was crazy bits of orthodoxy that he had tried to sneak in on her."[41] At one point Lucinda says to Ed, "You're wishy-washy. . . . That's the trouble with clergymen—they're afraid to cross anybody. They always want everybody to like them." She then says, "I never went in for the religious chazerei [ridiculous ideas]."[42] Lucinda's position is in stark contrast to Shoshanna Fetner (*God's Ear*), who says to her husband, Rabbi Yussel Fetner, "I always wanted to be a rebbetzin . . . with a house and a congregation . . . and interesting people in a Jewish neighborhood."[43]

In the fictional world, there are not many novels or short stories that feature the rabbi as a central character and even less that feature the rebbetzin as a key player. Undoubtedly, Miriam Small in the Weekday *Rabbi* series is a significant character. Myra Rosenstock (in Marilyn Greenberg's *The Rabbi's Life Contract*) and Ellen Rosen (in Margaret Abrams' *Awakened*) both have very important roles. Further, the character of Madelaine Stern (*A Place of Light*) is exceptionally well drawn. Yet, for the novel to center on the rebbetzin is a rare phenomenon. Rare though they may be, there are in fact two books which meet this narrow criterion, and both make their point in the novel's title. These works are by British author David Benedictus, *The Rabbi's Wife* (1976), set in London, and by Sylvia Tennenbaum, whose contribution is set in New York, *Rachel, the Rabbi's Wife* (1978).

Susannah Arnatt, the rebbetzin in *The Rabbi's Wife*, certainly is supportive of her husband, who is a Progressive rabbi in London. She attends committee meetings and religious services, and she is involved teaching some of the teens. She had been attracted to her husband "simply because he was a rabbi." Nonetheless, Susannah, while present at religious events, is singularly uninvolved. "Organized religion seemed to Susannah as hopeless as sex education, making public confusion out of private doubt and anxiety." She wonders to herself how her husband's congregants personalize God. "As a sort of Old Testament radio announcer? A white-bearded Prince Philip? A haughty professor? Or did any of them grasp the need for an

> abstract divinity?"[44] While these make for wonderful questions, they are not followed through in the novel, for on Yom Kippur she is kidnapped by Arab terrorists and much of the rest of the novel focuses on more political themes.
>
> The other rebbetzin-centered novel, *Rachel, the Rabbi's Wife*, portrays a rebbetzin who struggles with her congregational role. Her husband serves a Conservative congregation. Rachel may, or may not, love her husband, Seymour. She certainly does not love the rabbinate. She is described as a "reluctant rebbetzin."[45]
>
> Rachel responds to her rebbetzin-hood by detaching herself from her responsibilities. In the words of the novel, "Conversations with congregants dropped through Rachel's mind like stones through a clear pond." She is unable to remember when there are Sisterhood meetings, or when people phone and leave messages. She dresses in a nonconformist manner. "The night of the Sisterhood meeting . . . Rachel wore one of her more outlandish outfits." Rachel is seen, and sees herself, as an outsider. Right from the beginning of the novel, it is clear that she has not been a help for her husband: ". . . there were many voices raised in criticism against her. She was accused of being incomprehensible, difficult, cold, and snobbish. She was cited for being lax in her ritual observances, a Jewish illiterate. Because she knew that there was some truth to all the charges, she took them to heart, suffered, became more incomprehensible still."[46]

With the changes brought about by the women's movement, a number of the expectations of the rabbi's spouse clearly have been challenged, though to what extent challenged successfully is a matter of debate. In the mid-1980s, Hadassah Ribalow Nadich (1985) had argued that the women's movement and the changing times have "brought a cultural upheaval in many areas." She suggested that many "young Jewish women are no longer satisfied to play the role of the traditional rabbi's wife whose function they interpret as 'making the rabbi look good.'" Nadich noted that women today "are entering all professions and a young woman who marries a rabbi will perhaps not be satisfied to be part of a team. She wants to be a lawyer, a doctor or a psychologist so as to establish her own identity. Thus, the congregation no longer can look to the rabbi's wife for involvement in synagogue life." She feels that congregations have recognized these changes, and "many have accepted the fact that when they engage a rabbi, they are not taking on his wife as well."[47] Nadich's optimistic viewpoint notwithstanding, not all congregations have been ready to give up their expectation of the rabbi's spouse. A decade later, at the aforementioned program on the Changing Role of Clergy Spouses held in Denver in 1996, comments were made that "She [!] needs to be involved." "She [!] needs to be seen." "She [!] is more than 'just a congregant.'" Coincidentally, at that forum in Denver, part of the panel included a woman-Cantor's husband. He was asked how he is, or would prefer to be, addressed. He replied: "What do you call a Cantor's husband? Call him 'Lucky.'"[48] His reply notwithstanding, not all rebbetzins or rebbitz' (male rabbinic spouses) would necessarily feel similar. He also explained that early on in their marriage, they had decided that they would follow her career path, that he would adjust to her schedule.

> In the final novel of the Weekday *Rabbi* series, *That Day the Rabbi Left Town*, Rabbi Small's successor explains to the pulpit search committee that "his wife was no part of the deal; that [they] . . . were not to expect her to play the part of the traditional rebbetzin because she had her own interests"—for she is a practicing lawyer. The committee takes the news with a poise rarely displayed in that community.[49]

One of the difficulties experienced by rabbis, and certainly rabbi-spouses, is that they are always in the proverbial "fish bowl." Participants at the Denver forum expressed ideas similar to the comment by Shuly Schwartz, that part of congregational assumptions are "that women who married rabbis automatically shared their husbands' sense of calling and would be able to live life in the public eye."[50] These congregational assumptions are not always correct. Carolyn Hoyt (1993) explained she married a rabbi, but sometimes she feels that she wedded an entire congregation. "When my husband signed his contract, I signed on as well. But there were some things I did not bargain for." She goes on to explain, "For starters, the line between our public and private lives is thin at best. In every imaginable setting, we run into congregants—people who, for all their good intentions, expect godly behavior from my husband and from me as well. A woman once picked out a six-pack of Budweiser from our shopping cart, held it high over her head, and asked if her temple dues were going to support our drinking habit."[51] That not all rabbinic spouses are as comfortable in their public role as some congregants might think is succinctly summed up in the title of an article that appeared in the mid-1980s in a Rabbinic journal: "Two's Company: Three Thousand's a Crowd: Reflections of a Rebbetzin's Husband's Wife."[52]

A rebbetzin explains that she has found "that much of being married to the rabbi is social. It is everything from the *oneg* Shabbat to the seemingly endless receptions." She goes on to say that people assume that she is an adjunct of her husband. "I have also found that being married to a rabbi, I become privy to intimate details about people's lives. Sometimes these are things they tell me as a surrogate for Steve. Sometimes I think they think that I am paid to listen as well. But, the real reason is that I am safe. I am little lower than the rabbi. By talking to me, you don't have a real problem, just something it might be nice if the rabbi knew." Being the rebbetzin, however, definitely has its problems. As she explained, "sometimes as the spouse of a rabbi you become the target for other people's *mishegas*" [craziness].[53] People are angry, disappointed, frustrated, saddened about their own lives, their own spouses, their own children, their own parents, their own jobs, their own economic position—all which have *nothing at all to do with the rabbi, much less the rabbi's spouse*—but the rebbetzin becomes the "target" for their anger.

Coincidentally, in her 1985 article, Nadich went on to address the issue of the woman-rabbi's spouse. "Will there be expectations for his participation in congregational life? This presents a new sociological phenomenon that only the future will be able to assess." "What about the husband, who cannot pursue his career in the city where his wife has a pulpit? Will the husband feel an obligation to attend functions much as the *rebbetzin* has done?" Apparently she herself does not see the woman-rabbi spouse paralleling the experiences of rebbetzins. "Probably the rabbi's husband will concentrate on his own career and leave the congregation to his wife."[54]

As I noted in the chapter on women rabbis, there are a very limited number of fictional examples of women rabbis, so we can make only preliminary suggestions of how woman-rabbi spouses deal with their situation. Among the fictional examples,

> in the British production "Love hurts" the Warburgs are in the process of divorce. He is a professor. He was teaching in London, where she had her pulpit, but he decides to move to Birmingham to take a position there. In the case of Rabbi Lynda Klein (*A Place of Light*), her husband, Elliot, is a cardiac surgeon. He works at the local hospital in their Midwestern city. She is considering a change of pulpits, but she realizes that she is trapped. "She couldn't ask Elliot to follow her to some congregation in some tiny town where the nearest hospital was in the next county." As it is, we learn that he had given up a "great East Coast practice" for her.[55] The only other spouse of a woman rabbi whose profession is mentioned is merely identified as a successful bankruptcy attorney working in Manhattan.[56]

The rabbinic spouse takes on a whole new phenomenological life when *both* the rabbi and the rabbi's spouse are rabbis! Oftentimes, rabbinic couples seek to find a city large enough where both can serve as rabbis. In some rare instances, the rabbinic couples serve as co-rabbis of the congregation.

> In terms of fiction, there is a passing reference to a rabbinic couple in Erich Segal's *Acts of Faith*, though the woman-rabbi does not seem to be the co-rabbi.[57]

CHILDREN

As the rabbi's spouse is part and parcel of the rabbi's family life, so are their children. There are enormous pressures on the rabbi's family. Complaints which are familiar to *all* rabbinic families are listed in Polner's book. "Rabbi, how come your kid doesn't wear a yarmulke?" "Rabbi, why doesn't your child sit still at services?" "Rabbi, why does your son have such long hair?" "Rabbi, do you think it is proper to allow your daughter to wear such skimpy clothes?" "Rabbi, your wife comes so rarely to services."[58] As a rabbi, as the son of a rabbi, and as someone who served as a congregational rabbi for 21 years, I can personally attest that each and every one of these rings true. I either have literally heard these selfsame criticisms or know colleagues who tell me that they have heard these exact questions from their congregants.

In real life, children of rabbis, much as children of Protestant ministers and Greek Orthodox priests, find that they are treated differently simply because their parent is a clergyperson. Some children deeply resent being categorized as "the rabbi's son" or "the rabbi's daughter." Like it or not, and most do not, the rabbi's child is often judged in a different manner than his or her peers. They are regarded as "automatically"—or perhaps the term should be "genetically"—religious; religiously knowledgeable; and certainly better behaved than their peers.

Recently, a rebbetzin shared this observation:

> Our children are not immune to the impact of rabbinical life either and, therefore, our choices for them are sometimes skewed. As much as we try to have them be "like everybody else," it is inevitable that they will be singled out. Our children did attend the Jewish Center overnight camp near Buffalo. After "*Rabbi Mason's son* was called up to lead *Birkat Ha Mazon* [the blessings after the meal]" after dinner one night at camp, the kids never returned. Our daughter now goes to a Canadian camp (where they barely know what a rabbi is), and our son goes to Eisner (where he is far from being the only R.K. [Rabbi's Kid]) because we feel camp is one place where they should be able to be who and what they want without the baggage of being our kids."[59]

> The heroine of *The Launching of Barbara Fabrikant*, a rabbi's daughter, is a freshman in college. She has just met her new roommate, Marsha. After some desultory conversation, Barbara reluctantly mentions that her father is a rabbi. Marsha's first reaction is ecstatic. She explains that she, too, is Jewish, and then continues: "'I've never known a rabbi's daughter before,' Marsha says. 'Are you holier than most people? Do you keep kosher?'"[60] At one point in the novel, Barbara and some of her girlfriends take the commuter flight from Boston to New York. They are a little nervous about the safety of the flight. One of her friends says to Barbara: "We're counting on you . . . to keep the plane up. It's probably better than having a nun aboard, to have a rabbi's daughter."[61]

At a symposium on "The Modern Rabbi" a rabbi's son, then 19, explained that the rabbi's children regard their parents as human and sometimes they will go out of their way to prove this. "Surely, the rabbi's children do not regard the daily work of their rabbi as something mystical." He explained that at times he would very carefully and publicly retell a "dirty joke" that his father told in the privacy of their home. He would also publicly acknowledge its source.

> I must say however, that I am discreet in this slight violation of trust: I only retell the good ones. Such efforts to make the rabbi seem more "normal" and less lofty, more "regular" and less sacred, have various ramifications. For one thing, by making public such "human" traits, the rabbi's child can confirm his own belief in his father's humanness. And perhaps more important than helping to shape the child's image of his father, these efforts to humanize fortify the child's attitude toward himself. After all, if one can prove that his father is normal, then he is less likely to be branded "Son of Saint"—a dreadful epithet for the youngster seeking acceptance.[62]

> Rabbi David Small (the Weekday *Rabbi* series) is a rabbi's son. He speaks of the "added burden that will fall on our child as a rabbi's son. . . . Because your father is a public figure, everyone expects more of you, and you feel guilty when you don't come up to expectations."[63]
>
> Joseph Melamed (in Maurice Wohlgelernter's short story "Hardball") is a rabbi's son, but he clearly has little interest in academics. When he is 12, his father complains that he knows nothing. "'And another year to your Bar-Mitzvah,' [his father] . . . added as an afterthought. 'What an embarrassment you'll be in front of the entire congregation.'
>
> "Joe reddened with shame."[64]

Rabbi's children are often ambivalent about their parent's professions. On one hand there is the fact that you are always, in one sense or another, in the public eye and judged differently. On the other hand, at times as the rabbi's child you can be accorded a certain respect that comes to you by virtue of your being the rabbi's child.

> In the novel Rabbi Small continues his description of the pros and cons of being the rabbi's child:

> As a youngster, you can't imagine how often I wished my father owned a shoe store or went to work in an office like the fathers of the other boys. Believe me, I envied the boys whose fathers earned a

> living in the ordinary way. But there were compensations, and much of it was fun. When I went to synagogue on a Friday night with my mother, and I saw my father in the pulpit conducting the service, delivering his sermons, I always felt that the synagogue was ours, that I was being taken there as other boys were occasionally taken to their father's office on Saturday.[65]

When, several years ago, I first read Rabbi Small's words in *Saturday the Rabbi Went Hungry*, I think that my hair stood on end. It was absolutely eerie. Uncanny. I was transported back in time to the second grade. I remember vividly to this day how, one winter morning, we were literally going around the room telling each other about our father's occupation. I was the only child in that class whose father was a clergyman, much less a rabbi. I certainly was the only Jewish child in the class. I remember trying to think of an alternate occupation for my father. For some reason, I had decided to say he worked at an automobile service station, pumping gas. Whether my teacher detected my anxiety, or it was simply serendipitous, when it came to my turn, Mrs. Black said simply, "And we know, David, that your father is a rabbi." To my great relief, she then went on to the next student. In time I grew more comfortable with my role. Here again, I could easily relate to fictional Rabbi Small's description. Without doubt, there were compensations, and much of it was fun. Often, going to synagogue on a Friday night with my mother, and I saw my father in the pulpit conducting the service, delivering his sermons, I felt that the synagogue was ours, that I was being taken there as other boys were occasionally taken to their father's office on the weekend.

> Clearly not all rabbi's children have the positive experience of Rabbi David Small. Barbara Fabrikant tells a friend: "Being a rabbi's daughter is from hunger."[66] Even allowing for adolescent exaggeration, it is clear that she has had to live a very circumscribed life.

A rabbi's child explains that one of the "negatives" of being part of a rabbi's family is that you inevitably see "the underside of things." While on one hand this takes away from the mystery and awe of the rabbinate, you do see your parent in a more respectful way. You recognize that the "rabbi/parent" has to deal with a variety of difficult circumstances, for example on occasion doing a morning funeral and an afternoon wedding. It is the rabbi who consoles as well as who congratulates. The rabbi's spouse can play an enormously important role, this rabbinic-son explained: "My mother's best friend once said that most families have to be flexible, but that ours has to be completely elastic. It is the rabbi's spouse who provides the stability within that elasticity. For when my father is running around catering to others, it is my mother who takes care of the family—organizing, disciplining, explaining. And she is not only a mother—she is a surrogate everything." Turning to the rabbi/parent, he explains that the rabbi really is the key.

> He must be honest about himself and his job. He must . . . be able to explain why he attended the board meeting instead of the basketball game. He must assure his children and his congregation that his roles of parent and rabbi are not mutually exclusive. He must be able to say to his disappointed child that "he is a rabbi, too," and to his disappointed congregant that "he is a daddy, too." He must assure both constituencies that although he may occasionally disappoint them, he never deserts them."[67]

Though a number of novels offer a voice to rabbinic children,[68] perhaps the fullest development of a dialogue between a rabbi and his or her child is found in Myron S. Kaufmann's novel *Thy Daughter's Nakedness*. The Gordons have four children who range from pre-teen to 21. Much of the novel centers on the life of their daughter, Millicent. In one poignant passage, Millicent comes to her father to discuss the whole question of Judaism's attitude toward sex and premarital relations. Her father, Rabbi Ed Gordon, tries to answer her out of the traditional sources, both Biblical and post-Biblical. The discussion goes on for some time and highlights the difficulty of trying to relate the maintenance of traditional religious standards and yet to be informed by the freer attitudes and life styles of the twentieth century. That her father is not totally convincing in his arguments is less important than the fact that Millicent feels that she can discuss these issues with her father, the rabbi, or perhaps with the rabbi, her father.[69]

Millicent is several stages ahead of her "peer," Barbara Fabrikant. Though once again her observations have to be

> understood tongue-in-cheek, for *The Launching of Barbara Fabrikant* is written in a humorous vein, we learn that when it came to Barbara's sexual education, her parents found it impossible to deal with matters directly. She explains to her roommates that the subject was not really dealt with in her home. "Dad and my uncle [a doctor] separated the sex lectures between them; my father gave the moral side and my uncle took care of the disgusting details. From neither of them did I learn anything." She goes on to explain that she fared no better with her mother. Her mother limited their discussion to a short explanation about sanitary napkins. "This is the one bit of sexual information my mother ever passed on, otherwise she won't talk about sex at all. She disapproves of it entirely."[70]

Real-life rabbis are not unaware of their dual roles as rabbi and parent. "A rabbi's schedule raises havoc with my home life," we hear from one rabbi. Another, whose father also was a rabbi, says that as "the son of a rabbi I knew that the life of a clergyman is not what one might call a sheltered existence. I try not to say or infer to my children that they must lead a super-good existence because of my position. . . . Nevertheless, it is difficult. . . . Plans are forever being interrupted because of congregational obligations."[71] How do rabbis cope with their dual roles? *The honest answer is, with difficulty*. Most rabbis would agree in principle with the earlier advice that rabbis must assure their children as well as their congregation that their roles of parent and rabbi are not exclusive, that rabbis need to be able to say to their disappointed children that they are rabbis in addition to being parents and to be able to say to disappointed congregants that they are parents as well as rabbis. *The reality is that this is extremely hard*. Looking to the next generation of rabbis, Peter Rubinstein (1990) wonders if rabbis "who have children, or who are intent upon spending substantial time with a spouse, will face the decision of either working part-time (20 hours a week), taking time away from careers, or demanding that a full-time rabbinic position be viewed within the 40-hour work week framework."[72]

Rabbis clearly need to spend time with their children. Successful parenting involves a lot of work, and certainly in today's society the "absentee parent" is not an acceptable option for most families. As Rubinstein further observed, if "the rabbi's position is allowed to have time limitations, we will have a better chance of keeping our . . . rabbis in the congregational workplace."[73]

> One can only hope that in real life that rabbis, whether congregational rabbis or rabbis in other fields, will do better than the observation of one rabbi's child who said to another rabbi's child, "Fathers like ours don't know how to love. They live too much indoors."[74]

NOTES

1. Liebman, C. S. (1974). "The Training of American Rabbis," in *Aspects of the Religious Behavior of American Jews* (New York: Ktav Publishing), pp. 11, 13. [This article originally appeared in the *American Jewish Year Book 1968*, ed. Morris Fine and Morris Himmelfarb, vol. 69 (New York: American Jewish Committee and Philadelphia: Jewish Publication Society, 1968)]. See Lenn, T. (1972). *Rabbi and Synagogue in Reform Judaism* (New York: Central Conference of American Rabbis), p. 322.

2. Liebman, "The Training of American Rabbis," p. 12.

3. Cohn-Sherbok, D. and L. (1994). *The American Jew: Voices from an American Jewish Community* (Grand Rapids, MI: William Eerdmans Publishing), pp. 8, 13, 17, 21, 25, 140, 33.

4. Blankfort, M. (1956). *The Strong Hand* (Boston, Toronto: Little Brown and Co.), p. 89; Falk, H. (1972). *Days of Judgment* (New York: Shengold), p. 46.

5. Elkins, S. (1987). *The Rabbi of Lud* (New York: Charles Scribner's Sons), p. 11.

6. Lerman, R. (1989). *God's Ear* (New York: Henry Holt), p. 1.

7. Kemelman, H. (1964). *Friday the Rabbi Slept Late* (New York: Crown), p. 56.

8. Appel, A. (1986). *The Rabbi of Casino Boulevard* (New York: Saint Martin's); p. 83, Tennenbaum, S. (1978). *Rachel, the Rabbi's Wife* (New York: William Morrow), p. 143.

9. Kemelman, H. (1996). *That Day the Rabbi Left Town* (New York: Fawcett Columbine), p. 37 f.

10. Schreiber, M. (1991). *The Rabbi and the Nun* (New York: Shengold), p. 32 f.; Tarr, H. (1968). *Heaven Help Us!* (New York: Random House), p. 25; Leokum, A. (1969). *The Temple* (New York and Cleveland: NAL/World Publishing), p. 30; Gordon, N. (1965). *The Rabbi* (New York: McGraw-Hill), p. 35.

11. Davidson, A. and Wertheimer, J. (1987). "The Next Generation of Conservative Rabbis: An Empirical Study of Today's Rabbinical Students," in *The Seminary at 100. Reflections on the Jewish Theological Seminary and the Con-*

servative Movement, ed. Nina Beth Cardin and David Wolf Silverman (New York: The Rabbinical Assembly and The Jewish Theological Seminary of America), p. 35.

12. Cohn-Sherbok, D. (1993). *Not a Job for a Nice Jewish Boy* (London: Bellew Publishing), pp. 4, 5.

13. Cohn-Sherbok, D. and L., p. 33.

14. Schreiber, p. 32.

15. Tennenbaum, p. 152.

16. Tarr, *Heaven Help Us!*, p. 26.

17. Potok, C. (1967). *The Chosen* (New York: Simon and Schuster), p. 219.

18. Blankfort, p. 91.

19. Leokum, p. 56; Fast, H. (1984). *The Outsider* (Boston: Houghton Mifflin), p. 31.

20. Schwartz, S. R. (1995). "'We Married What We Wanted To Be': The *Rebbetzin* in Twentieth-Century America," *American Jewish History: 83* (June): 224.

21. Abrams, M. (1954). *Awakened* (Philadelphia: Jewish Publication Society of America), p. 169.

22. Schwartz, pp. 224 f.

23. Lenn, pp. 369, 371.

24. Lenn, pp. 374–375.

25. Lenn, p. 374.

26. Kemelman, H. (1973 [1972]). *Monday the Rabbi Took Off* (Greenwich, CT: Fawcett Crest), pp. 219 f. Note: the speaker is Betty Deutch, not Miriam Small.

27. Lenn, p. 376.

28. Ellyn Hutt, "*Ezer k'Negdo*: A Helper Opposite Him," personal communication to David J. Zucker, February 24, 1997.

29. For a discussion about Rebbetzins in recent fiction, see my article "Rebbitzens and Women Rabbis: Portrayals in Contemporary American Jewish Fiction." *CCAR Journal* 42:1 (Winter/Spring 1995), pp. 1–12.

30. Kemelman, *Friday the Rabbi Slept Late*, pp. 54, 63.

31. Kemelman, *Monday the Rabbi Took Off*, p. 53.

32. Kemelman, H. (1973). *Tuesday the Rabbi Saw Red* (New York: Arthur Field Books), pp. 217 f.

33. Kemelman, H. (1992). *The Day the Rabbi Resigned* (New York: Fawcett Columbine), pp. 4, 5, 7.

34. Polner, M. (1977). *Rabbi: The American Experience* (New York: Holt, Rinehart and Winston), p. 155 f.

35. Polner, p. 157.

36. Sundheim, A. (1981). Symposium on "Today's Rabbinate: the Per-

sonal Equation." *Central Conference of American Rabbis Yearbook: 90* (New York: Central Conference of American Rabbis), p. 154.

37. Schwartz, p. 228.

38. Feldman, E. (1996). *Tales out of Shul: The unorthodox journal of an Orthodox Rabbi* (New York: Shaar Press/Mesorah Publications), p. 51.

39. Longstreet, S. (1969). *Pedlock Saint, Pedlock Sinner* (New York: Delacorte), p. 60.

40. Shapiro-Rieser, R. (1983). *A Place of Light* (New York: Pocket), pp. 185, 267.

41. Kaufmann, M. S. (1968). *Thy Daughter's Nakedness* (Philadelphia and New York: J. B. Lippincott), p. 74.

42. Kaufmann, *Thy Daughter's Nakedness*, p. 494.

43. Lerman, p. 59.

44. Benedictus, D. (1976). *The Rabbi's Wife* (London: Blond and Briggs), p. 17. While technically not set in North America, I include this novel because it is so rare in that the central character is a rabbi's wife.

45. Tennenbaum, p. 19 f.

46. Tennenbaum, pp. 16, 26, 377 (see also p. 23).

47. Nadich, H. R. (1985). "The Rabbi's Spouse," *The Jewish Spectator* 50:2 (Summer):18.

48. To the best of my knowledge the earliest reference to this appellation ["Lucky"] appears in a talk where the speaker explains that congregants frequently ask "what do you call the husband of a rabbi, to which the standard reply coined by [Rabbi] Roz Gold is—'lucky.'" Prinz, D. (1981). Symposium on "Today's Rabbinate: the Personal Equation." *Central Conference of American Rabbis Yearbook: 90*. (New York: Central Conference of American Rabbis), p. 149.

49. Kemelman, *That Day the Rabbi Left Town*, p. 33.

50. Schwartz, p. 225.

51. Hoyt, C. (1993). "All Eyes Upon Us." *Women's Day* (April 6): 58.

52. The article by Didi Carr Reuben appeared in the *Journal of Reform Judaism* 33:1 (Winter 1986), pp. 37–41. This and other articles that deal with both the stereotypes and rebbetzins' reactions to those images are found in Schwartz, p. 226, n. 12.

53. Mason, P. (1994). "The Rabbi: On Love and Loss." *Central Conference of American Rabbis Yearbook: 103*. (New York: Central Conference of American Rabbis), p. 66 f.

54. Nadich, p. 18.

55. Shapiro-Rieser, pp. 244, 262.

56. Kane, p. 299.

57. Segal, E. (1992). *Acts of Faith* (New York: Bantam), p. 259.

58. Polner, p. 158.

59. Mason, p. 67.

60. Rose, L. B. (1974). *The Launching of Barbara Fabrikant* (New York: David McKay Company), p. 43.

61. Rose, p. 185.

62. Stern, D. E. (1981). Symposium on "Today's Rabbinate: the Personal Equation." *Central Conference of American Rabbis Yearbook: 90* (New York: Central Conference of American Rabbis), p. 146.

63. Kemelman, *Saturday the Rabbi Went Hungry*, p. 69.

64. Wohlgelernter, M. (1994). "Hardball." *Jewish Spectator* 59:2 (Fall): 48.

65. Kemelman, *Saturday the Rabbi Went Hungry*, p. 69.

66. Rose, p. 106.

67. Stern, D. E., p. 147.

68. Probably the best known rabbinic father/son relationships are found in Chaim Potok's *The Chosen* and *The Promise* (New York: Alfred A. Knopf, 1969). There, however, the plot consciously centers around the "non-communication," the "silence" imposed on his son by the Hasidic leader, Rabbi Saunders.

69. Kaufmann, *Thy Daughter's Nakedness*, pp. 307 ff.

70. Rose, p. 132.

71. Polner, p. 159.

72. Rubinstein, P. J. (1990). "The Next Century," in *Tanu Rabbanan: Our Rabbis Taught CCAR Yearbook 1989, vol. 2* ed. Joseph B. Glaser (New York: Central Conference of American Rabbis), p. 150. See Grossman, S. (1995). "The Dual Nature of Rabbinic Leadership" in *Conservative Judaism* 48:1 (Fall): 46.

73. Rubinstein, p. 151.

74. Ozick, C. (1983). "The Pagan Rabbi" in *The Pagan Rabbi and Other Stories* (New York: E. P. Dutton), p. 5.

9

Assimilation, Intermarriage, and Patrilineality

ASSIMILATION

Jews who live in the open societies of North America are not faced with many of the historic barriers they knew in the past. Anti-Semitism, as discussed in an earlier chapter, is at an all-time low. The marketplace is open to Jews. They are found in all professions and occupations. There are no restricted areas where Jews are required to live. Indeed, most congregants throughout North America voluntarily choose the location of their housing based much more often on the reputation of the local school district than on proximity to their synagogue. Indeed, most Jews today do *not* live within walking distance of their synagogue. No longer is there the social pressure to attend services that existed in the small villages of Eastern Europe. Most Jews who are in business would say that shutting their doors on the Jewish Sabbath no longer is an economic reality. Their clientele are likely as not Mr. Brown as Ms. Cohen, Ms. Smith or Mrs. Jones as Mr. Levy. Life in suburbia is not like life in the *shtetl*.

As the Jews move into new situations, they adjust, acculturate, and assimilate. Their neighbors and their neighborhoods are not exclusively Jewish. From living in a small but majority island community within an alien world, many, if not most, Jews in North America now live as a minority without the psychological protection of the community around them being totally or even largely Jewish. Jews live and work next to non-Jews. Their children are educated in schools with non-Jewish children and play soccer, football, baseball, and basketball with non-Jews. In the supermarket, Jewish men and women mix and rub shoulders with non-Jews. In the beauty shop, the person in the next chair may be as easily Mrs. Calhoun as Ms. Goldberg, not to mention Ms. Wong or Mrs. MacDonald. Indeed two of the six principles, which it is claimed "arous[e] the deepest loyalties and passions of American Jews," are that "there is nothing incompatible in being a good Jew and being a good American" and further that the continued "separation of church and state" is absolutely essential in order to protect "Jews and Judaism in America."[1]

For many Jews this good Jew/good American and church/state separation lends itself to a world where assimilation becomes more likely.

Furthermore, as Jews distance themselves from their synagogue, physically or psychically, the greater is their degree of assimilation, and the more likely they are to see and treat their rabbis as religious specialists. In a sense, congregants move from being "community participants" to "religious consumers." Closely correlated with the subject of assimilation are the rubrics of intermarriage and mixed marriage. These items, both highly charged and highly emotive, are dealt with in a separate section below.

In his study of politics, religion, and family life in present-day America, Charles S. Liebman (1973) points to the conflicting attitudes of Jews in the United States. Not without good reason did he title his book *The Ambivalent American Jew*. The majority of Jews, says Liebman, are "torn between two forces: the desire for acceptance by the gentile society and the attraction of non-Jewish values and attitudes, and the desire for group identity and survival as a distinct community. This phenomenon is, of course, not unique to Jews, but the intensity of both forces is probably more pronounced among the Jews than in any other group in American society."[2] Liebman speaks of a "survival-integration continuum" where the "extreme survival position is represented by some Hasidic groups, popularly labeled as ultra-Orthodox. Such groups tend to be indifferent to the rest of the American Jewish community and quite incapable of communicating with them." He goes on to explain that it "is difficult to find articulation of an extreme integration or assimilationist position. If one merely wants to be integrated into American society without any concern for group survival, the first sensible thing to do is to stop talking about it, which simply attracts attention."[3]

American Jews, by and large, think of themselves as Americans. They do not feel that they are "Jews" who are "now dwelling" in America. America has long considered itself a melting pot of various peoples. While this rich integrationist mix may be somewhat overstated (and has been challenged by some American sociologists), the idea is basically sound. It is not coincidental that the three largest Jewish religious organizations are called the Union of *American* Hebrew Congregations (Reform); the United Synagogue of *America* (Conservative); and the Union of Orthodox Jewish Congregations of *America* (Orthodox). In the mid-1960s, Jewish historian Jacob Radar Marcus noted it "is deemed un-American not to belong 'to the church or synagogue of your choice,' and the typical suburban Jew is in this, as in other respects, very much a conformist."[4] While in succeeding decades the percentage of synagogue affiliation may have dropped, the generalization remains a constant.

This integrationist pattern can be contrasted with the British Jewish community. As Barnet Litvinoff succinctly observed: "The Englishman's mind is an island, and his country has never been a melting pot. You are always a foreigner there if you bear the traces of foreign ancestry." American Jews may refer to themselves as Jewish and to their neighbor as a Catholic or Protestant, or alternately as a Scot or Irishman (meaning the neighbor is of Scottish or Irish ancestry), or they might speak of themselves as New Yorkers and their neighbor as a Nevadan or Californian. English Jews, by contrast, think of themselves as Jews and their neighbors as English.[5] Yet even in Great Britain, assimilation is on the increase and a major concern for the Jewish community.

Sociologists of the Jewish community, explains Paul Ritterband in "Modern Times and Jewish Assimilation" (1995), are divided into accomodationists/optimists, and assimilationists/pessimists. There is data, naturally, to support both positions. On one hand, the American Jewish community is more vibrant and successful than any in the past. "Jews have become major figures in American academic and intellectual life . . . the House of Representatives and Senate have three times as many Jews proportionately as their number in the population would predict." There are also Jews once again on the Supreme Court. By the same token, even though the most Jewishly committed have increased their commitments, the "less committed Jews have more and more opened themselves up to the forces of assimilation."[6]

Rabbis and, certainly more specifically, congregational rabbis constantly work with Jews who are struggling with the contradictory pulls of integration/survival. Children in their religious schools are more likely to be called Barbara and Brittany than Beruriah or Bracha, more often Bryan and Brandon than Benjamin or Benzion. Ritterband suggests, based on the 1990 National Jewish Population Survey, that "Jews have become the most secularized of all the ethnic groups in America of European origin."[7] Secularization presents itself in different ways, ranging from a change of surname to a basic indifference to matters Jewish.

Change of Name

In the 1990s, with the virtual integration of Jews into American society, a change of name as a method to achieve assimilation is not as common as it was in the earlier part of the twentieth century. The following interchange (actually set in Britain in the mid-1960s) nonetheless has a certain contemporary relevance.

> "There are some twelve hundred Jews living here, and of these you can reckon that about two hundred are lost to Judaism—I mean so lost that only the *goyim* [non-Jews] know them as Jews. I know four Colquhouns who were born Cohen, three MacLuskies who were born Laski, and two Macdonalds who were born Malchaski."
>
> "Name changing isn't a sign that they are lost as Jews."
>
> "No, but it's a sign that they would like to be lost."[8]
>
> Yet a change of name does not of necessity mean that the family is lost to the Jewish community. In America we learn that Rabbi Gordon Shepherd's family name used to be Shapiro.[9] In another instance we read: "Kind is a funny name for a rabbi, isn't it?
>
> ". . . I mean, it's not very Jewish."
>
> "It used to be Rivkind. My father changed it when I was a little boy."[10] Among the laymen, but one example among many, includes

this quip by a rabbi about a very active member of the synagogue: "Dore Redmont, an easy name to remember because I'm sure it used to be Isadore Rosenberg."[11]

Non-Participation (*in Synagogue or in Matters Jewish*)

Synagogue affiliation and synagogue participation is an important way to determine the Jewish activity of an area. The synagogues as a group contain the largest number of active Jews in the community. Yet, membership in and of itself does not determine the degree of Jewish activity. The vast majority of Jews live on the two coasts of the United States. There are major concentrations in the Northeast/mid-Atlantic corridor from Boston through New York to Philadelphia and on to Baltimore and Washington, D. C., as well as south Florida on the East Coast. On the West Coast, Jewish population is highest in California.

Given the concentration of Jews in New York and California, it is not surprising that the following statements are set in those two areas. In San Francisco, Rabbi Michael Kind (*The Rabbi*) hears this description about his synagogue: "They started Temple Isaiah eight years ago. You know why? The other Reform temples demanded too much time. Too much personal commitment. Your people want to be Jews, but not to the extent that it's going to take any of the free time they came to California to enjoy. Yom Kippur and Rosh Hashonah. That's all, brother."[12] In New York, Rabbi Davis (*Coat Upon A Stick*) remarks to a woman: "You sound like suburban league . . . Community Center . . . and trips to synagogue on the High Holy Days, in the car, . . . sherry parties . . . cocktail parties . . . Broadway plays."[13]

"Some of My Best Friends" (*Are Not Jewish*)

Another path to assimilation is taken by people who like to associate primarily with non-Jews, often to the exclusion of Jews. They will rationalize that this is merely "building bridges" between the communities, but the fact, nonetheless, is one of assimilation.

Dave Schoenfeld, a synagogue lay leader in Cypress, Georgia, proudly tells the Rabbinic Placement Director about his hometown community, the congregation which Rabbi Michael Kind (*The Rabbi*) will serve for a period of time. "We live very closely with our Christian neighbors. . . ."[14] Hugh Marshall, of Fair City, explains to Chaplain David Cohen that though there are only 60 families in the community, they are all "very active in the Community Chest, Red Cross, hospital drives, and . . . even raising money for church-building funds."[15] That layman nearly has apoplexy when Chaplain Cohen proposes to speak about the State of Israel when there will be non-Jews in the congregation. The previously mentioned lay leader is involved in Rabbi Kind's dismissal when the rabbi preaches on integration (again in front of a congregation where non-Jews are present). After all, what will "they" think?

"All Religions Are Equal"

"'I don't think it's the best,' said Conrad. 'I just happen to be in it, that's all. All religions are equal.'"

"'One religion can't be better than another,' Roy . . . said flatly."[16]

We have here other examples of assimilationist Jews who would downgrade or downplay any differences between Judaism and Christianity. These are often the same people who have Christmas trees but call them "Chanukah bushes" in December and who will have Easter eggs in the spring for their children so that the youngsters will "not feel different." In one novel, since Chanukah (which is based on a lunar calendar) begins that year in late November instead of mid-December, a woman buys enough Chanukah candles to light each night all the way through to Christmas.[17]

"But You Don't Look Jewish . . ."

Finally, there are women and men who take great pride in the fact that they "do not look Jewish." Real-life sociologist Charles S. Liebman notes:

"Nothing pleases most Jews more than to be told that they don't look Jewish or behave Jewishly, that they cannot be distinguished in their appearance, dress, speech, attitudes, or behavior from the non-Jew. . . . While this is all true, Jews still want to be Jews. They don't flock to Christian ministers for conversion . . ." Yet at the same time, Jews "are scandalized by intermarriage, insist that a non-Jewish partner in a marriage convert to Judaism. . . . They support the State of Israel financially, politically, and emotionally when such support must surely raise the specter of dual national loyalty, if not outright disloyalty to America; but they are outraged by the idea that the State Department discriminates against Jews in its personnel policies."[18]

> Some people, including a rabbi, look non-Jewish naturally,[19] while others, including a rabbi's daughter (*The Launching of Barbara Fabrikant*) help nature along.
>
> "'Well, isn't this a nice surprise,' Mrs. Green says. 'You know you don't look Jewish.'
>
> "'I had a nose job.'
>
> "At this Marsha laughs so hard that tears run down her cheeks. 'So did I,' she finally gasps . . . When she catches her breath she says, 'You have a beautiful nose. It's just like mine.'
>
> "'I know.' We laugh again, the Nose Sisters."[20]
>
> One might wish to debate whether helping nature along is or is not a sign of assimilation, but in many cases it is again a sign that they would like to be lost among the crowd.
>
> These are some of the problems that rabbis face in their communities. Undoubtedly if people wish to assimilate successfully, all they need to do is take the trouble to go to another town and divorce their past, as does the main character in Arthur A. Cohen's *The Carpenter Years.*

The statement by sociologist Charles Liebman that nothing "pleases most Jews more than to be told that they don't look Jewish or behave Jewishly, that they cannot be distinguished in their appearance, dress, speech, attitudes, or behavior" from non-Jews, as well as the incidence of plastic surgery to change appearances to look "less Jewish" is probably less relevant at the end of the twentieth century than it was in the 1960s or 1970s. Jews today, as many other ethnic groups, display little inhibition about their ethnicity. This is one of the positive benefits of a society that celebrates diversity and pluralism. The negative side to the celebration of diversity is that there is considerably less religious/social pressure in the Jewish community for the non-Jewish partner in a relationship to convert to Judaism. This whole issue of intermarriage/ mixed marriage is taken up presently.

INTERMARRIAGE/MIXED MARRIAGE

On every list of serious issues that face the North American Jewish community, intermarriage ranks among the top categories. There have been hundreds of books published on the subject, thousands of articles written, tens of thousands of sermons and discussions about this phenomenon. There is a budding industry that devotes itself just to the questions that are faced by intermarried couples.

In the mid-1980s, Sociologist Steven M. Cohen wrote that

> the most crucial and fundamental trend leading one to anticipate growing frequencies of intermarriage entails the growth in assimilation generally. For Jews, as for other major American religious groups, religious commitment is closely associated with the likelihood of marrying within the faith. Hence, declining commitment to the ethnic as well as to the religious aspects of Jewish identity will serve to lower barriers to intermarriage. Indeed, studies have demonstrated an increasing acceptance by both Jews and Gentiles of interreligious marriage owing to increased secularity and intergroup tolerance.[21]

Paul Ritterband suggests that by the 1990s, the "proportion of Jews who are third- and fourth-generation Americans has grown enormously and with that growth there has been a substantial increase in rates of intermarriage and falling away from the community. Concurrently, there has been a decline in the community's inhibition about intermarriage so that we now have a joint age cohort and generational effect of intermarriage." Basing his information on the 1990 National Jewish Population Survey, he explains that the "most recent rate reported for intermarriage (that is, married between 1985 and 1990) was 52 percent, up from nine percent for those married prior to 1965." Furthermore, he reports that most

> intermarriages, as recorded in communal surveys, leads to syncretism or religious neutrality in the home, a state of mind that almost inevitably terminates in cultural Christianity. The growing intermarriage rate is accompanied by a low rate of Jewish retention of children of such marriages. In recent mixed marriages, 28% of the children are reported as being reared as Jews, 31% as being reared with no religion, and 41% as being reared in some non-Jewish religion (in most instances one can presume that the religion is the Christian faith of the non-Jewish parent.)[22]

It is important to note that Ritterband refers to two different phenomena: "intermarriages" and "mixed marriages." Studies of intermarriage alternately refer to the religious upbringing of the partners, to their religion at the time of the marriage, or to their current religious affiliation. The term "intermarriage" in this context generally is used to define a marriage where one of the partners was born Jewish and one was not, whether or not the non-Jewish partner has converted. In some intermarriages, the non-Jewish partner does convert to Judaism, and the term often used for this subgroup is "Conversionary marriage." "Mixed marriage" generally refers to marriages where the Jewish-born and the non-Jewish born partners each retain their religion.

Rabbi Mark L. Winer, addressing his colleagues at a national convention in 1994, suggested the rise of Jews marrying out of the faith is less the result of low levels of Jewish identity than three confluent sociological trends. These trends, he explained, were "1) the increasing acceptability of Jews as marital partners, 2) the expanding conviction that any group identity is irrelevant to marital choice and 3) the waning concept of the desirability of marriage 'till death do us part' and the resultant growth of the frequency of divorce."[23] He develops his theme to suggest that the decline in anti-Semitism is as much to account for the acceptability of Jewish marriage partners than Jewish willingness to marry out. Further, the combination of the ideas of "Romantic love" with a general American view that devalues the importance of any group identity in successful marriage choice also leads to intermarriage. Winer also quotes sociological data to suggest that "intermarriages are four to twelve times more frequent among remarriages after divorce than among first marriages." Winer quotes the 1990 National Jewish Population Study and notes that the overall intermarriage rate between 1985 and 1990 was 52 percent. Yet, the rate for first marriages is closer to

20 percent. He adds further that since "almost half of the marriages in the Jewish community are remarriages after divorce, the intermarriage rate among the previously divorced approximates 85%."[24]

> In novels in North America the issue of conversion (someone considering conversion, someone in process of conversion, or someone who has converted) generally appears as a sub-plot, not as the major theme of the work.[25] In the fiction, as in real life, many people choose to convert because they are intertwined, engaged, or married to someone who is Jewish. Though we find conversions, or at least initial inquiries about conversion, in all of the major American movements, it is significant that where the "rabbi's fiancée" is the convert-to-be, she voluntarily does so through the Orthodox authorities: This, in spite of the fact that the rabbis are Reform. Yet, not surprisingly, both of these rabbis have traditional leanings (David Mendoza in *Pedlock Saint, Pedlock Sinner* and Michael Kind in *The Rabbi*).[26]

In his study on Jews and intermarriage, Louis A. Berman (1968) points out that oftentimes the non-Jewish partner is reaching toward Judaism just as the Jewish partner is retreating from it. This situation, he explains, allows for moments of humor. "About *your* becoming a good Jew," a rabbi explains, "I am not worried. But what of your [born-Jewish] husband; do you think we can make a Jew out of him?" Berman continues:

> Responding to a young lady's inquiry about conversion to Judaism, a rabbi began to explain the various steps she must take to become an observant Jew. Her fiancé impatiently demanded to know why his future wife had to become a *religious* Jew. "Why can't she be like me?" His fiancée interjected, "But Honey, I can't be like you; you're a *born* Jew. I was born Italian. The only kind of Jew I *can* become is a religious Jew."[27]

Yet even after conversion, the matter does not really rest. A point that occurs in real life, yet is only touched upon in the fiction is the difficulty that some converts encounter following conversion. Berman explains that conversion does not automatically confer acceptance upon the convert. Adherence

> to the religion of Judaism does not make a person authentically Jewish in the eyes of the Jewish community, which (a) makes an implicit distinction between Judaism and Jewishness, and (b) defines Jewishness according to how thoroughly one's kinship is bound up with other Jews. By this implicit standard, the intermarried convert to Judaism is at best only half Jewish because only half of his [her] extended family is Jewish. Hence the distress of those converts to Judaism who discover that despite their best efforts to lead a thoroughly Jewish life, they are not recognized as being "really" Jewish.[28]

As Lena Romanoff explains in her book *Your People, My People: Finding Acceptance and Fulfillment as a Jew By Choice*, "one of the most serious problems facing all converts . . . [is] lack of acceptance by other Jews."[29] Stated very explicitly, many a female convert has been referred to as "the *shiksah*" and male converts as "the *shaigetz*" [the masculine equivalent of *shiksah*] or as "the *goy*," this despite sincere attempts to integrate into the Jewish community. A recent guidebook to conversion to Judaism notes that while some in-laws and family members are accepting of the person's decision to convert, others remain quite resistant. Clearly, Jewish families differ as much as non-Jewish ones. Some are kind, caring, and welcoming, with or without a good knowledge of Judaism. "Some are observant, but unwelcoming toward converts. Some are ignorant about Judaism and hostile to a convert."[30]

With the high incidence of intermarriage/mixed marriage, "marrying out" of the faith is not seen as "shameful" as in earlier generations. As noted earlier, in recent years there is considerably less religious/social pressure in the Jewish community for the non-Jewish partner in a relationship to convert to Judaism. A greater acceptance notwithstanding, intermarriage continues to be a serious issue of discussion in the Jewish community.

> It is this very issue of the likely non-acceptance—or acceptance-with-reservations—of a person who has converted to Judaism that impels the Placement Director, Rabbi Sher, to discourage Rabbi Michael and Leslie Kind (*The Rabbi*) from going into the congregational rabbinate. Leslie is a convert to Judaism.[31] Despite Rabbi Sher's advice, the Kinds opt for the congregational rabbinate. Later in the novel, when the Kinds have just moved to a different city, where Michael is about to serve a new congregation, Leslie tells Michael that she dreads going

> to services, she hates seeing the new women congregants. "Those . . . *yentehs* [busybodies] . . . flock to the temple, not to pray, not even to hear the new rabbi, but to see the *shickseh*."[32] On the other hand, Rabbi Peretz Vogel (Jerome Weidman's *The Temple*) is married to a woman who is not Jewish, and this does not seem to be a significant issue for the congregation.[33] Likewise, Rabbi Arthur Bloom (*The Rabbi of Casino Boulevard*) is married to a non-Jewish woman, and that is not an impediment for his congregation.[34]

Despite the chilly reaction that face some converts, by and large, rabbis enjoy teaching converts to Judaism. Here are men and women who are seeking to learn about the faith and fate of Judaism, who are willing to study on a serious, adult level. Oftentimes, a special bond develops between the rabbi and the convert. Louis A. Berman points out that the rabbi "appreciates her intelligence and sensitivity, enjoys her fresh and honest interest in Judaism. The rabbi may feel quite embarrassed and irritated toward the discourtesy of those who question her sincerity or honesty, and outraged at the 'surly stand-offishness' which born-Jews may direct toward the convert."[35]

> Rabbi Ed Gordon (*Thy Daughter's Nakedness*) is teaching a course on Talmud. While a number of his congregants are taking the course, it is the young woman who is converting who is the real joy of the class. "Betsy had a quick intelligence and an openness to ideas, with no ax to grind. More and more when he addressed the little class . . . he was in fact talking to Betsy and wishing that the others would shut up."[36] While Betsy's parents-in-law initially are very pleased with her conversion, their appreciation sours when she makes religious demands upon her husband and will not eat at their home because they do not observe the dietary laws.

In real life, parents come to rabbis and then ask them to speak to their children about the proposed marriage with someone who is not born Jewish. Berman suggests that the parents may not meet a sympathetic ear. "The distressed parents may seek help from a rabbi, but get little sympathy or comfort from him. Did they give their child a Jewish education? Did they observe the customs of the Jewish religion? How often do they attend the synagogue? It becomes apparent that the parents are concerned with something other than religious values *per se*."[37]

> In Philip Roth's novel *Portnoy's Complaint*, we learn of the saga of his cousin, Hershie, who while still in high school was going with a non-Jewish girl. The family argued and argued. "When all else failed, Rabbi Warsaw was asked to join with the family one Sunday afternoon, to urge our Hershie not to take his young life and turn it over to his own worst enemy. . . . He remained in consultation with the defiant boy and the blighted family for over an hour."[38]

As noted above, "mixed marriages" are where the Jewish-born and the non-Jewish born partners each retain their religion. Virtually every rabbi among the mainstream religious traditions within American Judaism has had couples come to him or her and ask if the rabbi would either perform their marriage or recommend the name of a rabbi who would perform that marriage. Oftentimes, the rabbi will meet with the couple and point out the difficulties that they will encounter should they go ahead with their plans. Rabbis clearly prefer endogamy: marriage within Judaism. If the rabbi cannot convince the couple to change their minds, which is probably an unlikely possibility, then the rabbi may suggest that the non-Jew might consider conversion. The success rate of rabbis convincing couples *not* to enter into a mixed married union is very limited. By the time that the couple comes to the rabbi, in most cases they have determined to follow through with their plans. At times, in real life as in the fictional world, the Jewish partner has come to the rabbi under duress. He or she walks into the rabbi's study an angry person, probably irate with his or her parents who have insisted that "at least they go to see the rabbi." In a number of cases, this misplaced fury is taken out on the rabbi. Alternately, when rabbis are not successful in convincing the couple from desisting from their plans, the rabbis are blamed for their failure.

> In Myron S. Kaufmann's *Thy Daughter's Nakedness*, we find the example of a young man who has decided to "marry out" of the faith. When his parents learn of this and the fact that he says that he intends to drop his religion altogether, "his

parents made him go to Ed [Rabbi Ed Gordon] to discuss it, but Ed did not succeed in changing the boy's mind." In their discussion, it becomes clear that "the boy has scarcely any religious training, and his family's affiliation was of the most inactive and marginal kind." It is obvious that the boy has already made up his mind. Rabbi Gordon correctly comes to the conclusion that in a couple of hours, "he could not impart a sense of tradition that had been absent for a lifetime." In the novel, the young man's parents are furious that Rabbi Gordon could not dissuade the young couple from their plans.[39]

The unnamed young man in that novel, however, at least was polite, an improvement over the couple who comes to see Rabbi Lichtman in Philip Roth's novel *Letting Go*. After relating the fact that they eventually had to go to a Justice of the Peace to get married, the narrator explains that Paul and Libby had been surprised that they could not find a rabbi to marry them: "In the study of the third rabbi they visited, Paul rose up out of his seat and cursed him.

"'Isn't there a hot rabbi who performs marriages on kitchen tables? In all of this city is there no man low enough to unite two people who want to be united?'

"'Try City Hall,' the rabbi said. . . . 'Get united civilly.'"

Rabbi Lichtman then explains, "I marry Jew and Jew. . . . That's all."

When Paul retorts that they are Jew and Gentile, the rabbi explains that the Jewish ceremony is for Jews. Paul shouts at the rabbi and is verbally very abusive. Having lost his temper also, Rabbi Lichtman finally says, "You're a secular, *be* secular! Don't come tramping your muddy feet in my synagogue for sentimental reasons!"[40]

Though it takes place in Great Britain and it is two lay people speaking, the following remark sums up fairly well the prevailing view among rabbis and others who work with mixed married couples. "Mixed marriages mean mixed up children. Goyim should marry goyim and Jews should marry Jews."[41]

While the ideal may be that Jews should marry Jews, as we have seen above, this is not what is taking place in the American Jewish community. Jews are marrying non-Jews, some of whom are converting to Judaism. The percentage of marriages where the non-Jewish partner does convert, however, is decreasing, as there is more acceptance of "out-marriage." When the non-Jewish partner is a male, the children of his Jewish wife are universally accepted as Jewish. When, however, a Jewish man marries a non-Jewish woman, and she chooses not to convert, then there is considerable controversy concerning the status of their children. How the modern Jewish community has dealt with this issue of "patrilineality" is considered below.

PATRILINEALITY

While the ordination of women was regarded as a major departure from past practice and was roundly disparaged—certainly by Orthodox (as well as by a number of Conservative) rabbis—it paled as an issue in comparison to the reaction which followed the Reform movement's decision to formally embrace "patrilineality." Though patrilineality had been the norm for determining Jewishness in the Biblical period, roughly the first 2,000 years of Judaism, since the Rabbinic period and until the present, approximately another 2,000 years, "matrilineality," or determining that only a child born of a Jewish mother is Jewish, has been the accepted standard.[42] The change from patrilineality to matrilineality, some would argue, came about because of the high incidence of rape by Roman soldiers within the occupied Palestinian Jewish community. In order to preserve family integrity, they suggest, the rabbis decided that any child born of a Jewish mother was Jewish. Others date the change from patrilineality to matrilineality to the time of Ezra, in the mid-fifth century Before the Common Era. Shaye J. D. Cohen places the change in the Mishnaic period, about 1,800 or 1,900 years ago, and suggests that the transition came about through the influx of Roman ideas and the rabbinic interest in mixtures of all sorts. Furthermore, he argues that by the first century in the Common Era, the idea had taken hold within Judaism that a gentile woman "'converted' to Judaism not through marriage with a Jewish husband (as was the practice in biblical times) but through a separate ritual (immersion in water). . . . If [a gentile woman] converts to Judaism, her children are Jewish; if she does not, they are gentiles." Cohen then concludes that there "is no evidence that the matrilineal principle was introduced in response to any particular social need."[43] Whatever are the real origins of matrilineality, it is clear that this has been normative Jewish thinking for two millennia.

> In Herbert Tarr's *So Help Me God!*, a rabbi makes the case for patrilineality: "Whatever obscure reasons for the second-century ruling that only the child of a Jewish woman is considered a Jew—before that Jewishness had been patrilineal—that practice must end. Makes no sense for religion to be determined by the mother, and lineage and Hebrew name by the father. The offspring of *either* Jewish parent should be regarded as a Jew."[44]

While the weight of 2,000 years of Jewish traditional law is a powerful force, both Reform and Reconstructionist Judaism maintained that changes needed to be made in that principle for both ideological and practical reasons. Equalization of status between men and women was one consideration. Further, Jewish men were marrying non-Jewish women, and often the couple wished to rear their children as Jews. Consequently, for dozens of years in America, in addition to acknowledging matrilineality, Reform and Reconstructionist Jews had in many cases accepted patrilineality *de facto*. At its 1983 national convention, the Reform movement's Central Conference of American Rabbis adopted patrilineality as its official, *de jure* position.[45] As explained in Chapter 2, the resolution stated that "the child of one Jewish parent is under the presumption of Jewish descent. This presumption of the Jewish status of the offspring of any mixed marriage is to be established through appropriate and timely public and formal acts of identification with the Jewish faith and people." While this decision merely confirmed current practice, it unleashed a storm of protest from both the Orthodox and Conservative rabbinate, a storm that continues virtually unabated to this day, primarily among the Orthodox and traditional-leaning Conservative rabbinate. Among the arguments that were raised in protest to the Reform position was that this would set up needless divisions within the Jewish community. Orthodox, and possibly Conservative, Jews would not, or could not, marry Reform or Reconstructionist Jews because there would be a question about one's true "Jewishness." The Reconstructionist movement had adopted an affirmative position on Patrilineality years before the Reform movement did so.

"Patrilineality" as an issue which divides Orthodox, Conservative and Reform Jews is highlighted by Rabbi Daniel Winter (*An Eye for an Eye*) at a retreat organized for rabbis from all of these movements.[46] Patrilineality also comes up as a subject at a dinner party in Andrew Kane's novel *Rabbi, Rabbi*. It is clear that even among Reform rabbis there is not a unanimity of views. "Rabbi Samuels, an ardent proponent of fathers having equal say in the religion of their children, was arguing that if men and women were to be considered truly equal in all aspects, then the man's religion should be as strong a determinant as the woman's in deciding the religion of the child."[47] Reform Rabbi Rebecca Kleinman counters with the argument that the issue of patrilineality will create an incredible division within the Jewish community. The children of Conservative and Orthodox would be unable to marry Reform children because by "their definition," the Reform children would not be Jewish. Then Orthodox Rabbi Yaakov Eisen points out that at least one knows for certain who the mother is, though he admits that the state of affairs today is significantly different from other periods in Jewish history when "Jewish women were being raped on a fairly regular basis." Another female rabbi present dismisses Eisen's statement with the reply that his is "a weak argument . . . because it's the usual Orthodox stuff of resolving present inequities by referring to historical conditions that no longer exist."[48]

When Rabbi Arthur Bloom (*The Rabbi of Casino Boulevard*) meets with some of the professors at his seminary, one of them argues the case for matrilineality "because it can always be established who a child's mother is, while fatherhood remains elusive."[49]

The issue of Patrilineal descent will continue to divide Jews for many years to come. Orthodoxy is unlikely to change its position on the status of Jews, and by the same token there is no indication that Reform or Reconstructionist Jews will bend either. Sociologist Egon Mayer (1995) writes about the fact that most American Jews have accepted the principle of patrilineal descent as a legitimate basis of Jewish identity. While the Orthodox overwhelmingly remain opposed, they are in the minority. Nearly half of Conservative Jews accept patrilineality, as do 70 percent of nondenominational Jews.[50]

NOTES

1. Charles S. Liebman, quoted in Woocher, J. S. (1986). *Sacred Survival: The Civil Religion of American Jews* (Bloomington and Indianapolis: Indiana University Press), p. 94 f. The full list is:

   1. That there is nothing incompatible in being a good Jew and a good American.
   2. That separation of church and state is an essential for protecting Jews and Judaism in America.
   3. That Jews constitute one indivisible people and that denominational differences must not be permitted to threaten this essential unity.
   4. That problems of theology are somewhat irrelevant, and that insuring the physical and spiritual survival of the Jewish people is more important than theological disputation.
   5. That Jewish rituals are valuable forms of Jewish self-expression and help unify the family, but that individuals must be free to select and adapt Jewish practices to conform with modern norms.
   6. That every Jew must work for the survival of Israel, but need not live there.

2. Liebman, C. S. (1973). *The Ambivalent American Jew* (Philadelphia: Jewish Publication Society), p. 23.

3. Liebman, *The Ambivalent American Jew*, p. 25 f.

4. Marcus, J. R. (1964). "Background for the History of American Jewry," in *The American Jew: A Reappraisal*, ed. Oscar I. Janowsky (Philadelphia: Jewish Publication Society of America), p. 13.

5. Litvinoff, B. (1969). *A Peculiar People: Inside World Jewry Today* (London: Weidenfeld and Nicolson), p. 169. Cf. Gordon, N. (1965). *The Rabbi* (New York: McGraw-Hill), p. 21 "I have very good neighbors. Lovely Irishers."

6. Ritterband, P. (1995). "Modern Times and Jewish Assimilation," in *The Americanization of the Jews*, ed. Robert M. Seltzer and Norman J. Cohen (New York and London: New York University Press), p. 377 f.

7. Ritterband, p. 379. See p. 391, n. 2.

8. Bermant, C. (1966 [1965]). *Ben Preserve Us!* (New York: Holt, Rinehart and Winston), p. 30.

Again in Britain, the biting satire of Welsh physician/poet Dannie Abse parodies the Jew who has chosen to opt out of his Jewishness. He changes his own name; he chooses the names of the gospel's writers (!) for his sons; moves to a non-Jewish neighborhood; and then joins an exclusive [read: no-Jews allowed] golf-club:

> "Consider the mazzle of Baruch Levy
> who changed his name to Barry Lee,
> who moved to Esher, Surrey,
> who sent his four sons—Matthew, Mark,
> Luke and John—to boarding school,
> who had his wife's nose fixed,
> his own hair dyed,
> who, blinking in the Gents,
> turned from the writing on the wall
> (KILL JEWISH PIGS)
> and later, still blinking, joined the golf club.
>
> With new friend, Colonel Owen,
> first game out, under vexed clouds,
> thunder detonated without rain,
> lightning stretched without thunder,
> and near the 2nd hole,
> where the darker green edged
> to the shaved lighter green,
> both looked up terrified.
> Barbed fire zagged towards them
> to strike dead instantly
> Mostyn Owen, Barry Lee's opponent.
> What luck that Colonel Owen
> (as Barry discovered later)
> once was known as Moshe Cohen."

Abse, D. (1976). "Tales of Shatz." *Jewish Chronicle Literary Supplement* (June 4): v [5]. This poem, in slightly modified form, appears in *Voices Within the Ark: The Modern Jewish Poets*, ed. Howard Schwartz and Anthony Rudolf, (Yonkers, NY: Pushcart, 1980), pp. 823–825.

9. Levin, M. (1965 [1963]). *The Fanatic* (New York: Pocket), p. 36, cf. p. 32.

10. Gordon, p. 172.

11. Tarr, H. (1968). *Heaven Help Us!* (New York: Random House), p. 22.

12. Gordon, p. 282.

13. Fruchter, N. (1987 [1962]). *Coat Upon A Stick* (Philadelphia: Jewish Publication Society), p. 130.

14. Gordon, p. 214.

15. Tarr, H. (1963). *The Conversion of Chaplain Cohen* (New York: Avon), p. 172.

16. Kaufmann, M. S. (1968). *Thy Daughter's Nakedness* (Philadelphia and New York: J. B. Lippincott), p. 537.

17. Tarr, *Heaven Help Us!*, p. 101 ff.

18. Liebman, *The Ambivalent American Jew*, pp. 24–25. For fictional examples where Jews are pleased when they are told that they don't look Jewish, see Kaufmann, M. S. (1957). *Remember Me to God* (Philadelphia and New York: J. B. Lippincott), p. 191; Tarr, *The Conversion of Chaplain Cohen*, pp. 173–174.

As the twentieth century comes to a close, the rate of intermarriage has increased enormously. With this has come a *greater* acceptance of "outmarriage." Consequently, Liebman's point that Jews are scandalized by intermarriage, and that they insist that the non-Jewish partner in a marriage convert to Judaism is not as valid in the 1990s. I address this matter in a section to follow.

19. Tarr, *Heaven Help Us!*, p. 2.

20. Rose, L. B. (1974). *The Launching of Barbara Fabrikant* (New York: David McKay Company), p. 43.

21. Cohen, S. M. (1983). *American Modernity and Jewish Identity* (New York: Tavistock Publications), p. 123.

22. Ritterband, p. 382 f.

23. Winer, M. L. (1995). "Our Vision of the Future: Personal Status and K'lal Yisra-eil," *Central Conference of American Rabbis Yearbook 104* (1994), (New York: Central Conference of American Rabbis), p. 63.

24. Winer, p. 63.

25. Examples of novels where conversion to Judaism appears as a subplot include: Kaufmann's *Thy Daughter's Nakedness*, pp. 167 ff.; Gordon, pp. 194 ff.; Longstreet, S. (1969). *Pedlock Saint, Pedlock Sinner* (New York: Delacorte), p. 226 ff.; Abrams, M. (1954). *Awakened* (Philadelphia: Jewish Publication Society of America), p. 320; Levine, M. with Kantor, H. (1985). *The Congregation* (New York: G. P. Putnam's Sons), p. 203 ff.; Jacobs, I. (1972). *Ten For Kaddish* (New York: W. W. Norton), p. 212.; Kemelman, H. (1981). *Conversations with Rabbi Small* (New York: William Morrow), pp. 24 ff., *That Day the Rabbi Left Town* (New York: Fawcett Columbine, 1996), p. 116; Appel, A. (1986). *The Rabbi of Casino Boulevard* (New York: Saint Martin's), p. 191.

26. Longstreet, *Pedlock Saint, Pedlock Sinner*, p. 226 ff.; Gordon, p. 194 ff.

27. Berman, L. A. (1968). *Jews and Intermarriage: A Study in Personality and Culture* (New York: Thomas Yoseloff), p. 232 f.

28. Berman, L. A., p. 306.

29. Romanoff, L. with Hostein, L. (1990). *Your People, My People: Finding Acceptance and Fulfillment as a Jew By Choice* (Philadelphia, New York: Jewish Publication Society), p. 128.

30. Epstein, L. J. (1994). *Conversion to Judaism: A Guidebook* (Northvale, NJ and London: Jason Aronson), p. 52.

31. Gordon, p. 206 f.

32. Gordon, p. 278.

33. Weidman, J. (1975). *The Temple* (New York: Simon and Schuster), pp. 228–232.

34. Appel, p. 284 f.

35. Berman, L. A., p. 149.

36. Kaufmann, *Thy Daughter's Nakedness*, p. 234.

37. Berman, L. A., p. 250.

38. Roth, P. (1969). *Portnoy's Complaint* (New York: Random House), p. 57. Cf. Gordon, p. 320.

39. Kaufmann, *Thy Daughter's Nakedness*, p. 511.

40. Roth, P. (1962). *Letting Go* (New York: Random House), p. 102 f.

41. Bermant, C. (1971). *Now Dowager* (London: Eyre and Spottiswoode), p. 40.

42. A great deal has been written about the subject of matrilineality/patrilineality. In 1985, the respected journal *Judaism* devoted a whole issue to this one subject, asking rabbis and scholars from all schools of thought within Judaism to share their thoughts. Cohen, S. J. D., Bleich, J. D., Cohen, J. J., and others. (1985). "The Issue of Patrilineal Descent: A Symposium." *Judaism* 34:1 (Winter): 5–135.

43. Cohen, S. J. D. (1985). "The Matrilineal Principle in Historical Perspective." *Judaism* 34:1 (Winter): 13. For the argument proposing matrilineality stemming from the time of Ezra, see Zlotowitz, B. M. (1985). "A Perspective on Patrilineal Descent." *Judaism* 34:1 (Winter): 129–135; "Patrilineal Descent," in *The Jewish Condition*, ed. Aron Hirt-Manheimer (New York: Union of American Hebrew Congregations Press, 1995), pp. 260–267.

44. Tarr, H. (1979). *So Help Me God!* (New York: Times Books), p. 244.

45. Umansky, E. M. (1995). "Feminism and American Reform Judaism" in *The Americanization of the Jews*, ed. Robert M. Seltzer and Norman J. Cohen (New York and London: New York University Press), pp. 277 f. See also Schaalman, H. E. (1988). "Patrilineal Descent: A Report and Assessment," *Central Conference of American Rabbis Yearbook 97*, pp. 110–111; and also Lipman, section on "Lineality," in "*Tanu Rabbanan: Our Masters*," pp. 47–49.

46. Telushkin, J. (1992 [1991]). *An Eye for an Eye* (New York: Bantam), p. 46.

47. Kane, A. (1995). *Rabbi, Rabbi* (New York: Saint Martin's), p. 216.

48. Kane, p. 217. See also pp. 122–123. Though they will eventually receive ordination, technically, Rebecca Kleinman and Yaakov Eisen are still pursuing their studies, Kleinman at the Reform seminary, the Hebrew Union College-Jewish Institute of Religion, and Eisen at the Orthodox, Yeshiva University.

49. Appel, p. 198.

50. Mayer, E. (1995). "From an External to an Internal Agenda," in *The Americanization of the Jews*, ed. Robert M. Seltzer and Norman J. Cohen. (New York and London: New York University Press), p. 424.

10

God, Israel, and Tradition

Jewish theology is wider than an inquiry about the relationship between God and humankind, or the special relationship between God and the people Israel, or the problem of good and evil. Jewish theology needs to be understood as part of the ongoing covenant with God which links Jewish history with the Land of Israel and the Jewish people. Modern Jewish theology addresses issues including Chosenness, the Holocaust, and the reestablishment of the State of Israel.[1] Whenever Jews—and even more so rabbis—in real life, as in the fiction, speak, they have to be heard as reflecting their historical past. The horror of the Holocaust is everpresent in Jewish minds, even as all Jews are bound up with the fate of the State of Israel. Jews speak of a *shalshelet ha-kabbalah* [a chain of transmission] which links all generations of Jewish life and which reflects the Jewish encounter with God. Judaism today is but a point on a continuum which reaches back to the first Jews, Abraham and Sarah. It is because of this interdependence of God, Israel, and Tradition that they are joined together in this chapter.

GOD

Belief and Action

Orthodoxy, explains Gilbert Rosenthal, sees Judaism as a religious way of life. It is predicated on a belief in God and in God's Torah, which was initially revealed at Mount Sinai and then explicated by succeeding generations of sages. It is in the area of Torah and Halakhah [Jewish law and traditional practice] that Orthodox Judaism has concentrated its creative genius, rather than placing an emphasis on defining God. "Orthodoxy has little to say about God except to repeat the standard theological formulations of doxology: God exists; [God] is one; [God] is a personal God; [God] is omnipotent, omniscient, omnipresent, eternal and compassionate; [God] is spirit rather than form."[2]

Rosenthal's observations are borne out by two recent statements presented at a Symposium (1996) sponsored by the editors of the magazine *Commentary*, titled "What Do American Jews Believe?"[3] It is not the *nature* of God that Orthodox rabbis address, rather what God wants of humankind, which is to follow God's commandments. Rabbi Norman Lamm, President of Yeshiva University, has written that theology is essentially a monologue by humans about God. It has its place, he suggests, "on the periphery of the consciousness of a believing Jew. In the center, however, stands God, and man must not merely *think about* Him, but *respond to* Him as part of the dialogue between man and his Creator." Lamm continues, explaining that in "Judaism, the will of God is made known to man in the Torah, mostly in the form of *mitzvot*, commandments. These commandments are, by their very nature, binding. They summon man to obey . . . we may understand or not understand a commandment, prefer one *mitzvah* to another, but all God's will must be obeyed."[4] Orthodox Rabbi Saul J. Berman takes a similar position: "The more I study the Torah the more I am convinced that it is the revealed word of God." Further, Berman states, "I believe that the Torah is the expression of God's wisdom for the Jewish people, and ultimately for all of humanity. Therefore, every *mitzvah* of the Torah is the bearer of meaning and of potential for perfection."[5]

Conservative Judaism presents a broader spectrum of belief systems. Rabbi Elliot N. Dorff writes that when we turn to the issue of theology, "the Conservative Movement seems to be . . . seriously disjointed." Thinkers associated with the Conservative movement represent a variety of viewpoints. There are those who are "genuinely eclectic in their thought" such as Simon Greenberg, Louis Jacobs, and Dorff himself. In addition, some take specific approaches. Among those he mentions are

> naturalism (e.g., Mordecai Kaplan) and humanism (Eugene Kohn), pantheism (Jacob Kohn), predicate theology (Harold Schulweis), rationalism (Jacob Agus, Ben Zion Bokser, Robert Gordis), Hegelianism (Milton Steinberg), organic thinking *à la* Whitehead (Max Kadushin), existentialism of both atheistic (Richard Rubenstein) and theistic (Herschel Matt, Seymour Siegel, Arnold J. Wolf) sorts, phenomenology (Abraham [Joshua] Heschel), narrative theology (Michael Goldberg), and linguistic analysis (Neil Gillman).

A wide variety of views to be sure, but one which Dorff suggests "are linked not so much by a particular view of God, but rather by their common, historical view of Judaism as a developing civilization and by their stress on Jewish law in its evolving form."[6]

In the aforementioned "Symposium," Rabbi Ismar Schorsch, Chancellor at the Jewish Theological Seminary, explains that for him "God is both transcendent and immanent, incomprehensible and knowable. . . . God is a verb and not a noun, an ineffable presence that graces my life with a daily touch of eternity."[7] His colleague, Rabbi Elliot N. Dorff, who is Provost at the University of Judaism in Los Angeles writes that he believes "in a personal God Who interacts with us individually and collectively, as much female as male in characteristics." He explains that

> Jewish religious law is authoritative for me both as the practice of my people and as God's revelation. Our understanding of what God wants of us, however, continually develops, a position which the rabbis of the Talmud held, too. We must determine the content of Jewish law, however, as a community, not solely as individuals, for otherwise Jewish law loses its coherence and authority. The evolving nature of our community and our understanding of revelation explains why we need to make adjustments in Jewish law, dropping or reinterpreting some of the practices in the tradition and adding others.[8]

Reconstructionist Judaism was founded by Mordecai M. Kaplan. His theology came to be called "transnatural" because he believed that "the divine works through nature and human beings. He neither identified God with things in the world (natural) nor did he consider God to be beyond or detached from the world (supernatural)."[9] As was noted in Chapter 1 (The Rabbi in America), the Reconstructionist Movement has grown and developed, and while Kaplan's philosophy remains at the core of its ideology, now "Kaplan's teachings are viewed not as the end of the story, but as the beginning."[10] In recent years, Harold Schulweis' "predicate theology" has been a strong influence within the Reconstructionist Movement, as has the thinking of Harold Kushner, who argues that "God is neither all-powerful nor present everywhere." Schulweis "suggests that we refer to God not as subject, but as predicate." As Rebecca T. Alpert and Jacob J. Staub, the authors of *Exploring Judaism: A Reconstructionist Approach*, explain, for Reconstructionists, "Schulweis's terminology . . . would say that it is more important, for example, to believe that justice, kindness, and compassion are godly, than that God is a Person possessing the attributes of justice, kindness, and compassion. This is another way of expressing the importance of human responsibility to bring *godliness* into the world."[11]

In the "Symposium" on the beliefs of American Jews, Rabbi David A. Teutsch, President of the Reconstructionist Rabbinical College, explains that "I very much feel the presence of the divine in nature, in community, and in the workings of my own heart. It is up to us to seek God, however, because God is not a divine person Who intrudes in our lives or makes individual decisions, but rather the unifying dimension of our reality that is the ground of being and morality."[12]

Virtually since its inception, Reform Judaism has had much to say about the nature of God. "Clearly, the traditional supernatural concept of a deity who speaks to . . . [humankind], suspends the natural order of the universe through miracles, and is described in the Bible and rabbinic literature in human, anthropomorphic terms was unacceptable to Reform theologians."[13] As with the Conservative Movement, there are a wide variety of beliefs and theological positions. The spectrum of beliefs include neo-Orthodoxy, various notions linked to existentialism, naturalism, and a clear rejection of authoritarian supernaturalism. In the Reform Movement's "Centenary Perspective" (1976), the section which dealt with God explained that Reform Jews continue to affirm God and that Reform Jews "ground our lives, personally and communally, on God's reality and remain open to new experiences and conceptions of the Divine." Furthermore, it affirmed that "human beings, created in God's image, share in God's eternality despite the mystery we call death." Rabbi Sheldon Zimmerman, the President of the Hebrew

Union College-Jewish Institute of Religion, in the *Commentary* "Symposium," wrote that he believes "in God, the Creator of the universe and all that exists, the ongoing creative source of its unity, harmony, order and meaning. God has established a covenental relationship with all humankind . . . calling all of us to an ethical life of justice and peace." Zimmerman goes on to explain that it is his belief that "God entered history as a redemptive force at the time of the exodus from Egypt and as a guarantor of an age of justice and peace for all humankind at the end of history. We humans are called to work together cooperatively and with God to bring this ultimate time into being."[14] Zimmerman's colleague, Rabbi Eric H. Yoffie, President of the Union of American Hebrew Congregations, expresses a similar vision: "I believe in God Who gave Torah to the people of Israel in a process of revelation beginning at Sinai." He goes on to explain that "the heart of Torah is *mitzvah*—the individual divine command." Yoffie then explains where he differs from Orthodoxy, for while Orthodox thinkers would say *all* of the *mitzvot* are equally binding (see Lamm and Berman's comments, above), Yoffie explains that Reform Jews, with their concept of personal autonomy, have to decide which of the *mitzvot* (commandments) are binding and which are not. "I must *examine* each *mitzvah* and ask the question: do I feel commanded in this instance as Moses was commanded?"[15]

Given the variety of theological positions that we find throughout Judaism, which range from a more traditional approach with Orthodoxy to the many different positions taken by rabbis in the Conservative, Reconstructionist, and Reform movements, Rabbi David Small clearly overstates his case when he posits to a classroom of college students (in *Tuesday the Rabbi Saw Red*) that in Judaism "we have no theology, at least not in the generally accepted sense."[16]

In that same discussion, Rabbi Small makes some other rather startling comments. He says that Judaism does not have a theology, because

> we don't need one. . . . Our religion is based on the idea of a single God, a God of Justice. If you think about it, the concept of justice demands a single God because it implies a single standard. And because He is infinite, He is unknowable to finite minds. We don't forbid the study of Him . . . but we consider it pointless. . . . So

because we believe it's pointless to know the unknowable, we have no theology.[17]

Perhaps these words ("we have no theology") are placed in Rabbi Small's mouth simply to be provocative. It is quite clear from earlier works that he is much more knowledgeable. For example, as was mentioned in Chapter 2 (Mainstream Rabbis and Sectarian Orthodox Rabbis), Rabbi Small stated that faith as such is not required of Jews. He also refers (in *Sunday the Rabbi Stayed Home*) to the teaching of the prophet Micah, who explained that what God expects of us is to walk in God's ways (Micah 6:8). Then, Rabbi Small says that people can walk in God's ways and still have doubts about God's existence. "After all, you can't always control your thoughts." Furthermore, he notes that faith "is not a requirement of our religion. . . . I suspect it's a kind of special talent that some have to a greater degree than others."[18]

Indeed (again, as mentioned in Chapter 2), in *Monday the Rabbi Took Off*, Rabbi Small made it quite clear that Judaism places more emphasis on our deeds than our particular faith, or the nature of that faith, at any given moment. When asked if he believes in God, Rabbi Small replied that this is a difficult question to answer because it depends on a number of variables when you ask if "I believe in God."[19] The mere fact that Rabbi Small can offer (among many others) three different variables concerning God, *all ideas within mainstream Jewish belief*, shows that he is well aware that Judaism and theology are not incompatible.

Just as Rabbi Small is deliberately provocative in his statement to the college students that Judaism lacks a theology in the generally accepted sense, so in a similar manner Rabbi Ed Gordon clearly overstates his case when (in *Thy Daughter's Nakedness*) he says, "Human beings weren't made to be theologians—it's a waste of time. We haven't the capacity." Rabbi Gordon's point is that God wants us to be moral human beings. "The question is how to live. . . . All we have is a working hypothesis—to live as if there were a moral law, as if the world were made by God. That's why it says 'love God,' instead of 'believe in God.'" He then is asked if someone loves God and

> then does something because of that love, does this not mean that you believe in God as well? Rabbi Gordon quickly agrees. "Sure. And it's the only kind of belief that means anything. But 'love' instead of 'belief' keeps your eye on what you can understand. Who cares how you interpret your beliefs, as long as you come up with the right action?"[20]

Rabbi Gordon's statements, that "human beings weren't made to be theologians" and that it does not matter how you "interpret your beliefs" notwithstanding, the fact is that there are a wide spectrum of belief systems in Judaism. It is correct that Judaism does not have an organized continuous and required systematic theology. Nonetheless, the explication of beliefs is a matter of considerable weight. While Judaism has a fairly wide latitude in terms of interpretation, there are areas into which one could move which are beyond Judaism. For example, if you "interpret your belief" to claim trinitarianism, this is beyond Judaic thought. If you claim that God is absolutely amoral and capricious, this too is beyond standard Judaic thought. "One can live fully and authentically as a Jew without having a single satisfactory answer to . . . doubts [about God]; one cannot, however, live a thoughtful Jewish life without having asked the questions."[21]

Certainly we can have doubts, and there are so-called "radical Jewish theologians" such as Richard Rubenstein (*After Auschwitz* [1966], *Morality and Eros* [1970]), but having doubts about God's existence, or serious questions as to how God and humans interact, is different from a categorical denial of God's existence or God's relationship with the Jewish people.

> In the novel *Acts of Faith*, Rabbi Deborah Luria suggests that we may pray to God but we cannot be sure that God cares to give us an answer. She preaches in a sermon that ". . . we must be ready to serve a God who sends us no angel, neither to rescue us, nor to tell us that what we are doing is right."[22] This theology of a "distant God" is a marked transit from her religious background, for she is the daughter of a Hasidic "Rebbe."
>
> Her theology also is far from the more traditional approaches of Rabbis Michael Kind (Noah Gordon's *The Rabbi*) and Rabbi Joshua Kaye (Mordecai Schreiber's *The Rabbi and the Nun*), both of whose prayers to God indicate their belief that

> God hears, and responds, to our requests.[23] Likewise, Rabbi Diane Warburg ("Love hurts") clearly believes that one can have a personal relationship with God, though this does not mean that we will have instantaneous replies to our questions. For example, during a personal crisis in her family's life, she rolls her eyes upward and says to God, "I could use a ruling on this . . . O.K., a hint." Earlier in the series she had responded to her good friend's question why life had to be such a mess, "Do not expect an immediate answer, He's thinking about it."[24]

Belief in God is a multifaceted, multilayered question. Periodically, congregants will come to rabbis and raise questions about the existence of God. As there are no irrefutable proofs in real life, so with the fictional rabbis there are no sure answers.

> Rabbi Max Gross (*The Rabbi*) asks rhetorically: "Do you think I have scientific knowledge of God? Can I go back in time and be there when God speaks to Isaac or delivers the Commandments? If this could be done there would be only one religion in the world; we would all know which group is right." He then goes on to say, "About God, you don't *know* and I don't *know*. But I have made a decision in favor of God."[25]
>
> Similarly, Rabbi Leo Berdick (*The Strong Hand*) can say, "Belief can be the struggle to believe!" To illustrate his point, Rabbi Berdick tells the story of a pious rabbi who paused in his daily prayers when he came to the phrase, "I believe with perfect faith . . . that the Creator . . . is the author and guide of everything that has been created." The rabbi realized that he had some doubts and that he could not honestly pray these words. After struggling within himself he came up with a solution. "I'll not say, 'I believe with *perfect* faith,' . . . I will pray, 'Oh that I *might* believe with perfect faith.'"[26]

Real-life Rabbi Leonard S. Kravitz has written about the difficulties of theological language. The mere question "Do you believe in God?" presents all kinds of problems.

> First of all, which God is meant? Or more clearly put: which God, according to which theological synthesis? Are we asked to affirm

belief in the God Who is reported to have said: "Thou shall not suffer a witch to live?" Are we being asked about the God Who, the rabbis tell us, *davens* with *tefillin* [prays with phylacteries] like any *posheter Yid* [simple Jew]? Is it the Creator God . . . of Saadia. . . . Or is it the intellectually cognizing subject, the intellectually cognized object, and the intellect of Maimonides? . . . Are we being called to affirm the Ground of Being? Or, perhaps, the Power that makes for Salvation? . . .

A further question: what does it mean "to believe?" The phrase itself relates to a philosophical system. . . . For a follower of Dewey, "to believe" might mean to affirm as useful, rather than to affirm as ultimately true, since ultimate truth is not available to him.

Moreover, a particular thinker might operate out of diverse systems, at different times, for different reasons.[27]

Rabbi Kravitz' statements are certainly echoed by Rabbi David Small in his reply to the question of "Do you believe?" As touched on earlier, Rabbi Small explains that it all depends on a number of variables when you ask if "I believe in God." These variables include, do you mean the "I" of today, or yesterday, or of several years ago? The word "believe" is another variable: Is it the same kind of belief as in "two and two make four? Or the way that I believe that light travels a certain number of miles per second, which I myself have never seen demonstrated but which has been demonstrated by people whose competence and integrity I have been taught to trust?" Furthermore, there is the variable of God. Do you mean God as an ineffable presence, or a God who is aware of our being, and responsive to our call, or a God who is far beyond human knowledge? The rabbi concludes with this statement: "I suppose I have the feeling of belief and certainty some times and lack it at others."[28]

Theodicy

Theodicy, the attempt to justify the goodness of God in the face of the manifest and manifold evil which is present in the world, has vexed Jewish thinkers. In the classical argument, either God is capable of preventing evil, and *will not* do so, or God would wish to prevent evil, and *cannot* do so. In the first case, God is not all-merciful, and in the latter God is not all-powerful. In the modern period, the Holocaust requires some form of response on the issue of theodicy.

Rabbis after 1945 have all been affected in one way or another by the Holocaust. The annihilation of six million Jews and the destruction of East European Jewish life and culture has changed the way human beings have understood their relationship with God. Turning to the "Symposium" on contemporary Jewish Belief, it is instructive to refer to the responses of the various thinkers on the question posed by the editors of *Commentary*, namely how the Holocaust has influenced these rabbis' faith, religious identity, and observance. Norman Lamm (Orthodox) explains that the "Holocaust, incomprehensibly cruel, has shaken my faith—but not destroyed it." Further, he writes that the confluence of the Holocaust, and the reestablishment of the State of Israel "has stretched the perimeters and deepened the quality of my faith, and made me more tolerant of . . . those who lost their faith." He continues that "it has made me more consciously Jewish and, at the same time, less tolerant of pat answers and simplistic formulations about the truly overarching questions of life and destiny."[29] Saul J. Berman (Orthodox) writes that he struggles "sporadically, but intensely, with the integration of the Holocaust into my religious *Weltanschauung*. I have no answers, only observations." Among his observations are "how thin is the patina of Christian civilization," and that "in the aftermath, Christian society has still not learned the Jewish concept and practice of *teshuvah*, 'return.'" He also mentions that he remains "unresolved on the question of the uniqueness of the Holocaust in Jewish history."[30]

Conservative leader Ismar Schorsch explains that the "black hole of the Holocaust has blurred my vision . . . [and that he is influenced by] the concept of a self-limiting God. I am numbed by the human capacity to do evil and the divine reluctance to save us from ourselves."[31] Elliot N. Dorff (Conservative) states that for him, the "Holocaust is undoubtedly a most egregious example of the depths to which humans can sink, but it does not, despite the arguments suggested to the contrary, pose a philosophical problem for Judaism different from other examples of human depravity. For free will to mean anything, bad uses of it must be possible."[32]

Reconstructionist David Teutsch acknowledges that the Holocaust has impacted him, but "that has not been critical in determining my observance or identity as a Jew. Rather, it has deepened the demand I make upon myself for rigorous moral action, and the passion with which I believe each of us has a solemn obligation to make moral demands on the people around us."[33]

Though not mentioning the Holocaust by name, Reform leader Eric Yoffie states that "Anti-Semitism, on the most modest or most massive scale, is a profound evil, requiring an aggressive and immediate political response. But it has no impact on my faith, which is rooted in commitment to Torah."[34] Sheldon Zimmerman (Reform) states that the "Holocaust challenged our too-easy reliance on rationalism and modern values. What can it mean to be truly human in the face of such human evil? . . . What specific obligations do we as Jews have to and for each other and our people in the face of such profound evil directed against us and our existence? There can be no easy answer to these questions. . . ."[35]

Fictional rabbis have a variety of reactions to the Holocaust. Along with Rabbi Zimmerman, they might say there can be no easy answers to these questions. Some fictional rabbis find their faith destroyed. Some apportion blame to God, at least to the extent that they say that all that takes place is God's will. Others hold both God and humankind responsible, while still others, reflecting the words of Rabbi Dorff, would say that just as God must accept the inevitable fruits of human freedom, including bad uses of it, among which is our egregious capacity for evil, so do we as humans need to accept that the Holocaust was a human-inspired and human-caused event. Like Rabbi Lamm, certainly some of the fictional rabbis are less tolerant of pat answers and simplistic formulations about the truly overarching questions of life and destiny.

An Orthodox Rabbi, Joshua Tzuker (*Pedlock Saint, Pedlock Sinner*) seems to have lost his faith over the Holocaust. "I said to myself: Is God good, does good or bad have any meaning? Does Auschwitz scratch out God? Or was that catastrophe God's punishment of the Jews? Was Hitler an instrument of God's will?"

He then says: "Would that I believed. . . ."[36]

A different answer is given by Reb Saunders, the Hasidic Rabbi in Chaim Potok's *The Chosen*. Since Potok's books, *The Chosen* and its sequel, *The Promise*, are set in the 1940s and early

1950s, the issue of the Holocaust weaves through those novels. Reb Saunders labels the Holocaust as the will of God, something to be endured. "The world kills us," says Reb Saunders. He then speaks of the Jewish communities of Poland, Lithuania, Russia, Germany, and Hungary—all gone now into heaps of bones and ashes. "How the world drinks our blood. . . . How the world makes us suffer. It is the will of God. We must accept the will of God." Though he states that we must bow to God's judgment, yet he also asks, "Master of the Universe, how do you permit such a thing to happen?"[37]

A similar view of the universe—that all is God's will—is offered by the Hasidic rabbi who is the father of (Hasidic) Rabbi Yussel Fetner in Rhoda Lerman's novel *God's Ear*. According to him, all is planned by God, and yet we have free choice. This is what he tells his son, Rabbi Yussel.

"It's truth, Yussele. Everything's intended. There are no coincidences." Rabbi Yussel then replies: "This *universe* is intended? Hah!"

His father answers, *"It's truth. Hitler, hot dogs, camels . . ."*

"And what about free choice, for God's sake?"

"Yussele, maybe you should think about whether free choice is also intended?"[38]

Some time later, Yussel's father says to him, *"The paradox is, He gives you free choice but He's the only One Who knows the consequences."*[39]

That humankind truly has free choice and yet God knows the consequences is one of the ongoing paradoxes of the novel. In whichever way one understands that question, it is clear from what he says that in the older rabbi's thoughts, the Holocaust was part of God's intention. How do we know this? Remember the rabbi's statement: *"It's truth Yussele. Everything's intended. There are no coincidences."*

In Chapter 1 (The American Rabbi) reference was made to an Orthodox rabbi, Aaron Baltner (*A Marked House*) who apportions blame to both God and human beings.

"Millions of Jews humiliated, tortured and killed. . . . What was the reason, save that they were Jews? . . . Where was God when it took place, our omniscient, omnipotent and loving God? . . . Will He let the human race destroy itself without lifting a finger to save it? We need God's love and mercy. We are nothing without God." He then continues, addressing God, "Be the God we were taught to believe in. Take pity on all. Let the Creator and all Creation atone. Let there be a new day from now on." Rabbi Baltner questions God's apparent absence during the Holocaust, and while he holds humanity responsible, Baltner takes the matter further: he asks God to atone for not acting out the role of an all-powerful, all-knowing, beneficent deity.[40]

Still another answer is provided by Chaplain David Cohen in Herbert Tarr's novel *The Conversion of Chaplain Cohen* (again as mentioned in Chapter 1). Chaplain Cohen says, "I've thought about it, I've questioned, I've sought the answer. But there is no ready one . . . not for me . . . and I can't pretend there is an ultimate answer that anyone can fathom.

". . . Yesterday, alas, another note fell due—notice not of God's failure, but of the world's."[41] In Chaplain Cohen's mind, the Holocaust is an example of humankind's infinite capacity for evil.

In Andrew Kane's *Rabbi, Rabbi*, the question of theodicy comes up in a Talmud class at Yeshiva University. Yaakov Eisen asks his professor: "But the Torah explicitly states that if the Jews observe the *mitzvahs* [commandments], God will be good to us, and if not, He will punish us. Doesn't this mean that the Holocaust and other sufferings are merely punishments?" Rav Liebowitz replies:

> We do not take the Torah literally. . . . We are a bit more sophisticated than that. . . . Maybe the Torah speaks of reward and punishment in reference not to this world, but to the world to come? And if there is reward and punishment in this world, maybe we as humans don't understand how it is meted out? God's presence is hidden in the world, and He doesn't have to reveal a damn thing to us! The humility to accept this is the real essence of faith.

The rabbi then adds this thought: "The rationality of man can go only so far. It can accomplish great things, put men on the moon, cure diseases. But it cannot know God. Faith is the willingness to accept a reality beyond that which you can know or sense."[42]

When I periodically wrestle with the terrible tragedy of the Holocaust, I find that my faith is shaken but not destroyed. The Holocaust is a terrible, extreme example of the depth of depravity to which humans can sink. It does not, however, pose a philosophical problem for Judaism different from other examples of the depravity of humankind. Simply because we are human, we possess the God-given gift of freedom of choice; we are responsible for our actions as human beings, including an excessive capacity for evil.

I believe in a self-limiting God. While God *is* omniscient and omnipotent, God chooses not to look into the future in order to permit humankind free will. Likewise, God chooses not to use the full power of the divine, again allowing humankind to exercise its free will. Along with hundreds of thousands of others, I lost family in the Holocaust: My grandparents were murdered by the Nazis, and my uncle was interned at Buchenwald. In my mind, was God absent during the Holocaust? I think not. For me, God was present in the life-affirming moments when people, Jews and non-Jews alike, reached out for each other, to protect, to care, to show compassion, sometimes putting their very own lives in danger in the process. Paraphrasing William Styron's words at the close of his novel *Sophie's Choice*, I say that the question to ask is not, "Where was God?" but rather where was humankind? There surely are no acceptable answers.

Rabbi Mauricio Brodsky (in Allegra Goodman's book *The Family Markowitz*) lives in New York. He works for the Jewish-Catholic Dialogue Foundation, an organization probably similar to the Anti-Defamation League of B'nai B'rith's Department of Interfaith Affairs in New York. He explains that he lost family in the Holocaust and that he is angry with God. He also says that at times he does certain things and he is sure that God, likewise, is angry with him.

> Do I worry that God is angry with me? [Rabbi Brodsky asks rhetorically.] Certainly not. So he is angry with me. So what? I am angry with God! He let my family die. For this I will never forgive him. Always I have this argument with God. I ask him, why did you fail us? Men may fail. How can you, ever? What is this study of evil? . . . there is no answer. What is this thing, theodicy? My family went to the ovens, and that's it.[43]

Fictional Rabbi Brodsky and I come to the same answer from different positions. In any event, however, he and I both would say, what is this study of evil, what is this thing, theodicy? There is no answer.

Radical Theology

In the modern period, two individuals, Rabbi Mordecai M. Kaplan and Rabbi Richard Rubenstein, are each exemplars of a radical approach to theology. Kaplan taught at the Jewish Theological Seminary for many decades, and Rubenstein was ordained by JTS. Steven T. Katz, in his work *Jewish Philosophers* (1975), describes Kaplan's philosophy as a blend of religious naturalism and humanism. It challenges "both the belief in historical revelation and those theologies grounded on metaphysical interpretations of revelation." Katz continues, "Kaplan's views undermine the accepted forms of worship, ritual, and religious authority."[44] Richard Rubenstein is the author of *After Auschwitz* (1966). According to Katz, in Rubenstein's view, "the only honest response to the death camps is the rejection of God, 'God is dead,' and the open recognition of the meaninglessness of existence . . . there is no Divine Will nor does the world reflect Divine concern." Yet having said this, Rubenstein believes that Jews after Auschwitz are still Jews, and carry with them the shared Jewish experience. For "Jewish man only Jewish experience can be authentic."[45]

> In Chaim Potok's *The Promise*, Rabbi Abraham Gordon is a great scholar who teaches at the Zechariah Frankel Seminary, which is a thinly veiled reference to the Jewish Theological Seminary. We learn that Rabbi Gordon was a humanist and a naturalist. "For him supernaturalism and mysticism were irrelevant to modern thought. Revelation was a fiction. . . . Religion was the creation of man; its purpose was to make meaningful certain aspects of human existence."[46] We also learn that a number in the Orthodox world consider his works the writings "of an apostate" and that Gordon had "been put into cherem." "Cherem," the narrator explains " is the Hebrew term for excommunication."[47] Since there is no single recognized authority in modern Judaism, the excommunication was only

binding on those who supported or agreed with the excommunicators. The description of Gordon's philosophy, his teaching at the Zechariah Frankel [Jewish Theological] Seminary, and his being excommunicated by the more strident wing of Orthodoxy all mesh with the philosophy and life of Mordecai Kaplan.

Rubenstein, or, rather, Rubenstein's association with the "God is dead" school, is not so much featured in a fictional setting as it is mistakenly not featured! In a classroom setting, Rabbi David Small states in *Tuesday the Rabbi Saw Red* that the "God is dead" issue "concerns Protestant theologians rather than Jewish rabbis."[48] He is, in this instance, wrong on both counts: The matter was not limited to Protestant theologians, and indeed rabbis have been very concerned about the subject.

ISRAEL

As was mentioned in Chapter 1 (The Rabbi in America) the reestablishment of the State of Israel in 1948 had a profound effect on world Jewry. In the immediate period following the atrocity of the Holocaust, Israel's rebirth gave Jews a way to work through their grief. It provided a sense that the future could be filled with hope. "Tragedy and triumph" are associated with the Holocaust and Israel's establishment as a sovereign state. The incredibly strong connections between Jews worldwide and the State of Israel were summed up by sociologist Jonathan S. Woocher's remarks that "American Judaism recognizes only one heresy which subjects the perpetrator to immediate excommunication: denial of support to the State of Israel."[49]

The solid rabbinical support for Israel in today's world can be seen in virtually countless ways, from the number of rabbis who actively work on Israel's behalf to those who preach and teach about Israel to the hundreds of "Israel-centered" resolutions passed by the national rabbinical organizations at their annual conferences. In Chapter 5 (Congregational Rabbis and Their Communities) mention was made of the Jewish concerns in 1967 when many Christian religious leaders were apparently indifferent, or displayed outright hostility, to Israel's security needs.

Orthodox Rabbi Normal Lamm, writing about the Holocaust and the reestablishment of the State of Israel in the aforementioned *Commentary* "Symposium," explains that the "emergence of Jewish independence, especially after the Holocaust, has reinforced my faith—but not convinced me that we necessarily live in messianic times. The confluence of both in my consciousness has stretched the perimeters and deepened the quality of my faith, and made me more tolerant of both those who have lost their faith and those who clearly perceive the footsteps of the messiah in the state of Israel."[50] His colleague, Rabbi Saul J. Berman, sees the reestablishment of Israel as an opportunity "to create a more perfect state, a more ethical society, expressive of the deepest values of Jewish law and thought . . . the formative stages of a process that will shape the next 2,000 years of Jewish history."[51] Conservative Rabbi Ismar Schorsch writes, "I celebrate the rebirth of a democratic and dynamic Israel. . . . Israel [is] at the center of Jewish pride, healing and unity. . . . Israel belongs to all Jews, whether secular or religious, Reform or Orthodox."[52] Conservative Rabbi Elliot N. Dorff expresses a similar idea. He writes of his privilege "to live during the time of the Jewish return to the state of Israel." He glories in its Jewish creativity and the example Israel provides for Diaspora Jewry to enrich its own Jewishness. He goes on to say, "I do not, however, think that Israel is the only place where Jewish life can be lived; Israel and the Diaspora both can and must teach each other."[53]

Reconstructionist Rabbi David A. Teutsch writes of the state of Israel being an important part of his identification with the Jewish people, and it likewise is a source of pride and identity for him.[54] Reform leader Rabbi Eric Yoffie speaks of Israel's establishment as a blessing, "because Israel restores to a segment of the Jewish people control over its own destiny." Nonetheless, he observes that "the religious impact of the Jewish state on my personal faith and observance has been limited," and he notes that "a dynamic, non-fundamentalist religious life in Israel has yet to emerge."[55] His colleague Rabbi Sheldon Zimmerman writes of "the miraculous birth" of Israel and how Jews, and more specifically Reform Jews, need to "be informed and formed by it . . . [for we] are linked in a connection that is being formed, reformed, and reinterpreted as it is lived out in our time."[56]

Though there are a plethora of Orthodox institutions in Israel, the Conservative, Reconstructionist, and Reform movements are also well represented there by schools, synagogues, and social institutions. A day does not go by when there are not hundreds of American rabbis in Israel, studying, touring, leading missions, spending their sabbaticals.

> Marilyn Greenberg's *The Rabbi's Life Contract* literally begins in Israel as Rabbi and Mrs. Joshua Rosenstock are about to return from a year's sabbatical there. Likewise, a sizable section of Rhonda Shapiro-Rieser's *A Place of Light* is set in Israel. Rabbi Small twice visits Israel (in *Monday the Rabbi Took Off* and *One Fine Day the Rabbi Bought A Cross*). As noted in Chapter 1, Rabbi Small explains that Judaism is more than just a system of beliefs or ritual practices. It is that, but in addition it is "a way of life, but more than that, [Judaism is] . . . intertwined somehow with the people themselves, with the Jews as a nation. And the two, the religion and the people, are somehow tied in with the place, Israel . . . it is not significant merely because we happened to come from there, but rather because it is the particular place assigned to us by God."[57]

Though Israel is today (for nearly all Jews across the theological spectrum) a place of great pride and importance, though not spared from critical comments, in the years leading up to 1948, a small group of Sectarian Orthodoxy was absolutely opposed to its formation.

> A fictional spokesman for the opposition to Israel's establishment was Reb Saunders, a major character in Chaim Potok's *The Chosen*.
>
> Who are these people? Who are these people?" he thundered. "Apikorsim! [agnostics, atheists, heretics.] Goyim! Ben Gurion and his goyim will build Eretz Yisroel [the Land of Israel]? They will build for us a Jewish land? They will bring Torah into this land? Goyishkeit [non-Jewish values] they will bring into the land, not Torah! God will build the land, not Ben Gurion and his goyim! When the Messiah comes, we will have Eretz Yisroel, a Holy Land, not a land contaminated by Jewish goyim."[58]

The rabbinic opposition to Israel by that time period, however, was very limited, as David Ellenson makes abundantly clear in "Zion in the Mind of the American Rabbinate in the 1940s." While at the turn of the century the Jewish Theological Seminary had been the center of Zionist thought, by the 1940s Zionism had become much more widespread. The influence of such great Reform stalwarts as Rabbis Abba Hillel Silver and Steven S. Wise, to name but two, and the adoption of the pro-Zionist stance in the 1937 Columbus Platform by the Central Conference of American Rabbis meant that there had been extensive inroads to Zionism in the Reform movement. "Reform and modern Orthodox rabbis increasingly came to parallel their Conservative peers in fashioning a uniquely American form of the Zionist dream."[59]

TRADITION

How rabbis, and Jews, generally, understand the place of "religious tradition"—how the religious past informs the present—is one of the ways which mark the divisions between Orthodox and non-Orthodox Jews. Turning again to the *Commentary* "Symposium," where some leading voices of American Jewish religious leadership were asked to present their views, significant differences in the approaches of the various denominational leaders emerge.

Rabbi Lamm's words quoted earlier speak directly to the question of the authority of tradition. "In Judaism, the will of God is made known to man in the Torah, mostly in the form of *mitzvot*, commandments. These commandments are, by their very nature, binding. They summon man to obey . . . we may understand or not understand a commandment, prefer one *mitzvah* to another, but all God's will must be obeyed."[60] Rabbi Saul J. Berman, as noted earlier, has stated that he believes "that the Torah is the expression of God's wisdom for the Jewish people, and ultimately for all of humanity. Therefore, every *mitzvah* of the Torah is the bearer of meaning and of potential for perfection." Since the distinctive values of the Torah are taught through laws which govern human relationships, "their ritual enactment . . . serves as symbolic communication" and transmits those values to the next generation.[61]

Addressing the place of Torah, understood here as "Jewish tradition," Conservative Rabbi Ismar Schorsch explains that, in his view, "Torah offers a regimen for curbing our passions, a prescription for this-worldly salvation."[62] His colleague Rabbi Elliot Dorff's earlier remarks are very clear on the subject of the place of the past informing the present: Jews have to look at the past and then decide how to interpret that past in this time. "We must determine the content of Jewish law . . . as a community. . . . [We] need to make adjustments in Jewish law, dropping or reinterpreting some of the practices in the tradition and adding others."[63]

Mordecai Kaplan's famous dictum, the "past has a vote, not a veto," still informs Reconstructionist thought today. As Rabbi David A. Teutsch explains, central "to our struggle as Jews is the obligation to distinguish those parts of our inherited tradition that continue to have meaning from those that do not."[64]

Reform Rabbi Eric Yoffie understands the past in a similar way. He writes that as "a *mitzvah*-inspired liberal Jew, the only option that I have is to decide for myself what binds me. I will seek the guidance of rabbis and teachers, but ultimately I must *examine* each *mitzvah* and ask the question: do I feel commanded in this instance as Moses was commanded?"[65] Rabbi Sheldon Zimmerman says that the Torah is the story of the Jewish people's encounter with the divine. It frames our understanding of the meaning of Jewish life and God's demands of us. Yet, he allows that there "are times when we do not hear the voice of Sinai in the laws of earlier or present generations, when the law does not take on the power of *mitzvah* (living commandment) for us." He suggests that for Reform Jews, "Torah is process, not a finished written or oral product."[66]

> In the fiction, one of the clearest statements of Orthodoxy's notion of the inviolability of traditional teaching is found in Potok's *The Promise*. Reuven Malter is studying at Yeshiva University, called in the book the Samson Raphael Hirsch College. One of his Talmud professors questions him if he accepts the traditional teaching that God revealed the whole Torah to Moses on Mount Sinai and that the teachings of the Talmud are also, in that sense, of divine revelation.
>
> Rav Kalman asks, "'Tell me, Malter, do you believe the written Torah is from heaven?' He was asking me if I believe the Pentateuch had been revealed by God to Moses at Sinai." Rav Kalman then goes further. "You believe that every word in the Torah was revealed by God blessed is He to Moses at Sinai?" Rav Kalman then takes the matter still further. "'Do you believe the oral Torah was also given to Moses at Sinai?' He was asking

me whether I believed the various discussions of the Talmud had also been revealed by God to Moses at Sinai."[67]

A Conservative rabbi who grew up within the Sectarian Orthodoxy of Borough Park in Brooklyn explains his understanding of one of the major divisions between Orthodox and Conservative Judaism: "According to the Orthodox, I really don't believe in the same God as they do because I think oral law [the Talmud] is not as holy as the written law [the Bible.]"[68]

Rabbis wrestle with traditional texts seeking to find answers for the modern world. Depending where they place themselves along the religious continuum, they will accept or feel able to reject certain traditional teachings as valid and binding. Having said this, nonetheless, there are many Jews who consider themselves to be, using sociologist Chaim Waxman's criteria (see Chapter 2, Mainstream Rabbis and Sectarian Orthodox Rabbis), philosophically or ideologically "Centrist" Orthodox. They are meticulously observant of Halakhah (Jewish law and traditional practice) but are, nonetheless, philosophically modern. This means, at a minimum, to have a positive perspective on general education and knowledge; and, from a religious perspective, being a part of—and having responsibility for—both the larger Jewish community as well as society in general. When they come up against a principle which is articulated in the tradition, but one which they find goes against their very sense of right and justice, they are faced with heart- and mind-wrenching decisions. Do they bow to the authority of traditional teaching or opt for what they understand as a more righteous, but less authoritative, position?

Yonason Sacks (1993), in a discussion about Rabbinic Authority, ably informs us about the issues at hand:

> For the man of faith . . . obedience and authority are not as much predicated on consent as they are on profound belief in a God of creation, revelation and redemption. Such an individual perceives of God as a *mezaveh* [a "Commander"] who issues commands; always seeing himself as an "*'ẹved lifnei ha-melekh*," a servant before The King. For him, fulfillment of the divine will and the belief in reward and punishment are religious principles of faith. As such, the major thrust of religious inquiry is not to analyze the basis of obligation or authority, but rather to comprehend the scope and content of Torah Law.[69]

It is an ideological "Centrist" Orthodox Jew, in fact a rabbi and a graduate of the Rabbi Isaac Elchanan Theological Seminary at Yeshiva University, who finds himself wrestling with the question of how to deal with a young woman who has been married and widowed but whose husband's death cannot be verified. According to traditional Jewish law, she is an *agunah*—literally "chained"—the Hebrew term for a woman who is unable to remarry because she does not have a Jewish divorce, either because of her husband's refusal or his inability to do so. The problem is particularly vexing, for the woman in question is the fiancée of Rabbi Leo Berdick (*The Strong Hand*).[70]

Since he is unable to break with the bonds of tradition, Rabbi Berdick has no choice. He has to end his engagement. "God knows it isn't what I want. No one wants it. But I can't change the law by myself! I can't." The narrator then comments that it "was as if some strong hand was moving him . . . the hand of an absolute derived from God."[71]

In another novel, Israel Jacobs' *Ten for Kaddish*, the same issue of the status of an *agunah* is discussed. There, the rabbi, who was reared in a traditional Orthodox family and who went to a yeshiva high school but apparently received his ordination from the Jewish Theological Seminary, comes to a different conclusion.

> I've thought about it and thought about it. . . . Because someone a couple of thousand years ago laid down a law, doesn't mean we're forever bound to it. God's will is sifted through the minds of human beings. Man interprets His will. Two thousand years ago it was interpreted one way. We can interpret it another way. God's will is immutable. We can't change that, but we can change our interpretation of it.[72]

Finally, rabbinical student Rebecca Kleinman (*Rabbi, Rabbi*) explains her position, why, in part, she moved from her parents' Orthodoxy to her present Reform ideology. "I am Reform. . . . And as for me, that means that I have to make choices . . . [as do the] rabbinical students in my school. . . . Each makes his or her own moral decisions, and each is ready and willing to accept the responsibility for those decisions. . . ." She goes on to say, "I don't see myself as abandoning the tradition or the values that my parents taught me; I see myself as reshaping them, making room for new ideas. . . ."[73]

NOTES

1. See Eisen, A. (1991). "Jewish Theology in North America: Notes on Two Decades." In *American Jewish Year Book 1991*, ed. David Singer and Ruth R. Seldin, vol. 91. (New York: American Jewish Committee and Philadelphia: Jewish Publication Society), pp. 3–33.

2. Rosenthal, G. S. (1986). *Contemporary Judaism: Patterns of Survival*. Second Edition (New York: Human Sciences Press), p. 57.

3. Berber, D., Berman, S. J., Blumenthal, D. R., and others. (1996). "What Do American Jews Believe? A Symposium." *Commentary* 102:2 (August): 18–96.

4. Lamm, N., respondent. (1996). "What Do American Jews Believe? A Symposium." *Commentary* 102:2 (August): 59.

5. Berman, S. J., respondent. (1996). "What Do American Jews Believe? A Symposium." *Commentary* 102:2 (August): 21.

6. Dorff, E. N. (1991). "The Concept of God in the Conservative Movement." *Judaism* 40:4 (Fall), pp. 430–431, 441.

7. Schorsch, I., respondent. (1996). "What Do American Jews Believe? A Symposium." *Commentary* 102:2 (August): 82.

8. Dorff, E. N., respondent. (1996). "What Do American Jews Believe? A Symposium." *Commentary* 102:2 (August): 29.

9. Alpert, R. T. and Staub, J. J. (1988). *Exploring Judaism: A Reconstructionist Approach* (Wyncotte, PA: Reconstructionist Press), p. 20.

10. Alpert and Staub, p. 5.

11. Alpert and Staub, p. 21.

12. Teutsch, D. A., respondent. (1996). "What Do American Jews Believe? A Symposium." *Commentary* 102:2 (August): 88.

13. Rosenthal, p. 112.

14. Zimmerman, S., respondent. (1996). "What Do American Jews Believe? A Symposium." *Commentary* 102:2 (August): 95.

15. Yoffie, E. H., respondent. (1996). "What Do American Jews Believe? A Symposium." *Commentary* 102:2 (August): 93.

16. Kemelman, H. (1973). *Tuesday the Rabbi Saw Red* (New York: Arthur Fields Books), p. 198. See Eisen, "Jewish Theology in North America."

17. Kemelman, *Tuesday the Rabbi Saw Red*, p. 198.

18. Kemelman, H. (1969). *Sunday the Rabbi Stayed Home* (New York: G. P. Putnam's Sons), p. 58.

19. Kemelman, H. (1973 [1972]). *Monday the Rabbi Took Off* (Greenwich, CT: Fawcett Crest), p. 186.

20. Kaufmann, M. S. (1968). *Thy Daughter's Nakedness* (Philadelphia and New York: J. B. Lippincott), p. 170.

21. Gordis, R. (1988). *Emet Ve-Emunah: Statement of Principles of Conservative Judaism* (New York: The Jewish Theological Seminary of America, The Rabbinical Assembly, United Synagogue of America, Women's League for Conservative Judaism, Federation of Jewish Men's Clubs), p. 17.

22. Segal, E. (1992). *Acts of Faith* (New York: Bantam), p. 384.

23. Gordon, N. (1965). *The Rabbi* (New York: McGraw-Hill), p. 6; Schreiber, M. (1991). *The Rabbi and the Nun* (New York: Shengold), p. 253. See also Rabbi Sara Weintraub's comments, Goldman, A. J. (1987). *The Rabbi is a Lady* (New York: Hippocrene), pp. 86, 227 f.

24. Marks and Gran, Series 2, Episode 8, "Just a Bit of Business"; Series 2, Episode 1, "Strictly Business." An Executive Director of the Series "Love hurts," Joanna Willett, confirmed this analysis in personal correspondence with David J. Zucker, December 15, 1995.

25. Gordon, p. 134.

26. Blankfort, M. (1956). *The Strong Hand* (Boston, Toronto: Little Brown and Co.), p. 138.

27. Kravitz, L. (1973). "What Does It Mean To Believe In God?" in *Central Conference of American Rabbis Journal* 20:1 (Winter): 29.

28. Kemelman, *Monday the Rabbi Took Off*, p. 186.

29. Lamm, pp. 59–60.

30. Berman, S. J., pp. 21–22.

31. Schorsch, p. 82.

32. Dorff, *Commentary* "Symposium," p. 30.

33. Teutsch, p. 88.

34. Yoffie, p. 94.

35. Zimmerman, p. 95.

36. Longstreet, S. (1969). *Pedlock Saint, Pedlock Sinner* (New York: Delacorte), pp. 437–438.

37. Potok, C. (1967). *The Chosen* (New York: Simon and Schuster), p. 190 f.

38. Lerman, R. (1989). *God's Ear* (New York: Henry Holt), p. 83.

39. Lerman, p. 208.

40. Twersky, J. (1968). *A Marked House* (New York: Thomas Yoseloff), p. 226.

41. Tarr, H. (1963). *The Conversion of Chaplain Cohen* (New York: Avon), pp. 309–310.

42. Kane, A. (1995). *Rabbi, Rabbi* (New York: Saint Martin's), pp. 83, 84.

43. Goodman, A. (1996). "Mosquitoes," in *The Family Markowitz* (New York: Farrar, Straus & Giroux), p. 130.

44. Katz, S. T. (1975). *Jewish Philosophers* (New York: Bloch), p. 198.

45. Katz, pp. 224, 226.

46. Potok, C. (1969). *The Promise* (New York: Alfred A. Knopf), p. 63.

47. Potok, *The Promise*, pp. 62, 112.

48. Kemelman, *Tuesday the Rabbi Saw Red*, p. 198.

49. Woocher, J. S. (1986). *Sacred Survival: The Civil Religion of American Jews* (Bloomington and Indianapolis: Indiana University Press), p. 77.

50. Lamm, p. 59.

51. Berman, S. J., p. 22.

52. Schorsch, p. 82.

53. Dorff, *Commentary* "Symposium," p. 30.

54. Teutsch, p. 88.

55. Yoffie, p. 94.

56. Zimmerman, p. 95, 96.

57. Kemelman, *Monday the Rabbi Took Off*, p. 39.

58. Potok, *The Chosen*, p. 198.

59. Ellenson, D. (1995). "Zion in the Mind of the American Rabbinate during the 1940s," in *The Americanization of the Jews*, ed. Robert M. Seltzer and Norman J. Cohen (New York and London: New York University Press), p. 195.

60. Lamm, p. 59.

61. Berman, S. J., p. 21.

62. Schorsch, p. 82.

63. Dorff, *Commentary* "Symposium," p. 29.

64. Teutsch, p. 88. See also Alpert and Staub, p. 29.

65. Yoffie, p. 93.

66. Zimmerman, p. 95.

67. Potok, *The Promise*, p. 167.

68. Kellerman, F. (1991). *Day of Atonement* (New York: William Morrow) p. 65.

69. Sacks, Y. (1993). "The *Mizvah* of '*Lo Tasur*': Limits and Applications." *Tradition* 27:4 (Summer): 49. See also the references to Rabbinic Authority at the close of Chapter 1 (The American Rabbi).

70. Blankfort, p. 184.

71. Blankfort, p. 294.

72. Jacobs, I. (1972). *Ten For Kaddish* (New York: W. W. Norton), p. 272. See p. 181 for the reference to the *agunah*.

73. Kane, p. 129 f.

11

Non-Congregational Rabbis

As noted in previous chapters, the predominance of rabbis in fact and in fiction *who serve professionally as rabbis* (as opposed to having rabbinic ordination and then serving in some other occupation) do so in a congregational setting. In this chapter, I consider those rabbis who serve as rabbis but do so *outside of the congregational setting*. Broadly, this means four major categories: Administrators, Teachers/Scholars, Chaplains, and "Free Lancers."

The Rabbinical Council of America is the professional organization of the "Centrist" Orthodox rabbis. Nearly two-thirds of their members serve congregations; another 15 percent to 20 percent are in chaplaincy-related positions, either civilian or military; perhaps as much as 10 percent are in Jewish communal service; and about 10 percent are involved in Educational Administration or Bureau jobs. Explains Rabbi Steven M. Dworkin, Executive Vice President of The Rabbinical Council of America,[1] specifically, in terms of Yeshiva University graduates, about half enter some form of Jewish communal life, 20 percent go to pulpits; and the remainder go into educational or more generalized Jewish communal service.

In 1995, the Rabbinical Assembly, the professional association of the Conservative rabbinate, counted 1,385 members. Of these numbers, 755 actively serve congregations, 131 are in educational positions, 50 are in organizational life, and fewer than a dozen are Hillel rabbis. Since 222 of these rabbis are retired, it would suggest that at the present nearly two-thirds of the present membership serve congregations in either a full-time or part-time capacity. Though this may be correct, according to Rabbi Joel H. Meyers, Executive Vice President of The Rabbinical Assembly, in recent years, on average, half of the ordination classes entered pulpit work and the other half entered other fields of Jewish communal service.[2]

The Reconstructionist movement's Reconstructionist Rabbinical College was founded in 1968. It first began to ordain rabbis in 1974. As of 1996, of its 185 graduates, 110 men and 75 women, the largest group (91, just short of 50 percent) serve congregations. Another 23 serve as Chaplains, divided fairly evenly between Hillel and the military or hospitals (less than 15 percent of the total). Thirty-two are involved in some form of education, and another 16 are employed in communal service. Statistical information was not available as to which rabbis were serving on a part-time basis and those serving full-time.[3]

In his study of the Reform rabbinate, Lenn reported that in the early 1970s, more than three quarters of the graduates were serving congregations in a solo position or as the Senior, Associate, or Assistant rabbi. The vast majority were doing so in a full-time capacity. Faculty members or Administrators accounted for fewer than 10 percent, and Chaplains and Hillel rabbi accounted for fewer than five percent each for full-time employed rabbis.[4] Lenn further notes that most rabbis who teach full-time do so in a Jewish setting, and those who teach part-time do so in non-Jewish colleges and universities.

In the mid-1990s, approximately half of the 1,800 Reform rabbis served congregations on a full-time basis; and when one adds retired rabbis who largely served as congregational rabbis, the number moves to about 66 percent. Rabbis serving in non-congregational positions have risen 85 percent between 1964–1989; and in that same period, rabbis serving in secular occupations rose 176 percent; a phenomenal increase. These are significant changes over 25 years, though it was not clear how many in each category serve full time and how many on a part-time basis.[5]

ADMINISTRATORS

As with any major organization, there is a need for people to develop a vision for the association itself, to work out a plan, and then to administer the day-to-day affairs of the group. This is true for religious organizations no less than secular ones. There are literally dozens upon dozens of women and men, rabbis and lay people, who serve as staff members at the national and regional level for all of these groups. This is true of the congregational organizations of the various movements: the Union of Orthodox Jewish Congregations of America; the Conservative movement's United Synagogue of America; the Jewish Reconstructionist Foundation; and the Reform movement's Union of American Hebrew Congregations. In addition, there are literally hundreds of *national* Jewish organizations, secular as well as religious. The American Jewish Committee, together with the Jewish Publication Society, publishes an annual *American Jewish Year Book*. It features literally pages upon pages of national Jewish organizations in the United States and Canada. Among the categories are Community Relations; Cultural; Israel-Related; Religious, Educational Organizations; Schools, Institutions; and Social Welfare. Many of these groups have rabbis serving in senior positions on their staffs.

One of the most prominent and influential national organizations is the umbrella Conference of Presidents of Major American Jewish Organizations. Its mission is to strengthen the U. S.-Israel alliance and to protect the security and dignity of Jews abroad. It speaks and acts both nationally and internationally on issues which concern its approximate 50-member agencies. When he served his term as its president, Reform Rabbi Alexander Schindler was very outspoken in his views.

> Rabbi Alvin Blumenfeld (*The Rabbi and the Nun*) is described as "the rising leader of American Jewry, heir to Stephen Wise and Abba Hillel Silver." He serves a major congregation in the Midwest and we are told that he has recently become president of the Conference of Presidents of Major Jewish Organizations. He speaks of the difficulty of wearing the two hats, serving his large congregation and serving as president of a national Jewish organization.[6]

Each of the professional rabbinic organizations has an apparatus which serves to place rabbis in congregational life. In the Reform movement, the Placement Commission is a joint venture of the rabbinical seminary, the rabbinical professional body, and the congregational union. It has many purposes. Among these are that it serves as an employment agency, a body to recommend the credentials of qualified candidates, a labor union, a central supply pool of rabbis, and a professional standards measuring group. Describing the rabbinic placement process in the Conservative movement some years ago, the head of the Placement Commission explained,

> A rabbinical change can start in one of several ways. The congregation approaches our Placement Commission with a request. Rabbis notify us of their desire to make a change. Also, deaths and resignations present obvious placement needs. . . .
>
> Periodically, we send out lists to our member rabbis informing them of possible openings. We also send a questionnaire to the requesting congregations asking them for information that would help rabbis in deciding whether they are interested in being considered. After all, we are not a hierarchy; we do not assign rabbis to congregations, or congregations to rabbis. Basically we try to match the proper rabbi to the proper post.[7]

In fact, the placement process has been somewhat modified in subsequent years. While questionnaires are still sent to the congregations seeking a new rabbi, and rabbis within the movement are regularly informed of openings, new guidelines have been developed which allow rabbis to be in more direct contact with those congregations with whom they would wish to interview.

Fictional examples of Rabbi-Administrators are portraits of those people who serve as the Placement Directors for their rabbinical movements. These directors walk a careful line between their colleagues who wish to serve congregations and the congregations who want just the "right" person for the position. References to Placement Commissions and, even more, to Directors of Placement do appear in the fiction. In Arkady Leokum's novel *The Temple*, the process of selecting a rabbi is spelled out directly. Congregations approach the Placement Commission with clear ideas of what, at least in principle, they want in a rabbi. Leokum mentions that the Commissions set standards in terms of years of experience and possible size of congregation. Up to 10 years out of the seminary, there are limitations on the size of the congregation you can serve. After that, one is "deemed competent" to serve any size. Further, they set up panels made up of rabbis' résumés, which then are offered to the congregations to make their selections.[8]

Some of the fictional Placement Commissioners are portrayed sympathetically. Rabbi Sher in Noah Gordon's *The Rabbi* offers care and counsel to the protagonist of the novel, Rabbi Michael Kind. When Kind marries a convert to Judaism, the Placement Director suggests that a Hillel chaplaincy or a job with one of the cultural foundations might be an easier berth than a congregation. The campus is less narrow-minded, he advises, and congregational boards are made up of parents who will see Rabbi Kind's decision as a bad example for their children.[9] Rabbi Kind, however, is committed to serving a congregation, and the novel centers on his experiences as a congregational rabbi. Toward the end of the novel he opts to seek a new position. He meets with Rabbi Sher's successor, Rabbi Milt Greenfield.

"'I know of an opening that's a real challenge,' Rabbi Greenfield said.

"Michael grinned. 'Your predecessor . . . once said the same thing to me. . . . Only the way Sher put it was "I've got a lousy job for you.' They both laughed."[10]

As explained above, the role of a Placement Commission includes trying to match up congregations and rabbis. The Placement Director tries to be an honest broker, but the congregation and the rabbi do not always work out well together. Then the process begins all over again. Occasionally, however, the Placement Director can do something to heal the breach.

In Jerome Weidman's novel *The Temple*, Rabbi Dr. Bieberman, the head of the Placement Committee, is a consummate politician. He also is quite pompous. He explains that as the head of the Central Rabbinical Assembly's Placement Committee, it

> is his business to place rabbis in American congregations. He acknowledges that synagogue rabbinic search committees, often called "pulpit committees," are made up of "substantial people in the community. Successful businessmen. Doctors. Lawyers. People with money. Movers and shakers . . . they have to come to me. I give them what they want." He goes on to say that his office is "the engine room of American Judaism. . . . A man who comes to me for a rabbi is coming to me for a link in the chain that holds American Judaism together. I can't afford to give him a link that could break." Bieberman, however, goes on to say when a rabbi takes on a position and does not succeed, that the fault may not be the rabbi's, it may be the congregation which is at fault. "A link doesn't always break because it is weak. Sometimes a link breaks because the fastenings to the other links in the chain are weak."[11]

Once again, it should be stressed that the rabbinic-congregation interview process has changed considerably in recent years. The Placement Directors help to facilitate placement; today they do not "place" the rabbis by themselves.

Rabbi-Administrators are found not only within the denominational movements, be it the seminary/yeshiva, the congregational union, or the rabbis' professional group. As mentioned earlier, they are also part of the bureaucracy of Jewish life.

> Reference is made in the fiction to the "chief executive . . . [of a] vast fund-raising agency," a former congregational "rabbi who has given up his pulpit for this all-important community labor."[12] In another novel, Gerda Charles' *The Crossing Point*, which is set in England, Rabbi Sol Tarsch is head of the Hebrew Academic Institute, but his forte is fund-raising. Someone in his office explains, "This time His Excellency has received a call to South America. Apparently they can't raise funds without him. Not during the English winter, they can't. What d'you bet when atomic warfare breaks out on earth the President of the Congregation on the moon will suddenly discover he needs Tarsch to conduct a Zionist campaign!"[13]

TEACHERS/SCHOLARS

With the flowering of Jewish academic studies on the university level throughout North America in the 1960s and 1970s, we find rabbi-teachers and rabbi-scholars on many campuses. Some of these teachers/scholars will go directly from seminary to a full-time academic life, others will earn additional graduate degrees. Still others serve for a while in congregational life and then are drawn to academia. As a critical mass, however, the largest group of rabbi-teachers or rabbi-scholars are found in the world of the yeshivas. I touched on that phenomenon earlier in Chapter 2 (Mainstream Rabbis and Sectarian Orthodox Rabbis). In addition to the world of the yeshiva, most of the faculty who teach at the rabbinical seminaries are rabbis in their own right. Though by the period of the 1990s more and more of the faculty are American-born and trained, this is a relatively new phenomenon. In the period following World War II, many of these rabbi-teacher/scholars were European-born, or at least European-educated. This was true right across the board from the "Centrist" Orthodox movement's Rabbi Isaac Elchanan Rabbinical Training Seminary (RIETS) at Yeshiva University to the Conservative movement's Jewish Theological Seminary to the Reform movement's Hebrew Union College-Jewish Institute of Religion.

Some of the world's most famous Talmudic scholars serve on the faculty at Yeshiva University. At Yeshiva University, a major component of study is the Talmud. This, too, is reflected in the fiction.

> The best known books which portray these men are Chaim Potok's novels *The Chosen, The Promise*, and *In the Beginning.* The fictional Samson Raphael Hirsch Seminary and College (*The Chosen*), which bears a striking resemblance to Yeshiva University, where, in fact Potok studied, "was a rigidly Orthodox school . . . with European-trained rabbis, many of them in long, dark coats, all of them bearded."[14] Potok often sees these men as a kind of folk-hero. They may be harsh and demanding, but because they are so sincere in their desire and efforts to maintain traditional Judaism, at least by their lights, their sometimes tyrannical behavior is excusable. It is in Potok's novels that we meet Rav Schwartz. "He was an old man with a long, gray beard who wore a black coat and was constantly

smoking cigarettes. He was a great Talmudist, but he had been trained in a European yeshiva, and I didn't think he would take kindly to the scientific method of studying Talmud. I had once suggested a textual emendation in class . . . I didn't think he even understood what I had said."[15] We also meet Rav Gershenson, another brilliant Talmudist, who clearly understands the scientific study of Talmud but refuses to allow his student, Reuven Malter, to use that method in class. It was not an acceptable form of study at that yeshiva.[16]

It is in *The Promise* that we meet Rav Jacob Kalman. Described as a great Talmudist, a man who had taught at one of the great yeshivas in Vilna before World War II, he had spent two years in a concentration camp in the north of Poland. It was further rumored that he had escaped and fought with the Partisans. Rav Kalman "valued nothing but Talmud and knew nothing but Talmud."[17] He is given the class in the Talmud tractate *Chullin*, which is a prerequisite for ordination. Rav Kalman, always immaculately dressed in black, is bearded, and he seems to radiate darkness. "He was an angry, impatient, sarcastic teacher. . . . There was nothing humorous about Rav Kalman. . . ."[18] Rav Kalman has little patience for America, or American Judaism.

> His tirades were frightening. He talked about Hollywood as the symbol of American values; he ranted against . . . television; there was little about America he seemed to like. On occasion his tirades were based upon events occurring in the school. Students and teachers were attacked by name. A projected college course in Greek mythology was canceled because he labeled it paganism.[19]

At one point, the great Talmudist explodes with a searing critique of Jewish life in America.

> "In America, everything is called Yiddishkeit [Judaism,]" Rav Kalman said. "A Jew travels to synagogue on Shabbos [Shabbat, the Sabbath] in his car, that is called Yiddishkeit. A Jew eats ham but gives money to philanthropy, that is called Yiddishkeit. A Jew prays three times a year but is a member of a synagogue, that is called Yiddishkeit. Judaism"—he pronounced the word in English, contemptuously: Joo-dah-eeism—"everything in America calls itself Judaism."[20]

More than a generation after the time of Rav Kalman, a man very much in his image is portrayed in Andrew Kane's novel *Rabbi, Rabbi*. Rabbi Eliezer Trachtenberg is American-born, he is in his mid-forties, yet, like his fictional colleague, he is dogmatic and has little patience with Jewish life in present-day America. Rabbi Trachtenberg's ". . . entire *weltanschauung* was clearly of another time, at least several centuries earlier. His uniform consisted of a long black caftan and a wide-rimmed felt black hat, both of which had certainly been stylish in Poland during the 1600s. The buttons on the caftan were deliberately placed on the left side, symbolically representing a rejection of the Gentile world, in which buttons for men's jackets and coats are typically sewn on the right."[21] At one point, Rabbi Trachtenberg expresses his considerable disdain for a bar mitzvah celebration that had cost thousands upon thousands of dollars. The main character in the novel, Yaakov Eisen, thinks to himself that Rabbi Trachtenberg would be appalled to know that many leaders in the Reform movement felt similarly about such an extravagant waste of money. "If Trachtenberg knew that some of his sentiments were shared by members of the Reform rabbinate . . . I'm sure he would conjure up some rationalization to distance himself from any conceivable association with his liberal enemies."[22]

Clearly not all professors of Talmud or other subjects are so contemptuous of life in America. In Chaim Potok's *In the Beginning*, the master Talmudist Rav Tuvya Scharfman "adopted the language of the baseball field and made it on occasion the controlling metaphor of his relationships to his students."[23]

While in the fiction Talmud professors are exclusively men, in real life in recent years women have also made a name for themselves as students and professors of Talmud,[24] for example, Judith Hauptman at the Jewish Theological Seminary, to name but one.

CHAPLAINS

Rabbis serve as Chaplains in a variety of settings. These include as military Chaplains; Hillel Directors (the Jewish group at university); health-care related Chaplains in hospital, hospice, or long-term care facilities; as well as prison and jail Chaplains. There is an active professional organization for chaplains of all varieties, though most serve in hospitals, hospices, or long-term care facilities. The National Association of Jewish Chaplains has its national office in New Jersey. It has an annual national convention, publishes a newsletter, and has set criteria to certify Jewish chaplains.

Military Chaplains

The oldest form of Jewish Chaplaincy can be traced to the Bible, for in Deuteronomy 20:2–4 it relates that Moses instructed the people that a priest was to accompany them in war to strengthen their morale. From Moses to the American Civil War is a long period of time, but it is in the early 1860s that we first learn of a Jewish Chaplain who is appointed for the Union forces. This first Jewish Chaplain, Michael Allen, served briefly in the summer of 1861, but he was forced to resign because he was neither an ordained clergyman nor a Christian. In 1862, Congress passed legislation indicating that chaplains needed to be both ordained and recommended by some ecclesiastical body. This allowed for Jewish Chaplains to serve in the armed forces. The first rabbi to receive a commission as military chaplain was Reverend Jacob Frankel of Philadelphia in 1862.[25] Jewish Chaplains have served in most wars and military combat since that time, certainly in World War II; the Korean Conflict; Viet Nam; and, more recently, in the Gulf War of 1991–1992. During World War II, there were as many as 265 chaplains on duty. Since that time, their numbers have decreased, and in 1996 there were 43 chaplains serving in the military full time, another 89 who were serving on a part-time basis, and 56 who were on "reserve duty." The part-time chaplains were largely civilians who provided religious services at military facilities on a contract basis.[26]

Military Chaplains are chaplains first and only secondarily are they denominational chaplains. This is in both senses of the words denominational. They are chaplains first and Christians, Jews, Muslims, or whatever after that. Further, when they work within their specific religious setting, they are generically Protestants, not Baptists, Presbyterians, Lutherans, or Episcopalians. Likewise, the Rabbi/Chaplains are generically rabbis, whether their ordination is through Orthodox, Conservative, Reconstructionist, or Reform auspices.

Chaplains fill a number of roles: They are religious leaders, teachers, spiritual advisors, and pastoral counselors. Since they work with non-Jewish colleagues (primarily Roman Catholic and Protestant Christians—but in the contemporary period Muslims, Buddhists and other religious leaders as well), interfaith or inter-religious dialogue is often part of their day-to-day activity. One of the most difficult roles for military chaplains, as for rabbis in general, is to deal with people who are dying, to provide a sense of comfort in their final hours or moments.

Real-life Rabbi Louis Barish relates the occasion when a young Army doctor was brought to Walter Reed Hospital in Washington, D. C. The patient knew he was dying, and he asked Chaplain Barish for a prayer book. He also expressed his desire to talk, asking about Judaism's teachings about life beyond death. Though sinking rapidly, the patient was determined to stay alive until he could see his family one more time. Chaplain Barish prayed throughout the night, and miraculously the dying man was able to survive to see his family the next day, shortly before he died. Upon reflection, Rabbi Barish explains that the dying man had "appeared to draw great satisfaction from our quiet talks. Eventually, he gave me back the faith I had taught him."[27]

> Chaplain Leo Berdick (*The Strong Hand*) had volunteered to serve his country during World War II. Stationed in the Pacific Theater, he is working in a first aid tent in the Philippines when a load of recent casualties is brought in. One of them is a Jewish doctor whom Berdick had met aboard ship.
>
> "Go ahead," Dr. Toll said. I didn't know what he meant then. "Say the prayers."
>
> . . . He was quite clear-minded and strong until the end.
>
> . . . I said the *Vidui*, the Hebrew prayer over the dying . . .
>
> How I hated death in those days! The whole world dies with every man's death . . . Before the war, I could not imagine how much I could love human beings.
>
> . . . Sometimes I felt helpless, a consoler, a mourner.[28]

Not all of a chaplain's duties are harrowing or upsetting. He or she, often through the good offices of the Jewish Welfare Board, brings kosher food to Jewish personnel. Chaplain Louis Barish has written about his Passover experiences during the Korean Conflict.

> In April 1953, a week before Passover, six mud-covered jeeps pulled into an Army supply point located at the edge of Seoul. The inscriptions written in bold type on the front and rear of these jeeps told the story of six Jewish Chaplains at work in Korea. "Kosher Caravan" was the first to arrive, after a long and arduous drive over tortuous roads. The "Rough Riding Rabbi," the "Rabbi From Brooklyn," "Shema Yisroel," "Aron Hakodesh," and the "Red Sea Special," followed in rapid succession . . .
>
> Our mission was to examine the multitude of crates with Passover supplies, to determine whether everything was accounted for . . . Would the Jewish Welfare Board correctly interpret our needs? Would the supplies get to us on time?
>
> . . . To the Jewish troops at Little Gibraltar, Bunker Hill, in the Punch Bowl, at Heartbreak Ridge . . . the question whether we had adequate ammunition in Korea was less important than the question, "Are we going to have Passover services; have the kosher supplies arrived; how about a Haggadah?" The supply line from JWB to our men in Korea was as significant to their spiritual life as the connections between the Pentagon and the war front were to their physical security.[29]

From Passover 1953 to the High Holiday season 1956 is a short distance. Chaplain Gershon Loran (in Chaim Potok's novel *The Book of Lights*) had just finished conducting Rosh Hashanah services in Ascom City in Korea.

> He rode back to the battalion in a typhoon. His assistant drove the jeep . . . along flooded roads . . . .
>
> Two days later there was a half-page story in *Stars and Stripes* about the High Holiday services. His picture was in the paper, as well as his jeep with the blue and white wooden tablets wired to the front bumper. . . .
>
> [A few days later soldiers] came from all over the division to attend the services of the Festival of Booths. . . .
>
> . . . On the table lay the palm frond and citron he had been sent airmail from the Jewish Welfare Board in the States.[30]

While there are numerous references to chaplains serving in wartime in both the factual and fictional world, as mentioned earlier, chaplains have a variety of activities and a significant amount of their time is spent in pastoral counseling. Real-life Rabbi Martin Siegel, who served in the Marine Corps, recalls that as a chaplain he spent less time on theology than practical counseling. "I didn't spend much time pontificating about God. The men had practical, not spiritual problems—the sergeant hated them; their girlfriend was pregnant; they were in debt—and I provided practical services."[31]

Since there are many more non-Jewish than Jewish personnel in the armed services, it holds to reason that Jewish chaplains will counsel non-Jews as well. In her research concerning Jewish chaplaincy in the United States Armed Services, Jennifer Weiner reports that occasionally Jewish chaplains were consciously consulted by non-Jewish personnel because those service persons felt they would be less obligated by religious counsel, or that the chaplain would not challenge their religious beliefs. While she found that one chaplain stated that he did not counsel non-Jews, and another rarely counseled non-Jews unless assigned to be the "duty chaplain," it was also mentioned that some chaplains who had developed specialties in ministry such as marriage counseling had actually built up a large interfaith following. On the whole, however, most Jewish chaplains reported that, in terms of counseling, being the Jewish chaplain was neither a help nor a hindrance in their counseling.[32]

> Chaplains counsel in the field. In Korea, Chaplain Gerson Loran (*The Book of Lights*)
>
> felt pride in his involvement; he was a part of them. He managed in ways not clear to him to gain their trust. Noncoms came to him with their lives open; he counseled men from cities and suburbs, farms and towns, from Texas and Maine and the Dakotas, from the Ozarks, the Adirondacks, the Sierras—and somehow he was liked. He could not understand it, could not grasp it; he was liked by men whose lives he could not begin to conjure in visions.[33]

A fair amount of time involves listening, especially with young or new servicemen and servicewomen, and as the problems are often homesickness or girlfriends or boyfriends left behind, the chaplain finds that her clientele, given the proportion of non-Jews to Jews, are more often Protestants and Roman Catholics because homesickness or love-sickness is not a "religious denominational" issue.

Chaplain David Cohen (*The Conversion of Chaplain Cohen*) thinks that

> sometimes it seemed that instead of people coming to him with problems, it was the reverse—the same problem would frequently return to him with different people.
>
> Usually awaiting David in his chapel office each morning was at least one airman, summoned the day before in response to a letter or phonecall from his mother saying her son (1) hadn't written home in ten months, and she was worried; or (2) hadn't written home in three days, and she was worried; or (3) was going to get married, and she was worried; or (4) was returning with his wife to live with her, and. . . .
>
> A variation of the worried mother were the letters from the cast-off sweetheart who wondered if the former boyfriend had lost her address; was working on a secret undercover mission that prohibited letter-writing; or that she was pregnant by him or someone else who she had never loved anyway.
>
> "Never once did an ex-sweetheart suggest the possibility that the negligent boy friend might be (1) married, or (2) unconcerned, or (3) might have enlisted in the Air Force just to get away from her."[34]

Military chaplains and, likewise, prison chaplains find that they have to walk a narrow line between their responsibilities to the Military command or the prison Administration and to their "congregation." For several years, I served as a part-time chaplain visiting federal and state prisons and county jails. On one hand, the chaplain needs to have a deep respect for the law. If the law enforcement authorities know that you can be trusted, and they respect your judgment, then you can be a much more credible advocate for the people whom you visit. By the same token, among prisoners, just as among servicemen and servicewomen, there are those who want to play the system for all that it is worth. If chaplains are successfully manipulated, then they lose their effectiveness. In one of his novels, Herbert Tarr explains that military chaplains need to walk a "tightrope" between military authority and ecclesiastical authority. A similar tightrope exists for prison chaplains.

At the close of their military chaplaincy school, the candidates are told that the

> chaplain is not only a chaplain. He is something more. Just because he wears the same uniform as other officers and is subservient to military command . . . these things do not mean he is to be an apologist for the military.
>
> The chaplain is, first of all, a spokesman for God.
>
> That is why in the military the chaplain is always a displaced person. And he must forever remain a D.P. if he's to be any good as a chaplain. . . . For a chaplain's value is determined by his ability to walk the tightrope between military authority and ecclesiastical authority.[35]

Chaplains work closely with their troops, but they rarely are found in combat zones. Still, there are chaplains who are killed in action. As this is true of the factual world—for two Jewish chaplains did die in Viet Nam[36]—so, likewise, we find in the fiction that there is an example of a death.

> When we first meet Rabbi Chaplain David Mendoza (*Pedlock Saint, Pedlock Sinner*), he is just in the process of being discharged from the Army. At the end of the novel, he returns to active duty and is killed in Viet Nam.[37]

Hillel Chaplains

On many college and university campuses, there are rabbis who serve as Hillel counselors. Their role is to encourage and to provide Jewish programming for the students at their setting. On many campuses, there is a separate building which serves as the Hillel House. In addition to formal and informal programming, Shabbat and holiday services are usually centered at Hillel. There are about 300 Hillel organizations across North America. Hillel rabbis come from all of the major movements in North America. As with their military counterparts, Hillel rabbis are first and foremost rabbis, and their "denominational" differences are understood to be secondary to their primary mission in working with students and faculty. As military chaplains, at times, they are also involved in counseling.[38] Because they are role models at an important juncture in the formative lives of Jewish students, Hillel rabbis at times become one of the reasons that students choose the rabbinate.

There are limited references to Hillel rabbis in the fiction. The glimpses we do see, however, are revealing. Rabbi Joe Wasserman, a Hillel director in Los Angeles, clearly influences Joshua Kaye (*The Rabbi and the Nun*) to pursue a rabbinic career.[39]

Realistically, however, not all Hillel rabbis are happy in their posts. In Kemelman's *Sunday the Rabbi Stayed Home*, Rabbi Small visits a colleague who is a Hillel rabbi at a university. When Small remarks that a college-centered position seems attractive, his friend explains that, in fact, he misses the "real world" of the congregational rabbinate.[40]

Often the Hillel Foundation at a particular campus is financially supported through the local Federation. With this support may well come certain expectations. Richard Rubenstein served as the Hillel Rabbi at the University of Pittsburgh for about a dozen years. He explains that as long as the Federation was not a major supporter, he could continue his work on the campus. Yet when the local Pittsburgh Federation decided to "control" Hillel, he knew that his days there were limited. He refused to work in an environment where he would not be free to speak his mind. As he wrote, he "knew that the price of financial support for Hillel from the Federation would be simple: Get rid of Richard Rubenstein."[41]

While Rubenstein's experience certainly is not true for all Hillel Foundations, it is eerily similar to an episode involving fictional Rabbi Joshua Kaye (*The Rabbi and the Nun*). When he leaves his congregation, he moves to Los Angeles and becomes involved with the local Jewish university student group. A friend and mentor of his, Rabbi Joe Wasseman, serves as the Director of the Jewish Student Union (the "Hillel" group). Rabbi Kaye works with the students and, in a short while, they have set up a havurah and established a meeting place which they title the HOUSE OF PEACE. Rabbi Kaye is also involved in various social-justice causes, and specifically he is actively supporting the California Farm Workers strike. One day, his older colleague phones and explains that he and Rabbi Kaye need to meet immediately. At the meeting is Howard Friedman, "a member of the board of governors of the university and vice president of the Jewish Community Federation of Greater Los Angeles." Friedman explains that the Federation technically owns the property where the HOUSE OF PEACE is situated. He goes on to say that the Teamsters Union, which is opposed to the Farm Workers strike, is planning to make a sizable donation to the Federation, and the Federation would hate to lose that money "because of some student activists." If the students do not give up their work with the strike, then they will have to give up the house. When Friedman leaves, Rabbi Wasseman tells his younger colleague that this is not a battle that can be won. "Money is the bottom line. It pays my salary. It pays for that house. It pays for everything. Go try to do something about it. You really can't. In the end the Howard Friedmans are always the ones who call the shots."[42]

THE FREE-LANCER

In an evaluation of the American rabbinate at mid-century, "The American Rabbi: A Religious Specialist Responds to Loss of Authority," Jerome E. Carlin and Saul H. Mendlovitz (1958) devote a section to the Free-Lancer. They explain that the Free-Lancer generally is ordained from an American yeshiva [seminary], yet he rarely is affiliated with a synagogue, school, or any other formal arm of the Jewish community. "He makes his living by selling certain rabbinic services to the large number of Jews who have no formal membership in a synagogue, or who are members of congregations or prayer-circles which have no rabbi." The Free-Lancer, they explain further, is generally a firm believer in Orthodoxy but he appears as a modern, that is, he speaks English and wears modern clothing. "His purpose is not community service, but the sale of *services*; his functions consist in performing religious rites for a fee." The authors actually quote a Free-Lancer who succinctly sums up his vocation in these words: "Actually, I'm a specialist in weddings, funerals and burials, and dedicating monuments. I deal in intangible commodities."[43]

Carlin and Mendlovitz go on to explain that this Free-Lancer oftentimes is found at cemeteries where he anticipates the needs of his services by mourners when they ask him to participate by chanting prescribed ritual prayers. He then does this for a fee.

Though merely a tangential figure in the novel, an anonymous Free-Lancing rabbi is described in Bruce Jay Friedman's *About*

> *Harry Towns*. "He was a fellow the [funeral] chapel kept on tap in case you didn't have any particular rabbi of your own in mind . . . the rabbi, a homely fellow with . . . wan Talmudic features. . . . And damned if this faded little mysterious house rabbi didn't get her . . . it was as if he had known her all his life."[44]
>
> Unlike the Free-Lancer mentioned above, Rabbi Jonas Lifschitz is absolutely central to the short story "The Silver Crown," by Bernard Malamud. Rabbi Lifschitz is not only a Free-Lancer, he is in the tradition of the Hasidic wonder-rabbis. An old man living in poverty, Rabbi Lifschitz, is approached by the main character in the story, Albert Gans. Gans claims that he wants to hire the rabbi to save the life of Gans' father, who is ill in the hospital. Gans then is told that for a certain sum of money, the rabbi can fashion a silver crown. The rabbi will then offer this crown to God. "The crown is not a medicine, it is the health of your father. We offer the crown to God and God returns to your father his health."[45]

Carlin and Mendlovitz offer the criteria of the Free-Lancer as someone who performs religious services for a fee, who generally is a firm believer in Orthodoxy, but who appears as a modern and whose purpose is not community services as such but offering services when needed. At the end of the twentieth century, the definition of a Free-Lancer can be expanded. In areas of major Jewish population concentration, New York, Chicago, Los Angeles, and Miami, to name but a few, Free Lancers are to be found in all of the denominational bodies. Rabbis who will perform ceremonies—marriages, funerals, bar mitzvahs and bat mitzvahs, conversions for a fee—often will advertise in the Jewish press.

A Free Lancer with a very different clientele is Rabbi Amos Feigelbaum of "Metropolis," a typical American city described in Dan and Lavinia Cohn-Sherbok's work *The American Jew: Voices from an American Jewish Community* (1994). Rabbi Feigelbaum is a jeweler by trade, but he also is trained as a *mohel*, someone who performs ritual circumcisions. Rabbi Feigelbaum is American-born. He studied in Israel and received his *semikhah* (ordination) there. He explains that he is a specialist: circumcisions are the *only* rites he performs. "I do it for everyone in the community, from the Reform and Reconstructionists to the *Hasidim* and super-Orthodox."[46]

A recent book dealing with Jewish life in America quoted a *New York Times* article which suggested that the rabbinate was becoming a popular career for young Jews. The article raised the question if, in the 1990s, there was not a conscious movement away from "the materialism of the 1980s toward more spiritual concerns."[47] In their search for *more spiritual concerns*, some rabbis have sought answers from the Eastern traditions and then tried to incorporate these concepts into Judaism. Rabbi Wayne D. Dosick, serving a congregation near San Diego, California, suggests in his book *The Best is Yet To Be: Renewing American Judaism* (1988) that he sees among his congregants a great hunger for the sacred and a craving for the transcendent, for the enduring, the eternal. He explains that for the modern synagogue to thrive, it needs to "see where its people are. The Synagogue must explore the cults, yoga, est, TM, the health club and all the other 'secular religions,' and see what the attraction is, what these groups and practices offer, what they have that Judaism does not." He goes on to suggest that instead of replacing them, "let the Synagogue learn from them, by taking the best of the modern disciplines and stirring them together with Judaism to find new forms, new modes, new expressions of faith and spirituality."[48] In like manner, Rabbi Zalman Schachter-Shalomi, who is a well-respected figure in the Jewish Renewal movement, has written of his studying with both Sufi and Buddhist teachers.

Though he may be several steps beyond both Rabbi Dosick's and Rabbi Schachter-Shalomi's thoughts, a Free-Lancing rabbi found in some recent fiction, coincidentally set in California, would seem to have blended the East and the West. His answer is Zen Judaism. In Alice Kahn's novel (*Fun With Dirk and Bree*), published in 1991, we read of the following program:

> *Rabbi Sheldon Birnbaum of the Temple Without Walls presents:*
>
> *Wine, Men, Women, and Song: a special weekend for couples who are in trouble, in conflict, or interested in relationship renewal.*
>
> *Rabbi Birnbaum is the leading practitioner of Zen Judaism, a school of thought that combines the ancient wisdom of the East, the ancient wisdom of the Middle East, and the land of plenty called California to improve our sense of inner and outer peace.*

The announcement for the program ends with the words "*Om Shalom*."[49]

NOTES

1. Rabbi Steven M. Dworkin, Executive Vice President, The Rabbinical Council of America, personal communication to David J. Zucker, December 15, 1995.

2. Rabbi Joel H. Meyers, Executive Vice President, The Rabbinical Assembly, personal communication to David J. Zucker, December 26, 1995.

3. "Reconstructionist Rabbinical College 1996–97 Fact Sheet." Wyncotte, PA: Reconstructionist Rabbinical College, 1996.

4. Lenn, T. (1972). *Rabbi and Synagogue in Reform Judaism* (New York: Central Conference of American Rabbis), p. 24. Fewer than 10 percent of the rabbis were reported as fully employed under the category of "Other." In terms of part-time employment, a fairly large number, 41 percent were listed as "Faculty and/or Administration." The large size of this number probably indicates that many rabbis, in addition to pulpit work, *also* teach on a part-time basis. Nearly 30 percent determined that they were "other" in terms of part-time employment.

5. Rabbi Elliot L. Stevens, Executive Secretary, Central Conference of American Rabbis, personal communication to David J. Zucker, December 11, 1995.

6. Schreiber, M. (1991). *The Rabbi and the Nun* (New York: Shengold), p. 13 ff.

7. Polner, M. (1977). *Rabbi: The American Experience* (New York: Holt, Rinehart and Winston), p. 41.

8. Leokum, A. (1969). *The Temple* (New York and Cleveland: NAL/World Publishing), p. 78 f.

9. Gordon, N. (1965). *The Rabbi* (New York: McGraw-Hill), p. 206 f.

10. Gordon, p. 355.

11. Weidman, J. (1975). *The Temple* (New York: Simon and Schuster), p. 306.

12. Levin, M. (1965 [1963]). *The Fanatic* (New York: Pocket), p. 325.

13. Charles, G. (1961 [1960]). *The Crossing Point* (New York: Alfred A. Knopf), p. 9.

14. Potok, C. (1967). *The Chosen* (New York: Simon and Schuster), p. 208.

15. Potok, *The Chosen*, p. 212.

16. Potok, *The Chosen*, p. 250 f.

17. Potok, C. (1969). *The Promise* (New York: Alfred A. Knopf), p. 63.

18. Potok, *The Promise*, p. 105 f.

19. Potok, *The Promise*, p. 107.

20. Potok, *The Promise*, p. 109. See also Ullman's analysis of the "Traditional Rabbi" in chapter one of his thesis. William, A. M. (1985). "The Rabbi in American Jewish Fiction." Unpublished rabbinic thesis, Hebrew Union College—Jewish Institute of Religion, Cincinnati.

21. Kane, A. (1995). *Rabbi, Rabbi* (New York: Saint Martin's Press), p. 167.

22. Kane, p. 196 f.

23. Potok, C. (1975). *In the Beginning*, (New York: Alfred A. Knopf), p. 410.

24. Greenberg, B. (1993) *Moment* 18:6 (December): 51. "Is Now The Time for Orthodox Women Rabbis?" p. 51.

25. Eichorn, D. M. (1962). "A History of the American Jewish Military Chaplaincy," in *Rabbis in Uniform*, ed. Louis Barish (New York: Jonathan David), p. 5. See also Weiner, Jennifer (1996). "The Role of the Rabbi in the United States Armed Forces." Unpublished rabbinic thesis, Hebrew Union College-Jewish Institute of Religion, Cincinnati, 1996, Chapter 1.

26. Rabbi David Lapp, National Director Jewish Welfare Board. Phone conversations with David J. Zucker, August 1, 1996. For a portrait of some Jewish cadets and Chaplain/Major [Rabbi] Ben Romer, the Jewish Chaplain at West Point, see Gilbert, B. M. (1996). "At West Point." *Reform Judaism* 25:1 (Fall): 42–45.

27. Barish, L. (1962). "Preparing to Die," in *Rabbis in Uniform*, ed. Louis Barish, (New York: Jonathan David), p. 203.

28. Blankfort, M. (1956). *The Strong Hand* (Boston, Toronto: Little Brown and Co.), p. 141 f.

29. Barish, L. (1962). "Religious Services—Passover in Korea–1953," in *Rabbis in Uniform*, ed. Louis Barish, (New York: Jonathan David), p. 142 f.

30. Potok, C. (1981). *The Book of Lights* (New York: Alfred A. Knopf), pp. 196, 198.

31. Siegel, M. (1971). *Amen: The Diary of Rabbi Martin Siegel*, ed., Mel Ziegler (New York and Cleveland: World), p. 151.

32. Weiner, chapter 4.

33. Potok, *The Book of Lights*, p. 171.

34. Tarr, H. (1963). *The Conversion of Chaplain Cohen* (New York: Avon), p. 186 f.

35. Tarr, *The Conversion of Chaplain Cohen*, p. 110 f.

36. Weiner, Chapter 1.

37. Longstreet, S. (1969). *Pedlock Saint, Pedlock Sinner* (New York: Delacorte), pp. 21, 464.

38. Miralee Goldsmith, B'nai B'rith Hillel Foundation National Headquarters, Washington, DC. Personal communication to David J. Zucker August, 1996.

39. Schreiber, p. 33.

40. Kemelman, H. (1969). *Sunday the Rabbi Stayed Home* (New York: G. P. Putnam's Sons), p. 18.

41. Rubenstein, R. L. (1974). *Power Struggle* (New York: Charles Scribner's Sons), p. 183.

42. Schreiber, p. 180 f.

43. Carlin, J. and Mendlovitz, S. H. (1958). "The American Rabbi: A Religious Specialist Responds to Loss of Authority," in *The Jews: Social Patterns of An American Group*, ed. Marshall Sklare (Glencoe, IL: The Free Press) pp. 386, 387.

44. Friedman, B. J. (1974). *About Harry Towns* (New York: Alfred A. Knopf), p. 124. The ultimate "Free-Lancer" is the protagonist of Stanley Elkins' (1987) novel, *The Rabbi of Lud* (New York: Charles Scribner's Sons). He is employed full time by a cemetery in New Jersey.

45. Malamud, B. (1973). "The Silver Crown," in *Rembrandt's Hat* (New York: Farrar, Straus & Giroux), p. 10.

46. Cohn-Sherbok, D. and L. (1994). *The American Jew: Voices from an American Jewish Community* (Grand Rapids, MI: William Eerdmans Publishing), p. 127.

47. Bershtel, S. and Graubard, A. (1992). *Saving Remnants: Feeling Jewish in America* (New York: Free Press), p. 143 f., quoting Ari Goldman, "More and More Young Jews Are Picking Careers as Rabbis." *The New York Times*, 24 May 1991.

48. Dosick, W. D. (1988). *The Best is Yet To Be: Renewing American Judaism* (Chestnut Ridge, NY: Town House Press), p 165 f.

49. Kahn, A. (1991). *Fun with Dirk and Bree* (New York: Poseiden Press), p. 162.

12

Rabbis View the Rabbinate

Many rabbis are by nature eloquent and articulate. They describe well their profession: the joys and sorrows, the opportunities and frustrations. In *Letters of Faith*, the late Rabbi Manuel Laderman of Denver addresses a letter "To a Future Rabbi." It begins with these words: "I admire your spirit. It is a tribute to your strong convictions that you are considering the rabbinate as your life work. You are brave." In this letter, Rabbi Laderman describes the rabbinate as a cultured profession, one that is honorable, a growing profession, one which provides a decent though not an excessive income. He also states that it "is a Jewish profession. You have the opportunity of working with and helping in every area of Jewish concern."

He goes on to explain, however, that the "rabbinate is a hard profession. . . . You are always on call. Your days and your nights are never your own." He counsels that a rabbi must love people. This is important, for being a rabbi brings many heartaches. When you deal with human beings, ". . . you are subject to all the disappointments that people can bring—betrayal of trust, failure in loyalty, callousness in idealism." People, Laderman points out, are unpredictable.

The greatest rabbinical headache, he advises, is the self-searching question: "Am I getting an answer to my efforts?" He also notes that the rabbi is the worst judge in drawing up a balance sheet of one's own effectiveness. Mere statistical information is not of help. The "'still small voice' works often quite unbeknownst to you." As was mentioned in Chapter 6 (Congregants View Their Rabbis), the sad, but realistic fact is that the "best laity in the world will never fully understand all that you stand for as a rabbi," for you want more than they are willing to do and be.

Delegation of activity [or more to the point, the terrible temptation *not* to delegate]—letting someone else take the responsibility for the job which you could do faster and more efficiently, and probably better—is a great problem in the rabbinate. Planning, programming, and preparing are rabbinical jobs; the execution needs to be done by others.

Rabbi Laderman also stressed the importance of preaching. A rabbi is the "interpreter of the tradition and literature of Judaism." What the rabbi says *should* be flavored with the richness of Jewish lore. Yet herein lies a problem: Our basic texts are not as familiar to the people in the pews as they were to Jews in past years. Furthermore, unlike Christians who come to church to be moved by a sermon, and who offer high praise to a minister or priest when they say that the sermon moved them, and that they applied it to themselves, Jews will say "the rabbi spoke very well," as if the rabbi were an entrant in an oratorical contest. Nonetheless, he advised, "preach from the heart; prepare well before preaching; be aware that you are fulfilling a sacred task when you stand in the pulpit."

Central to the rabbinate is *teaching*. Teaching is not a *part* of a rabbi's work, it is "all your work. You will find yourself always teaching. Sometimes formally, in a classroom atmosphere; often informally, in a discussion or in conversation."[1]

He points out that seminarians often complain that they are required to study and learn about subjects which seem to have no possible future use in the practical rabbinate. He suggests that this is especially true of the Orthodox seminaries. Here I have to disagree with Rabbi Laderman. I do not think that the complaints are limited to the Orthodox seminaries. In my experience, rabbis in all of the seminaries complain that they have to learn about subjects that they will never come across in the practical rabbinate. In my time, I complained to a senior faculty member at the Hebrew Union College. I questioned why we had to learn such words as the Hebrew or Aramaic terms for barley corn, turnips, rue, white cassia, or wild garlic, much less garden orach, wild-lupine and dwarf-onion, which appeared in the Mishna tractate *Kilayim*. I was told: "David, we want you to learn for the sake of learning, not because you necessarily will be using those terms." Rabbi Laderman's words, however, were absolutely correct when he suggests that never again will you "have the time to study as much as you do" in seminary. A common complaint, especially among congregational rabbis, is that they just find it very difficult to make the time to study. Laderman, however, advised the future rabbi that none of the knowledge you acquire goes to waste when you teach your congregation how to love God and follow God's commandments. In all honesty, however, I am still waiting for the apt moment when I shall be able to teach about rue, wild-lupine and garden orach.

I also remember the anecdote told by a colleague who both served a large congregation and managed to study. For many years, this rabbi had successfully set aside the morning hours of eight to 10 for study and research. It was difficult at first, he explained. "My secretary would answer the phone and say, 'I am sorry, you cannot speak to the rabbi now, he is busy studying.' People got very angry. They were upset with me. I found that I had to take another tack, one which worked amazingly well. I simply instructed my secretary to leave out one word. Now my secretary says, 'I am sorry, you cannot speak to the rabbi now, he is busy.'"

Counseling is another area in which rabbis are involved. Here Laderman offers some cautions: You do not know as much as those who make psychotherapy a full-time profession. Refer, refer, refer.

He continues with some observations on pastoral and social visitation; the importance of paying attention to administrative duties; and then he raises the "great intangible" of community leadership. He suggests that the middle way is most desirable, not to go "all out" so that your congregation will be neglected, but by the same token, not to turn your back on communal responsibilities. Rabbi Laderman then closed with the thought that rabbis need to take care of their bodies and their souls. "Keep your health, maintain your vigor, and hold on to a sense of humor." Finally, always remember that a rabbi is a master of learning. Find the time, make the time, to study.[2]

While many rabbis would agree with much of Rabbi Laderman's advice, younger colleagues would probably take issue with his comment that as rabbis you "are always on call. Your days and your nights are never your own." In Chapter 7 (Women Rabbis) it was noted that one of the most significant legacies of the feminist movement has been the notion that rabbis need to establish a proper balance between their professional and their personal lives and that the congregations need to be supportive of this request. Rabbi Susan Grossman explains that the congregation benefits from the rabbi setting time boundaries. "When I set limits on what my congregants can reasonably ask of my time, I explain to them that if I can't do it [i.e., make time for my own family], how can I ask them as doctors, lawyers, executives, busy people to make time for their families as well."[3]

> In *A Place of Light*, Madelaine Stern is portrayed as an "exemplary rebbetzin." Nonetheless, she is quite clear about the time demands of the congregational rabbinate. At one point, she turns to her husband and says, "You will do what you have done for the last twenty years, Aaron. You will go off to the synagogue and leave me to manage things alone." She is not a happy woman. At the close of the novel, she offers some advice to her husband's successor, Rabbi Lynda Klein. She says: "God doesn't demand human sacrifices, and neither should the congregation. If you give them one, you're leading them astray."[4]

Rabbi Laderman's point that the rabbinate is a "hard profession" but one which can bring enormous joy and personal gratification is reflected in the following observation of the rabbinate: "The congregational rabbinate ranks among the most rewarding and unique contemporary vocations. Participants in few other callings potentially touch the lives of entire families: parents, children, and grandparents. Rabbis relate to their congregants as teacher, friend, confidant, priest, pastor, and companion through life cycles and life crises."[5] The congregational rabbinate does bring much joy, but likewise it brings its share of woe. As noted in Chapter 6 (Congregants View Their Rabbis), the list of expectations of the rabbi is seemingly endless and, at times, contradictory. The rabbinate, as with many professions where people work with their fellow human beings, can be both exhilarating and emotionally exhausting. This is especially true of those who work in the public eye, in the proverbial "fish bowl." The rabbinate is made up of great stress and enormous satisfactions.

STRESS

A survey of articles written in the last few decades about the rabbinate by rabbis themselves and by laity include these titles: "Portrait of the Inauthentic Rabbi," (Maurice Shudofsky 1954); "The Rabbinate: A Restless Body of Men" (Ephraim Greenberg 1960); "The Vanishing American Rabbi" (Benzion C. Kaganoff 1964); "The American Rabbi in Transition" (Max J. Routtenberg 1966); "The Conservative Rabbinate—In Search of Professionalism" (Viviana Z. Zelizer and Gerald L. Zelizer 1973); "Rabbinic Dilemmas" (Norman B. Mirsky 1974); "The Changing American Rabbinate: A Search for Definition" (Stanley Rabinowitz 1975); "Inner Dynamics of the Rabbinate" (Jack H. Bloom 1981); "Rabbis & Their Discontents" (Howard Singer 1985); "Eating up the Rabbi" (Gary A. Tobin 1987); "The Endangered Rabbi" (Arthur Gross Schaefer and Eric Weiss 1994).[6] Many articles which ask directly or indirectly, What is the Future of the Rabbinate?

When rabbis, or the rabbinate as a profession, are described as "inauthentic," "vanishing," "in transition," or "discontented," it should send serious signals to the Jewish community. Are the rabbis still "restless"? If so, what are some of the implications for the rabbinate and the Jewish community? If the congregations *are* "eating up the rabbi," can there be any doubt that the rabbinate is "endangered"? What does this mean? What causes this phenomenon? How will this effect the future of Judaism in the twenty-first century?

Though the rabbinate without question provides enormous satisfactions, and most rabbis would repeat their choice to go into the rabbinate, the level of gratification does not contradict the fact that there is an *inordinate amount of stress* in the rabbinate. A study titled "Role-Related Stress in the Rabbinate" explained that psychological distress in the rabbinate is very high, indeed. Comparisons were made with the data which was gathered following the nuclear reactor accident at Three-Mile Island in Pennsylvania. At Three Mile Island, "the mean scale score of *males* residing in a 20-mile radius of the reactor during the month following the accident was 0.983." The comparable index for the general population sample was 0.915. *Rabbis, by way of contrast weighed in with a distress level of 1.104.* The study of the rabbis dealt with "data collected from the rabbis [where they were asked to] attest to their experience of distress over the immediate previous *one-year* period. Thus this sample of rabbis admits to an experience of *chronic* psychological distress at a level *higher* than the brief period of peak distress felt by males in reaction to the Three Mile Island accident."[7]

Why the stress and distress? One common answer is that rabbis have both the most visible and the least understood functions in the Jewish community. Even those Jews who are affiliated with congregations do not comprehend the role(s) of the rabbi. Gary A. Tobin (1987), in an article/op-ed piece titled "Eating up the rabbi," suggests that modern ". . . rabbis are being asked to be so many things to so many people, that, with rare exceptions, they cannot possibly succeed." Tobin goes on to suggest that congregants expect the rabbi to be an entertainer who delivers sermons and speeches; a modern library able to spit out relevant religious answers at will; someone to offer religious meaning, humor, or appropriate pathos at life cycle events; a magnet for potential members; a counselor; "a leader, helping to give the synagogue direction and purpose, but not too fast and not too far away from the centrist majority." The list goes on. The "rabbi is supposed to *turn on* and inspire children . . . to inculcate Judaism into the reluctant preadolescent" and adolescents as well! "While parents abandon ritual practice and synagogue attendance, the rabbi is supposed to be a modern role model." Tobin continues, "But when things go wrong at a synagogue . . . the rabbi is the first to be blamed. If membership isn't booming, if the children aren't learning enough, if the building is too old or in the wrong place, firing the rabbi usually seems to be the best solution."

In Tobin's view, the

> rabbi has been eaten up . . . because the spiritual leadership and guidance he might have provided has been subverted to power politics, glad-handing, and obligatory interesting but banal speeches.
>
> Congregational rabbis cannot be expected to survive in the political milieu of contemporary synagogue life without adopting some of the behaviours of the congregations they serve. They cannot be all things to all people without becoming defeated or manipulative themselves. Tragically, as the congregations eat up the rabbis, they are also destroying the spiritual soul of contemporary Judaism.[8]

Gary Tobin's metaphor of "eating up the rabbi" can be understood on several levels. It can be "destroying" the rabbinate; destroying the "relationship" between rabbis and their congregations; destroying the "effectiveness" of the rabbinate or a particular rabbi; it can even mean, on a more (im)personal, more visceral level, destroying, that is, literally *killing* a rabbi.

Some years ago, Elliot B. Gertel (1984), in an analysis of "The Image of the Rabbi in Modern American Literature," suggested that one common fictional depiction of the rabbi is as a "tragic hero" and more specifically as a "Christ-figure." He draws on the idea developed by Richard Rubenstein in his autobiography *Power Struggle*. "Rubenstein . . . recalls his feeling while serving as a rabbi that Jews want to see their rabbis dead because they have no Christ-figure or eucharist to satisfy their cannibalistic urges each week as the Mass does for Catholics. This, Rubenstein suggests, is why congregants persecute rabbis, who thus become vulnerable to ulcers and heart attacks or madness."[9]

> Gertel offers the example of Israel Jacobs' novel *Ten For Kaddish*, where Rabbi Morris Kleinman does die at the end of the novel. The cause of death is a heart attack brought upon by the ongoing stress of his congregation. Following the rabbi's death, one of his congregants, a woman who was one of his strong supporters, comments on the rabbi and his relationship with the synagogue. "The whole congregation betrayed him." She then asks, "Why did they crucify their rabbi?" A few moments later she wonders why the congregation has humiliated the rabbi, why they have abused him so badly.[10]
>
> *The Rabbi Is a Lady* focuses nearly entirely on Rabbi Sara Weintraub. She is the widow of Rabbi Sam Weintraub, who recently died. The story begins after the Weintraubs have served in their "prosperous, suburban Long Island community . . . for fifteen years." With the focus on Sara Weintraub, it is easy to forget a small detail that is mentioned, almost in passing, in the second paragraph of the novel, namely the cause of Rabbi Sam Weintraub's death. "Rabbi Sam, as he was affectionately known, had died after a brief illness. His heart gave way. . . ."[11]
>
> In another novel, an internist who has worked specifically with rabbis—"dozens of them"—explains to Rabbi Joshua Kaye that he, the rabbi, would "be surprised to learn how many

rabbis suffer from one form or another of intestinal disorders." Clearly rabbis are not exposed to the same germs, so what then is the common denominator? "Congregations, of course. What do congregations do to rabbis? To use the old Jewish expression, [they, the congregants] eat out their *kishkes* [intestines, guts]. That's right. They put you guys under such stress, they force you to internalize so much, they make you play the nice guy, always smiling, always ready to please, while all the while you eat out your insides, and, sooner or later, your insides begin to strike back."[12]

Richard Rubenstein wrote about rabbinic stress and rabbi-as-scapegoat in *Power Struggle*. Elsewhere, Rubenstein penned a short story titled "A Rabbi Dies." To hearken back to Gary A. Tobin's image, this anonymous rabbi was "eaten up" by his congregation, though in Rubenstein's eyes, he was a willing sacrifice. In this story, a Conservative rabbi is pictured as colluding with his congregation in his own death. After asking rhetorically if the rabbi wanted to die, the narrator explains that there "are all kinds of suicides." There are the obvious suicides, such as jumping out of a window, but there are also the "little suicides, an ulcer, chronic overweight, hypertension . . . and the biggest little suicide of them all, the coronary." In the story, the rabbi is pictured as being very hard on himself, very self-critical. He never measures up to the rabbinic figure of his own father. His father was a Talmudic scholar who barely made a living. The rabbi of the story is, by all outward American standards "successful." Unlike his own father, this rabbi headed up a very large, very affluent congregation. His children were married, his wife was seen as the ideal life partner for him, he was well respected in the Conservative movement. In the narrator's view, the dead rabbi "succeeded in the rabbinate but, in his own eyes, he had failed."

"He was a driven man and he paid a terrible price."

Later, it is suggested that the rabbi "was a perfect target" for the congregation's misplaced anger with whatever slights they had felt from the Christian community. "He did not dare to retaliate. It could have been at a committee meeting. An objection was raised, not for the sake of the objection, but for the sake of wounding the rabbi. It could have been at a social occa-

> sion. Humor can be vicious. . . . He could as little afford to return his congregants' hostility as they could afford to retaliate against gentile aggression. He was the congregation's Jew."
>
> The officers of the congregation are depicted as a "rough, tough, hardened group . . . self-made men." They are rich, bitter, and opinionated as well. "They had a peculiarly ambivalent attitude toward our rabbi. They recognized his importance and his authority, yet he was their hired hand."
>
> In the narrator's view, "in all likelihood, his death was not entirely accidental. He may have at least consented to it. I suspect that something within him yearned for it."[13]

GREAT SATISFACTIONS

Though there are many frustrations and incredible stresses in congregational life, the fact is that most rabbis love serving in their positions. There is enormous satisfaction in being the one who offers comfort and consolation to a mourner, the one who serves as officiant at a life-cycle ceremony, being the one who acknowledges another milestone in a Jewish life. Whether it is at a *brit milah* [circumcision], at a bar mitzvah, a bat mitzvah, Confirmation, or wedding ceremony, the rabbi often sets the tone for these sacred occasions. Lenn reports that generally speaking, rabbis are quite satisfied with their lives. In his study, more than 80 percent of the rabbis indicated that they were reasonably pleased with the way that things have worked out for them. The American Reform rabbinate, at least in terms of their careers, seem to be a reasonably happy lot.[14] The Conservative rabbinate tells a similar story. "There are two spheres of activity which give me greatest satisfactions. One is education," explains a Conservative rabbi. "The second sphere . . . is personal contact with my congregants, including visitation and counseling. Many hours of my day are spent listening to people talk. In addition there are moments in my congregants' lives that require emotional and spiritual support." Another rabbi indicates his satisfaction at influencing "young people to a deeper commitment to Judaism." He goes on to mention the help he can give to someone who is ill or bereaved. Still another rabbi writes, "I like the congregational rabbinate because it gives me great satisfaction to be surrounded in different ways by fellow Jews. My vocation is an avocation as well."[15]

Reflecting on his rabbinate, retired "Traditional" Orthodox Rabbi Daniel Goldberger (1994) writes of the many satisfactions in his long and distinguished career in Denver. "Teaching . . . [t]he study of Torah and the instruction of others in the history, values, texts and ideas of our people and faith have been a continual source of deep satisfaction." He indicates that it is good to know that some of his sermons or addresses moved his listeners to action. He also notes the personal gratification "derived from the heartfelt handshake of a mourner after a funeral who tells you that you have been helpful in softening the blow of a bereavement." Likewise, he writes of the hug of a little child to whom you represent a dear friend; "the gratitude of some troubled individual who has come to you with a heavy burden and needs a sympathetic ear"; the many hours wherein you offer counsel to people struggling with life's problems; "the intellectual stimulation" of grappling with the great issues of the world; and not least, "the conviction that you have turned the hearts of some people to prayer, to the study of Judaism, to the intensification of Jewish living, and to the ongoing support for strengthening Eretz Yisroel [the Land of Israel] and its people." He concludes by saying it is in these things "that one finds the greatest rewards of the rabbinate, and which make of it a sacred calling."[16]

In Dan and Lavinia Cohn-Sherbok's *The American Jew: Voices from an American Jewish Community*, rabbis speak of their experiences. Generally, they are very happy. The Orthodox rabbi describes how proud he is that he has been able to build up his congregation to where now there are a great number of children to teach. The Traditional rabbi left the rabbinate for a number of years and worked as a family counselor. Then he returned. "I was missing the people. I had enjoyed the rabbinate," he explained. The Reform rabbi said, "I've been in this congregation for 23 years. By and large this has been a wonderful experience." The Conservative rabbi noted, "In general my congregation doesn't look over my shoulder. They respect me. I can do as I think best." A former congregational rabbi who was in academia spoke glowingly of many happy years in congregational life but explained that there were pitfalls there as well. A congregational rabbi who was also a college professor spoke of the joy of building up institutions: the synagogue, a museum, a broadly based academic Center for Jewish studies.[17]

Fiction, by its very nature, thrives on dramatic moments and, generally, there is more drama in conflict than moments of contentment. Nonetheless, there are fictional accolades for the rabbinate. Rabbi David Hartman (*The Outsider*) has served his congregation for 25 years. He speaks of the many compensations. He praises his congregation, who have sat and listened to him over the years. He prides himself on his sermons and notes how people tell him that they have been "cheerfully stolen by Catholic priests, Lutheran ministers, Baptist ministers, Presbyterian ministers, Congregational ministers, and of course rabbis."[18]

Days of Judgment comes to a close in the midst of the High Holidays. Just before Yom Kippur, the Cohens receive a flurry of phone calls. "The rabbi and his wife never fully realized how many close, loyal friendships they had formed over the years with the various people they had advised and encouraged or helped in times of need."[19]

Rabbi Charles Shaphan Pedlock, the protagonist of *Pedlock Saint, Pedlock Sinner*, through dint of hard work and a fair amount of politics becomes the "successful" Chief rabbi of his congregation. He builds a marvelous campus above Muholland Drive: The parking lot alone is five acres. At the dedication exercises, 16 rabbis attend, as well as representatives from all the major Jewish organizations, a group from various Eastern rabbinical seminaries, plus local, state, and national dignitaries, all there to honor him on his day of triumph.[20]

Rabbi David Small, of the Kemelman Weekday *Rabbi* series, serves his congregation for 25 years. That he is able to succeed in working with his often feisty, petty, and contentious boards is one of the greater mysteries of the mystery series itself. In any event, after a quarter century, he decides that he wants to explore other areas. He chooses to take early retirement and moves into academia.[21]

In *The Rabbi*, Michael Kind serves at a number of pulpits, but then he settles very successfully in Woodborough, Massachusetts. At the close of the novel, he thinks about how many sermons he has delivered over the years. "So many services, so many words. He grinned in the dark. Not so many as still stretched in front of him; he felt it in his bones, he could almost reach out and touch it, a ladder of Sabbaths to be climbed into the future."[22]

A QUIZ

Serving in the rabbinate has many possible permutations. Many rabbis do serve congregations, but that is only one possibility. Some will be happy there; for others it will be a less natural "fit." Dan Cohn-Sherbok tried the congregational rabbinate but found that this was not the place for him. Academia was much more his natural environment. As an academic, he wondered if there was any method that could be created to advise potential congregational rabbis how well (or how unlikely) they were temperamentally suited for congregational life. He came up with what he describes as the differences between "Dog Rabbis" and "Cat Rabbis." Congregational life, he explains, "is designed for dog rabbis. A good [congregational] rabbi must behave like a dog, loving everyone, greeting each person with enthusiasm, rounding everyone up and metaphorically wagging his tail. Right or wrong, this is ultimately what congregations want: A rabbi must be friendly and public-spirited, he cannot be a solitary recluse." Cats, he points out, *are* solitary creatures. "They like only specific individuals, and then only when they are in the mood. They are wary and cautious with strangers. And after only a little socializing, they have had enough. They prefer to be alone."

Since most rabbis do not assess the realities of congregational life in the light of their own temperament, Cohn-Sherbok devised the "Dog Rabbi/Cat Rabbi" quiz. He explains that he recommends it "to all rabbis as a means of determining whether they are better suited to the rough-and-tumble of congregational life or to a more quiet and peaceful existence as a university teacher or institutional administrator."[23]

This is the quiz in its entirety. A brief evaluation follows.

Are you a Dog Rabbi or a Cat Rabbi?

1. It is your birthday. Would you prefer to celebrate (a) with a large party with all your friends or (b) with a quiet evening in a restaurant with your spouse?

2. When you have company at home, at the end of the evening do you (a) urge them to stay or (b) long for them to go?
3. For your vacation, would you prefer (a) to lead a tour to Israel or (b) sun yourself on a quiet beach?
4. If you could only have one, would you choose to have attached to your synagogue (a) a pre-school or (b) a library?
5. Does the thought of being alone for an afternoon (a) make you uneasy or (b) fill you with relief?
6. If your spouse leaves town for a few days, do you see it as a chance (a) to catch up with old friends or (b) catch up with some reading?
7. Does the thought of your eldest son's next PTA meeting fill you (a) with enthusiasm or (b) with dread?
8. Be honest. Do you prefer officiating at (a) weddings or (b) funerals?
9. When you see an acquaintance on the other side of the street, is your first impulse (a) to cross over and say hello or (b) pretend you haven't seen him or her?
10. Do you believe you have (a) many acquaintances and a few good friends or (b) far too many acquaintances and few good friends?

If you scored mostly (a)s, then you are a Dog Rabbi. The active rabbinate is clearly for you. But if you scored mostly (b)s, then you are a Cat Rabbi—this should be a cause for reflection. You no doubt entered the rabbinate because you are committed to the Jewish faith and wish to study and teach about tradition. But the congregational rabbinate demands more than this. It is not enough simply to love Judaism. A good congregational rabbi needs to love his congregants and enjoy being with them.[24]

While Cohn-Sherbok's quiz is very amusing, it is so very accurate. While he makes no pretense of presenting a scientific study, if you take the test seriously, most of us really do fit generally into one pattern or the other. Not only that, but at some time in our lives, we are more Dog Rabbi-like and, at others, presumably more Cat Rabbi-like. For 21 years, I served in the traditional definition of a congregational rabbi. Many of those years were very happy, and at the time I was more Dog Rabbi than Cat Rabbi. Yet, today, serving as the Chaplain in a long-term care facility, working with women and men who are mostly in their eighties, nineties, and a few a century old, I find that I have changed:

I have become more Cat Rabbi-like. Undoubtedly, these men and women are my congregation. I love them and enjoy being with them. Yet, they are clearly very different from the pre-school/religious school/bar mitzvah or bat mitzvah/confirmation congregation that we think of when most of us describe congregational life.

Unquestionably, there are many stresses and strains working with the elderly. Not the least is that you work daily with people who are in physical distress and likewise who face a certain amount of mental distress. By definition, these are people who do not have a long life-expectancy. It is painful knowing that there are serious time limits on the relationships you can realistically build with your congregants. Yet, at the same time, there are moments of true delight, of wonderful insights and incredible joy. As Abraham Joshua Heschel had once observed, "to be retired is not to be retarded." Old age has its down sides, but there are many, many moments of merriment.

Being a rabbi is hard work. Yet time and again, I have found that there are unique dividends. There *is* something special serving in a profession where the goals allow you to teach, to counsel, and to touch the lives of entire families. Rabbis oftentimes are confidant, priest, pastor, and companion through life cycles and life crises. Rabbis learn in order to teach, and they teach by their personal example, all the while bringing their congregants closer to the performance of God's commandments. It is a rewarding life.

NOTES

1. Laderman, M. (1991). "To A Future Rabbi," in *Letters of Faith* (Denver: Hebrew Educational Alliance), pp. 113–122.

2. Laderman, pp. 122–124.

3. Grossman, S. (1995). "The Dual Nature of Rabbinic Leadership" in *Conservative Judaism* 48:1 (Fall): 46.

4. Shapiro-Rieser, R. (1983). *A Place of Light* (New York: Pocket), pp. 185, 184, 287.

5. Menitoff, P. J. (1987). "Diverse Expectations in Congregational-Rabbinic Relations" in *Journal of Reform Judaism* 34:4 (Fall), p. 1.

6. The articles by Bloom, Greenberg, Rabinowitz, Routtenberg, and the Zelizers are found in *The Rabbinate in America: Reshaping An Ancient Calling*, ed. Jacob Neusner (New York and London: Garland, 1993). The other articles are listed in the Bibliography of this book.

7. Freedman, L. R. (1985). "Role-Related Stress in the Rabbinate: A Report on a Nationwide Study of Conservative and Reform Rabbis," in *Proceedings of the Rabbinic Assembly 1984*, Vol. 46. (New York: The Rabbinical Assembly), p. 45.

8. Tobin, G. A. (1987). "Eating up the rabbi," in *The Jerusalem Post* (April 13): 5.

9. Gertel, E. B. (1984). "The Image of the Rabbi in Modern American Literature." *Conservative Judaism* 37:3 (Spring): 55. See also Rubenstein, R. L. (1974). *Power Struggle* (New York: Charles Scribner's Sons), pp. 123 ff., 133 ff.

10. Jacobs, I. (1972). *Ten For Kaddish* (New York: W. W. Norton), p. 275, see also p. 278.

11. Goldman, A. J. (1987). *The Rabbi is a Lady* (New York: Hippocrene), p. 1.

12. Schreiber, M. (1991). *The Rabbi and the Nun* (New York: Shengold), p. 52 f.

13. Rubenstein, R. (1971). "A Rabbi Dies," unpublished work, quoted in Neusner, J. (1972). *American Judaism: Adventure in Modernity* (Englewood Cliffs, NJ: Prentice Hall), pp. 47–48, 50, 55, 47.

14. Lenn, T. (1972). *Rabbi and Synagogue in Reform Judaism* (New York: Central Conference of American Rabbis), p. 94.

15. Agus, J. B., Brief, N., and Charry, E. (1975). "The Congregational Rabbi and the Conservative Synagogue: A Symposium," *Conservative Judaism* 29:2 (Winter): 19, 35, 70.

16. Goldberger, D. (1994). "Some Parting Reflections." [Denver, Colorado] *Intermountain Jewish News* (August 26): 5.

17. Cohn-Sherbok, D. and L. (1994). *The American Jew: Voices from an American Jewish Community* (Grand Rapids, MI: William Eerdmans Publishing), pp. 10 f., 19, 25 f., 23. 38 ff., 98.

18. Fast, H. (1984). *The Outsider* (Boston: Houghton Mifflin) p. 294. For a factual example of rabbis "borrowing" colleagues' materials, see Feldman, E. (1996). *Tales out of Shul* (Shear Press, New York: Mesorah Publications) p. 35 ff.

19. Falk, H. (1972). *Days of Judgment.* (New York: Shengold) [First mention of Falk is in Chapter 1] p. 216.

20. Longstreet, S. (1969). *Pedlock Saint, Pedlock Sinner* (New York: Delacorte), p. 462.

21. Kemelman, H. (1996). *That Day the Rabbi Left Town* (New York: Fawcett Columbine), p. 10.

22. Gordon, N. (1965). *The Rabbi* (New York: McGraw-Hill), p. 388.

23. Cohn-Sherbok, D. (1995). "Dog Rabbis and Cat Rabbis." *CCAR Journal* 42:1 (Winter/Spring): 22.

24. Cohn-Sherbok, "Dog Rabbis and Cat Rabbis," p. 23.

Epilogue: The Future of the Rabbinate

According to one legend, Adam said to Eve, "We are living in a time of crisis." "Yes," she replied, "and I have some foreboding about the future."[1] From time immemorial, people have agonized about the difficulties of their present situation and darkly pondered the days to come. After all is said and done, having viewed the rabbinate in fact and fiction, it is realistic to ask, "Does the rabbinate *really* have a future?" Are those writers noted in Chapter 12 (Rabbis view the Rabbinate) correct in suggesting that rabbis and the rabbinate are facing a dangerous, uncertain, transitional, discontented, period ahead? Is rabbinical stress but the prelude to rabbinic demise? Alternately, is Simon Schwartzfuchs correct when he asserts in his scholarly work *A Concise History of the Rabbinate*, that the rabbinate has "an assured future"?[2]

It is clear that rabbis in contemporary North America fill a great variety of roles. Many are found in congregational life, many others are in education, chaplaincy, administration, social work, and organizational life. There are rabbis who have earned *semikhah* (ordination) and continue their studies in yeshivot, while still others do not serve as rabbis at all but rather go into business, law, medicine, or other occupations.

Rabbis today are a new breed of men and women, radically different from their predecessors over the centuries, and yet they share a great deal with those who preceded them in the pre-modern world. As in the past, many contemporary rabbis serve within the Jewish community. Some observers of the present-day rabbinate lament that rabbinic authority does not have the "honor" or "reverence" that it did in past. Yet, some of that honor or reverence was more theoretical than practical. Lay people then, as now, often have very strong opinions and great influence. Rabbis who are economically dependent upon their communities are not a phenomenon that was introduced in the twentieth century, much less the last half of the century. Rabbis in the past, just as in the present, needed to know about the Jewish world and the wider world in which the Jews lived. David B. Ruderman (1987) explains that to

> know only Jewish texts was never enough. On the contrary, an overwhelming number of rabbis living in both western and eastern Europe regularly fostered cultural liaisons with the outside world. Many were versed in literature, philosophy and science. . . . Above all, the medieval and modern rabbi continue to share a common psychological condition. They remain communal role models whose personal authenticity is measured by their ability to know and live the law. . . .
>
> Undeniably the rabbi has suffered some loss of political power to lay groups within the Jewish community; the rabbi also sees his or her exclusive claim to expertise in Jewish matters somewhat eclipsed by the new breed of Judaic scholars in university and seminary settings.

The fact is, however, that not all rabbis in the past were great scholars, nor did they have the time or inclination for unlimited study. Rabbis knew—and continue to know—a great deal of the erudition of past Jewish learning. Rabbis in the past "performed the unique function of mediating between esoteric scholarship and the needs of the lay community. Little has changed in this respect."[3] Some rabbis are more scholarly than others. Each of the movements can be rightfully proud that they have provided scholars of note, some who also serve congregations. Rabbis today, and certainly congregational rabbis, generally fill a role that is not part of the expectation of scholars. They learn in order to teach, and teaching leads to performance of God's commandments. Though teachers of Torah, at times rabbis become, as it were, the symbolic Jews of their communities. Jack H. Bloom has suggested that congregational rabbis have become the "exemplary Jews"—spokespeople for Judaism, performers of commandments on behalf of their communities.[4] Yet, having said this, rabbis are seen as fulfilling a unique role: They represent an ideal, not the least part of which is as the voice of tradition and the person who has specialized knowledge in interpreting God's will. "By studying, applying, and living the Torah, the rabbi remains, in the language of Salo W. Baron, 'the chief protagonist in the drama of Jewish communal survival.'"[5] For this reason alone, the rabbinate has an assured future. Yet what will the rabbinate look like in the twenty-first century?

Social scientists do not have a great record in predicting the future. As the Yiddish phrase aptly explains, *A mensch tracht un Gott lacht*—A human plans, and God laughs. Consequently, the suggestions which follow can only be offered conditionally. If the century to come is a reflection of the last decades of the twentieth century, we can expect that the face of the rabbinate will look very different from what we see now. The most striking change will be a much greater percentage of women rabbis. The graduating classes of the Jewish Theological Seminary, the Reconstructionist Rabbinical College, and the Hebrew Union College-Jewish Institute of Religion feature very high numbers of women. Whether the century to come will also find Orthodox women rabbis is unknown. I would guess that this will eventually happen. Women are serious students and scholars of Torah and Talmud. In time, their call to achieve *semikhah* (ordination), along with men, shall come about. Perhaps one way to realize this will be that they serve synagogues made up exclusively of women.

Rabbis increasingly will be products of their own specific movements: Orthodox, Conservative, Reconstructionist, and Reform. In the past, in terms of familial background, there was a fair amount of "crossover" from Orthodox to Conservative or Reform, or from Conservative to Reform. Rabbis grew up in one religious environment (Orthodox, Conservative) but then took their training as rabbis in a movement that was more liberal (Conservative, Reform). Indeed, if anything, there is a shift somewhat toward the religious right. If the current patterns continue, rabbis generally will be *more* observant than their families-of-origin.

The last 20 years or so has seen a resurgence of Orthodoxy, both Mainstream and Sectarian, in a variety of areas across North America, including Greater New York, Boston, Philadelphia, Baltimore, Toronto, South Florida, and Greater Los Angeles/Southern California. These communities will need a variety of Orthodox rabbis to serve them, and so in turn they will probably produce their own cadre of leaders.

Alan Silverstein (1987) explains that, on average, today's Conservative rabbi, unlike his predecessors, is neither "a middle-aged or older father figure, nor a veteran of Orthodox, pious upbringing. Indeed the rabbi can no longer even be expected to be a male. More and more, the rabbi seems to be similar to, rather than in contrast to, his congregants. Like laypeople, the rabbi of today can be a person of any age, of any religious background (including Jews-by-Choice), and can be either a man or a woman."[6]

Peter J. Rubenstein addresses the issue of the Reform rabbinic community in the coming century, but what he suggests is probably very similar to what will be the case for the non-Orthodox rabbinate more generally. Among his points: An increasing number of rabbis will be married to spouses who were not Jewish at birth. Some of these spouses will not be Jewish when they marry. Indeed, some rabbis will choose not ever to marry and will not have children. Sexual orientation will not be a determining issue in terms of the rabbinate. Oftentimes, the rabbinate will become a second career for women and men. He further posits that with the increase in the number of available opportunities for rabbis to serve in the community, this may result in a shortage of rabbis.[7] Again, if present trends continue, rabbis will choose to serve in part-time positions. Another phenomenon might be that for leaders, synagogues will have co-rabbis with very specific duties assigned to each person.

So why are there certain voices who question if rabbis and the rabbinate have a future at all? My answer is that Jews like to *shraiy gevald* [cry "woe"].[8] Jews like to wring their hands, individually or collectively, and mutter their dark foreboding about the coming generations. They ask if there will be any future generations of Jews. This phenomenon is not unique to the Jews and Judaism. There are other ethnic, religious, and even political groups which have regarded themselves as the final generation. That the phenomenon exists elsewhere, however, is another question. Jews have become so good at voicing their concerns that we forget this is not something new. Early in the Bible, Abraham complains to God: "what can you give me, seeing that I shall die childless . . . you have granted me no offspring" (Genesis 15:2–3). What a lesson! The first Jew is complaining that there will not be a second generation. We do not have to wait long for another example. Shortly afterwards, Rebekah complains to Isaac that their son Esau has "married out" and that their other son, Jacob, is still a bachelor. Her complaint clearly is: Am I ever going to see Jewish grandchildren? (Genesis 27:46).

When we move forward in time to the period of the prophets, we find numerous examples where these patriots who spoke for God projected little hope for the future of the Jewish people. Amos cries out, "Hear this word which I take up over you in lamentation, house of Israel: maiden Israel is fallen, not to rise again . . . the city that marches out a thousand strong shall have a hundred left, and the one that marches out a hundred strong shall have but ten left" (Amos 5:1–3). The prophet is saying that in the future a mere remnant composed of 10 percent will survive. First Isaiah voices a similar concern (see Isaiah 5:9 f.; 30:17).

In the book of Lamentations, composed following the destruction of the Temple in Jerusalem more than 2,500 years ago, we read: "Behold, see our disgrace. Our heritage has passed to aliens . . . we have become orphans, fatherless, our mothers are like widows . . . gone is the joy of our hearts, our dancing is turned into mourning . . . truly [God], you have rejected us" (Lamentations 5:1–3, 15, 22).

Consider the period of the Talmud. In the Mishna (*Sotah* 9.15), a catalogue of misfortunes is listed, all which suggest that the future is very bleak. "When Rabbi Meir died, there were no more makers of parables. When ben Azzai died, there were no more industrious scholars. When ben Zoma died there were no more interpreters [of Torah]. When Rabbi Yehoshua died, goodness ceased to exist. . . . When Rabbi Akiva died the glory of the Torah came to an end. When Rabbi Hanina ben Dosa died, people of great deeds ceased to exist." The list goes on to suggest that the future is intolerably bleak. The Mishna continues: "The people shall wander from town to town and none will show them compassion."

As Simon Rawidowicz explains, the person who

> studies Jewish history will readily discover that there was hardly a generation in the Diaspora period which did not consider itself the final link in Israel's chain. Each always saw before it the abyss ready to swallow it up. . . . Each generation grieved not only for itself but also for the great past which was going to disappear forever, as well as for the future of unborn generations who would never see the light of day.[9]

The fact is that we as Jews—or simply we as human beings—have had very little success in predicting the future. We do not know how the years ahead will play out. If we could actually know what will transpire—*and therefore be unable to change it*—we would lose our sanity. How so? Because in addition to the wonderful pieces of good news that the years ahead will bring, such as the eradication of certain diseases and illnesses, we would also know that the period ahead likewise will bring certain acts of horror and carnage as human beings treat other human beings in an inhumane way. We would go insane because we would know the future with certainty and completely be unable to modify it.

As a Jewish people, we have transcended the tragedies of the destruction of the First Temple in Jerusalem well over *2500* years ago, and the destruction of the Second Temple 1,900 years ago. We have transcended the devastation of the Crusades, the Chmielnicki massacres in the Ukraine, the pogroms of Russia and Russian Poland, and we will transcend the tragedy of the Holocaust. It is well over 2,000 years since, as recorded in the book of Esther, wicked Haman plotted the destruction of the Jews of Shushan, and the 127 provinces of King Ahasuerus, which ranged from India to Nubia. Still, we continue to celebrate Haman's downfall and the triumph of good over evil as we annually observe the festival of Purim. Whatever else, we Jews have long memories!

So, when all is said and done, how are the Jews doing in this last decade of the twentieth century? Should we really be fearful of the future, should we be wringing our hands? I do not think so. The fact is that Jews and Judaism are doing very well. I am much more persuaded by the argument of Charles E. Silberman. Silberman writes: "Judaism [is not] seriously threatened by the new openness of American society. . . . It is true that an open society makes it easier for Jews to abandon their Jewishness, but it also reduces the temptation to try, for Jewishness is no longer perceived as a burden, still less an embarrassment. . . . Today . . . young Jews are comfortable with their Jewishness, whether they express it in religious or secular terms. . . ."[10]

I am neither myopic nor naive about the fact that there are problems that Jews and Judaism face in America and elsewhere. We do not live in a perfect society. Nonetheless, along with Silberman, I am convinced that

> the end is *not* at hand; for all the talk about intermarriage and assimilation, Judaism is not about to disappear in the United States. On the contrary . . . the overwhelming majority of American Jews are choosing to remain Jews—some kind of Jews, if not necessarily the kind their grandparents and great-grandparents were. . . . In some segments of the American Jewish community, moreover, generational change is now accompanied by an intensification, not a diminution, of religious observance. We are, in fact, in the early stages of a major revitalization of Jewish religious, intellectual, and cultural life—one that is likely to transform as well as strengthen American Judaism.[11]

In every generation, we have had leaders who felt that they stood at the abyss, that the future was bleak beyond words. In their own time, and in their own idiom, they were deeply concerned about Jewish "continuity." The fact is that they were wrong. We have flourished, and we shall continue to flourish. The future will not look as it does today. Were we living 500 years ago, in post-1492 Spain or Turkey or Poland, a world that had just seen the expulsion of Iberian Jewish life, we could not have imagined the varied faces of late twentieth century Jewry. Were we living in the countryside of Eastern Europe, or Lithuania or Germany, 200 years ago at the end of the eighteenth century, in the midst of the emerging revolutions of the Hasidic-Mitnagged-Haskalah worlds, we could not have imagined the flourishing communities of late twentieth-century Jewry. How then can we correctly envision Judaism's future, much less the role and functions of rabbis and the rabbinate some 200, much less 500, years into the future?

Will there be a thriving Jewish life in North America? As Stanley F. Chyet (1994) explains,

> Obituaries of the American Jewish community are always ready. That is understandable enough. It has never been possible to assume a high level of Jewish education as a general Jewish pattern, and now it is equally impossible to assume a general pattern of affiliation with a synagogue or taking a Jewish mate—yet the community *qua* community does not falter, its middle-class character somehow reinforced by a religio-ethnic glue which appears stronger than all the counterforces in our morally neutral American society.[12]

Wherever we find Jews, Jewish life, and rabbis and the rabbinate in the centuries ahead, it will be different from what we know today.

We have evolved as a people, influenced by both internal and external forces. That will continue to be the pattern. The role of rabbis is to educate Jews in the present, for by definition it always is the present generation which makes the decisions, lays the policies, and directs the activities which touch on the generation to come. By building a proper framework in our time we will not silence those who *shraiy gevald*, but we will be secure in the knowledge that we have done our part to forge the links which connect us to the future.

Simon Schwartzfuchs has written that the "history of the last thousand years, and even more that of the last century, shows that no Jewish community has ever endured for a lengthy period if deprived of the services of the rabbi. The nature of postexilic Judaism makes survival impossible without a teacher and a guide."[13] The rabbis will continue to be both those teachers and those guides. Furthermore, as America continues as a largely secular society, the average layperson will feel that the rabbi is closer to God, and can provide a necessary link between earth and heaven. Rabbis will continue to be called upon to fill many roles.

Though neither a prophet nor a prophet's son, I would venture to guess that as we look to the years ahead, there will be many flourishing centers of Jews and Judaism, just as both rabbis and the rabbinate will be flourishing. I am just as sure that there will be those who will be wringing their hands, looking at their own lives, and looking forward in despair for the future of Jews and Judaism. They will, I predict, be *shraiying gevald* and giving speeches about Jewish "continuity" or its equivalent idiom of the time. Likewise, rabbis will be deeply involved in teaching Judaism and providing answers to the questions what it means to be a Jew and how to live a Jewish life, and they will also address matters of "spirituality" or its equivalent phrase of the time.

> In the Prologue, I quoted from Harry Kemelman's fifth novel of the Weekday *Rabbi* series, *Tuesday the Rabbi Saw Red.* There, Rabbi David Small said that in the past, the rabbi's basic job was to "to guide and teach the community. Well, that's still his job, only now his community is less plastic, less docile, less interested, and even less inclined to be guided. It's a much harder job than it used to be. . . .
>
> "We say it's hard to be a Jew, and it's even harder to be a rabbi, I suppose, who is a kind of professional Jew."[14]

It *is* hard to be a Jew, and it is *harder* to be a rabbi. Yet, as was stated in an earlier chapter, the rabbinate is a cultured profession; it is one that is honorable. It is a Jewish profession, perhaps the most Jewish of professions. Rabbis have the opportunity of working with and helping in every area of Jewish concern. Rabbis are in a position to influence the future of Judaism. What could be more exciting and rewarding!

NOTES

1. My rendition of this conversation is based on the opening lines of Selma Weintraub, (1987). "Dreams Are Realized in Accordance with Their Interpretation," in *The Seminary at 100. Reflections on the Jewish Theological Seminary and the Conservative Movement*, ed. Nina Beth Cardin and David Wolf Silverman (New York: The Rabbinical Assembly and The Jewish Theological Seminary of America), p. 411.

2. Schwartzfuchs, S. (1993). *A Concise History of the Rabbinate* (Oxford, UK and Cambridge, USA: Blackwell), p. 145. "An Assured Future" is the title of the final chapter of his book!

3. Ruderman, D. B. (1987). "Rabbi and Teacher," in *Contemporary Jewish Religious Thought*, ed. Arthur A. Cohen and Paul Mendes-Flohr (New York: Charles Scribner's Sons), pp. 745, 746.

4. Bloom, J. H. (1981). "The Inner Dynamics of the Rabbinate," *Proceedings of the Rabbinical Assembly* 42, pp. 132 ff. The article is quoted in Neusner, J. (1993). *The Rabbinate in America: Reshaping An Ancient Calling*, ed. Jacob Neusner (New York and London: Garland), pp. 2–7.

5. Ruderman, pp. 746–747. Ruderman quotes Salo W. Baron, *The Jewish Community*, 2 (1942), p. 77.

6. Silverstein, A. (1987). "A New Image of the Rabbinate," in *The Seminary at 100. Reflections on the Jewish Theological Seminary and the Conservative Movement*, ed. Nina Beth Cardin and David Wolf Silverman (New York: The Rabbinical Assembly and The Jewish Theological Seminary of America, 1987), p. 430.

7. Rubinstein, P. J. (1990). "The Next Century," in *Tanu Rabbanan: Our Rabbis Taught, CCAR Yearbook 1989, Vol. 2.*, ed. Joseph B. Glaser (New York: Central Conference of American Rabbis), p. 137.

8. See my article, in a slightly altered form, "Jewish 'Continuity' and the 'Ever-Dying' Jews." *Jewish Spectator* 61:1 (Summer 1996), pp. 21–24.

9. Rawidowicz, S. (1967). "Israel: The Ever-Dying People." *Judaism* 16:4 (Fall): 424.

10. Silberman, C. E. (1985). *A Certain People: American Jews and Their Lives Today* (New York: Summit), p. 25.

11. Silberman, p. 25.

12. Chyet, S. F. (1994). "American Jews: Notes on the Idea of a Community." *American Jewish History* 81:3–4 (Spring, Summer): 338–339.

13. Schwartzfuchs, p. 147.

14. Kemelman, H. (1973). *Tuesday the Rabbi Saw Red* (New York: Arthur Fields Books), pp. 258–259.

Bibliography: Fiction

Abrams, Margaret. *Awakened*. Philadelphia: Jewish Publication Society of America, 1954.

Abse, Dannie. "Tales of Shatz," *Jewish Chronicle Literary Supplement* (June 4, 1976), p. v. This poem, in slightly modified form, appears in *Voices Within the Ark: The Modern Jewish Poets*, ed. Howard Schwartz and Anthony Rudolf, pp. 823–825. Yonkers, NY: Pushcart, 1980.

Agress, Hyman and Frances. *The Firing of Rabbi Levi*. New York: Manor Books, 1978.

Appel, Allan. *The Rabbi of Casino Boulevard*. New York: Saint Martin's, 1986.

Ashe, Penelope. *Naked Came the Stranger*. New York: Dell, 1975 [1969].

Bellow, Saul. *Herzog*. New York: Viking Press, 1964.

———. "The Old System." In *Mosby's Memoirs and other stories*, pp. 43–83. New York: Viking Press, 1968.

Benedictus, David. *The Rabbi's Wife*. London: Blond and Briggs, 1976.

Bermant, Chaim. *Ben Preserve Us*. New York: Holt, Rinehart and Winston, 1966 [1965].

———. *Now Dowager*. London: Eyre and Spottiswoode, 1971.

Blankfort, Michael. *The Strong Hand*. Boston, Toronto: Little, Brown and Co., 1956.

Brian, Lee. "With Tenderness." In *Reconstructionist*, 46:8 (December 1980), pp. 20–27.

Butler, Samuel. *The Way of All Flesh*. Garden City, NY: Doubleday and Co., 1944 [1903].

Charles, Gerda. *The Crossing Point*. New York: Alfred A. Knopf, 1961 [1960].

Chyet, Stanley F. "The Wise Men of Wentworth." In *Chicago Jewish Forum*, 21:1 (Fall 1962), pp. 34–36.

Cohen, Arthur. *The Carpenter Years*. New York: New American Library, 1967.

Elkins, Stanley. *The Rabbi of Lud*. New York: Charles Scribner's Sons, 1987.

Falk, Harvey. *Days of Judgment*. New York: Shengold, 1972.

Fast, Howard. *The Outsider*. Boston: Houghton Mifflin, 1984.

Friedman, Bruce Jay. *About Harry Towns*. New York: Alfred A. Knopf, 1974.

Fruchter, Norman. *Coat Upon A Stick*. Philadelphia: Jewish Publication Society, 1987 [1962].

Gillette, Glenn and Jeanne and Zucker, David J. "Here and Now." In *Jewish Spectator*, 61:2 (Fall 1996): 43–49.

Gold, Herb. *Fathers*. New York: Arbor House, 1966.

Goldman, Alex J. *The Rabbi Is a Lady*. New York: Hippocrene, 1987.

Goldman, William. *Boys and Girls Together*. New York: Bantam, 1965 [1964].

Goodman, Allegra. "The Succession." In *Total Immersion: Stories*, pp. 27–48. New York: Harper and Row, 1989.

———. "And Also Much Cattle." In *Total Immersion: Stories*, pp. 139–167. New York: Harper and Row, 1989.

———. "Mosquitoes." In *The Family Markowitz*, pp. 100–137. New York: Farrar, Straus & Giroux, 1996.

———. "The Art Biz." In *The Family Markowitz*, pp. 28–44. New York: Farrar, Straus & Giroux, 1996.

———. "One Down." In *The Family Markowitz*, pp. 234–262. New York: Farrar, Straus & Giroux, 1996.

Goodman, Paul. "A Prayer for Dew." In *Breakthrough: A Treasury of Contemporary American-Jewish Literature*, ed. Irving Malin and Irwin Stark, pp. 116–121. Philadelphia: Jewish Publication Society, 1965.

Gordon, Noah. *The Rabbi*. New York: McGraw-Hill, 1965.
Green, Gerald. *The Last Angry Man*. New York: Pocket Books, 1959 [1957].
Greenberg, Marilyn. *The Rabbi's Life Contract*. Garden City, New York: Doubleday and Co., 1983.
Haase, John. *The Nuptials*. New York: Simon and Schuster, 1969.
Harris, Mark. *The Goy*. New York: Dial, 1970.
Jacobs, Israel. *Ten For Kaddish*. New York: W. W. Norton, 1972.
Kahn, Alice. *Fun With Dirk and Bree*. New York: Poseiden Press, 1991.
Kane, Andrew. *Rabbi, Rabbi*. New York: Saint Martin's, 1995.
Kaufmann, Myron S. *Thy Daughter's Nakedness*. Philadelphia and New York: J. B. Lippincott, 1968.
———. *Remember Me To God*. Philadelphia and New York: J. B. Lippincott, 1957.
Kellerman, Faye. *The Ritual Bath*, New York: Arbor House, 1986.
———. *Sacred and Profane*, New York: Arbor House, 1987.
———. *Milk and Honey*. New York: William Morrow, 1990.
———. *Day of Atonement*. New York: William Morrow, 1991.
———. *Grievous Sin*. New York: William Morrow, 1993.
Kemelman, Harry. *Friday the Rabbi Slept Late*. New York: Crown, 1964.
———. *Saturday the Rabbi Went Hungry*. New York: Crown, 1966.
———. *Sunday the Rabbi Stayed Home*. New York: G. P. Putnam's Sons, 1969.
———. *Monday the Rabbi Took Off*. Greenwich, CT: Fawcett Crest, 1973 [1972].
———. *Tuesday the Rabbi Saw Red*. New York: Arthur Fields Books, 1973.
———. *Wednesday the Rabbi Got Wet*. New York: William Morrow, 1976.
———. *Thursday the Rabbi Walked Out*. New York: William Morrow, 1978.
———. *Conversations with Rabbi Small*. New York: William Morrow, 1981.
———. *Someday the Rabbi Will Leave*. New York: William Morrow, 1985.
———. *One Fine Day the Rabbi Bought a Cross*. New York: William Morrow, 1987.
———. *The Day the Rabbi Resigned*. New York: Fawcett Columbine, 1992.
———. *That Day the Rabbi Left Town*. New York: Fawcett Columbine, 1996.

Leahy, Syrell Rogovin. *A Book of Ruth*. New York: Simon and Schuster, 1974.

Leokum, Arkady. *The Temple*. New York and Cleveland: NAL/World Publishing, 1969.

Lerman, Rhoda. *God's Ear*. New York: Henry Holt, 1989.

Levin, Meyer. *The Fanatic*. New York: Pocket, 1965 [1963].

Levine, Morton, with Hal Kantor. *The Congregation*. New York: G. P. Putnam's Sons, 1985.

Longstreet, Stephen. *Pedlock Saint, Pedlock Sinner*. New York: Delacorte, 1969.

———. *Pedlock & Sons*. New York: Delacorte, 1966.

Malamud, Bernard. *The Assistant*. New York: Farrar, Straus & Giroux, 1957.

———. "The Magic Barrel." *The Magic Barrel*, pp. 193–214. New York: Farrar, Straus, and Cudahy, 1958.

———. "The Silver Crown." In *Rembrandt's Hat*, pp. 3–29. New York: Farrar, Straus & Giroux, 1973.

Markfield, Wallace. *To An Early Grave*. New York: Simon and Schuster, 1964.

Marks, Laurence and Maurice Gran. Allan McKeown and Joanna Willett Executive Producers. "Love hurts." London: Alomo Productions, SelecTV, 1992–1993. [Twenty episodes. Series 1—Episodes 1–10: "Crawling From The Wreck"; "Take It To The Limit"; "Walk Right Back"; "Relative Values"; " Cured"; "Stormy Weather"; "A Day In The Life"; "Charity Begins At Home"; "Who's Sorry Now?"; "Let's Do It." Series 2—Episodes 1–10: "Strictly Business"; "Cold Comfort"; "The Max Factor"; "Your Money Or Your Life"; "Band of Gold"; "Face The Music"; "If The Cap Fits"; "Just A Bit Of Business"; "For A Few Dollars More"; "Love For Sale."]

Ozick, Cynthia. "The Pagan Rabbi." In *The Pagan Rabbi and Other Stories*, pp. 1–37. New York: E. P. Dutton, 1983.

Pollack, Eileen. "The Rabbi in the Attic." In *The Rabbi in the Attic and Other Stories*, pp. 85–120. Harrison, New York and Encino, California: Delphinium Books, 1991.

Potok, Chaim. *The Chosen*. New York: Simon and Schuster, 1967.

———. *The Promise*. New York: Alfred A. Knopf, 1969.

———. *My Name is Asher Lev*. New York: Alfred A. Knopf, 1972.

———. *In the Beginning*. New York: Alfred A. Knopf, 1975.

———. *The Book of Lights*. New York: Alfred A. Knopf, 1981.

Ragen, Naomi. *The Sacrifice of Tamar*. New York: Crown, 1994.

Richler, Mordecai. *The Incomparable Atuk*. London: Andre Deutsch, 1963.

———. *Saint Urbain's Horseman*. New York: Alfred A. Knopf, 1971.

Rose, Louise Blecher. *The Launching of Barbara Fabrikant*. New York: David McKay Company, 1974.

Roth, Philip. "Defender of the Faith." In *Goodbye, Columbus and Five Short Stories*, pp. 173–214. Boston: Houghton Mifflin, 1959.

———. "The Conversion of the Jews." In *Goodbye, Columbus and Five Short Stories*, pp. 149–171. Boston: Houghton Mifflin, 1959.

———. "Eli the Fanatic." In *Goodbye Columbus and Five Short Stories*, pp. 261–313. Boston: Houghton Mifflin, 1959.

———. *Portnoy's Complaint*. New York: Random House, 1969.

———. *Letting Go*. New York: Random House, 1962.

Rubenstein, Richard L. "A Rabbi Dies," unpublished work, 1971. In Neusner, J. *American Judaism: Adventure in Modernity*. Englewood Cliffs: Prentice-Hall, 1974, pp. 46–59.

Schisgal, Murray. "The Rabbi and the Toyota Dealer." [A play.] In "Closet Madness And Other Plays." New York: Samuel French, 1984.

Schreiber, Mordecai. *The Rabbi and the Nun*. New York: Shengold, 1991.

Segal, Erich. *Acts of Faith*. New York: Bantam, 1992.

Shapiro-Rieser, Rhonda. *A Place of Light*. New York: Pocket, 1983.

Singer, Isaac Bashevis. "The Bishop's Robe." In *A Crown of Feathers and other stories*, pp. 137–149. Greenwich, CT: Fawcett, 1974 [1973].

———. "The Joke." In *A Friend of Kafka*, pp. 159–180. New York: Farrar, Straus & Giroux, 1970.

———. "A Pair." In *Passions and other stories*, pp. 202–217. New York: Farrar, Straus & Giroux, 1975.

Tarr, Herbert. *The Conversion of Chaplain Cohen*. New York: Avon, 1963.

———. *Heaven Help Us!* New York: Random House, 1968.

———. *So Help Me God!* New York: Times Books, 1979.

———. *A Woman of Spirit*. New York: Donald I. Fine, 1989.

Telushkin, Joseph. *The Unorthodox Murder of Rabbi Wahl*. Toronto and New York: Bantam, 1987.

———. *The Final Analysis of Dr. Stark*. Toronto and New York: Bantam, 1988.

———. *An Eye for an Eye*. New York: Bantam, 1992 [1991].

Tennenbaum, Silvia. *Rachel, the Rabbi's Wife*. New York: William Morrow, 1978.

Twersky, Jacob. *A Marked House*. New York: Thomas Yoseloff, 1968.

Wallant, Edward Lewis. *The Human Season*. New York: Harcourt Brace Jovanovich, 1960.

Weidman, Jerome. *The Temple*. New York: Simon and Schuster, 1975.

———. *Last Respects*. New York: Random House, 1971.

Welles, Penelope. *Babyhip*. New York: E. P. Dutton, 1967.

Wohlgelernter, Maurice. "Hardball." *Jewish Spectator* 59:2 (Fall 1994): 46–55.

Wouk, Herman. *Marjorie Morningstar*. Garden City, New York: Doubleday and Co., 1955.

Bibliography: Nonfiction

Ackerman, David M. "The Seminary [JTS] Rabbinical School Curriculum." *Conservative Judaism* 44:4 (Summer 1992): 47–61.

Adler, Rachel. "A Stumbling Block Before the Blind: Sexual Exploitation in Pastoral Counseling." *CCAR Journal* 40:2 (Spring 1993): 13–43. Responses by Rabbi Jeffrey K. Salkin and Rabbi Julie R. Spitzer, 43–54.

Agus, Jacob B., Neil Brief, Elias Charry, et. al. "The Congregational Rabbi and the Conservative Synagogue: A Symposium." *Conservative Judaism* 29:2 (Winter 1975): 3–96.

Ahlstrom, Sidney E. *A Religious History of the American People*. New Haven and London: Yale University Press, 1972.

Alpert, Rebecca T. "Reconstructionist Rabbis" [a section of] "The Making of American Rabbis" in *Encyclopedia Judaica Yearbook 1983/5*, pp. 101–105. Jerusalem: Keter, 1985.

Alpert, Rebecca T., and Jacob J. Staub. *Exploring Judaism: A Reconstructionist Approach*. Wyncotte, PA: Reconstructionist Press, 1988.

Angoff, Charles. "The Future of European Jewry: The Need for an Enquiry." *The Jewish Quarterly* 8:4 (Autumn, 1961): 8–11.

Barish, Louis. "Religious Services—Passover in Korea-1953." In *Rabbis in Uniform*, ed. Louis Barish, pp. 142–144. New York: Jonathan David, 1962.

———. "Preparing To Die." In *Rabbis in Uniform*, ed. Louis Barish, pp. 203–204. New York: Jonathan David, 1962.

Berenbaum, Michael G. "The Situation of the American Jew." In *Events and Movements in Modern Judaism*, ed. Raphael Patai and Emanuel S. Goldsmith , pp. 231–249. New York: Paragon House, 1995.

Berger, David, Saul J. Berman, David R. Blumenthal, et al. "What Do American Jews Believe? A Symposium," *Commentary* 102:2 (August 1996): 18–96.

Berman, Louis A. *Jews and Intermarriage: A Study in Personality and Culture*. New York: Thomas Yoseloff, 1968.

Berman, Saul J. Respondent, "What Do American Jews Believe? A Symposium," *Commentary* 102:2 (August 1996): 21–23.

Bershtel, Sara and Allen Graubard. *Saving Remnants: Feeling Jewish in America*. New York: Free Press, 1992.

Biale, David. *Power and Powerlessness in Jewish History*. New York: Schocken, 1986.

Bitton-Jackson, Livia. "New Roles for Jewish Women." In *Events and Movements in Modern Judaism*, ed. Raphael Patai and Emanuel S. Goldsmith, pp. 285–302. New York: Paragon House, 1995.

Bloom, Jack H. "The Inner Dynamics of the Rabbinate." *Proceedings of the Rabbinical Assembly 42* (1981), pp. 132–137. Quoted in *The Rabbinate in America: Reshaping An Ancient Calling*, ed. Jacob Neusner (New York and London: Garland, 1993), pp. 2–7.

Borowitz, Eugene B. *Reform Judaism Today*. New York: Behrman House, 1978.

———. *Sh'ma*, ed. Eugene Borowitz, 27:527 and 27:528 (February 7 and 21, 1997), and relevant articles by Zevulun Charlop (Rabbi Isaac Elchanan Theological Seminary at Yeshiva University); William Lebeau (Jewish Theological Seminary); Norman J. Cohen (Hebrew Union College-Jewish Institute of Religion); Daniel Gordis (Ziegler School of Rabbinic Studies, University of Judaism); David Teutsch (Reconstutionist Rabbinical College); Ronald D. Price (Institute of Traditional Judaism); Zalman Schachter-Shalomi (ALEPH, Alliance for Jewish Renewal); and Shohama Wiener (Academy for Jewish Religion.)

Bush, Lawrence. "Can We Accept a Congregation That Does Not Worship God?" *Reform Judaism* 23:2 (Winter 1994): 25–27.

Cardin, Nina Beth. "The First Generation of Women's Rabbinate." *Conservative Judaism* 48:1 (Fall 1995): 15–20.

Carlin, Jerome, and Saul H. Mendlovitz. "The American Rabbi: A Religious Specialist Responds to Loss of Authority." In *The Jews: Social Patterns of An American Group*, ed. Marshall Sklare, pp. 377–414, Glencoe: The Free Press, 1958.

Charlop, Zevulun. "Orthodox Rabbis" [a section of] "The Making of American Rabbis" in *Encyclopedia Judaica Yearbook 1983/5*, pp. 84–90. Jerusalem: Keter, 1985.

———. "Rabbinic Education: Then, Now and Tomorrow." *Sh'ma* 27:527 (February 7, 1997): 1–3

Chyet, Stanley F. "American Jews: Notes on the Idea of a Community." In *American Jewish History* 81:3–4, (Spring, Summer 1994): 331–339.

Cohen, Norman J. "The Changing Face of Rabbinic Education." *Sh'ma* 27:527 (February 7, 1997): 3–5.

Cohen, Shaye J. D. "The Matrilineal Principle in Historical Perspective," *Judaism* 34:1 (Winter 1985): 5–13.

Cohen, Shaye J. D., J. David Bleich, Jack J. Cohen, et al. "The Issue of Patrilineal Descent: A Symposium." *Judaism* 34:1 (Winter 1985): 1–135.

Cohen, Steven M. *American Modernity and Jewish Identity*. New York: Tavistock Publications, 1983.

Cohn-Sherbok, Dan. "Dog Rabbis and Cat Rabbis." *CCAR Journal* 42:1 (Winter–Spring 1995): 21–23.

———. *Not a Job for a Nice Jewish Boy*. London: Bellew Publishing, 1993.

Cohn-Sherbok, Dan and Lavinia. *The American Jew: Voices from an American Jewish Community*. Grand Rapids, MI: William Eerdmans Publishing, 1994.

Cowan, Jennifer R. "Survey Finds 70% of Women Rabbis Sexually Harassed," *Moment* 18:5 (October 1993): 34–37.

Davidson, Aryeh and Jack Wertheimer. "The Next Generation of Conservative Rabbis: An Empirical Study of Today's Rabbinical Students." In *The Seminary at 100. Reflections on the Jewish Theological Seminary and the Conservative Movement*, ed. Nina Beth Cardin and David Wolf Silverman, pp. 33–46. New York: The Rabbinical Assembly and The Jewish Theological Seminary of America, 1987.

Davidson, Jessica R. "When the Rabbi is a Woman." *Congress Monthly* 58:6 (September/October 1991): 10–14.

Davis, Moshe. *The Emergence of Conservative Judaism*. Philadelphia: Jewish Publication Society, 1965.

Dershowitz, Alan M. *Chutzpah*. Boston: Little, Brown and Co., 1991.

Dinnerstein, Leonard. *Anti-Semitism in America*. New York, Oxford: Oxford University Press, 1994.

Dorff, Elliot N. "The Concept of God in the Conservative Movement." *Judaism* 40:4 (Fall 1991): 429–441.

———. Respondent, "What Do American Jews Believe? A Symposium," *Commentary* 102:2 (August 1996): 29–30.

Dosick, Wayne D. *The Best Is Yet To Be: Renewing American Judaism*. Chestnut Ridge, New York: Town House Press, 1988.

Dresner, Samuel H. "From Jewish Inadequacy to a Sacred Community." In *Federation and Synagogue: Towards A New Partnership*, pp. 26–51. Los Angeles: The Susan and David Wilstine Institute of Jewish Policy Studies, The University of Judaism, 1994. See also the other essays in this pamphlet: Arnold Eisen. "Working Towards Cooperation and Pluralism"; and Barry Shrage. "Bringing Federations Closer to Synagogues."

———. *The Jew in American Life*. New York: Crown, 1963.

Eckardt, A. Roy and Alice L. "Silence in the Churches." *Midstream* 13:8 (October 1967): 27–32.

———. "Again, Silence in the Churches," Appendix in A. Roy Eckardt. *Elder and Younger Brothers: The Encounter of Jews and Christians*. New York: Charles Scribner's Sons, 1967.

Eichorn, David Max. "A History of the American Jewish Military Chaplaincy." In *Rabbis in Uniform*, ed. Louis Barish, pp. 1–33. New York: Jonathan David, 1962.

Eisen, Arnold. "Jewish Theology in North America: Notes on Two Decades." In *American Jewish Year Book 1991*, ed. David Singer and Ruth R. Seldin, vol. 91, pp. 3–33. New York: American Jewish Committee and Philadelphia: Jewish Publication Society, 1991

Ellenson, David. "Zion in the Mind of the American Rabbinate during the 1940s." In *The Americanization of the Jews*, ed. Robert M. Seltzer and Norman J. Cohen, pp. 193–212. New York and London: New York University Press, 1995.

Epstein, Lawrence J. *Conversion to Judaism: A Guidebook*. Northvale, NJ and London: Jason Aronson Inc., 1994.

Fein, Leonard J., et. al. *Reform is a Verb: Notes on Reform and Reforming Jews*. New York: Union of American Hebrew Congregations, 1972.

Feldman, Emanuel. "I Could Have Used Some Rabbinic Authority." *Tradition* 27:4 (Summer 1993): 1–3.

———. "Rabbinic Authority: A Special Issue," ed. Emanuel Feldman. *Tradition* 27:4 (Summer 1993): 1–157.

———. *Tales out of Shul: The unorthodox journal of an Orthodox rabbi*. New York: Shaar Press/Mesorah Publications, 1996.

Fishman, Priscilla. *The Jews of the United States*, ed. Priscilla Fishman. New York: Quadrangle/New York Times Book, 1973.

Fishman, Sylvia Barack. "The Impact of Feminism on American Jewish Life." In *American Jewish Year Book 1989*, ed. David Singer and Ruth R. Seldin, vol. 89, pp. 3–62. New York: American Jewish Committee and Philadelphia: Jewish Publication Society, 1989.

———. *A Breath of Life: Feminism in the American Jewish Community*. New York: Free Press, 1993.

Fox, Karen L. "Hearing the voice of survivors of sexual misconduct." Paper presented at a symposium at the Pacific Association of Reform Rabbis titled "Rabbi's Sexual Misconduct: Collegial Response and Methodology of Teshuvah [Repentance] and Communal Healing." January 1994.

Freedman, Leslie R. "Role-Related Stress in the Rabbinate: A Report on a Nationwide Study of Conservative and Reform Rabbis." In *The Rabbinic Assembly Proceedings 1984*, pp. 43–50. New York: The Rabbinical Assembly, 1985.

Gelerenter-Liebowitz, Shoshana. "Growing Up Lubavitch." In *Daughters of the King: Women and the Synagogue*, ed. Susan Grossman and Rivka Haut, pp. 238–242. Philadelphia and Jerusalem: Jewish Publication Society, 1992.

Geller, Laura. "From Equality to Transformation: the Challenge of Women's Rabbinic Leadership." In *Gender and Judaism: The Transformation of Tradition*, ed. T. M. Rudavsky, pp. 243–253. New York and London: New York University Press, 1995.

Gertel, Elliot. "The Image of the Rabbi in Modern American Literature." *Conservative Judaism* 37:3 (Spring 1984): 51–61.

———. "A Novel Approach to Conservative Judaism." *United Synagogue Review* (Winter, 1991).

Gilbert, Beth M. "At West Point." *Reform Judaism* 25:1 (Fall 1996): 42–45.

Goldberger, Daniel. "Some Parting Reflections." In [Denver, Colorado] *Intermountain Jewish News*. (August 26, 1994): 5.

Gordis, Daniel. "Visions from a new rabbinical school." *Sh'ma* 27:527 (February 7, 1997): 5–6.

Gordis, Robert. *Emet Ve-Emunah: Statement of Principles of Conservative Judaism*. New York: The Jewish Theological Seminary of America, The Rabbinical Assembly, United Synagogue of America, Women's League for Conservative Judaism, Federation of Jewish Men's Clubs, 1988.

Goss, Julie. "Women In The Pulpit: Reworking the Rabbi's Role." *Lilith* 15:4 (Fall 1990): 16–19.

Gottschalk, Alfred. "Reform Rabbis" [a section of] "The Making of American Rabbis." In *Encyclopedia Judaica Yearbook 1983/5*, pp. 96–100. Jerusalem: Keter, 1985.

Greene, Melissa Fay. *The Temple Bombing*. Reading, MA: Addison-Wesley, 1996.

Greenberg, Blu. "Will There Be Orthodox Women Rabbis?" *Judaism* 33:1 (Winter 1984): 23–33.

———. "Is Now the Time for Orthodox Women Rabbis?" *Moment* 18:6 (December 1993): 50–53, 74.

Greenberg, Simon, editor. *The Ordination of Women as Rabbis: Studies and Responsa*. New York: Jewish Theological Seminary, 1988.

———. "The Rabbi as *Darshan*." *Judaism* 40:4 (Fall 1991): 471–483.

Gross-Schaefer, Arthur "Breaking the Silence: Rabbinic Sexual Misconduct." *Sh'ma* 24:473.

———. "Teshuvah and Rabbinic Sexual Misconduct." *CCAR Journal* 42:2 (Summer/Fall 1995): 75–80.

Gross Schaefer, Arthur and Weiss, Eric. "The Endangered Rabbi." *Jewish Spectator* 59:2 (Fall 1994): 25–29.

Grossman, Lawrence. "Jewish Communal Affairs." In *American Jewish Year Book 1991*, ed. David Singer and Ruth R. Seldin, vol. 91, pp. 177–203. New York: American Jewish Committee and Philadelphia: Jewish Publication Society, 1991.

Grossman, Susan. "The Dual Nature of Rabbinic Leadership." *Conservative Judaism* 48:1 (Fall 1995): 43–48.

Gurock, Jeffrey S. "Resisters and Accomodators: Varieties of Orthodox Rabbis in America, 1886–1983." In *American Jewish Orthodoxy in*

Historical Perspective, pp. 1–62. New York: Ktav Publishing, 1996. This article originally appeared in *American Jewish Archives* (Cincinnati, November 1983), pp. 100–187.

———. "The Winnowing of American Orthodoxy." In *American Jewish Orthodoxy in Historical Perspective*, pp. 299–312. New York: Ktav Publishing, 1996. This article originally appeared in *Approaches to Modern Judaism II* (Chico, CA, 1984), pp. 41–54.

Hammer, Reuven. "Conservative Rabbis" [a section of] "The Making of American Rabbis." In *Encyclopedia Judaica Yearbook 1983/5*, pp. 91–95. Jerusalem: Keter, 1985.

Harvey, Van A. *A Handbook of Theological Terms*. New York: Macmillan, 1964.

Hauptman, Judith. "Conservative Judaism: The Ethical Challenge of Feminist Change." In *The Americanization of the Jews*, ed. Robert M. Seltzer and Norman J. Cohen, pp. 296–308. New York and London: New York University Press, 1995.

Heilman, Samuel C. "Orthodox Jews: An Open or Closed Group?" In *Uncivil Religion: Interreligious Hostility in America*, ed. Robert N. Bellah and Frederick E. Greenspahn, pp. 115–131. New York: Crossroads, 1987.

Helmreich, William B. *The World of the Yeshiva: An Intimate Portrait of Orthodox Jewry*. New York: Free Press, 1982.

Hoyt, Carolyn. "All Eyes Upon Us." In *Women's Day*, pp. 58, 66. April 6, 1993.

Hutt, Ellyn. "*Ezer k'Negdo*: A Helper Opposite Him," February 24, 1997.

Hyman, Paula E. "Ezrat Nashim and the Emergence of a New Jewish Feminism." In *The Americanization of the Jews*, ed. Robert M. Seltzer and Norman J. Cohen, pp. 284–295. New York and London: New York University Press, 1995.

Jacob, Walter. "Dialogue in the Twentieth Century." In *Toward a Theological Encounter*, ed. Leon Klenicki, pp. 67–84. New York, Mahwah: Paulist Press, 1991.

———. "Private Ordination—Need We Be Concerned?" *CCAR Journal* 44:1 (Winter 1997): 3–8.

Jacobs, Phil. "What's Behind Rabbi's Touch?: When a kiss results in a violation of trust." [Detroit] *The Jewish News*, July 8, 1994, 1 ff.

Karff, Samuel E. "The Rabbi as Religious Figure." In *Tanu Rabbanan: Our Rabbis Taught CCAR Yearbook 1989, vol. 2*, ed. Joseph B. Glaser, pp. 71–88. New York: Central Conference of American Rabbis, 1990.

Karlin-Neumann, Patricia. "Dealing with Rabbis who have committed acts of sexual misconduct." Paper presented at a symposium at the Pacific Association of Reform Rabbis titled "Rabbi's Sexual Misconduct: Collegial Response and Methodology of Teshuvah [Repentance] and Communal Healing." January 1994.

Karp, Abraham J. "Overview: The Synagogue in America—A Historical Typology." *The American Synagogue: A Sanctuary Transformed*, ed. Jack Wertheimer, pp. 1–34. Cambridge, New York: Cambridge University Press, 1987.

Katz, Steven T. *Jewish Philosophers* New York: Bloch Publishing, 1975.

Kensky, Allen. "Women in the Rabbinate: The First Ten Years." *Conservative Judaism* 48:1 (Fall 1995): 3–4.

Klenicki, Leon. "Jewish-Christian Dialogue." In *A Dictionary of the Jewish–Christian Dialogue, Expanded Edition*, ed. Leon Klenicki and Geoffrey Wigoder, pp. 100–103. New York, Mahwah, New Jersey: Paulist, 1995.

———. *Toward A Theological Encounter: Jewish Understandings of Christianity*. Leon Klenicki, ed. New York, Mahwah, New Jersey: Paulist, 1991.

Kohn, Daniel B. "Modern Congregants: Jewish by Proxy?" *Jewish Spectator* 59:1 (Summer 1994): 26–28.

Kosovske, Howard "Sexual Exploitation: A Jewish Response" *CCAR Journal* 41:3 (Summer 1994): 5–20.

Kravitz, Leonard S. "What Does It Mean To Believe In God?" *Central Conference of American Rabbis Journal* 20:1 (Winter 1973): 27–30.

Laderman, Manuel. "To A Future Rabbi" *Letters of Faith*, pp. 113–124. Denver: Hebrew Educational Alliance, 1991.

Lamm, Norman. Respondent, "What Do American Jews Believe? A Symposium" *Commentary* 102:2 (August 1996): 59–60.

Lawson, Martin S. "Duty of Rabbi to disclose knowledge of sexual misconduct of a colleague." Paper presented at a symposium at the Pacific Association of Reform Rabbis titled "Rabbi's Sexual Misconduct: Collegial Response and Methodology of Teshuvah [Repentance] and Communal Healing." January 1994.

Lenn, Theodore. *Rabbi and Synagogue in Reform Judaism*. New York: Central Conference of American Rabbis, 1972.

Liebman, Charles S. *The Ambivalent American Jew*. Philadelphia: Jewish Publication Society, 1976.

———. "The Training of American Rabbis." In *Aspects of the Religious*

Behavior of American Jews, pp. 1–110. New York: Ktav Publishing, 1974. [This article originally appeared in the *American Jewish Year Book 1968*, ed. Morris Fine and Morris Himmelfarb, vol. 69. New York: American Jewish Committee and Philadelphia: Jewish Publication Society, 1968.]

———. "Orthodoxy in American Jewish Life." In *Aspects of the Religious Behavior of American Jews*, pp. 111–187. New York: Ktav Publishing, 1974. [This article originally appeared in the *American Jewish Year Book 1965* ed. Morris Fine and Milton Himmelfarb, vol. 66 (New York: American Jewish Committee and Philadelphia: Jewish Publication Society, 1965)].

———. "Jewish Survival, Antisemitism, and Negotiation with the Tradition." In *The Americanization of the Jews*, ed. Robert M. Seltzer and Norman J. Cohen, pp. 436–450. New York and London: New York University Press, 1995.

Lipman, Eugene J. "The Changing Self-Image of the Rabbi." *Dimensions* [New York: Union of American Hebrew Congregations]. Spring, 1970: 27–29.

———. "*Tanu Rabbanan*: *Our Masters Have Taught Us*." In *Tanu Rabbanan: Our Rabbis Taught, CCAR Yearbook 1989, vol. 2*. ed. Joseph B. Glaser, pp. 39–70. New York: Central Conference of American Rabbis, 1990.

Litvinoff, Barnet. *A Peculiar People: Inside World Jewry Today*. London: Weidenfeld and Nicolson, 1969.

Lunin-Pack, Jesse. "1995 Audit of Anti-Semitic Incidents." [Prepared by Jesse Lunin-Pack] New York: Anti-Defamation League, 1996.

Marcus, Jacob Radar. "Background for the History of American Jewry." In *The American Jew: A Reappraisal*, ed. Oscar I. Janowsky, pp. 1–25. Philadelphia: Jewish Publication Society of America, 1964.

———. *United States Jewry 1776–1985*. 4 vols. Detroit: Wayne State University Press, 1989–1993.

Marder, Janet. "How Women are Changing the Rabbinate." *Reform Judaism* 19:4 (Summer 1991): 4–8, 41.

———. "Sexual Misconduct: How Vulnerable Are Synagogues?" *Reform Judaism* 23:2 (Winter 1994): 16–18, 20, 81–82.

Marx, Jeffrey A. "Healing the congregation in the aftermath of clergy sexual misconduct." Paper presented at a symposium at the Pacific Association of Reform Rabbis titled "Rabbi's Sexual Misconduct: Collegial Response and Methodology of Teshuvah [Repentance] and Communal Healing." January 1994.

Mason, Patrice. "The Rabbi: On Love and Loss." *Central Conference of American Rabbis Yearbook: 103*, pp. 63–69. New York: Central Conference of American Rabbis, 1994.

Mayer, Egon. "From an External to an Internal Agenda." In *The Americanization of the Jews*, ed. Robert M. Seltzer and Norman J. Cohen, pp. 417–435. New York and London: New York University Press, 1995.

Menitoff, Paul J. "Diverse Expectations in Congregational-Rabbinic Relations." *Journal of Reform Judaism* 34:4 (Fall 1987): 1–7.

———. "A Formula for Successful Rabbinical-Congregational Relationships." *CCAR Journal* 40:1 (Winter 1993): 35–43.

Meyer, Michael. *Response to Modernity. A History of the Reform Movement in Judaism*. New York and Oxford: Oxford University Press, 1988.

Mintz, Jerome R. *Hasidic People: A Place in the New World*. Cambridge and London: Harvard University Press, 1992.

Mirsky, Norman. "Rabbinic Dilemmas." *The Jewish Spectator* 39:1 (Spring 1974): 32–36.

———. "The Vision of Man Triumphant." *Unorthodox Judaism*, pp. 112–125. Columbus: Ohio State University Press, 1978.

Nadell, Pamela S. "The Women Who Would Be Rabbis." In *Gender and Judaism: The Transformation of Tradition*, ed. T. M. Rudavsky, pp. 123–134. New York and London: New York University Press, 1995.

Nadich, Hadassah Ribalow. "The Rabbi's Spouse." In *The Jewish Spectator* 50:2 (Summer 1985): 16–18.

Neusner, Jacob. *American Judaism: Adventure in Modernity*. Englewood Cliffs, NJ: Prentice-Hall, 1972.

———. *The Rabbinate in America: Reshaping An Ancient Calling*, ed. Jacob Neusner. New York and London: Garland, 1993.

Polner, Murray. *Rabbi: The American Experience*. New York: Holt, Rinehart and Winston, 1977.

Printz, Deborah. Symposium on "Today's Rabbinate: the Personal Equation." *Central Conference of American Rabbis Yearbook: 90*, pp. 148–150. New York: Central Conference of American Rabbis, 1981.

Rabinowitz, Louis Isaac. "Rabbi, Rabbinate." In *Encyclopedia Judaica*, vol. 13, p. 1445. Jerusalem: Keter, 1972.

Raphael, Marc Lee. *Profiles in American Judaism: The Reform, Conserva-*

tive, Orthodox and Reconstructionist Traditions in Historical Perspective. San Francisco: Harper and Row, 1984.

Rawidowicz, Simon. "Israel: the Ever-Dying People." In *Judaism* 16:4 (Fall 1967): 423–433.

"Reconstructionist Rabbinical College 1995–96 Fact Sheet." Wyncotte, PA: Reconstructionist Rabbinical College, 1995.

"Reconstructionist Rabbinical College 1996–97 Fact Sheet." Wyncotte, PA: Reconstructionist Rabbinical College, 1996.

Reisner, Neil. "Rabbis Under Stress." [Philadelphia] In *Jewish Exponent*, September 26, 1986, pp. 31–33.

Reuben, Didi Carr. "Two's Company: Three Thousand's a Crowd: Reflections of a Rebbetzin's Husband's Wife." In *Journal of Reform Judaism* 33:1 (Winter 1986): 37–41.

Ritterband, Paul. "Modern Times and Jewish Assimilation." In *The Americanization of the Jews*, ed. Robert M. Seltzer and Norman J. Cohen, pp. 377–394. New York and London: New York University Press, 1995.

Romanoff, Lena with Hostein, Lisa. *Your People, My People: Finding Acceptance and Fulfillment as a Jew By Choice*. Philadelphia, New York: Jewish Publication Society, 1990.

Rosenthal, Gilbert S. *Contemporary Judaism: Patterns of Survival*. Second Edition. New York: Human Sciences Press, 1986.

Rothkoff, Aaron. "Semikhah." In *Encyclopedia Judaica*, vol. 14, pp. 1146–1147. Jerusalem: Keter, 1972.

Rubenstein, Richard L. *Power Struggle*. New York: Charles Scribner's Sons, 1974.

Rubinstein, Peter J. "The Next Century." In *Tanu Rabbanan: Our Rabbis Taught CCAR Yearbook 1989*, vol. 2, ed. Joseph B. Glaser, pp. 133–155. New York: Central Conference of American Rabbis, 1990.

Ruderman, David B. "Rabbi and Teacher." *Contemporary Jewish Religious Thought*, ed. Arthur A. Cohen and Paul Mendes-Flohr, pp. 741–747. New York: Charles Scribner's Sons, 1987.

Sachar, Howard Morley. *A History of the Jews in America*. New York: Alfred A. Knopf, 1992.

Sacks, Yonason. "The *Mizvah* of *'Lo Tasur:'* Limits and Applications." In *Tradition* 24:4 (Summer 1993): 49–60.

Saperstein, Harold I. "The Origin and Authority of the Rabbi." In *Rabbinic Authority*, ed. Elliot L. Stevens, Vol. 90, Part 2. New York: Central Conference of American Rabbis, 1982: 15–27.

Sarah, Elizabeth. "Introduction." In *Hear Our Voice*, ed. Sybil Sheridan, pp. 1–2. London: SCM Press, 1984.

Schaalman, Herman E. "Patrilineal Descent: A Report and Assessment," *Central Conference of American Rabbis Yearbook 97* (1988): 110–111.

Schnall, David J. "The Way (They Say) We Are: Using Quantitative Data to Explore the Parameters of Orthodoxy." In *Tradition* 27:2 (Winter, 1993): 69–80.

Schorsch, Ismar. Respondent, "What Do American Jews Believe? A Symposium." In *Commentary* 102:2 (August 1996): 81–83.

Schwartz, Shuly Rubin. "'We Married What We Wanted To Be': The *Rebbitzen* in Twentieth-Century America." In *American Jewish History* 83 (June, 1995): 223–246.

Schwartzfuchs, Simon. *A Concise History of the Rabbinate*. Oxford, UK, and Cambridge, USA: Blackwell, 1993.

Selengut, Charles. "Themes in Modern Jewish Theology." In *Events and Movements in Modern Judaism*, ed. Raphael Patai and Emanuel S. Goldsmith, pp. 125–143. New York: Paragon House, 1995.

Seltzer, Robert M. *The Americanization of the Jews*, ed. Robert M. Seltzer and Norman J. Cohen. New York and London: New York University Press, 1995.

Sharot, Stephen. "The British and American Rabbinate: A Comparison of Authority Structures, Role Definitions and Role Conflicts." In *A Sociological Yearbook of Religion in Britain 8*, ed. Michael Hill, pp. 139–158, London: SCM Press, 1975.

Shudofsky, Maurice M. "Portrait of the Inauthentic Rabbi." In *Reconstructionist* 20.5 (April 23, 1954): 19–25.

Siegel, Martin. *Amen: The Diary of Rabbi Martin Siegel*, ed. Mel Ziegler. New York and Cleveland: World, 1971.

Silberman, Charles E. *A Certain People: American Jews and Their Lives Today*. New York: Summit, 1985.

Silverstein, Alan. "A New Image of the Rabbinate." In *The Seminary at 100. Reflections on the Jewish Theological Seminary and the Conservative Movement*, ed. Nina Beth Cardin and David Wolf Silverman (New York: The Rabbinical Assembly and The Jewish Theological Seminary of America, 1987): 427–432.

Singer, Howard. "Rabbis and Their Discontents." In *Commentary* 79:5: (May 1985): 55–58.

Sklare, Marshall. *America's Jews*. New York: Random House, 1971.

———. *Conservative Judaism: An American Religious Movement*. Lanham, MD, New York, and London: University Press of America, 1985 [1972].

Springer, Mychal. "A Rabbinate on the Fringe." In *Conservative Judaism* 48:1 (Fall 1995): 83–86.

Stern, David Eli . Symposium on "Today's Rabbinate: The Personal Equation." *Central Conference of American Rabbis Yearbook: 90*, pp. 145–147. New York: Central Conference of American Rabbis, 1981.

Stern, Elizabeth Weiss. "Practical Realities of the Rabbinate." In *Papers of the Women's Rabbinic Network Conference*, pp. 26–31 (March 21–24, 1993), Oakland, California.

Stevens, Elliot. *Rabbinic Authority*, ed. Elliot L. Stevens, Vol. 90, Part 2. New York: Central Conference of American Rabbis, 1982.

Stutz, Christine. "Natural Wonder: Gila Ruskin Redefines the Role of the Rabbi." In *Baltimore Jewish Times*, 227:8 (Feb. 23, 1996): 52–56.

Sundheim, Adrienne. Symposium on "Today's Rabbinate: The Personal Equation." *Central Conference of American Rabbis Yearbook: 90*, pp.153–157. New York: Central Conference of American Rabbis, 1981.

Telushkin, Joseph. *Jewish Literacy*. New York: William Morrow, 1991.

Teutsch, David A. Respondent, "What Do American Jews Believe? A Symposium." In *Commentary* 102:2 (August 1996): 88–89.

Tobin, Gary A. "Eating up the rabbi." *The Jerusalem Post*, April 13, 1987, p. 5.

Turkel, Eli. "The Nature and Limitations of Rabbinic Authority." In *Tradition* 27:4 (Summer 1993): 80–99.

Ullman, Alan M. "The Rabbi in American Jewish Fiction" Unpublished rabbinic thesis, Hebrew Union College-Jewish Institute of Religion, Cincinnati, 1985.

Umansky, Ellen M. "Feminism and American Reform Judaism." In *The Americanization of the Jews*, ed. Robert M. Seltzer and Norman J. Cohen, pp. 267–283. New York and London: New York University Press, 1995.

———. "Women's Journey toward Rabbinic Ordination." In *Women Rabbis: Exploration and Celebration*, ed. Gary P. Zola, pp. 27–41. Cincinnati: HUC-JIR Rabbinic Alumni Association Press, 1996.

Waxman, Chaim I. "Dilemmas of Modern Orthodoxy: Sociological and Philosophical." In *Judaism* 42:1 (Winter 1993): 59–70.

Weiner, Jennifer. "The Role of the Rabbi in the United States Armed Forces." Unpublished rabbinic thesis, Hebrew Union College-Jewish Institute of Religion, Cincinnati, 1996.

Weintraub, Selma. "Dreams Are Realized in Accordance with Their Interpretation." *The Seminary at 100. Reflections on the Jewish Theological Seminary and the Conservative Movement*, ed. Nina Beth Cardin and David Wolf Silverman (New York: The Rabbinical Assembly and The Jewish Theological Seminary of America, 1987): 411–421.

Wertheimer, Jack. "The Conservative Synagogue." *The American Synagogue: A Sanctuary Transformed*, ed. Jack Wertheimer, pp. 111–149. Cambridge, New York: Cambridge University Press, 1987.

———. "Recent Trends in American Judaism." In *American Jewish Year Book 1989*, ed. David Singer and Ruth R. Seldin, vol. 89, pp. 63–162. New York: American Jewish Committee and Philadelphia: Jewish Publication Society, 1989.

Wilkes, Paul. *And They Shall Be My People: An American Rabbi and His Congregation*. New York: Atlantic Monthly, 1994.

Winer, Mark L. "Our Vision of the Future: Personal Status and K'lal Yisra-eil." In *Central Conference of American Rabbis Yearbook 104*, pp. 58–69. New York: Central Conference of American Rabbis, 1995.

Woocher, Jonathan S. *Sacred Survival: The Civil Religion of American Jews*. Bloomington and Indianapolis: Indiana University Press, 1986.

Wurzburger, Walter S. "Centrist Orthodoxy—Ideology or Atmosphere." In *Journal of Jewish Thought* (1:1985): 67–75.

Yoffie, Eric H. Respondent, "What Do American Jews Believe? A Symposium." In *Commentary* 102:2 (August 1996): 93–95.

Zelizer, Gerald L. "Conservative Rabbis, Their Movement, and American Judaism." Responses by Jonathan D. Sarna, Jenna Weissman Joselit, and Henry Feingold. In *Judaism* 44:3 (Summer 1995): 292–313.

Zimmerman, Sheldon. Respondent, "What Do American Jews Believe? A Symposium." In *Commentary* 102:2 (August 1996): 95–96.

Zlotowitz, Bernard M. "A Perspective on Patrilineal Descent." In *Judaism* 34:1 (Winter 1985): 129–135.

———. "Patrilineal Descent." In *The Jewish Condition*, ed. Aron Hirt-Manheimer, pp. 260–267. New York: Union of American Hebrew Congregations Press, 1995.

Zucker, David J. "Rebbitzens and Women Rabbis: Portrayals in Contemporary American Jewish Fiction." In *CCAR Journal* 42:1 (Winter/Spring, 1995): 1–12.

———. "Jewish 'Continuity' and the 'Ever-Dying' Jews." In *Jewish Spectator* 61:1 (Summer 1996), pp. 21–24.

Index

About the Author

David J. Zucker serves as the Chaplain at Shalom Park, a continuum of care community near Denver. Ordained at the Hebrew Union College-Jewish Institute of Religion, he earned a Ph.D. at the University of Birmingham, England. A popular lecturer and teacher, he serves on the editorial board of the *Jewish Spectator*. He has published articles in *Judaism; CCAR Journal; Jewish Spectator; Midstream; Conservative Judaism; Studies in American Jewish Literature; Paintbrush*; and *Journal of Ecumenical Studies*. A former congregational rabbi, as well as a professor of Religious Studies, he approaches this subject of rabbis in fiction from both a professional and a personal perspective. He serves as the President of the Rocky Mountain Rabbinic Council. He lives in Aurora, Colorado with his wife, Donna. They have three children: Jeremy Daniel, Joshua Seth, and Ian Michael.